Fifty Years Around
the Third World

# FIFTY YEARS AROUND THE THIRD WORLD

## Adventures and Reflections of an Overseas American

*Haldore Hanson*

FRASER PUBLISHING COMPANY
Burlington, Vermont

Copyright © 1986 by Haldore Hanson

All rights reserved. No part of this book may be reproduced in any form or by any means without written permission of the publisher, except for reviewers, who may quote brief passages in an article or critical review.

Fraser Publishing Company
PO Box 494
Burlington, VT 05402
(802) 658-0322

Library of Congress Catalog Card Number: 86-082337
ISBN: 0-87034-080-8 pbk
ISBN: 0-87034-081-6 hc

Photographs by the author except as otherwise credited.
Maps by Northern Cartographic.

Edited, designed, and produced by Robinson Book Associates.
Typeset by PostScript, Inc.
Printed in the United States by Braun-Brumfield, Inc.

*To Berni*

# Contents

| | | |
|---|---|---|
| | Prologue | xi |

### PART ONE
## Old China     1

| | | |
|---|---|---|
| 1 | How I Got to China | 5 |
| 2 | My Peking Life On Eight Great Men Lane | 12 |
| 3 | "Red Bandits" Take Their Long March | 19 |
| 4 | Chicago Girl Flees Reds | 24 |
| 5 | Freelancing Through Chiang Kai-shek's China | 27 |
| 6 | Omens of Revolution | 34 |

### PART TWO
## War Correspondent     41

| | | |
|---|---|---|
| 7 | Japan Invades | 45 |
| 8 | Reporting the Guerillas | 51 |
| 9 | Travels with the Eighth Route Army | 58 |
| 10 | One Breach of Discipline | 65 |
| 11 | Interview with Mao Zedong in His Yan'an Cave | 70 |
| 12 | With Stilwell at China's War Base | 76 |
| 13 | Why Mao's Men Won the War | 83 |

### PART THREE
## Wartime America     85

| | | |
|---|---|---|
| 14 | Chicago: Newsman for the Associated Press | 87 |
| 15 | Washington: A State Department Program in China | 93 |
| 16 | Family in the Wartime Capital | 100 |
| 17 | Lobbyist | 102 |

| | | |
|---|---|---|
| 18 | Truman's Point Four | 107 |
| 19 | An Encounter With Senator McCarthy | 112 |
| 20 | Fallout from Communist Hunters | 120 |
| 21 | Virginia Cattle Farmer | 124 |

### PART FOUR
## My Work in the Third World — 129

| | | |
|---|---|---|
| 22 | Burma: With Prime Minister U Nu | 135 |
| 23 | Iran: Developing a River Valley | 142 |
| 24 | Pakistan: With President Ayub Khan | 150 |
| 25 | Family Matters in Asia | 160 |
| 26 | Africa's Green Revolution Falters | 169 |
| 27 | Nigeria: Biafrans | 176 |
| 28 | A Compulsive Collector | 179 |
| 29 | Culture Shock and the Ten Commandments | 182 |

### PART FIVE
## Plant Breeding for the Third World — 187

| | | |
|---|---|---|
| 30 | Dr. Borlaug Receives a Nobel Peace Prize | 195 |
| 31 | The Cloning of Research Institutes | 206 |
| 32 | A Donnybrook over the Green Revolution | 210 |
| 33 | Maize: A Potential Supercereal in the Third World | 213 |
| 34 | Neighbors to an Aztec King | 222 |

### PART SIX
## Return to Peoples China — 231

| | | |
|---|---|---|
| 35 | What the Beijing Airport Road Tells Us | 237 |
| 36 | I Learn from My Former Beijing Residences | 241 |
| 37 | Dr. Borlaug Examines Chinese Wheat | 246 |
| 38 | Briefing Travellers to China | 253 |
| 39 | My Trek to the Mountain Called Chomolungma | 258 |

### PART SEVEN
## We Retrace the Long March After 50 Years — 265

| | | |
|---|---|---|
| 40 | A Briefing on the Peoples Liberation Army | 269 |
| 41 | Great Changes in the Countryside | 274 |
| 42 | *The China Daily* Reports Our Trek | 278 |
| 43 | On the Road in Jiangxi | 283 |
| 44 | The Rice Revolution in Hunan | 288 |

| | | |
|---|---|---|
| 45 | Communes Where Some Get Rich First | 291 |
| 46 | Through A Poor Mountainous Province | 295 |
| 47 | A Family "Lives Well" on US$18.27 a Week | 298 |
| 48 | Sichuan Transport, Old and New | 303 |
| 49 | A Population Program Called 1×1=1 | 305 |
| 50 | A Shaanxi Harvest Seen Through American Eyes | 312 |
| 51 | Two Wheat Breeders at Wugong | 315 |
| 52 | How Well Is the PRC Meeting Basic Needs of Its People? | 325 |
| | Epilogue: The Third World in the Year 2000 | 328 |
| | Selected Bibliography | 329 |
| | Index | 333 |

## ILLUSTRATIONS

MAPS

| | |
|---|---|
| The Chinese Revolution | 2 |
| Peking in the 1930s | 3 |
| South Asia | 130 |
| Nigeria and West Africa | 132 |
| CIMMYT Research Stations (Mexico) | 190 |
| Peoples Republic of China | 266 |

PHOTOGRAPHS

Photographic section follows page 178

# Prologue

This book reports my adventures and reflections as an overseas American in the third world—through decades of residence in China, Burma, Iran, Pakistan, Nigeria, and Mexico.

Along the way the story offers insights from my careers as a war correspondent in China, a State Department officer in Washington, a cattle farmer in Virginia, a manager of development projects in Asia and Africa, the director of a world-famous agricultural research center in Mexico (sometimes called the home of the green revolution), and finally a return to China. This book is a smorgasbord of governments, national leaders, and life styles.

When I studied geography in school, the phrase *third world* did not exist. It came into use in the 1960s. Today news from the third world dominates international headlines. If a newspaper reports a famine in Africa, a civil war in Central America, a terrorist bombing in the mideast, or bank loan crises in Mexico, Brazil, and Argentina—these are events in the third world.

The *first world*, as most newspaper readers know, comprises the industrialized and capitalist countries of North America and Europe, plus outposts like Japan, Australia, and New Zealand. To avoid using the word *capitalist* in describing this group, the United Nations refers to the first world as *market economies*. The *second world* refers to the USSR and its Marxist neighbors in eastern Europe. Again, the United Nations avoids an ideological term by describing these countries as *centrally planned*.

The third world covers everyone else. It takes in all the western hemisphere south of the United States and all of Africa and Asia except Japan. Third worlders embrace 75 out of 100 people in the world population and three-fifths of the world land mass.

The term *overseas American*, as I use it, applies to at least 15 or 20 million

Americans who have spent a period of years at a post outside the United States. I think of Peace Corps volunteers and American scholars studying in foreign universities; Christian missionaries (a dwindling lot because most churches abroad now prefer local leadership); businessmen, bankers, journalists, and diplomats; and thousands of technical specialists employed in development programs. The largest group of Americans living abroad are members of the armed forces who spend years in the German Federal Republic, South Korea, or other defense posts. In absolute numbers our overseas Americans have exceeded the number of overseas Britons who were said—at the height of the British Empire—to approximate one Englishman in ten. Overseas Americans are an important part of our foreign relations, but there has been little popular literature written about them.

I was introduced to the third world as a freelance writer in China. I then spent 11 years in the Department of State at Washington, working on problems of developing countries. Since then I have lived three decades as economic advisor to the government of Burma, as finance officer for the construction of a high dam in Iran, as Ford Foundation representative in Pakistan and Nigeria, and as director of an international agricultural research institute in Mexico. Between assignments I never paused long enough, or investigated deeply enough, to formulate my ideas about underdeveloped countries. My experience outran my understanding. I made the decisions required for each day's work, but often I did not grasp the broader picture.

Only after I retired at nearly 70 did I find time to read more widely on the world events I had experienced and to assess my role as an activist in the third world. I wrote this book to help the nonspecialist reader see the third world as I knew it.

My story may include more about plant breeders than some readers would like, but I believe recent progress in agricultural research is an important factor in maintaining global stability. I have tried to present the work of economists and scientists as simply as possible, avoiding *jargon-speak*—at the risk of oversimplification.

Fifty years around the third world have convinced me that most developing countries will lag still farther behind the industrialized countries by the year 2000, and that this lag will continue to be a major problem.

I recognize two influences on myself. First, I was a Minnesotan; this means a midwestern environment, largely rural, and egalitarian. Minnesotans generally accept people on their merits and not for reasons of class; they believe that if you get up early and work hard, things will work out.

Second, I experienced the great depression of the 1930s and was deeply affected by it. In my student generation we told each other we did not want to accumulate large sums of money or to seek power for power's sake. We wanted to make a contribution to society—more than anything else, we wanted to leave a mark on a better world. That explains some judgments in this book.

A note from my style manual: for most names in Chinese, I have followed the *pinyin* spelling used by the Chinese government and by most western newspapers. For names of a few people who were famous before pinyin—such as Chiang Kai-shek and Sun Yat-sen—I have kept the old spellings. For current Chinese place names like Beijing (old name Peiping), Nanjing (Nanking), and Tianjin (Tientsin), I have generally used the current form when discussing Peoples China and the old spelling when describing the nationalist period before 1949. To its former residents, *Peking* is such a nostalgic name that it may appear anywhere in the book as a slip of the pen.

I have used both the metric system and the British-American measure of feet and pounds. For example, I prefer kilograms per hectare in agricultural research, but feet for the height of mountains and miles for the length of journeys.

The value of Chinese currency has varied during the half century covered by the book—from US$0.33 for the Chinese dollar in the 1930s, to US$0.50 for the Chinese yuan in 1983.

I am grateful for the help of many people. I benefited from suggestions of Robinson Book Associates and Fraser Publishing Company, both of Burlington, Vermont, and from coworkers in the third world, especially colleagues at the International Maize and Wheat Improvement Center in Mexico. In China I am indebted for travel and briefings by the Chinese Academy of Agricultural Sciences and the Military Museum, both of Beijing. Needless to say, any errors that still lurk in the printed book are my own.

>Haldore Hanson
>Director General Emeritus
>International Maize and Wheat Improvement Center (CIMMYT)
>Box 6-641,
>06600 Mexico, D.F. Mexico
>November 1986

> *Some scholars think that China is perhaps the only country in the world where the people eat less, live more bitterly, and are clothed worse than they were 500 years ago.*
>
> T. H. White and Annalee Jacoby, 1946

PART ONE

# OLD CHINA OF THE 1930s

The old China where I went to live in 1934 was a country with physical conditions not very different from medieval Europe. Four-fifths of the people lived in villages with uncertain food supply, life expectancy at birth of 36 years, and illiteracy of 84 percent. Village houses were made of mud blocks, thatched roofs, and paper windows; there was no running water. Cooking fuel in the kitchen was dried straw or charcoal. After sundown illumination was generally by candle. There were few motor vehicles; scheduled airlines were still in the future; and the building of railroads had only begun. The common transport for agricultural produce was by wheelbarrow, which meant that grain could not move more than 200 miles. China's rural areas had been ravaged for 4000 years by recurring famines, floods, droughts, and epidemics.

Among urban centers, three great ports along the Pacific littoral were dominated by foreign traders and industrialists; these were Shanghai, Canton, and Tientsin. Here the traveller encountered wharfs for modern ocean-going ships and extensive *godowns* (warehouses) displaying well-known corporate names such as Butterfield and Swire and Jardine Matheson (British shippers), British-American Tobacco Company, Standard Oil, Ford Motor Company, Shanghai Power Company, and Hongkong and Shanghai Banking Corporation. Close to these corporate facilities were foreign residential areas, walled, and guarded by

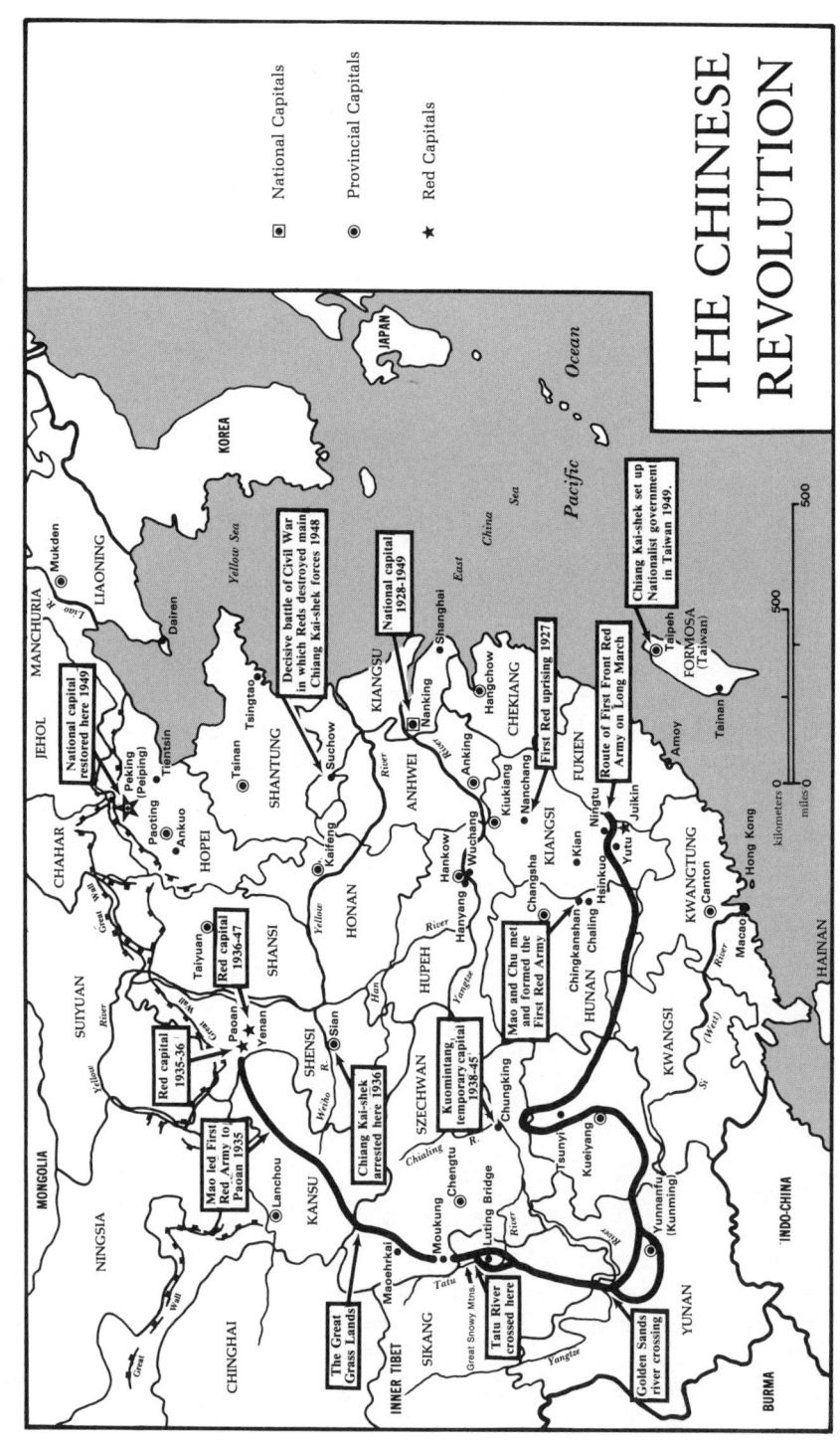

foreign troops. Except for treaty ports managed by foreigners, few places were equipped with electricity, telephones, or modern hospitals. The most plentiful resource was good-natured, intelligent, hard-working, and thrifty Chinese people. This was the old China when I arrived.

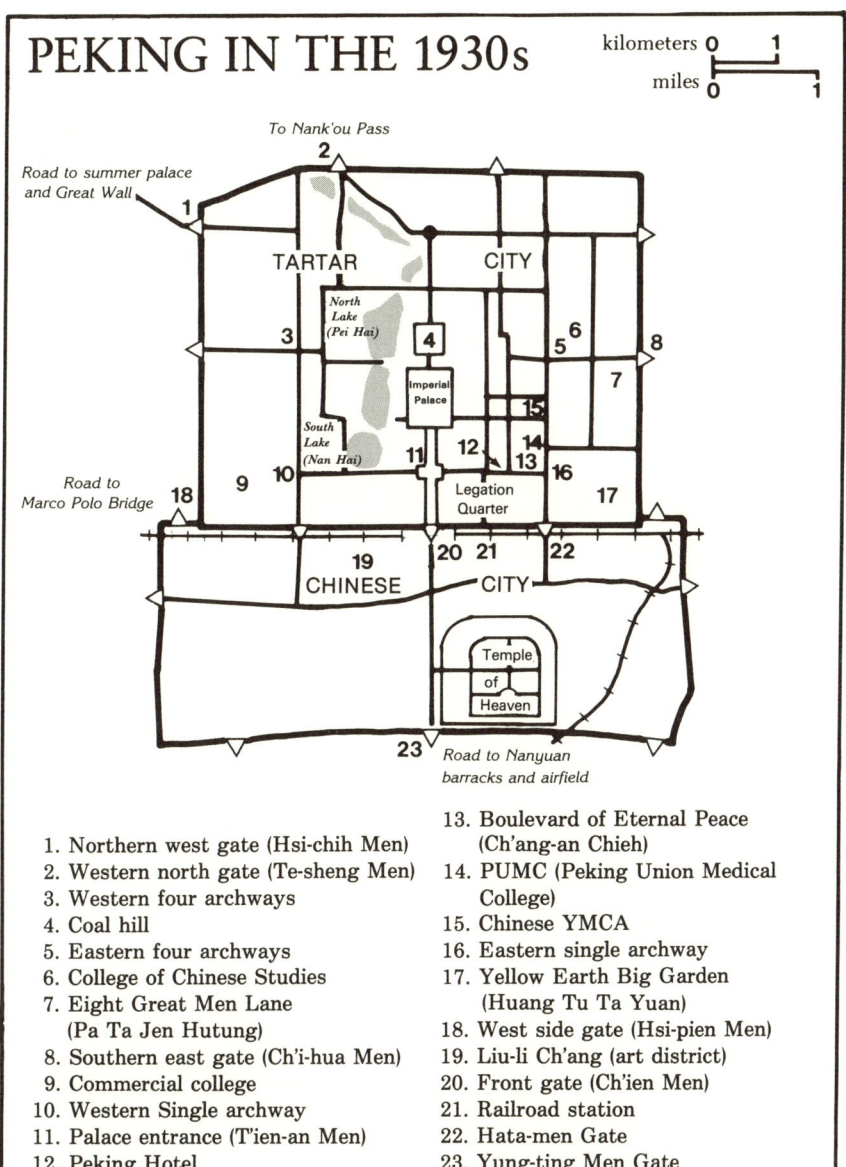

1. Northern west gate (Hsi-chih Men)
2. Western north gate (Te-sheng Men)
3. Western four archways
4. Coal hill
5. Eastern four archways
6. College of Chinese Studies
7. Eight Great Men Lane (Pa Ta Jen Hutung)
8. Southern east gate (Ch'i-hua Men)
9. Commercial college
10. Western Single archway
11. Palace entrance (T'ien-an Men)
12. Peking Hotel
13. Boulevard of Eternal Peace (Ch'ang-an Chieh)
14. PUMC (Peking Union Medical College)
15. Chinese YMCA
16. Eastern single archway
17. Yellow Earth Big Garden (Huang Tu Ta Yuan)
18. West side gate (Hsi-pien Men)
19. Liu-li Ch'ang (art district)
20. Front gate (Ch'ien Men)
21. Railroad station
22. Hata-men Gate
23. Yung-ting Men Gate

*Stowaway: an unregistered passenger.*

Webster's Dictionary

CHAPTER 1

# How I Got to China

When Commencement approached at Carleton College in 1934, Wall Street financiers were no longer leaping out of windows, but Phi Beta Kappa keys were still hanging in pawnshops and Ph.D.s were mowing lawns. Most of my classmates in the depression had no immediate job prospects.

The talents I had developed in school didn't seem salable; I had captained a nationally successful debating team; edited an award-winning high school yearbook; and won a trip to Europe in a letter writing contest. My winning letter, addressed to a Bengali student, described life in my home town of Duluth, Minnesota, a city of 100,000 at the head of Lake Superior.

So where did a new graduate turn in 1934?

An American newspaper editor whom I met had once worked for the *Japan Advertiser* in Tokyo. He assured me it was not difficult to find a job on English language newspapers in Asia. Also Walter Judd, a medical missionary on sabbatical leave from China, made China sound like a good place to start writing.

I had written an honors thesis on relations between Japan and China and had attended several international relations conferences sponsored by the Carnegie Endowment for International Peace. An Endowment officer offered me letters of introduction to professors in Japan and China.

And probably most important, a Chinese student spent a vacation with my family in Duluth. He said his family would welcome me as a guest in their Peking home.

That settled it. After Commencement I borrowed $125 from a Duluth bank, repayable in one year, and started on a journey that would lead to—jail!

My trip to the west coast was by low cost methods that were commonplace during the depression. I hitchhiked from Duluth to Minneapolis, rode a railroad locomotive from there to Chicago, and drove a second-hand automobile for an auto dealer from Chicago to San Francisco. I was amazed at the casual trust when the dealer advanced me the cost of gasoline enroute. This was in the days before drivers' permits or credit cards were available for identification.

When I arrived at San Francisco in July 1934, longshoremen's pickets stood along the wharves. A strike had begun against all U.S. and Canadian registered ships. The only ship likely to sail in the next two weeks, I learned, was the Japanese liner, *NYK Chichibu Maru*. Although I still had $100 in traveller's checks, enough to pay for steerage passage, little would be left when I arrived in Japan. All that stopped me from returning home, I think, was the loss of face after telling friends I was going to China.

Stowing away seemed to be my only option. I had read that when stowaways were caught, they were put to work as kitchen help and dropped at the next port. It sounded like working your way across. An hour before the *Chichibu* was scheduled to sail, I put on my last clean clothes, filled my briefcase with oranges and biscuits, took a taxi through the picket line on the wharf, and walked up the gangplank with a group of passengers. Then I paced the first class deck. A Japanese band played the "Star Spangled Banner" as the dockside cables were hoisted, and the Golden Gate Bridge soon disappeared behind us.

Now, what does a stowaway do? I began to feel conspicuous walking around with a briefcase. I had no plan for hiding. I reasoned that the sooner I was caught and put to work, the less dishonorable I would feel. At dinnertime I went into a public washroom, ate a few biscuits, and dropped the briefcase at the door of the baggage room. Later, when dancing began in the first class lounge, I joined the activity, still wondering when I would be detected. The suspense ended when a Japanese officer in a starched white uniform walked out on the dance floor, tapped me on the shoulder, and asked my cabin number. I excused myself from my dancing partner and outside the lounge informed the officer I had no ticket: consternation! The detective—for that was his role—grabbed me by the shoulder and marched me to the purser's office.

The purser was a stout, patriotic Japanese. He charged me with insulting the Japanese emperor, spying on the merchant marine, and causing trouble for imperial officers. I agreed with his last point. Trying to be a reporter, I asked how the detective had identified me. A slap on the cheek was the only reply. I asked to be put to work—any kind of work—and dropped at Honolulu. Now I learned for the first time that American law prohibits foreign vessels from carrying American citizens between two U.S. ports; by law the foreign carrier is required to imprison a stowaway and turn him over to American authorities at the next port. My pockets were emptied, and I was led to the brig, a bare jail cell about six feet square with one barred porthole looking out on a service deck. The cell was furnished with a wooden bed and iron toilet—no mattress, no blankets, no toilet paper. Three times a day a Japanese seaman opened a little trap door in the wall to push in a plate of rice and fish and a pair of chopsticks. The seaman seemed friendly but he spoke no English.

By the time I was taken from the ship at Honolulu I had slept in my clothes for five nights without bathing or shaving. Since I had no comb, my hair was unkempt. Still in that condition I was escorted to the city jail, photographed with a number across my chest, and lodged in a double cell with a fellow accused of rape.

A drunk in the cell across the corridor, an unshaven man with a raucous laugh, asked me my offense and shook his head with mock sadness when I told him. "It's too bad, sonny; you'll get six months," he said. "That's minimum. A guy's got only one chance around here. There's two judges, one tough and one easy. If you get Brown, he'll let you off." He broke into a guffaw of laughter.

The lenient judge must have been on the bench next day. He read the letters of introduction addressed to Japanese and Chinese professors and released me without a jail sentence—provided I leave Honolulu by the next Japanese ship and pay the minimum fare. I bought a steerage ticket and then had $12 in my pocket. To live as cheaply as possible for the week before the next sailing, I borrowed a blanket from the YMCA, stuffed it in my briefcase, and started on a walk around the island of Oahu. At night I stretched out under the beach palms. I ate mainly pineapples and crackers.

One night while walking beside the water after dark, I stumbled over a cairn of rocks—some kind of Buddhist shrine, I guessed—and cut a gash in my wrist. I let out a yelp at my bloodstained hand. A flashlight beam appeared out of the darkness, and a stranger came up to ask my difficulty. Miraculously it was a Nisei medical doctor from Honolulu who was vacationing in a tent on the beach. He sewed several stitches in the gash and invited me to stay for the night.

Another night I was bedded down near Pearl Harbor, the naval base, when a downpour soaked my blanket and chilled me. I was walking the ten miles back to Honolulu when a highway policeman stopped to give me a ride. "Where do you live?" he asked as we approached the city. I told him my situation. He offered to fix me up. He knew the manager of a sailors' home, a charitable place, no charge. There I spent my last day in Honolulu, playing cribbage with old sailors. When I sailed I was four decks below the dance music but still had nine dollars in my pocket and a friend awaiting me at Yokohama.

Seiichi Asada was 20 and a graduate of Tokyo's No. 1 high school, awaiting the results of his entrance examination for Tokyo Imperial University. I had learned that much about him during our two years of correspondence.

Asada took me to his home on a narrow lane that teemed with people wearing kimonos and wooden clogs. The houses were two-story wood and paper structures. These neighborhoods were later destroyed in the two great fire bombings of Tokyo by the U.S. Air Force in World War II. In my period at Asada's home we ate and slept on bamboo floor mats. We used public bathhouses managed by women attendants, which I found embarrassing. I discussed my reaction with Asada who merely shrugged.

With two other students we made a two-week camping trip around the five lakes of Mount Fuji, and we finished by climbing the 12,400-foot mountain. Thousands of Japanese students were making similar trips that summer, encouraged by a 50 percent student discount on the national railroads.

We boarded a southbound train at Tokyo one August night. Early the next morning we left the train, cooked our breakfast over a wood fire, and started walking on a mountain trail that took us up 5,000 feet in ten hours. The Japanese walked methodically, resting about five minutes every hour. I was impatient and set off at a faster pace, but as the sun grew hotter and midday approached, my calf muscles stiffened. I sat down to await the others and was glad thereafter to follow their routine.

We slept on rough lava flow that had hardened with parallel grooves in the surface. I cut a few evergreens for a mattress and was about to slide them under my blanket when Asada stopped me with the polite inquiry: "What you do?" I explained that I was making my bed a little softer, as Boy Scouts in America do. "We don't use," he said firmly. "Our army teach us to sleep on rocks." I later realized that these young men were participants in a national toughening program, preparing for a war. I recalled this conversation many times during the Japanese invasion of China.

Next day we hiked through a wilder mountain region. Farm huts clung to steep slopes. Rice paddies were little shelves held up by dry stone walls. Peasant women naked to the waist stood in the paddies hoeing weeds, their pendulous breasts swinging in rhythm with the hoe. I was surprised how quickly I was becoming accustomed to experiences that would have shocked my acquaintances in Minnesota.

On the last day of our trek we reached the summit of Mount Fuji, symbol of the cult of Japanese patriotism. Most Americans who have climbed the volcano belittle the achievement; they say it is only a 10-hour walk up trails that are well graded. That is true. Yet the fascination for me was the sight of thousands of pilgrims—men, women and children—climbing to the snowy summit, pausing to pray at Shinto shrines, and returning with the inner satisfaction that they had visited the holiest mountain in Japan.

During my Carleton years Japan's empire building was in full swing. In my sophomore year—on September 18, 1931—the Japanese Kwantung Army had staged a bomb blast on the South Manchurian Railroad. Blamed on the Chinese, it served as the pretext for Japanese seizure of Chinese Manchuria. In 1932-1933—my junior year—the Japanese army occupied the additional Chinese province of Jehol in Inner Mongolia, created a demilitarized zone between Peking and Tianjin, and forced China to sign the Tanggu Truce. That year Japan also walked out of the League of Nations. In my senior year the Japanese army forced Chinese customs officers in north China to accept large shipments of Japanese manufactured goods without payment of duty; the Japanese were thus making China pay for the Japanese military adventures.

Japan's territory grabbing began several decades before Manchuria. The starting point for the Japanese empire was the quick war between Japan and China in 1894-1895. To the surprise of Western nations, little Japan whipped its giant neighbor and, among its booty, took the island that Europeans call *Formosa* and the Chinese call *Taiwan*. This was the beginning of half a century of Japanese colonial rule in Taiwan that left an impressive foundation of roads, railroads, hydropower, literacy, and peasant associations that administered irrigation. These Japanese developments played an important role in the later economic success of Taiwan.

In 1904-1905 Japan fought another brief war in the Far East, this time with Russia, and to the world's even greater astonishment, Japan thrashed the Czarists. That time Japan took the southern half of the Russian railroad system in Manchuria; the southern half of the island of Sakhalin lying off the east coast of Siberia; and control of Korea, which Japan annexed in 1910.

During World War I Japan entered the struggle on the side of the Allies, and—having the Far East to itself—seized German holdings in the Chinese province of Shantung. Thus Japan became a modest colonial power. But these scattered territories did not fill Japan's primary economic need for raw materials and markets. While Great Britain, France, and the Netherlands had vast overseas territories to supply their trade, Japan still depended mainly upon its small home base. In these circumstances the Japanese army decided that military expansion to the Asian mainland was the best opportunity, with China as the primary target, and Manchuria as the starting point. A frontier region north of the Great Wall, Manchuria was an area larger than France and Germany combined. It was rich in coal and iron, grain fields, and grasslands. By the summer of 1934 when I arrived, Japan had not only swallowed up Manchuria but was pressing its next stage of empire building—separating the provinces of north China and creating another Manchukuo-like puppet government.

That summer I called on Japanese university professors, using my Carnegie introductions. These academics were enthusiastic about the work of the Japanese army in Manchukuo. A faculty member at a Christian university in Tokyo remarked to me, "I am eager to see the new empire; we hear such fine reports." Everywhere I found omens of war. A Tokyo department store gave its entire top floor to exhibits of national defense. A 30-foot-tall map of the Pacific Ocean emphasized with colored markers how the Japanese navy confronted the American navy. This was seven years before Pearl Harbor. A popular exhibit in this store, titled "How to Detect Spies," warned children to watch foreigners and especially to look in their coat lapels for miniature cameras.

Looking back on that visit in 1934, I now know that even more significant changes were occurring that no visitor could see. An obscure German army officer, a confidant of Hitler, was preparing a secret report in Japan on the Japanese army. His name was Colonel Eugene Ott, and his report prepared the way for the Tokyo-Berlin Axis of 1939.

My first view of China was from the sea, across the harbor of Tanggu in north China. That was September 1934. No commercial airplanes flew to China in those days; everyone went by sea. I was travelling with Edwin Beal, an American I had encountered in Tokyo who had loaned me the price of my boat passage. A Chinese language student, Beal later became head of the Chinese section at the Library of Congress in Washington. We sailed on a small coastal steamer from the Japanese port of Shimonoseki, crossing the Yellow Sea as deck passengers.

I clearly remember three Chinese scenes from that day of arrival. First, two sleek Japanese gunboats were riding at anchor in the port of Tanggu, sending coded messages to each other by flashing lights on their radio masts. These were the first of many foreign naval vessels I was to see in Chinese ports, carryovers of past invasions and foreign victories.

Second, a Chinese labor crew was unloading 55-gallon oil drums from a barge, and the workers sent out a rhythmic chorus across the water that sounded like "Hi ho, yo ho, hi ho, yo ho." The strong beat kept the workmen in step. The remarkable ability of the Chinese to work collectively predated the Marxists.

And third, our ship was soon surrounded by a flotilla of small harbor craft paddled by children who were selling fruit. A Canadian standing next to me at the ship's railing bought half a dozen small pears. He passed one to me with his pocket knife and advised me to peel it while he wiped a pear on his pants leg and ate it with skin and all. I asked why he did not follow his own advice. He said, "I have lived in China five years and acquired some resistance to common germs. When you have lived here five years, you can eat fruit without peeling, but newcomers need to be more careful." His warning was sound.

At Tanggu Ed Beal and I followed other ship passengers to a nearby railroad station and purchased "hard seats" to Peking. For the next four hours Chinese *gaoliang* (sorghum) glided past our window, the crop standing three to five meters high, turning brown in the chill September air. Oxen plodded along the dirt roads, pulling two-wheeled carts. Occasionally a swirling wind lifted a cloud of fine brown dust into the air, a sight still familiar to travellers in north China.

As our train approached Peking across the agricultural plain, I fantasized about the city walls, said to be ten meters high and seven meters thick, topped with battlements that had survived from the fifteenth century. The walls were built with tamped earth and faced with sun-dried bricks that were many times larger than western burned bricks. Marco Polo passed through this same countryside in 1275 A.D. on his way to the Mongol capital located a little to the north of modern Beijing. In 1934 Beijing was still reportedly the most populous walled city in the world with 36 kilometers of walls surrounding the northern or Tartar city, surmounted by nine gate towers, and another 14 kilometers of walls enclosing the southern or Chinese city, with seven gate towers. I was excited at the prospect of making this medieval city my home.

At the railroad station Ed Beal's spoken Chinese got us rickshas to the YMCA on Hadamen Street where a letter of introduction to the Y secretaries obtained rooms for the night. I had one gnawing problem: my money was finished!

> Peking lies at the same latitude as Philadelphia, Madrid and Ankara.
>
> World Atlas

CHAPTER 2

# My Peking Life on Eight Great Men Lane

The Chang family of Peking invited me to join their household. Dr. Chang Yu-ch'uan, the patriarch, was a balding, 54-year-old scholar, with a grey mustache and a frequent twinkle in his eye. He was American educated (University of California and Yale). The Changs lived at 26 *Ba Da Ren Hutung*—translated Eight Great Men Lane—in the east city near the Qihuamen city gate. Their door on the street was distinguished by a bright red color, a brass door knocker and a pair of stone lions outside the threshhold. Inside was a series of courtyards filled with fruit tress and surrounded by many rooms, with the rearmost courtyard assigned to the kitchen.*

On my first day the family protested my way of eating. I am naturally left-handed and from early childhood have used a spoon or fork in my left hand. But when I picked up chopsticks in my left hand, the family said that was not the correct way to eat in China. After some struggle I learned to tweak chopsticks in my right hand, and to this day I use a fork in my left hand and chopsticks in my right.

The Chang family consisted of father, mother and five children. The eldest son was studying in the United States, the next two sons were enrolled at universities in Peking, a daughter was in high school and the youngest son was

---

*\*Chang Yu-ch'uan* was the spelling used by this man in the 1930s under the Wade-Giles system, a way of spelling Chinese sounds in Roman letters, designed by two Englishmen and widely used by mapmakers and newswriters prior to the communist takeover. The Peoples Republic of China adopted a new system of romanizing in the 1960s, called *pinyin*, now used in official government publications. Dr. Chang's name in pinyin would be *Zhang Yuquan*.

in elementary school. I took half my meals with the family and was expected to help the children speak English at the table.

As the newest family member I occupied the guest room, a spacious chamber with a Louis XIV bed. My room stood beside the front gate, isolated from the family, thus causing minimum intrusion. I was called Old Chang's secretary, which meant only that I edited his English articles and translations. One of his projects, I remember, was writing an English description of the imperial porcelain collection that was to be sent for exhibition in London. We spent days in the palace museum discussing appropriate words for glazes and crackles. Another month's work was translating the Chinese guidebook for the Summer Palace, that wonderful collection of royal rooms built by the Empress Dowager in the foothills overlooking Kunming Lake.

Old Chang was a quiet, thoughtful, and admirable man who lived to 71. He died peacefully in 1951, two years after the communists came to power. My warm feelings for the Chinese and their country began with that period as a member of the Chang family.


Shortly after arrival, I enrolled at the College of Chinese Studies for tutoring in the spoken Chinese language, a course that continued part time for two years. The college was a branch of the University of California, located about five minutes by bicycle from the Chang residence, close to the Eastern Four Archways (*Dongsi Pailou*). My tutor's name was Mr. Ma. To this day I can hear his voice in the opening lesson while he taught the Chinese tones: "Repeat after me: Wo, ni, ta. Wo ni, ta." (I, you, he.)

I spent inadequate time studying the written language; eventually I came to recognize perhaps 1,000 characters—not enough to read a Chinese newspaper, which is said to require 5,000 characters. But my concentration on spoken Chinese soon enabled me to give instructions to a ricksha puller or a house servant, to order a restaurant meal, to bargain in the market, and to arrange a railroad ticket. My first demonstration in Chinese bargaining came from Prof. Knight Biggerstaff of Cornell University, who had arrived in Peking for a second period of residence with a prior knowledge of the language. He needed a wooden chest of drawers as a file cabinet. We bicycled together to the East Market, which was then called *Dongan Shichang*. At a furniture shop Biggerstaff spent five minutes giving extended greetings to the shopkeeper, then another five minutes deprecating the shop's merchandise. He then casually mentioned that he would be interested in a chest of drawers. Unfortunately, he said, he did not see anything of good quality. The shopkeeper lined up his best chests, and priced one at 30 Mexican silver dollars (US$10 at that time).* Now the bargaining followed this approximate sequence:

> Shopkeeper: $30
> Biggerstaff: 50 cents
> Shopkeeper: $20
> Biggerstaff: $1
> Shopkeeper: $15
> Biggerstaff: $1.25
> Shopkeeper: $10
> Biggerstaff: $1.50
> Shopkeeper: $7.00
> Biggerstaff: $1.60

Here the series of compromises broke down. Only after Biggerstaff started for the door did the two agree on a sale price of two Mexican dollars.

Years later, while I was living in Muslim countries of south Asia, I could safely begin bargaining at half the seller's opening price, but in China of the 1930s the buyer would be fleeced if he started that high. To pay for language lessons and provide pocket cash, I taught English conversation in the Commercial College near West Single Archway (*Xidan Pailou*). I rode my bicycle there for a two-hour class three days a week. These classroom conversations revealed aspects of Chinese life that I might otherwise have missed. I learned, for example, that some of my students had been married as early as age 13. Although they were several years younger than I, they already had one or two children; they were not yet employed and still were supported by their parents. It was difficult for an American to imagine such dependence within the extended family.

My students at the Commercial College said that I needed a name in Chinese characters that approximated the sound of my Western name. One group of students recommended *Han* (for Hanson) *Ha Do* (for Haldore). Another group chose the two characters *Han Sen*. I preferred the shorter name and had calling cards printed with the two character—*Han* for Korea and *Sen* for forest. I also learned to write my name in the air with the first finger of my right hand, as most Chinese do.

Riding to and from my teaching classes I varied my daily route to acquaint myself with the city. Some days I cycled past the Gate of Heavenly Peace at the front entrance of the palace (*Tiananmen*). Sometimes I followed the

---

*The Mexican dollar coin, about the size of the American silver dollar, had circulated in China for many years and remained in use until inflation during the Japanese war caused the coins to be melted down.

street behind the palace, passing Coal Hill and the North Sea Park. Coal Hill is a man-made elevation about 300 feet high at its central point and a quarter mile long, its skyline adorned by a series of red-pillared pavilions. The name refers to coal allegedly buried there for use by the imperial family in case of siege. The hill was originally created from earth diggings many centuries ago when the three royal lakes adjoining the palace were excavated. In my period the palace was locked and unoccupied.

Street-side food was found at major street corners. There were hawkers of low-cost food like roasted ears of corn, baked sweet potatoes, steamed bread (*mantou*), and roasted chestnuts. Some hawkers used wheelbarrows with charcoal fires. Others had shoulder poles with two round boxes at each end. One box contained the charcoal stove and foodstuffs for cooking, the other was filled with serving dishes and a bucket of water for dishwashing. This was China's pioneer fast food industry, preceding McDonald's. A ricksha puller could buy a small meal of noodles, vegetables and tea for a few coppers. In those days 30 coppers made 10 cents, and bargaining continued over a single copper.

Small children standing at these food stands would often point at foreigners like me, laugh loudly, and shout "*Yang gui zi*" ("foreign devil") or "*Dabizi*" ("big nose"). This was more a joke than a hostile act, and their lack of malice made it easy for me to laugh with them.

During long conversations with Old Chang, my host, I learned about his career. We often talked in the sunny courtyard under the fruit trees, both of us dressed in Chinese gowns. He rotated a pair of round stones the size of walnuts in his right hand as he talked about recent Chinese history. After some of these sessions I bicycled to the Social Science Research Library where I wrote notes on my expanding ideas about China. If I expected to become a news correspondent, I thought, I would need a fuller picture of Chinese events.*

Old Chang was a Cantonese, born in 1880 (about the age of my father), and he became one of the most highly educated Chinese of his generation. After preparatory schooling at Fuzhou and Tianjin he earned a B.A. degree at Tokyo Imperial University, a Bachelor of Laws at the University of California, and a Master of Laws at Yale (1904). His foreign study was

---

*\*Lao Chang*, translated "Old Chang," is an honorific and familiar expression that Chinese often use in addressing each other, much as Americans might refer to Abraham Lincoln as "Old Abe." The person so addressed is not necessarily elderly.

financed by the emperor as part of the government's modernizing effort. It proved to be too late. By the time Chang returned from seven years abroad, the emperor's goverment was tottering from revolutionary pressure.

In 1905, I learned, the emperor had appointed a commission of scholars to study the constitutions of western nations and to recommend an organic law for China. At 25 Chang had been named a member of this group and had served two years. Next he was appointed inspector of schools for north China where he helped introduce mathematics and science. By 1910, at age 30, he became president of the College of Communications at Peking (*Jiaotung Daxue*), a post he held until the emperor abdicated in 1912. Then Old Chang became counsellor to the Ministry of Foreign Affairs and concurrently secretary to the first president of China, Sun Yat-sen.

President Sun was a native of Guangdong province, and he talked to his secretary in their provincial tongue. Dr. Sun had spent his high school years in Honolulu, had earned a medical degree in Hong Kong, and was a baptised Christian. He gave up the practice of medicine at 26 to agitate against the Manchu emperor. Old Chang described Dr. Sun as a magnetic personality, a man effective at organizing traditional secret societies, but who controlled no army and mobilized no labor unions or peasants. He was an intellectual rebel.

The revolution of 1912 succeeded in ousting the emperor but failed to provide a successor. A new constitution—the one on which Chang and the imperial commission had labored—set up an elective parliament, but the parliament failed to function. Dr. Sun Yat-sen was elected president by his political party, but he was unable to govern. Within a few months he surrendered the presidential mandate to the former commander of the imperial armies, General Yuan Shi-kai, who preferred to rule without a constitution or parliament. When General Yuan died in 1916, China broke up into rival warlord areas, each controlled by a self-appointed military commander. Whichever warlord controlled Peking was recognized by the foreign governments as the national government of China.

After a decade of chaos, Dr. Sun Yat-sen was offered Russian help to organize a nationalist revolution and, though Sun declared publicly that he did not favor communism for China, he accepted the Comintern offer. The struggling Nationalist Party, known in China as the *Guomindang*, reorganized itself along Russian lines, with tight discipline from the top down. The 300 members of the Communist Party were invited to join the 50,000 members of the nationalist party, a merger that Dr. Sun considered harmless. Michael Borodin, a skilled Russian organizer, became Dr. Sun's expert on how to prepare a revolution. Whampoa Military Academy was established at Canton to train officers for a new nationalist army that would drive north to unify China. As director of the academy Dr. Sun chose an unknown nationalist party member, Chiang Kai-shek, age 36.

Chiang came from Zhejiang province. Born in 1887, by age 18 he was a cadet in China's imperial military academy at Baoding, near Peking. Later he spent four years in a Japanese military school at Tokyo where he met Dr. Sun and came under his revolutionary spell. Chiang returned to China in 1911—in time to participate in the military action that overthrew the Manchus. He then left soldiering and entered the business community at Shanghai where he was a part-time stockbroker, with many friends among the international traders. From there Dr. Sun selected Chiang to head the new military academy at Canton. Chiang's colleagues at Canton included a small but remarkable group of communists. Political training at the academy was entrusted to an unknown man named Zhou Enlai, later premier of Peoples China. An affiliated school at Canton trained revolutionary propagandists; this was headed by another little-known communist named Mao Zedong. On the faculty at Whampoa Academy was a Chinese named Nie Rongzhen, and under him a cadet named Lin Biao; both later became marshals in the Red Army. Of course, there were also cadets who would become generals in the nationalist army. It was a stellar mix.

Chiang Kai-shek led the armies in their successful march northward, capturing Shanghai, Nanking, Hankow and eventually Peking. In 1925 Dr. Sun died of cancer before the nationalist victory. Two years later Chiang Kai-shek repudiated the communists, and thousands of leftists in Shanghai and Hankow were massacred. Chiang Kai-shek established his government at Nanking. When I arrived in 1934, China was in the sixth year of Chiang's nationalist rule.

Peking of the 1930s was a city of 1.4 million Chinese and about 3,000 foreigners living within the walls. The Japanese and their colonials, the Koreans, were most numerous among foreigners (about 1,000), the Americans came next (about 500), and then the British (300). Foreigners, as we non-Chinese were called, got to know each other like residents of a village. The city had almost no industry, but it had 17 colleges and universities.

Among foreigners, those in the diplomatic community were the elite, many living within the Legation Quarter—a walled city within a walled city. Officially Nanking had become the capital of China in 1928, but most embassies and legations remained in Peking.

Foreign missionaries were also a large contingent. Presbyterians maintained their church, schools, hospital, and printing press in the north city near the drum tower. Methodists had a church, schools, and hospital at the southeast corner of the city near Hadamen Gate. Congregationalists were on *Dongshikou* in midtown with church and schools. Catholics were most numerous among the religious community, with many churches managed by foreign priests, mainly French. Another nonprofit group was comprised of medical doctors at Peking Union Medical College. This was the Rockefeller Foundation's largest project in Asia.

Scholars of the Chinese language were another small and prestigious group of foreigners in Peking, most of them under age 30. These included John and Wilma Fairbank from Harvard, Knight Biggerstaff of Cornell, Derk Bodde of Pennsylvania, Martin Wilbur of Columbia, and John DeFrancis of Yale. There were also European sinologues.

For me the most interesting people in the foreign community were the newspapermen, of whom there were no more than 20. Among the old timers were the American, John Goette of International News Service; the Australian, H. J. Timperley of *Christian Science Monitor*; the American, Hal Ekins of United Press; two Britons, Malcolm McDonald of the *London Times* and Frank Oliver of Reuters; and men representing French and German news agencies. Edgar Snow was there; he had arrived from the University of Missouri School of Journalism in 1928 and had become a correspondent for the *London Daily Herald*. When I met Snow, he was leading a quiet life at Yanjing University, engaged in part-time teaching, translating, and occasional newspaper writing. His book, *Red Star Over China*, came later.*

Peking in 1934–35 was a splendid place for me to savor the leisure of upper-class Chinese life. But if I wanted to learn about the problems of China, I had to get out and travel.

---

*Among the younger American correspondents were two from the press associations. F. M. Fisher, a Michigan man, had earned a B.A. degree from Yanjing University, served several years as city editor of the local English paper, *Peiping Chronicle*, then joined United Press. James White, a graduate of Missouri School of Journalism, came to Peking as an exchange student and later became Associated Press correspondent for north China.

> *When practically the whole Red Army was concentrated at Yudu, in southern Jiangxi, the order was given for the Great March, which began on October 16, 1934.*

Edgar Snow, 1937

CHAPTER 3

# "Red Bandits" Take Their Long March

October 16, 1934 was an average day in Peking. The weather was cool and dry. Newspapers reported nothing eventful. I held my English conversation class as usual at the Commercial College.

Yet something was happening that day that would make October 16, 1934 an historic date for China—the start of events that were dramatically changing the direction of Chinese history. At dusk that day in the southeastern province of Jiangxi the Red Army began its Long March; about 5:30 P.M. Mao Zedong set out with other leaders from the north gate of Yudu town toward Ganzhou—destination unknown.

The Long March was a fighting retreat by 100,000 communist troops from a revolutionary base the size of Switzerland in southeastern China. The march traversed 10,000 kilometers (6,000 miles) in a little more than a year (farther than from New York to Alaska by way of Mexico); the marchers crossed violent unbridged rivers and climbed snow-covered ridges; they confronted hostile tribesmen; they skirmished with warlord troops or nationalist armies almost every day, and frequently endured attacks by nationalist warplanes. Out of 100,000 Red troops, only 30,000 reached the new base.

The Long March was important because it enabled the Red Army to escape the encirclement of Chiang Kai-shek in southeastern China and to establish a new revolutionary base in the northwestern province of Shaanxi. The march placed the Red Army in position to fight a popular war against Japanese invaders, and to train thousands of patriotic Chinese students for the war effort.

The march was also a training ground for a strong and cohesive band of communist leaders. Brigadier General Samuel Griffiths of the U.S. Marine

Corps once wrote about the Long March: "From this trial emerged a group of tested leaders, supremely confident of their ability to shape the destiny of their party and their country. And from it, too, sprang an indoctrinated army endowed with a rich experience, convinced of the righteousness of its cause and equipped with the dynamic doctrine of guerilla and mobile warfare."

The Long March has been compared to other military epics in history—to Napoleon's retreat from Moscow, to Alexander's withdrawal from India, to Xenophon's retreat from Persia with 10,000 Greeks. But the Chinese Long March surpassed those events in several respects: It involved more men, it lasted a longer time, and it had greater impact on its contemporary period.

It was three years before the story of the Long March became widely known. Edgar Snow, the young American journalist, wrote the first detailed narrative in 1937, using eyewitness testimony from Mao Zedong and other survivors. Arthur Miller described Snow's *Red Star Over China* as "the best single reportage I have ever read and surely among the most influential ever written."*

Some background on the Red Army and its leaders is needed here. The picture I give in these pages was not known to me when I lived with the Chang family in Peking but is inserted here—many years later—based on briefings I received from the Peoples Liberation Army in Jiangxi.

To start, a communist insurrection in Chiang Kai-shek's army at Nanchang served the role of Bunker Hill in the American revolution—that is, an armed revolt was followed by years of struggle, ending in success for the revolution. On the night of August 1, 1927, 20,000 troops at Nanchang revolted, seized the city, and later formed themselves into the nucleus of the Red Army. The Nanchang uprising, as it came to be called, was led by Zhou Enlai, later the premier of the Peoples Republic. The list of military officers who participated reads like a *Who's Who* of the Chinese army—Zhu De, commander of the Eighth Route Army during World War II; Li Xiannian, president of China in the 1980s; Ye Jianying, president of the Chinese National Assembly in the 1980s; and five others who became marshals in the Red Army (Nie Rongzhen, Liu Bocheng, Chen Yi, Lin Biao, and He Long). August 1, the date of the uprising, is now a Chinese holiday.

The 1927 uprising was followed by a series of defeats for the Nanchang

---

*Other eyewitness testimony about the Long March appeared in profiles published by Helen Foster Snow (*Inside Red China*, 1939); in Marshal Zhu De's autobiography as told to Agnes Smedley (*The Great Road*, 1956); and in recollections by the German, Otto Braun, the only foreigner on the march (*A Comintern Agent in China*, 1982).

rebels, and for other communist bands that tried to seize and hold major cities south of the Yangtze River. Late in 1927 remnant troops under Mao Zedong—an estimated 700 men retreating from the failed "autumn harvest uprising" in Hunan province—occupied six counties in the wild and foggy mountains along the Jiangxi-Hunan border. This was a traditional forest hideout for bandits. Stragglers from other Marxist defeats arrived in 1928, including 900 troops under Zhu De and 1000 under Peng Dehuai. By the time the combined forces reached more than 4000, the communists had outgrown the food supply in the forest retreat. So they moved across southern Jiangxi to a more prosperous area centered on the city of Ruijin. This became their fighting base against Chiang Kai-shek for the next five years, 1929–1934. The territory held by the communists expanded to 24 counties with a population of 2.5 million. Communist troops grew to more than 100,000.

Communist successes in Jiangxi have now been attributed primarily to the effective leadership of two men—Mao Zedong and Zhu De. Although their story is familiar to many non-Chinese readers, some of their qualities are worth repeating here to explain why it has been difficult for other countries to imitate a Maoist revolution.

Mao Zedong and Zhu De met for the first time in April 1928 at the village of Maoping in western Jiangxi. Each had suffered defeats, and they came to discuss a joining of their small forces.

Mao was a Hunanese, then 35, son of a small landowner and grain trader. Zhu was a Sichuanese, age 42, and a career army officer. Both were college graduates. Mao earned his degree from Hunan Teachers College at Changsha; Zhu graduated from Yunnan Military Academy at Kunming, one of the earliest modern military schools in China. Mao never studied abroad; Zhu spent three years in Marxist classes in France, Germany and the USSR, supporting himself with factory jobs.

Both Mao and Zhu brought important credentials to their first meeting. Mao had been a delegate to a secret congress in 1921 at Shanghai that founded the Chinese Communist party. In 1922 he organized the Communist party in his home province of Hunan and began mobilizing a revolutionary peasant movement that enrolled the largest membership of any peasant organization in China. When nationalist and communist leaders assembled at Canton in 1924 to prepare the military conquest of the warlords, Mao was there. He maneuvered himself into key assignments, first as leader of the propaganda department, then as head of the peasant institute that trained agitators for peasant revolt. By 1927, Mao was probably the most knowledgeable man in China on the subject of peasant grievances and how to arouse the villagers.

Zhu De, the military commander in the partnership, had served 11 years in the warlord armies of Sichuan and Yunnan, receiving rapid promotions. When republican armies overthrew the emperor in 1912, Zhu commanded a battalion at 26. By 1916, when Yuan Shi-kai was president, Zhu at 30 was a brigadier general.

No biography of Zhu De gives a plausible explanation why he decided in 1922—like a "born again Christian"—to give up high office in Yunnan, kick his opium habit, and proceed for study in Europe. There he joined a branch of the Chinese Communist party, and returned to China in time to participate in Chiang Kai-shek's nationalist revolution. A Sichuan warlord and old friend appointed Zhu De the public safety commissioner at Jiangxi, and from that post—as mentioned earlier—he joined the Nanchang uprising of 1927.

The Red Army, as organized by Mao and Zhu, differed from traditional warlord armies, as the communists now see it, in four ways.

1. The leadership of the Red Army was half political and half military. The dual command began at the top, with Mao and Zhu, and extended down to the lowest squad. That double leadership still exists.

2. Peasants provided the main support of the Red Army; therefore Mao and Zhu believed the Red Army must follow a code of conduct that ensured friendly relations between troops and villagers.*

3. The Red Army needed food, uniforms, and arms that must be obtained

---

*Mao's eight rules of conduct were set to music and sung by the troops. They were translated:

1. Replace doors that are used for bed boards.
2. Speak politely to peasants.
3. Return borrowed objects.
4. Pay for everything damaged.
5. Be fair in business transactions.
6. Be sanitary; dig latrines a safe distance from houses.
7. Never take liberties with women; don't bathe in the sight of women.
8. Don't ill-treat prisoners.

This code was needed, the army has explained, because the soldiers, average age 22, were themselves peasants of little education, unmarried, high spirited, and only beginning to understand the revolution.

in a manner that did not place a heavy burden on the villagers as warlord armies had done.*

4. On the battlefield the Red Army faced nationalist forces that were stronger in troop strength and armaments. Therefore the Reds used evasive tactics. These factors were also set to music and sung by the troops. The most familiar song was translated:

> *When the enemy advances, we retreat*
> *When the enemy encamps, we harass*
> *When the enemy avoids battle, we attack*
> *When the enemy retreats, we pursue.*

Of course this quatrain did not explain fully the Red Army response to Chiang Kai-shek's five annihilation campaigns. During the first four encirclements (1929-1933), the Red Army deliberately drew the nationalist armies into the Red base, split the enemy into groups, concentrated Red Army strength against one enemy group at a time, thus establishing Red superiority at the point of contact. With these tactics the Red Army destroyed whole divisions, captured thousands of prisoners, and replenished its own supply of weapons. It was only in the fifth encirclement campaign of 1934, when Chiang Kai-shek's German advisors introduced a shrinking encirclement of concrete blockhouses, that the Red Army lost its mobility and was dislodged. That was the background of the Long March.

The term *Long March* was coined by the communist leadership after the retreat to northwest China. The march began one month after I arrived in China and continued for a year. The nationalist government claimed exaggerated victories over the communists, many deaths among the top communist leaders and communist troop casualties that exceeded the total communist forces. The route of the marchers was not clear in the press because Mao Zedong was often leading his troops with evasive tactics.

As we will see in the next chapter, the communist armies spread fear in China's foreign communities.

---

*Mao tested in Jiangxi the communist policies on land distribution, reduction of peasant debts and tax reform. For example, the tax scale in the old Jiangxi base took 15 percent of crops from best quality land, 5-10 percent from medium land, and nothing from poorest mountain land.

*Fenyang in 1936 was a town of 60,000 people—
surrounded by medieval walls.*

Walter Judd, M.D.

CHAPTER 4

# Chicago Girl Flees Red Army

In August 1935, news spread through Peking's bachelor community: "Young women have arrived in town." Two American college students, enroute to English-teaching posts in the interior, were stopping several days at the College of Chinese Studies. I volunteered my services as a guide, although I then had no expectation that one of them—several years later—would become my wife. Bernice (Berni) Brown had been a sophomore at Carleton when I was a senior, and Josephine Hamilton was a fresh graduate from Oberlin.

After dinner that first evening we three visited the Temple of Heaven under a full moon. It was an exotic experience for travellers to ride by ricksha through the darkened streets, listening to the pat-pat-pat of the ricksha puller's cloth shoes, peering through the pool of light thrown by the ricksha's oil lamps, and occasionally being startled by the ricksha's gong when the runner warned other rickshas approaching in the dark.

At the temple the great wooden gates were closed and barred. A stone mason crew had been repairing the temple, and the masons were sleeping on the floor just inside the gate. I pounded on the temple door and shouted *"Kai mur! Kai mur!"* ("Open the gate!")

For several minutes there was no sound, then low grumbling, then someone moving. I said in Chinese, "We are foreign visitors"; that assertion was presumptuous but effective. The drawbars were lowered with a loud scraping sound and the big gate was opened just enough for us to squeeze through, stepping cautiously over the sleeping forms of the renovation crew.

In the moonlight we walked around the marble platform that surrounds the temple, then down the long stone walk to the Altar of Heaven. Here the emperor had prayed annually for good crops. It was eerie to stand in the moonlight, the three of us seemingly alone in the silent city. Only arrogant foreigners were as privileged as the emperor had been.

The two student teachers were going to Shansi province, about 300 miles west of Peking. Oberlin had assigned Jo Hamilton to teach at a high school in the city of Taigu. Berni Brown's destination was a government high school at Fenyang, then a town of 60,000 with medieval walls 30 feet high, no paved streets, no electricity, and no telephones. The "running water" was delivered to homes by water carts pulled by oxen. Fenyang's most modern feature was an American hospital directed by the Protestant medical missionary, Dr. Walter Judd, who later became a congressman from Minnesota.

Assigning American students to teach English in Asia was a practice that long preceded the Peace Corps. Several colleges and universities including Carleton, Oberlin, Yale, and Cornell, had such programs in China. Carleton assigned one or two undergraduates here each year, usually for a two-year stay between their junior and senior years. The program was financed by student contributions and campus money-raising projects.

When Berni Brown made a Christmas visit to Peking, I asked her what it was like to teach in a Chinese high school. She said her students sat on backless wooden benches, each with an English textbook open. There were about 20 boys and 10 girls in each of four classes. Ages ranged from 12 to 17, but they looked younger. In September the students and teachers dressed alike in blue ankle-length gowns that buttoned at the throat.

When winter came, Fenyang temperatures dropped below freezing and the school rooms were unheated. Students came to class in quilted gowns, woolen stocking caps, and scarves. If the floors were scrubbed in the morning, a thin layer of ice formed under the students' feet. There was much coughing and sneezing. Then the Communists approached.


The Central Red Army had ended its Long March in October 1935 and encamped in Shaanxsi province, about 70 miles west of the Yellow River. Fenyang was about the same distance to the east of the river. After four months of rest the Reds made an exploratory feint in the direction of Fenyang. Their apparent purpose was to gather grain, money, medical supplies, and peasant recruits, and possibly to feel out the strength of Japanese forces for a later attack. They crossed the Yellow River swiftly on Chinese New Year, February 18, 1936. The garrison from Fenyang rushed to prevent the crossing, but too late. Fenyang reacted with near panic. Authorities began buying up food in anticipation of a siege. Oxcarts and rickshas were requisitioned to haul army supplies. Men teachers at the high school were pressed into service filling sandbags at the city gates. There were spy rumors. Five local laborers were beheaded on suspicion of being communists, and their heads were hung outside the magistrate's office. There was no court trial, so nobody knew whether the charges were true.

Fenyang's small foreign community made hurried plans to evacuate, sending their only automobile in relays to Taigu, the nearest rail connection. Berni left Fenyang on the last vehicle trip, but only after the *Chicago Tribune* had carried the inaccurate headline, CHICAGO GIRL FLEES REDS ON BIKE.*

The refugee school teacher proceeded to Peking to await developments. We began seeing much of each other, and the hothouse atmosphere of military threat speeded up a relationship that might otherwise have been merely a spring romance. After a month, Berni's high school announced it would be closed indefinitely. She was now unemployed. Although other schools in Peking offered her teaching posts, she decided to complete her studies in the United States.

Before she departed from Peking, we agreed on a tentative scenario: to be married in the United States in exactly three years, March 29, 1939. Our friends were skeptical about such a distant commitment, but our plans worked out, and the marriage is now approaching its 50th anniversary.

I stayed on in Peking, determined to gather materials for a China book—meanwhile supporting myself by freelancing.

---

*Many years later Berni was asked by an officer of the Peoples Liberation Army with whom she was travelling, "Why did you run away from the Red Army? Can't you see we are friendly?" Berni reminded the officer that in 1936, about the time she left Fenyang, Red Army troops in Anhwei province had seized two Americans, Rev. and Mrs. John Stam, and beheaded them. Also about the same time, two European missionaries, Alfred Bosshardt and Arnelis Haymen, were seized in Hunan province by Red troops under Commander He Long and held for ransom. Four coolie-loads of Mexican silver dollars were paid, and the prisoners were released.

The PLA officer professed to know nothing about these events. That is understandable, since the editing of revolutionary history is selective.

> The commonest conjugation in Chinese grammar is that of the verb "to squeeze": I squeeze, you squeeze, he squeezes; we squeeze, you squeeze, they squeeze. It is a regular verb.
>
> Lin Yutang, 1935

CHAPTER 5

# Freelancing through Chiang Kai-shek's China

It was now my second year in China. I shared a rented house in Peking near Hadamen Gate with an American scholar, John DeFrancis. He was working on a doctoral thesis about Mongolia. Our Chinese landlady, Mrs. Ruth Yang, had a five-room house with shady garden courtyard that she rented to us with one manservant and a mixed board of Chinese and western food for 100 Mexican silver dollars a month. That meant DeFrancis and I were each paying U.S.$17 *a month*. This will sound unbelievable to tourists who now pay US$80 *a day* in the Peoples Republic of China, but the low cost of living was only one of the remarkable aspects of Peking in the 1930s.

I began freelancing. I calculated that if writing would pay the cost of travel, I would make a series of two-month trips and return to Peking periodically for teaching and writing. I consulted Edgar Snow about his experiences with the writing market. When Ed was a newcomer, he served two years with the American editor of the *China Weekly Review*, J. B. Powell. The Review was a 40-page weekly news magazine, published in English at Shanghai. It paid low rates but was always willing to buy articles from writers outside its staff. In addition, Snow suggested a dozen English language newspapers in the treaty ports. The most likely prospects were the *Peiping Chronicle*, the *Peking-Tientsin Times*, and the *North China Daily News*. All three had British editors who welcomed travel reports from the interior.

Starting in the summer of 1935 I travelled half-time and within two years sold articles totalling 580 typewritten pages. The articles were potboilers but exposed me—I was then 23—to China of the 1930s. During my third year in China I moved my home base to Wuhan where I wrote editorials for the *Hankow Herald*, an English daily that served the commercial community of central China. I also taught English composition at a local university and became a stringer, or piece rate correspondent, for the Associated Press.

In 1935 China was undergoing a railroad construction boom. Most new rail routes were chosen to serve Chiang Kai-shek's military campaigns against provincial warlords, but the new lines also stimulated a flow of agricultural products (rice, wheat, cotton) from the interior to the coast and a return flow of city products like kerosene and cement. British treaty port editors asked me to describe first-hand the increased flow of trade.

I travelled the railroad routes of Peking-Shanghai, Peking-Hankow, Peking-Baotou (Inner Mongolia), Peking-Harbin (Manchuria) and Changsha-Nanning (Guangxi province). I sampled the Yangtze River steamship route and the sea route from Shanghai to Amoy. There was little air travel within China in those years. One German airline called Eurasia Aviation Corporation advertised a ten-hour daylight flight for 12 passengers from Shanghai to Chengdu with refuelling stops at Nanking, Chengchow, Sian, and Hanchung. A competing flight by CNAC (China National Aviation Corporation) flew 14 passengers from Shanghai to Chengdu in eight hours, with refuelling at Nanking, Hankow, Ichang and Chungking. That flight, the advertising said, was by a "powerful new DC2" at 200 miles an hour.

My travel articles sold best when I travelled the lesser-known rail routes. A report on a new narrow-gauge railroad in Shansi was reprinted in five treaty port newspapers because that territory was relatively little known to the commercial communities on the coast.

Governor Yan Xi-shan, who built the narrow-gauge line, chose a nonstandard width so that trains from Chiang Kai-shek's territory could not enter his province. The Shansi gauge was 39 inches between rails; the national gauge was 56 inches. German locomotives used on the Shansi tracks were standard size, but their wheels were set 39 inches apart. This caused the train to rock and held the average speed to 20 miles an hour.

"My god, you're not taking the warlord express!" exclaimed a friend at Taiyuan. I said I had heard good things about the profitability of the new route, and I thought it would make a good story in the coastal papers.

At Taigu station I bought a passenger ticket southbound to Tungkuan on the Yellow River, in third class, the only class available. The fare was Chinese $8.60, then equal to US$2.90. The 420-mile journey lasted 28 hours. About 30 passengers were standing on the platform at Taigu when the locomotive, coal tender and six boxcars wheezed to a halt at noon on a cold February day. Where are the passenger cars? I asked. Obviously I must be a novice traveller from the coast because the passenger cars were there in front of me—those boxcars, adapted for people by installing three wooden benches lengthwise, one bench against each wall and one down the center. Two window openings without glass were cut into each side of the car and a coal stove at one end tried vainly to offset the winter temperature. The six boxcars on this train were already crowded to the doors, so the trainmen attached an open flatcar with three-foot sides as a temporary passenger car until we reached the next station. I was accommodated on the air-conditioned flatcar.

Moving south, our train followed a series of black barren mountains on the left; on the right was the Fen River, a tributary of the Yellow River. We passed walled towns with watch towers over their gates, dating from turbulent dynasties. In contrast to the medieval countryside, our smoke-belching locomotive seemed very modern.

"Roast beef and biscuits!" was the cry at a small rail station about sundown. Enterprising farmers had barbecued a cow that they were selling for 20 cents a slice, and the wheat biscuits, big as saucers, were ten pieces for ten cents. This made up for the lack of a train diner.

At this station we exchanged our open carriage for a boxcar without benches. The Chinese passengers carried no bedding, but they wore sheepskin robes from throat to ankle and fur caps that pulled down over their ears. No one seemed cold.

Darkness came. An oil lamp at the end of the car cast a dim circle of light. Voices came from invisible forms, marked only by a circle of cigarettes glowing in the dark. I unrolled my wolfskin bedroll beside the stove, and though the floorboards jounced, I was soon asleep. Next morning farmers met the train at a station with wash basins and kettles of hot water for which the price was a few coppers. Some women sold hot tea. One baker's boy offered yesterday's steamed bread, cold but tasty, and Peking pears.

The last six hours of the trip we passed cotton-growing valleys; the station platforms were piled high with bales awaiting shipment. Close to the Yellow River the train rumbled cautiously through a man-made gorge in the loess hills, with earthen walls rising a hundred feet on each side of the train. Crumbling earth showered down on the carriages. When we emerged at the river, the landscape was blotted out by a whirling cloud of yellow sand that obscured the sun. I bargained for a baggage carrier, watching over my shoulder to see how much others were paying. At the river's edge the baggageman and I boarded a flat-bottom freight ferry that already had 18 passengers, and we immediately pushed off. At midstream the ferry was buffeted by the full force of the Yellow River. Polemen bent to the gunwales, pole against the shoulder, arms quivering under the pressure of the current. Ice cakes struck the side of the ferry and spray flew over the passengers. After 25 minutes of struggle, the navigator guided the ferry into a quiet backwater under the walls of Tungkuan city. My baggageman led me to a tolerable Chinese inn called the Great Golden Tower where I could await the arrival of the Lunghai express train to Sian next day. The innkeeper warned me to beware of pickpockets.

With 24 hours on my hands, I sought out the railroad office inside the walled city. Here I asked about the building of the narrow gauge and its traffic, which would add interest to a feature story. Foxy warlord Yan Xishan, I was told, had spent only 20 million silver dollars for the 420 miles of track and the rolling stock. First, he confiscated the land for the right of way without compensation: he argued that the railroad would raise the prices received by farmers, and that was true. Second, Yan divided the rail route into short stretches and commandeered the labor, animal power, and tools from all the villages within 100 *li* (33 miles) of the line. He set a deadline for each group of villages to complete their stretch. This conscription of cheap labor was the same system by which early Chinese emperors had built the Great Wall and the Grand Canal. The Shansi provincial army was employed on the mountainous stretches, but even this labor was charged against the neighboring villages at 10 cents a manday. The route I had travelled had been built in two years.

Already during the first year of operation, more than 100,000 tons of wheat and about the same amount of cotton had moved out of lower Shansi. The cost of agricultural freight had been greatly reduced: train freight now moved at 1.6 Chinese cents a ton-mile; bullock carts at 7 cents a ton-mile; and motor trucks at 16 cents. The greatest railroad benefit came later as the farmers increased their crops to take advantage of the new transport.

The years of Chiang Kai-shek's Nanking government have often been described as a do-nothing period in old China, but some of the developments under Chiang's rule were positive. The Peoples Republic of China later inherited these railroads and made full use of them.

Another salable topic for the freelancer was opium smoking. In Peking I collected information on the price of opium and other drugs and published the data in unsigned articles through the Tientsin papers. Gathering the information was simple: I hired a ricksha puller at the Peking Hotel to take me to the opium shops he knew. Opium was sold over the counter in shops managed by Koreans. When the British social worker, Muriel Lester, visited Peking on behalf of the League of Nations, the British Embassy asked me to help her. In one afternoon Miss Lester and I made drug purchases in more than 50 shops; the trade was officially illegal, but the law was not enforced by the warlord rulers of the province.

In the summer of 1936 I visited Fukien province to write several articles for the *North China Daily News*. At Amoy I made contact with the local opium ring through a circuitous channel: a European salesman for the B.A.T. (British-American Tobacco Company) had a Chinese male secretary whose brother was a friend of a local gangster. For ten silver dollars, the friend agreed to show me some of the drug lounges in Amoy. The city then was divided into 18 racketeer districts, each under one underworld figure who controlled narcotics, gambling, and prostitution. My guide could protect me in one district.

During the first two hours we visited lower-class dens that were patronized by coolies who appeared to be ricksha pullers and stevedores. They lay on the floor to smoke and paid only a few Chinese coppers for one pipeful. Later we visited upper-class lounges where prices were as high as 20 silver dollars for the evening. One hotel had a gambling hall on the second floor, an opium lounge on the third floor where hostesses joined in the smoking, and bedrooms on the fourth floor where a man of means could enjoy his opium dreams with a woman. My guide claimed that there was a physical urge aroused by opium; smoking lounges were often linked to brothels.

Late in the evening my guide said he was ready for a few puffs. He led the way beneath a restaurant to a cool, semi-darkened lounge with upholstered divans, where we were attended by men servants in white silk gowns. The guide agreed to demonstrate the smoking procedure so I could write a feature story.

My escort ordered a saucer of opium that was sufficient for six pipes. The opium looked like a pool of molasses, two inches in diameter. The smoker picked up an instrument that resembled a woman's hatpin, dipped the tip in the sticky opium and twirled the opium over the flame of an alcohol lamp. The bead of opium puffed up like a soap bubble, then burst, giving off its moisture and leaving a white crumb of dry opium on the pin. The smoker repeated this process several times until the opium residue was the size of a pea.

Now it was time to prepare the pipe. A tubular brass pipe about two feet long had a hole near its base that served a purpose like the bowl of a tobacco pipe. The smoker heated this hole over the alcohol flame, did the same with the bead of opium; then very deftly thrust the hatpin down the hole of the pipe. The opium clung to the pipe, and he withdrew the hatpin with a twisting motion.

The pipe was now ready. The smoker placed one end of the pipe in his mouth and held the other end over the alcohol flame. Then he puffed smoke into his lungs as rapidly as possible. For half a minute this puffing continued while the smoker used the hatpin to push the outer edge of the bead of opium toward the hole in the pipe. The opium gave off a sweet aroma. After finishing one pipeful the smoker drank a cup of strong tea and lay down to rest for about five minutes. He required about half an hour to prepare the six pipes and engaged in only three minutes of actual smoking.

Overcoming my fears, I tried a pipeful. I had no dreams and found only a sweet taste in my mouth. Experienced smokers later told me I did not inhale enough.

My notes of a novice opium smoker appeared on page one of the *North China Daily News.*

On my travels I often stayed overnight with foreign missionaries who were preaching the gospel in every Chinese province and in almost every town. In the 1930s there were reported to be 8,000 Protestant missionaries in China—mostly American—and 12,000 Catholic priests—mostly European. Because I was their paying house guest (call it nonprofit at US$2 a night) and often benefitted from their local information, I feel ungrateful if I now express doubts about their evangelical results, which to me appeared meager. More than one evangelist said defensively, "If I save two souls for Jesus Christ, I feel my life has been well spent." My skeptical reaction: What a bottom line!

Missionary hospitals and schools scored higher in my estimation. Mission high schools and colleges played a large role in China before 1949, especially the 13 Christian colleges supported by American mission boards. The best known were Yanjing at Peking, St. Johns at Shanghai, Nanking University and Ginling College for Women at Nanking, Lingnan at Canton, Central China University at Wuhan, and West China University at Chengdu. Chinese faculties trained for these American-supported institutions still play a role in the higher education of the Peoples Republic.

Agricultural missionaries in the 1930s were few but left their mark: The old research station at Nanking College of Agriculture has now become the Jiangsu Academy of Agricultural Sciences; the former research station at West China Union University has become the Academy of Agricultural Sciences for Sichuan province; and the small research station at Taigu, Shanxi, managed in the 1930s by Dr. Ray Moyer, a Cornell-trained missionary, has now expanded to become the Shanxi College of Agriculture.

Missionaries have been pictured by Chinese revolutionaries as living in luxurious western-style houses within walled compounds; they were said to have enjoyed more status and more comforts with servants than they would have received in their home country. In my experience, that picture is not representative. It is true, however, that missionaries persuaded themselves that the nationalist regime of Generalissimo and Madame Chiang—both Methodists—was a liberalizing force bringing good government to China. Not surprisingly, this image of China was broadcast in the United States by the same church constituencies that supported the missionaries. The churches thus became a China lobby that contributed at least two useful pressure campaigns—one to end the unequal treaties, the other for the United States to stop arming Japan during the invasion of China.

A century of missionary work from the 1840s to the 1940s waits to be adequately appraised; the need is to measure the impact on Chinese beliefs after liberation. An episode in 1983 illustrates my doubts. A middle-aged Chinese scientist working for the Ministry of Agriculture at Beijing confided to me that he had received both his primary and middle school education under American missionaries. Aha, I thought; I shall do a little research. Were your schools Protestant or Catholic? He looked puzzled. "I don't understand those words," he said, "but I remember my lower school was a Mary-school and my middle school was a Jesus-school." I concluded his first school was Catholic and the second Protestant, but he remembered nothing about dogma.

> *Most of the great pre-industrial societies of the world have experienced explosions of "peasant fury". . . . But no country has had a richer and more continuous tradition of peasant rebellion than China.*
>
> Jean Chesneaux, 1973

CHAPTER 6

# Omens of Revolution

Most Chinese, I found, lacked patience with statistics; they were satisfied with approximations. In the 1930s if an educated Chinese were asked the population of China, he might answer 400 million or 450 million and add the phrase *cha bu do*, meaning more or less. Yet any discussion of the peasant problem depended upon reliable statistics because farming was the occupation of 80 to 90 percent of the population *cha bu do*.

Four centers that I visited in 1936 and 1937 were studying the peasant problem. The first was the Mass Education Movement at Ding county, 100 miles south of Peking. The second was the National Agricultural Research Bureau at Nanking, a unit of Chiang Kai-shek's government. The third was Nanking University, where a remarkable American economist, John Lossing Buck, was conducting a classic farm survey in 23 provinces. Finally, Jiangxi provincial government was conducting a "rural reconstruction program" in the area formerly controlled by the communists. I found no agreed-upon wisdom among these four centers, but the information I gathered helped me to understand my later wartime visits to communist-held areas in northern China.

The Ding county program was headed by a former YMCA secretary, the dynamic Jimmy Y. C. Yen, whose activities received partial support from the Rockefeller Foundation in New York. Jimmy Yen's program began with a mass literacy drive—an effort to teach peasants and their families to read and write—and expanded to include village hygiene and simple scientific farming. It was a modest effort. Its greatest success was in training village leaders; the greatest shortcoming was its failure to face the problem of land rental. A family that pays half its crop in rent may not improve its status much by learning to read and write. Nevertheless, when communist-led guerillas were fighting the Japanese army in central Hebei, the communists told me they recruited their most dedicated officers from Ding county. So mass literacy probably awakened a new and intense nationalism.

The Nanking University study of peasant problems produced the most comprehensive data. Professor John Lossing Buck trained Chinese students to conduct 16,783 interviews all over the country. The study lasted four years, 1929 to 1933. When I interviewed Buck in 1935 in his university classroom, he was analyzing data with pencil and paper (no pocket calculators or large computers in those days). He gave me some of his basic findings:

> The average amount of land cultivated by a Chinese family was 3.3 acres. The average household contained 6.2 persons. That meant each half acre had to feed one person.
>
> On land ownership: two out of four farmers owned all the land they cultivated; one out of four was part renter; and one out of four was entirely a renter. Buck's figures show greater land ownership than those gathered by Mao Zedong in Hunan province. Mao calculated 70 percent were tenants. It is probable that Buck was correct for China as a whole, and Mao was correct in Hunan.
>
> The median rent charged to peasants was 49 percent of the crop, an appalling squeeze.
>
> The average peasant in Buck's survey had experienced famine three times in a lifetime. The typical famine lasted 11 months. During those famines an average of 5 percent of the people starved to death, 13 percent emigrated, generally to beg in a city, and 24 percent survived on tree bark and pasture grass.

The farmers, according to Buck's data, were driven into debt by a combination of high rents, high interest, and high taxes. The most common purpose of borrowing each year, according to the Buck survey, was to "roll over" the debt—that is, to extend the previous debt for another year and to add the current interest to the debt. The Buck survey concluded that farm debts were steadily rising during the years of the Chiang Kai-shek government.

I visited the Jiangxi "rural reconstruction program" in the spring of 1937, 2½ years after the main communist force had left the province on their Long March. Like the Ding county program mentioned earlier, the Jiangxi program stressed mass literacy, scientific agriculture, and village hygiene. It did nothing about land distribution and little about farm indebtedness or rent reduction. I wrote enthusiastically about the Jiangxi literacy program—especially the "little teacher movement" by which primary school children were trained to teach their parents to read and write—but the Jiangxi program could not halt the downward slide of China's peasant economy. I looked for something more favorable to say about the Jiangxi program but I did not find it.

Few writers in the 1930s were reporting the severity of the Chinese village problem and the likelihood of a peasant uprising. Yet China was then about one decade away from establishment of a communist regime. There were a few discerning observers like Lu Hsun, the short story writer; Fei Xiao-tung, the brilliant American-trained anthropologist; and Edmund Clubb, an American foreign service officer who pieced together the growth of Chinese communism. Clubb was eventually forced out of the State Department because of his efforts to report on the spread of communist influence. I cannot claim to be among those far-sighted observers.

In 1937 I met Agnes Smedley. She was an American correspondent representing the highly regarded *Frankfurter Zeitung*. Among news reporters Agnes had the reputation of knowing more about the communist side of the Chinese civil war than any other foreign reporter; it was said she had contacts with the communist underground. Other correspondents who claimed to know her well insisted she was not a communist but an angry social rebel whose hostility toward authority resulted from an impoverished childhood in a Colorado mining camp. I met Agnes in an apartment in the French Concession of Shanghai in a cloak-and-dagger atmosphere. Her address was not listed in the phone book, but J.B.Powell of the *China Weekly Review* gave me directions for finding her.

Agnes was a hefty woman of 44 with a profane tongue. She had been in China about eight years.

"Are you married?" I asked.

"I earn my living on my feet, not my back," she retorted.

I told her I recently visited the old Red Army base in Jiangxi to see the Guomindang's reconstruction program.

"What reconstruction, for Chrissake!" she exploded.

I ignored the sarcasm. My reply went something like this: "The reconstruction by the Guomindang has preserved part of the communist activities, especially the mass literacy classes and efforts to improve crops. As far as I could see, that work is useful. But the reconstruction has one great weakness; it does nothing about farm debts, or high rents, or the concentration of land holdings in a few hands. Isn't that the central problem?"

Agnes never commented. But when she did speak again, after a long pause, it was in a calmer voice. She mentioned that she had helped some travellers from the United States to visit Yan'an, and they had carried her personal letters to the communist leaders. The visitors had brought back requests for supplies, especially from Ma Haide, the American medical doctor at Yan'an who sent a list of drugs to be purchased. She was procuring these items to be carried to Yan'an, she hoped, by future travellers.

I never wrote about this conversation with Smedley. But almost 50 years later, long after her death in England in 1950 at 57, I learned she had done me a service. I asked Lu Zhengco, a retured guerilla general at Beijing, why he allowed me to travel in territory controlled by the guerillas during the Japanese war. He said he consulted General Nie Rongzhen who in turn consulted Agnes Smedley through the communist underground in Shanghai. Smedley replied that she considered Hanson a reliable reporter.

Agnes was the author of four or five books on China, all containing her angry, revolutionary view of the world. The best of these writings is *The Great Road: Life and Times of Zhu De*. It was published after her death.

Agnes Smedley's ashes are buried at Babaoshan, a cemetery a few kilometers west of Peking. Her inscription translates:

*In memory of Agnes Smedley,
American revolutionary writer
and
Friend of the Chinese people*

One topic strangely missing from my freelance writings were the unequal treaties during the century from 1842 to 1943. As an American living in China I benefitted greatly from the privileges wrung from China by foreign governments. In the 1930s the Legation Quarter in Peking contained at least five foreign military units—those of the United States, Britain, France, Italy, and Japan. The American community of 500 civilians in Peking was guarded by 200 "horse marines" mounted on Mongol ponies. The Japanese had 800 infantrymen inside Peking guarding 1000 civilians. These legation guards were authorized by the treaty settling the Boxer siege of 1900; the guards' primary function was to keep open the communications between Peking and the sea. It is difficult to conceive a parallel situation in Washington, D.C. It would require a walled compound covering half a square mile, possibly starting on Lafayette Square opposite the White House, containing foreign embassies, each guarded by its own armed forces. That is what the powers imposed on China.

Other "unequal" conditions were even more galling to China: foreign gunboats in Chinese harbors; foreigners collecting Chinese customs duties; foreigners managing the Chinese salt monopoly; 80 cities called "treaty ports" forcibly opened to foreign trade, foreign schools, foreign churches; and foreign residents exempt from Chinese laws and courts. Despite these inequalities, I believe Chinese critics go too far in blaming foreigners for China's poverty and mismanagement.

My freelance articles covered many other topics. At Tientsin I described the forced entry of Japanese commercial goods —especially refined sugar and synthetic fiber cloth—without payment of Chinese customs duty. I sold an article on this subject to the U.S. journal *Pacific Affairs*.

At Central China University I delivered a speech that was reprinted in *China Digest*, a pocket-size publication resembling the U.S. *Readers Digest*. Titling the speech "Ten Million Unfilled Chinese Jobs," I quoted Chinese government officials engaged in rural work, including the national soil survey, national road development, and rural health services. These agencies found most Chinese college graduates of the 1930s were unwilling to work in the rural areas for the prevailing salary of 100 silver dollars a month.

In October 1936 Chiang Kai-shek celebrated his fiftieth birthday, and his government ordered all newspapers in China to write articles lauding progress under Chiang's regime. I drew the assignment to write the editorial for the *Hankow Herald* and wrote a factual article praising Chinese educational progress.

On the night of December 12, 1936, I received a telegram at Hankow from the Associated Press stating that Chiang Kai-shek had been arrested at Sian by two of his own generals. AP requested that I spend the night at Hankow railroad station and interview the first evacuees arriving from Sian. Next day I telegraphed AP the details of martial law in Sian; this was the closest any reporter got to Sian that day. Negotiations for the generalissimo's safe release proved a turning point in the Chinese revolution.

One rebel leader was the Young Marshal from Manchuria, Zhang Xueliang. His father, known as the Old Marshal, had been overlord of Manchuria before the Japanese assassinated him in 1928. The Young Marshal took over his father's command, and his Manchurian troops were driven out of the northeast provinces by the Japanese. Now these same

Manchurian troops were stationed at Sian, under orders from Chiang Kai-shek to fight the communists. But the Manchurians considered it more important to fight the Japanese and regain their homeland.

A second rebel leader was General Yang Hou-cheng, also stationed at Sian. His troops were strongly influenced by the communist slogan, "Chinese should not fight Chinese."

Chiang Kai-shek remained a prisoner for 13 days. Little news leaked out, but we later learned that negotiations had centered on an eight-point rebel program. The two most important points were: (1) a truce in the civil war, and (2) armed resistance to any further Japanese aggression.

During the Sian negotiations the rebels invited a communist delegation headed by Zhou Enlai to join the talks. To the surprise of most people the communists advocated that Chiang be released and returned to leadership at Nanking. Consistent with this view, the generalissimo was freed on Christmas Day, 1936, having given oral approval to the rebel program.

One irony: The Young Marshal was placed under house arrest by Chiang Kai-shek after the Sian incident and has remained a prisoner of the nationalist government for 50 years. But his daring arrest of Chiang Kai-shek accomplished its immediate objective. When the Japanese began their invasion on July 7, 1937, both nationalist and communist troops resisted.

In June 1937, I moved back to Peking to work with a group of professors and journalists who had organized a fortnightly magazine called *Democracy*. If a Japanese invasion were coming that summer, as many believed, Peking would be the trouble spot. The magazine was short lived. After only five issues (May–July 1937) it was padlocked by the Japanese army because it advocated Chinese resistance.

*The volume of AP news had reached staggering proportions—1,000,000 words in every twenty-four hours.*

Oliver Gramling, 1940

PART TWO

# WAR CORRESPONDENT

Journalists, it is said, write the first draft of history. Several hundred American correspondents—some of the best of their generation—were assigned to China during the twelve years of fighting that began with the Japanese invasion of 1937 and ended with the communist triumph over Chiang Kai-shek in 1949. By-lines of that period included Tillman and Peggy Durdin, Henry Lieberman, and Walter Sullivan of the *New York Times*; A.T. Steele of the *New York Herald-Tribune*; John Hlavcek of the *New York Daily News*; John Hersey, and Theodore White of *Time-Life*.

How did American reporters view the convulsion in China? During the first two years, 1937–1939, China was a retreating underdog, pounded by the Japanese army and drawing sympathy in the news. China news often dominated the world front pages as the datelines moved from Peking to Shanghai, to Nanking, to Hankow. The communists were organizing guerilla warfare behind the Japanese lines, a development that fascinated the American public. At Hankow the correspondents first met and were captivated by the remarkable Zhou Enlai, a communist leader who was described in dispatches as "accessible, articulate and charming." This was a period of the united front between Chiang Kai-shek and the communists, a partnership that gradually fell apart.*

After retreating with the nationalist government to Chungking, the press corps found itself separated from the fighting. They were soured by nationalist propaganda, controlled by nationalist censorship, and surrounded by nationalist inflation, mismanagement, and corruption. In the eyes of frustrated correspondents Mao's capital in far-off Yan'an, blockaded by the nationalists, seemed a romantic center of Chinese hope.

After 1945 the press corps had to cope with a new political dimension. General Patrick Hurley, the American ambassador to China, resigned, alleging procommunism and disloyalty among State Department and embassy staff—charges that made China policy a poisonous issue.

What qualities did these correspondents display? They were young. Most were in their thirties and were college educated. Few spoke Chinese, yet this did not seem a handicap. There was no observable correlation between the best reporters and the best linguists.

Were these correspondents biased in favor of the communists? Not in my opinion. They seemed skeptical about the efforts of both sides to manipulate them.

Did American reporters in China cooperate with U.S. government officials? Yes; the relationship was close. When the Japanese army seized the cable office at Peking and stopped American press messages, the U.S. Embassy transmitted the news cables over embassy radio to Manila where the news was relayed commercially to New York.

---

*The "united front" between Chiang Kai-shek and the communists began with a written agreement in August 1937. The agreement authorized the communists to maintain in Shanxi province the Eighth Route Army of 45,000 troops, and the New Fourth Corps in the lower Yangtze valley, near Nanking, with a strength of about 10,000.

The agreement was shaky from the start. The nationalist government accused the communists of expanding their armies beyond the agreed-upon strength, of moving their armies to unauthorized areas, and of mobilizing large numbers of guerillas for use in a renewed civil war. On their part the communists suspected Chiang Kai-shek of withholding his best armed soldiers from the Japanese fighting.

The breakdown of the united front was gradual, but the turning point seemed to be the "New Fourth Incident." In 1940 Chiang ordered the communist New Fourth Corps to transfer from the Yangtze valley to northern China. Before the corps had completed its crossing of the Yangtze, one of Chiang Kai-shek's armies attacked the New Fourth, massacred part of the troops, and disarmed the remainder who had not yet crossed the river (January 6–14, 1941).

Thereafter the Yan'an border region was blockaded by nationalist forces, and Mao Zedong found it necessary to order communist troops in the border region to grow their own food. For the remainder of the Japanese war nationalist-communist relations remained wary, and within a year after the Japanese defeat full-scale civil war was renewed.

How well did correspondents serve as the eyes of the American public? Actually, they failed to communicate effectively to American readers that Chiang Kai-shek was losing popular support and that a communist victory in the civil war seemed inevitable. The American public was thus unprepared for the communist victory in 1949. Contrary to later interpretations in the McCarthy era, this failure was not the result of sympathy for communist ideology. These correspondents were competent journalists who were watching history unfold and reporting what they saw.

I shared their experience during 1937–1939, as described in the next few chapters.

> It is always easy to find an excuse to start a war.
>
> Matsumuro Koryo, chief of Japanese
> intelligence at Peking, 1936

CHAPTER 7

# Japan Invades

An express train hurtled northward toward Peking in June 1937 through fields of ripe wheat ready for harvest. Sitting alone in the dining car, I watched the villages glide by and wondered when war might begin. Eight miles outside the Peking walls our locomotive slowed for a steel bridge spanning the Yongding River, and a Chinese steward pointed downstream to the ancient white marble arches of the Marco Polo Bridge, named for the Venetian traveller because he stood on the bridge in the thirteenth century. He wrote in his *Travels*: "Its length is 300 paces, and its width eight paces, so that ten mounted men can—without inconvenience—ride abreast." Marco Polo must have calculated the width of the bridge with small Mongol ponies. The Chinese call the bridge *Lugouqiao*. Near the marble bridge is one of the strategic railroad junctions of north China. There rail lines coming out of Peking divide—one line goes to Tianjin and one to Wuhan. In 1937 the Marco Polo Bridge gained new fame, this time as the place where the Chinese-Japanese war of 1937–1945 began.

I had been back in Peking from Wuhan less than two weeks when my houseboy, Feng Lin, awakened me one morning with a rap on the bedroom door. "*Dapao, dapao* (Cannons!)," he called excitedly. I poked my head out the front door and heard distant rumbling; it could have been thunder but the sky was clear. The Japanese army had been holding night maneuvers around Marco Polo Bridge; such war games were not alarming in north China because American, British, and Italian troops also engaged in such exercises. In a diplomatic note of 1913, the Chinese foreign office had specified four locations near Peking where foreign garrisons could hold maneuvers. Marco Polo Bridge was one of them. Yet on this occasion there was greater apprehension than usual. The Japanese war games had continued for 13 days.

I telephoned the *Peiping Chronicle* and asked an editor what was happening. I learned that a Japanese officer had protested to the Chinese foreign office that someone fired on the Japanese in the dark the previous midnight; one Japanese soldier was missing. At daybreak the Japanese had begun shelling the Chinese garrison town of Wanping, close to the Peking city walls. I assumed this, like so many recent events, was another false alarm. The Japanese would probably demand the resignation of a Chinese official, and the incident would be closed. Not until days later did we conclude that we were witnessing an Asian Sarajevo.

Peking suffered acute jitters. I remember walking home from the telegraph office one night through a dark *hutung* (lane); the narrow roadway was dimly discernible between black walls that rose on either side. Doorways resembled dark caverns. A dog growled in the murk, then someone very close to me barked an animal-like command. I stopped. For a brief moment there was no sound or movement; then out of a doorway came the glint of a broadsword, slowly advancing, point foremost. "I am a foreigner," I said in Chinese in a low voice. The sword was lowered, but the shadowy swordsman drew closer until his face nearly touched mine. It was a Chinese sentry. He mumbled apologies and the cavernous doorway swallowed him up.

For the next two weeks troop trains arrived daily from Manchuria, bringing Japanese reinforcements. Sporadic firing continued at Marco Polo Bridge.

The Associated Press hired me as a reporter to supplement the work of its resident correspondent, J. D. (Jimmy) White. I was 25, and he was 27. White would supervise the office and attend Japanese press conferences in the Diplomatic Quarter. These were conducted by a stout, balding, English-speaking Japanese officer named Col. Junjo Hiraoka. My assignment was to report what was happening outside the city walls. Most correspondents in Peking were married and were reluctant to risk field trips. They also found it useful to stay close to the cable office. Jack Belden and I were among the few reporters who moved about. Together we travelled daily to Marco Polo Bridge.*

When a city passes from the control of one wartime combatant to another, the population experiences a moment of peril. On July 27, 1937 the commanding Japanese general in Tianjin issued an ultimatum: Unless all

---

*Belden was an American freelance writer, a graduate of Rutgers University. He had worked his way to the Far East as a seaman, and jumped ship at Hong Kong. I first met him in Peking, tutoring Chinese students in English. Later he wrote three war correspondent books, all highly praised: *Retreat with Stilwell*, describing the allied defeat in Burma; *Still Time to Die*, dealing with the North African war; and *China Shakes the World*, describing the liberation war in China. The last is a classic.

Chinese troops evacuated Peking within 24 hours, the Japanese would attack. That afternoon an eerie hush settled over the old capital. Before dark, peddlers in the side streets ceased their cries. Occasionally a grey Chinese military truck sped from one defense sector to another, but otherwise the streets were empty. The 1,400,000 residents remained indoors.

Next morning the buzz of an airplane awakened the city. A lone Japanese scout plane was dropping leaflets. My breathless servant brought a copy that translated:

BY THE WILL OF HEAVEN AND THE NORTH CHINA PEOPLE
THE JAPANESE ARMY IS DRIVING OUT
THE UNRULY CHINESE SOLDIERS

Many residents shook their heads at the possible destruction—a palace 600 years old, a priceless art museum, and 19 universities.

Still buttoning my shirt, I ran to a vacant field near my house to get a view of the American radio tower that rose 360 feet above the Diplomatic Quarter. High on the shaft was a black triangle, the distress signal of the American navy. This was the signal to call all Americans into the embassy where they could be protected by the American mounted marines. Not since the Boxer Uprising in 1900 had Peking faced such an emergency. The quiet of dawn was punctuated by distant shelling or bombing, initially toward the south where the Chinese defense force had its largest barracks at Nanyuan (South Field); later the sounds of battle were heard on the west, north, and east of the city. The Japanese were softening us up.

After breakfast I started on my bicycle toward the American embassy but was stopped by an amazing spectacle. Chinese soldiers were ripping up the asphalt on Hadamen Street near the YMCA, digging trenches across the tramcar line and piling up sandbags in the middle of the street. Yet the defenses faced toward the diplomatic quarter. I asked why. The Chinese officer waved his sword toward the embassies and shouted, "Eight-hundred Japanese soldiers in there!" The Chinese feared that when the ultimatum expired at noon, Japanese troops would rush out of their compound and open the city gates from the inside—a variant on the Trojan horse.

By 11 A.M. the American embassy had become a fortified village of canvas tents. More than 500 missionaries, doctors, and scholars were jostling together in one big party. Rooms were free; board was 55 cents a day. Most of the American community was gathered under the shadow of the radio mast.

Before noon word came that all telephone and telegraph lines outside the city were cut. Railroad tracks were torn up. Except for its embassy radios Peking was isolated.

At 11:45 A.M. I stood with several correspondents outside the diplomatic quarter at the gate where the Chinese expected the Trojan-like attack. At 11:58 we edged toward a drainage ditch where we could dive for cover. Then the Hongkong and Shanghai Bank clock tolled noon. Nothing happened.

A little past noon a report of Chinese victory stirred the city population. Chinese armies were said to have attacked and recaptured from the Japanese all the rail stations between Peking and Tianjin. But that night the Chinese troops withdrew and Peking became a Japanese-occupied city—for eight years. By an irony of history a similar "victory" was proclaimed by Russian troops when Napoleon's army neared Moscow. A mass was sung for the victorious troops of the Czar less than 24 hours before the Russian army abandoned its capital.

The day after the Japanese bombing and shelling I was the only correspondent to reach Nanyuan barracks. Early in the morning I left the south gate of Peking by bicycle. The sky was clear, the temperataure already hot. The distance from the city walls to the barracks was seven miles. I encountered no obstacle on the blacktop road until I come to a sandbag barricade about seven feet high, that spanned the road. I called to the sentry on the other side of the wall, expecting to see a Japanese cap pop up. Nothing happened. I clambered up the wall of sandbags and looked down at a grisly sight: a heap of Chinese corpses. Not a Japanese in sight. I climbed down to examine the victims. Most were villagers. I pulled my bicycle over the barricade and rode on slowly through increasing carnage. Soldiers lay sprawled in heaps. A spectacle like a surrealist painting set my nerves quivering. A Chevrolet car in the road ahead of me was rocking back and forth like a teeter-totter. Between the front wheels of the car protruded the writhing head of a horse. Four men sat in the car, nodding forward and backward like sleepy men at the opera. I spoke to them softly, but they were dead. It appeared that their vehicle had been ambushed while travelling at high speed and had crashed into the horse, tangling the live animal under the motor. Beyond this bizarre scene was a riddled staff car with two dead Chinese generals slouched in the back seat. Their driver had evidently run away at the moment of attack.

Slowly the shock penetrated. The silence was unnerving. I swerved my bicycle to avoid a corpse that moved. It was a wounded man lying on his back. He implored me to call his mother in Peking so she could come to him, but he could not remember her telephone number. I gave him a packet of toast from my pocket. A cup of water would have been more appropriate, but my canteen was empty.

I wandered through the barracks where 3000 men had been bombed out of their quarters the day before. The sleeping area was strewn with toothbrushes, shoes, dirty socks, cigarettes, pictures of sweethearts—everything that a soldier possesses. Hundreds of cavalry horses were milling around the barracks, still terrified by the explosions of the previous day. One horse nuzzled my handlebars, apparently begging for food, but I had nothing to feed him.

By midafternoon the stench of corpses filled the air, and my cable to the Associated Press was overdue. Famished, I cycled back to Peking to report that at least 1000 Chinese soldiers had paid the price of Peking's ineffective defense.

Nothing in life is so exhilarating," wrote Winston Churchill in 1898, "as to be shot at without result." Churchill was then a war correspondent for the *London Times* covering tribal wars on India's northwest frontier.

I experienced that same exhilaration on a warm afternoon in August 1937 as I cycled along a railroad embankment 15 miles north of Peking, headed for Nankou Pass. Nankou is a dip in the Great Wall that many tourists visit each year. But long before the tourists, Nankou was the invasion route through which mounted barbarian hordes from the north repeatedly invaded China. In 1937 the Japanese army chose the same route, but in reverse, moving northward out of Peking along a railroad leading to Inner Mongolia.

On the seventh day of the Japanese assault at the Great Wall, I slipped out of Peking to observe the battle. On the handlebars of my bicycle I tied an American flag about 12 by 15 inches. I was still a treaty port foreigner who thought no Japanese or Chinese soldier would intentionally shoot at a traveller protected by his flag.

To the left of the railroad was a barren streambed about half a kilometer wide; to the right—about 200 meters away—was a sorghum field with a lush crop standing four meters tall, an ideal hiding place for a sniper.

The first rifle shot out of the sorghum sounded like a firecracker. I don't know how close the bullet came to me, but it missed. Still thinking foreigners were sacrosanct, I dismounted, stretched the flag to all of its 15 inches and shouted in Chinese, "I am an American." No sound or movement came from the sorghum. After a pause I mounted and proceeded no more than 50 meters when three more shots went pop-pop-pop! I then abandoned faith in the treaties and pedalled toward my destination as fast as I could, zigzagging on the narrow path. Like Churchill, I was unscathed and exhilarated.

I returned to Peking that night to report a military standoff at the Great

Wall. A few days later the Chinese troops surrendered this gateway to Mongolia.

The great Chinese retreat had begun. Within 18 months Japanese armies occupied the principal Chinese railroads, and the Japanese navy closed the main seaports. Japanese forces were then thinly spread along the major transport routes with garrisons maintained in the cities. That was the pattern when a stalemate descended upon China. The situation remained substantially unchanged for seven years, 1939 to 1945.

Meanwhile, a different kind of war developed in the Japanese rear—a struggle that greatly influenced the Chinese revolution.

*Guerilla: One who engages in irregular warfare.*
Webster's Dictionary

CHAPTER 8

# Reporting the Guerillas

I was at the Beijing railroad station in January 1938 discussing the war with a missionary from Baoding when I noticed a lean Chinese with bushy hair, perhaps 30 or 35, edging closer to listen to our conversation. "The guerillas," I was saying, "may be the key to China's future. We get reports about sporadic attacks on the railroads in the rear of the Japanese army, but nobody has the facts about the guerilla organization."

After the missionary boarded a train, the eavesdropper beckoned me aside, introduced himself as a Chinese professor of chemistry, and asked why I was interested in the guerillas. I explained that I was a correspondent for an American news agency, and that we had been unable to make contact with the guerillas. He told me, "I shall travel shortly to guerilla headquarters in central Hebei, and when I return I will give you an interview." I handed him my card, and he disappeared in the crowd.

Two months later my telephone rang, and the same quiet voice said, "This is Professor Wang speaking." I was skeptical because I had checked his university affiliation and found he had introduced himself falsely. If he were willing to come to my room at the College of Chinese Studies, I agreed to see him.

For five hours the professor poured out a story that no responsible correspondent would cable without verification. It sounded like preposterous propaganda. He said a group of Chinese communists assisted by patriotic students from Peking had organized an isolated government behind the Japanese army administering 7 million people in central Hebei. Their nearest borders were only 50 miles from Peking. This government claimed that a defense corps of 500,000 volunteers was guarding the villages, and a small mobile army was attacking the Japanese-held railroad. The equipment of the guerillas included crude village arsenals, radio communications, telephones, newspapers, and outdoor theaters—all organized without money from the outside. I asked to see for myself and to take photographs.

A few days later I was sitting beside "Professor Wang" on a Japanese passenger train running southward from Peking. Young peasants approached the professor at stations to report on the strength of the local Japanese garrison. Wang took no notes, but later at his headquarters I saw him write a report on Japanese army strength. When we left the train at a small station, I was questioned briefly by Japanese military police and passed through the sentry post as a missionary. The professor hustled me into a nearby shop, obtained two bicycles from a back room, and within minutes we were pedaling across open fields.

"That village ahead of us," the professor said after half an hour's ride, "marks the boundary of guerilla territory." I strained my eyes at the guards in peasant clothes, armed with old rifles and broadswords. These were ordinary farm boys. They saluted self-consciously and examined our military passes.

As we cycled on, the atmosphere changed. Children gathering dry grass for the kitchen stoves were singing songs about "Japanese robbers." Sentries repeatedly asked for our travel permits. Peasants in the villages were wearing armbands to indicate their membership in new mass organizations. Twice we passed units of uniformed guerillas numbering 200 to 300 men moving up to the railway for night raids on Japanese garrisons.

In the first walled town Professor Wang entrusted our bicycles to a regimental commander in exchange for two horses and an armed guard of 30 cavalry. I was assigned a long-legged Japanese horse that had belonged to a Japanese major killed in battle near Baoding. As we trotted across the fields where Chinese farmers were preparing their summer sorghum, the guerillas made jokes about the enemy horseman in their midst. They said I must be a traitor (*hanzhien*) because my Japanese horse, which had previously thrown two Chinese riders, was friendly toward me. I pointed out that a Chinese rider sits flat in the saddle and bounces up and down with every stride of the horse. The Japanese carries his weight in the stirrups and "posts" every second stride as most Americans do. A Japanese horse would naturally prefer a western rider. Also, the flat Western saddle used by the Japanese was more comfortable for an American than the wooden Mongol saddle used by many Chinese cavalrymen.

When we reached the headquarters town of Anguo, thousands of guerillas were drawn up in review for their first foreign reporter. A column of cheery youths stretched perhaps a half mile long and four ranks deep, each man clad in a rumpled gray uniform and wearing a sleeve badge that read PEOPLE'S SELF-DEFENSE ARMY. The propaganda corps of students from Beijing universities shouted in English an anti-Japanese slogan: "Down with the Japanese robbers!" For the first time during the war I saw Chinese faces that were genuinely happy.

The commander-in-chief's headquarters was in the rear of the post office, a room about 20 feet square. From floor to ceiling it was papered with blueprint maps that showed in detail the villages, roads and creeks of central Hebei. Blue and red pins marked the location of Chinese and Japanese troops. As we entered, a small man in a grey uniform was standing with a radio message in his hand, silently moving the pins. He was introduced as Comrade Lu Zhengco, commander-in-chief of the central Hebei guerillas. He nodded his greetings and motioned me into a bedroom for our first interview. The room was bare of any decoration—just a stone bed (*kang*), two blankets and a washbasin. "My only luxury," he confessed, as he saw me eyeing his room, "is this pair of leather shoes marked U.S. MARINE CORPS." He said he bought them from a pawnshop in Peking.

Compared to the pompousness of Japanese officers at press conferences, this guerilla commander was quiet and self-assured. In answer to my questions General Lu said he had been born in 1903 in a farmer's family of Manchuria, where he had obtained a primary education before joining the army of warlord Zhang Zuolin. He later attended the Northeastern Military Academy. After the Japanese seized Manchuria in 1931, Lu had become a guerilla organizer in Jehol province and had fought with the volunteers until 1935. His knowledge of guerilla warfare came from experience as extensive as that of Lawrence in Arabia.

While we talked in the bedroom, our conversation was punctuated by the wailing sound of a radio transmitter in an adjoining room. The general opened a door, revealing three radio operators bent over a long table. "Our largest set is 75 watts," Lu explained. "It keeps us in contact with Chiang Kai-shek's zone commander and the Eighth Route Army headquarters, both in south Shanxi. The two smaller sets of 7½ watts each send orders to our troops here in Hebei."

The general excused himself to work on plans for an attack but sent his chief commissar—political officer—to escort me about the town. I was shown that guerilla barracks were actually school-houses and temples where bamboo matting was spread on the stone floors. As many as 64 men could sleep shoulder to shoulder in one room. Bedding rolls were lined up against the wall; above them hung washbasins and toothbrushes. The guerillas, I learned, were eating two meals a day, the menu consisting of a steamed grain (sorghum or millet) and a few vegetables. Their only delicacy was dried fish captured from the Japanese.

A guerilla arsenal was located in an old spinning mill with machinery operated by diesel motors. Its 120 workmen were turning out hand grenades, broadswords, and bayonets. The steel came from a truckload of war materiel stranded in central Hebei when war broke out. The hand grenades were smelted from the big native rice pans that are two feet wide and a half-inch thick; one pan provided enough iron for 20 or 30 grenades. Black powder was made from the soil.

The uniform factory was a novelty. Sixty Singer sewing machines—the old treadle model—had been gathered from tailor shops in different towns and assembled under one roof. With them, volunteer workers were producing several hundred summer uniforms a day. The cloth was a bright green to match the summer crops.

I visited the telephone office, which my guide claimed controlled 2,000 miles of rural lines. I inspected a hospital staffed by three doctors and 20 nurses. A printing shop, originally organized by missionaries, was turning out a semimonthly guerilla magazine and a daily news sheet with a circulation of 2,500. This was one of several news bulletins in the guerilla area.

Colonel Xia, the deputy commander, lighted his brass water pipe several nights later and settled back to tell me about an ambush. He was seated beside a wooden table with a kerosene lamp around which a group of guerilla officers were drinking tea and eating melon seeds. The group included a cross section of the guerilla staff—several political agents from the Eighth Route Army, a number of officers from the old Manchurian army, a few university students from Peking, and two local farmers.

"A villager," the colonel began, "reported eight Japanese motor trucks moving off the railway. Our guerillas hurried to the road and prepared a surprise attack. When the first Japanese truck entered the graveyard where we were hiding, the front wheels of the truck were blown off by a land mine and 40 Japanese soldiers leaped from their trucks to find shelter in the ditches. We harried them all afternoon and rushed the trucks about 8 P.M., finishing the survivors with hand grenades. Our booty included seven usable trucks, five artillery pieces, 800 shells and 70 rifles." As evidence the colonel pulled up his sleeve, revealing several Japanese officers' insignia including the stripes of a major; he had sewn them on his undershirt.

A dispatch rider was asked to tell of a skirmish on the previous day. "Four of us," the rider related, "were traveling on horseback when 12 Japanese motor trucks appeared behind us on the road. We galloped ahead, left one man to hold the horses in a grove of trees, and three of us hid behind grave mounds. When the trucks came abreast of us, we hurled four hand grenades apiece and escaped before the Japanese could attack. Our spies this morning reported that the Japanese suffered more than 40 casualties."

Early in the war, when the Japanese had no barbed wire entanglements around their railway stations, General Lu said the best record for nocturnal raids was established by the Ding County regiment of guerillas, composed entirely of local boys who attacked their native city nine times. "Even when they were not making an attack," the general added, "the men often went over the wall to visit their families." I later visited this regiment and found most of the men armed with Japanese rifles.

On another day over a bowl of cabbage and rice I asked General Lu to tell me the origin of his guerilla army in central Hebei. "I was an officer in the Fifty-third Chinese Army in 1936," he began. "My brigade of 5000 men was part of the old Northeast Army commanded by Marshal Zhang Xueliang, and therefore part of the national armies of Chiang Kai-shek." The general had been stationed at Xi'an at the time the Young Marshal arrested Chiang Kai-shek in December 1936, but his own brigade was not part of the police action. Subsequently Chiang Kai-shek odered the Northeast Army into Hebei to prepare for a Japanese attack. When the invasion began, General Lu was holding a 3-mile sector in the Chinese defense, 20 miles southeast of Peking. Lu's brigade fought a six-day engagement as the Japanese pushed southward through Hebei—that was September 1937—but by the end of one week the brigade had suffered 2,000 casualties and his men were far behind the retreating Chinese armies. Then a strange thing happened: The Japanese marched around Lu's position and ignored him. Lu was left in an area of shattered villages, terrified farmers, and Chinese bandit gangs. Lu and his officers began to organize a new defense force in the Japanese rear.

The general explained how he became affiliated with the communists. After the Xi'an incident, the communists had entered into a united front agreement with Chiang Kai-shek. The Eighth Route Army (new name of the Red Army) moved into Shanxi province to fight the Japanese. And as they advanced, they detached some of their officers to establish military and political academies on the Hebei border near the town of Fuping. Agents from these academies discovered Lu's defense organization in central Hebei, and they invited his 3,000 surviving troops to undergo six weeks of political training which Lu accepted. The men returned to central Hebei at the start of 1938 with a better concept of Chinese defense.

"Our present task," the general explained, "is to give the villagers something to fight for. Almost all the farmers have personal reasons for hating the

Japanese—houses have been burned, women raped, old people killed, cows and pigs carried off. There was no lack of ill feeling." But hatred, the general believed, was a poor battle cry. Farmers had always been bitter against the Chinese government but they had seldom revolted. To make these peasants fight against the Japanese we had to offer them something they prized. Following the program of the Eighth Route Army, we gave each village a democratic council.

In addition to a political voice, the general said, every farmer received some economic advantages. His rent was lowered 25 percent, and interest on his debts was restricted. The guerillas loaned their cavalry horses at plowing time to aid the farmers who had lost their animals. "We make each farmer feel that this is his war," said General Lu.

Mobilizing guerillas was a simple task, Lu claimed. In fact, he received more volunteers than he could handle. The officers' academy near Anguo turned out a quarterly class of 300 cadets, and the headquarters staff trained as many as 6,000 new guerillas a month. Nearly all the men brought their family rifles.

With General Lu, I attended a mass meeting only 15 miles from the railway at a walled town where peasants and their families gathered for a victory celebration. The men in the crowd were armed with old spears, flintlock rifles, buccaneer pistols, broadswords, and execution axes—these weapons signified their membership in the Village Self-Defense Corps. The men were poorly trained, poorly armed, and useful mainly to guard the roads.

Before this crowd of at least 5000, a 16-year-old boy leaped to the platform and led the farmers in anti-Japanese cheers. The older farmers mumbled the slogans self-consciously; the boys shouted like fanatics. "We won't be Japanese slaves!" "Down with the Japanese robbers!" "Long live the Chinese Republic!"

Eighth Route Army political officers harangued the crowd on the atrocities committed by the Japanese soldiers. Later, the Under-Fire Dramatic Club took the platform for a series of patriotic one-act plays.

Singing was important at mass meetings, and on this occasion there were three favorite songs. The first was the stirring military march, "Stand up, you who refuse to be bond slaves" (*Qilai*), which later became the national anthem of the Peoples Republic. The second was the snappy guerilla song, "We have no guns, we have no cannons." The third was the sad, hymn-like song of the Northeast volunteers, "My home is on the bank of the Sungari River."

After rendering these patriotic favorites, some soldiers raised a cry for a solo from the foreign visitor, and their call was reinforced by rhythmic clapping from the audience. I later learned this call for a solo was a favorite ploy of the guerillas. I have no singing range and only a wobbly pitch; besides, I was completely terrified when I was pushed to the center of the stage. In my state of confusion the only song I could think of was the nursery rhyme:

> *Three blind mice, three blind mice,*
> *See how they run, see how they run.*
> *They all ran after the farmer's wife,*
> *She cut off their tails with a butcher knife.*
> *Did you ever hear such a tale in your life,*
> *As three blind mice.*

An interpreter translated, and the crowd of peasants roared. No doubt the peasants lived in close proximity to mice.

Many years later President Jimmy Carter was attending a banquet at Peking when communist leaders of the Peoples Republic pressed him for a solo. The President chose the most appropriate song I can imagine for this purpose—a song called "Old McDonald Had a Farm." He drew wild whistles when he came to the many choruses:

> *A moo-moo here, a moo-moo there,*
> *A hee-haw here, a hee-haw there,*
> *A quack-quack here, a quack-quack there,*
> *An oink-oink here, an oink-oink there,*
> *A cackle-cackle here, a cackle-cackle there.*

Before President Carter finished, some of the Chinese joined him in the chorus.

I left the mass meeting and started my return journey to Peking. I had plenty of photographs to satisfy skeptical newspaper editors about the existence of the guerillas, and I carried an invitation to return during the summer of 1938 to visit other guerilla armies and units of the Eighth Route Army scattered across Shanxi province.

*The Eighth Route Army was a young, tough, enthusiastic army.*

Brig. Gen. Samuel B. Griffith, USMC, 1968

CHAPTER 9

# Travels with the Eighth Route Army

In May 1938 I received a hand-carried letter from the Shanghai office of the Associated Press. It said in effect, "Get through the Japanese lines and let the guerillas show you everything they've got. If the trip takes more than a month, send your dispatches by courier. Don't buy any airplanes but all reasonable expenses will be paid." I inserted a notice in the *Peiping Chronicle* that I was transferred to Shanghai and reserved a steamship berth. No one's suspicions were aroused when I then disappeared from Peking and travelled again by train into guerilla territory. The notes below are based on my diary of 1938.

At Ding County I met two professors from Peking who specialized in train wrecking. They had just returned from a "very successful" wreck of a Japanese military train. Both men were around 35 and unmarried; both spoke English. One had studied at Cornell University on an American fellowship. At first, they said, they had applied the technique of Lawrence of Arabia—burying a charge of dynamite under the rails, running a detonating wire into the fields, and posting a sentinel to touch off the explosion under the locomotive. When their dynamite supply ran out and Chiang Kai-shek failed to send more, the professors organized squads of guerillas to pull up the spikes on railroad curves, causing derailments. Then the Japanese learned to run light surveillance cars over the line in the early morning to spot the sabotage. "But we have a new trick for them now," said the former chemistry professor. He drew from his pocket a small piece of wood carved in the shape of a spike head and painted a rusty color. These wooden dummies were substituted for the steel spikes and were strong enough to support the surveillance car, making it almost impossible to discover the mischief from a moving vehicle. The professors wrecked three trains during the fortnight I was with them.

It was black when our party of 86 assembled to cross the Japanese-held railroad. We had orders to leave the guerilla border east of the railroad at 10 P.M., to cross the tracks at midnight, and to enter the western guerilla territory before dawn, a march of about 26 kilometers (16 miles). In addition to myself the party included 30 political students who had never been under enemy fire and 55 guerillas armed with rifles, broadswords, and hand grenades. The final instructions were: no talking, no smoking; tie all drinking cups to prevent rattling. If the enemy opens fire, fall to the ground and don't move without orders.

We started forward in single file, walking on a gravel road. Barking dogs brought peasants to their doors, where they stood with lantern in hand. By 11 P.M. it was so dark we could see only three feet ahead of us. I strained my eyes toward a fellow in front of me whose white ammunition belt bobbed up and down.

A whispered word of caution came back—"We are approaching the railroad." Suddenly a lantern appeared to our right. Everyone dropped to the ground. The gleam approached and passed only a few hundred feet from us, revealing in a feeble pool of light a Chinese farmer walking the tracks. He was a guard compelled to serve the Japanese. We rose again to cross the tracks when an ear-splitting crash shook the earth; a hissing sound passed overhead and ended in a dull boom. Artillery! Everyone again fell flat on the ground. Another explosion, another hiss, and before the shell burst, a crashing sound like stampeding cattle arose from a nearby cornfield. Japanese machine guns began firing from two directions. I was safe in a drainage ditch, but a youth lying next to me sprang to his feet and fled. Someone cried, *"Pao! Pao!"* ("Run! Run!") and our party was in panic, men retreating on hands and knees, then running in confusion.

Fifteen minutes passed. The sound of running had ceased and the machine guns were silent. I seemed to be alone. My watch said 12:15. I wondered how I would find the guerillas in the dark when a voice near me whispered *"Han xiansheng,"* my name in Chinese. It was an officer. He cursed the students who had run and explained that the Japanese had been shooting at another guerilla group up the line who were stealing rails.

We retreated together till we found the guerillas assembling in a village two miles from the railroad. There I encountered two peasants who had been carrying my baggage. They said they dropped my belongings at the railroad. My camera and films, my typewriter, and a confidential report on the guerillas—all were gone! I could imagine these items spread next morning on the desk of a Japanese intelligence officer. Two soldiers were assigned to look for my baggage and the rest of us retreated into guerila territory. I was so sickened by my loss I hardly noticed the cold floor of a schoolhouse on which we fell asleep at 4 A.M.

Three hours later I was awakened by a sentry who said a farmer had come to see me. The farmer was a fellow about 25, strong through the shoulders. He explained he was the one carrying the lantern along the railroad the night before, that he was arrested by the Japanese but released at 4 A.M.. The farmers in his village told him a foreigner with the guerillas had lost his baggage and he had come to offer help. Incredible as it seemed, this man living under threat of death from the Japanese now volunteered for service to the guerillas. Five hours later the same fellow reappeared on his bicycle, my packsack over one shoulder and my typewriter case strapped to his rear fender. He said a Chinese school teacher had picked up the baggage early in the morning and hid it in his house. But that was not the end of the story. Next night this same fellow led our guerilla party across the danger zone to the western guerilla district.

On reaching the town of Fuping I was delighted to learn that Captain Evans Carlson was arriving on horseback from the opposite direction. Carlson was an American Marine serving as assistant naval attache. He was the first American official to travel with the guerillas. Towards evening a clatter of hooves came up the stone street in front of the Fuping government headquarters and a tall man in sheepskin jacket, laced hunting boots, and sun helmet dismounted from the lead horse. We stayed up until midnight exchanging information. I was particularly interested in Carlson's impressions of the communist leaders he had recently visited and whom I was about to meet. Carlson characterized Mao Zedong as a "social dreamer, a genius living 50 years ahead of his time." Zhu De, Eighth Route Army commander, was "the prince of generals, a man with the humility of Lincoln, the tenacity of Grant, and the kindliness of Robert E. Lee." I swapped Carlson a cake of shaving soap for an ounce of pipe tobacco and we parted at dawn.

By horse we rode 50 *li* (17 miles) to the Shanxi-Chahar-Hebei border government, the civilian side of the guerilla movement. Governor Song Shaowen and his guards met us at the government headquarters and invited us for tea. The governor was a quiet thoughtful man of 29, a 1934 graduate of Peking University. He had served as a school teacher, as secretary to warlord Yan Xishan in Shanxi, and was now governor of a wartime united front government for three provinces. I asked him how communist this wartime arrangement was. He said that of the nine members of the government's executive committee, three come from the Shanxi provincial government, three from the communists, one from Chiang Kai-shek's Nationalist Party, one had been a Shanghai newspaper reporter, and one a school teacher—the last two without previous political connection.

I asked the governor how the border government came to be organized. He said that when the Japanese army had occupied Taiyuan, capital of Shanxi, an emergency conference had been held at the mountain town of Fuping in western Hebei on January 8-15, 1938, attended by representatives of warlord Yan Xishan, the communists and Chiang Kai-shek's nationalists. Out of this had grown the present united front structure.

In a village 20 kilometers from Mount Wutai I visited an Eighth Route Army officer sitting in a room papered with maps from which he directed 100,000 guerillas in the defense of the border government. General Nie Rongzhen was a communist officer of few words. In 1924 he had been a chemistry student in Paris studying for a doctoral degree. When the Chinese revolution began, he had moved to Moscow, taken a year's training in the political institute, and then had returned to China as instructor in Chiang Kai-shek's Whampoa Military Academy at Canton. He had joined the communist revolt at Nanchang in 1927, had fought through the civil war in Jiangxi, had survived the Long March and had emerged as a brigadier general. I found Nie dressed in a clean white shirt, a well-tailored uniform and handsome cavalry boots that he said he removed from a dead Japanese. He retained a Parisian pride in clothes and was the best-dressed man I met in the Eighth Route Army.

I asked Gen. Nie how he expected his guerillas to bring about a Chinese victory in the war. The general phrased his answer cautiously. "The first objective of the guerillas," he observed, "is not military but political. We aim to occupy all the territory behind the Japanese lines and between their railroad zones. In this way we can prevent the Japanese from using Chinese resources." The general reminded me that previous invaders of China had seized the country piece by piece, using China's own manpower and wealth from one province to conquer the next. Thus the Chinese had defeated themselves. "If our guerillas restrict the Japanese to the railroad zones," Gen. Nie believed, "the Japanese strategy of conquest will be defeated. At the same time we will also prevent the Japanese from collecting Chinese taxes."

Before we said goodby, Gen. Nie presented me with a pair of guerilla straw sandals. I wore them until they were reduced to shreds.

At Mount Wutai I spent an evening with Norman Bethune, a Canadian who was serving as medical director for the Eighth Route Army, and his surgical partner—Richard Brown, another Canadian. I had not heard of Bethune before, but within two years he became one of the best-known western names in China. He had been sent to China by the China Aid Council of New York to organize a field hospital. He died in 1939, a martyr to blood poisoning contracted in his surgical work. Mao Zedong wrote a eulogy to him that is required reading in most Chinese schools.

At 48 Bethune was tense, vigorous, and idealistic. He showed me through his "base hospital," which consisted of wards in village houses with one courtyard for surgical theater and a kitchen where he sterilized surgical instruments in a rice cooker. Sallow-cheeked wounded soldiers lay shoulder to shoulder, many without blankets, using bricks for pillows. "What happened to the wounded before you came?" I asked. "They lived or they died," the doctor answered with a shrug. "Bullet wounds in the arm or leg healed in a year, whereas under proper treatment they would take a few weeks."

Richard Brown, the second Canadian, was a veteran missionary doctor from Henan province who had served six months with Bethune and now had been called back by his hospital. He travelled with me on foot and horseback to the Yellow River.

The first night out we encountered one of China's pests. Fifteen minutes after we extinguished our candle, Brown and I were both scratching and the flare of a match revealed armies of flat brownish creatures the size of a typewriter "O" crawling in our blankets. In the light of a flashlight they scooted under the matting on the bed. I tried to sleep, thinking bedbugs could be no worse than mosquitoes, but soon the crawling sensation moved under my sheet, around my neck and across my face. The venom from Chinese bedbugs raised a slight fever, making sleep difficult. The doctor carried his folding aluminum cot into the courtyard where he thought he could escape the invaders; I moved my cotton blankets into a granary where I found fitful rest. Next morning I resolved never to sleep in a place where local people slept. It was preferable to remove a wooden door from its hinges and lay it across two chairs. Occasionally the altar in a Buddhist temple provided a clean night's sleep. Our soldier escorts didn't seem to be bothered by bugs, although they undoubtedly carried them in their uniforms.

The most interesting part of this travel was our introduction to the *real* Eighth Route Army: 200 Long March veterans accompanying a mule train of ammunition on a four-day march across the Zhengtai railway, which was in Japanese hands.

The army commander called for us at 5:30 A.M. in the village of Hongzedian. The mules were ready. The commander was a quiet, soft-spoken fellow about 30, uneducated except for Red Army schools, but we saw his mature judgment during our four days with him.

Troops from the old Red Army lined up in the village stone street. Their dress was a miscellany of khaki shirts and shorts, brown leggings, blue caps, straw hats hanging on their backs and rag sandals. About four out of five carried rifles, the others broadswords. The men were short in stature, probably averaging five feet three inches; nearly all were southerners from Jiangxi and Hunan.

On the march they formed a single file. Five men served as advance guards a half mile ahead of the main force, and each of 70 baggage mules was attended by a peasant. The column moved at a brisk pace—about four miles an hour—that they maintained hour after hour with only brief rests. Every ten minutes a political director blew his whistle, and the men shifted their rifles from one shoulder to the other.

About noon of the first day the sky clouded over and rain poured down; the soldiers merely put on their broad-brimmed straw hats and marched in silence. I marveled at the conditions they accepted without comment. A man in front of me shuffled his feet on a stony path because his sandals were worn away at the heel and were ready to drop off if he took a full stride.

As I marched with the Eighth Route Army, I wondered why these troops were such a successful fighting force. The first quality seemed to be their youthful enthusiasm. The average age in the unit was about 22. Some men only 20 had already served eight years in the Red Army, having started as Little Devils in Jiangxi.

A second quality I noted was the extraordinary personality of their officers, a combination of kindliness and determination. Every time we paused for a drink of tea, the leaders chatted with the farmers or sat down in a cluster of soldiers and got them laughing with a story. In each village the older farmers came out and cried, *"Hui lai la"* ("You are back") because these same soldiers had passed through a week earlier.

A third characteristic was their efficiency in getting work done. When we stopped for the night, men were immediately assigned to guard the trail, to care for the mules, to find sleeping space, to start the cooking, and to visit the farmers. Details were handled without a hitch. The principle of "absolute obedience" was violated only once while we travelled in this unit.

On the march I began to realize the homeless state of the soldiers. Most had left home at about 15 years of age and had not seen their parents since. They had no girl friends waiting for them. Nobody cheered for them when they won. They received no banquets or special food—always millet or sorghum and one vegetable.

They had no observable vices. Dr. Brown said that in performing 854 full physical examinations on the Eighth Route Army, he had found only 2 cases of venereal disease. They drank no alcohol, and they smoked their native pipes with locally grown tobacco. Their salaries were $1.00 silver a month, which they spent for shoes, fruit, and tobacco.

The only elements that broke the monotony of this austere life were the fellowship and self-education that they found among their peers. Some had fought side by side for years. They shared the grief when mutual friends were killed. They looked back on the same hardships and the same humorous experiences. They loved to reminisce. Clusters of friends were always smoking together, talking about the day's journey. They sang a great deal.

Another reason why this army fought well—probably the principal reason—was their political faith. All were confident of China's final victory. Each morning before the day's march began, or at the noon break, the squads of ten gathered on the ground to listen to a 15 or 20-minute talk about the mass movement, the world united front, or the weakness of Japanese "imperialism." The degree of political comprehension among them may be exaggerated, but their consciousness of their objective was very real.

*A single spark can start a prairie fire.*

Old Chinese saying

CHAPTER 10

# One Breach of Discipline

On the third day of the journey we rested till 5 P.M. in a village only 20 *li* (7 miles) from the Japanese-held Zhengtai railway. We then set out on an all-night march that was the most exhausting on this trek. Fortunately local villagers donated about 40 pairs of cloth sandals to the soldiers, enabling those who had been shuffling in rags to protect their feet.

We first climbed a ridge of 1500 meters (4600 feet) in less than two hours, and arrived just at dark on the summit. There we could look down on the railway two miles away, a Japanese danger zone.

The trouble began when we started the descent on steep mountain trails in the dark, stumbling over boulders, creeping along narrow ledges, always in single file, straining to see the man ahead. Rocks rolled down the mountainside. Mules in the baggage train brayed. The dogs in darkened villages came out to growl. But there was no pausing.

By starlight we could see the glint of a river far below us that we knew flowed beside the railway. The descent to the tracks was very steep for 3000 feet. The rolling stones became a small avalanche of gravel, finally rousing the Japanese sentries in the nearest garrison five *li* away (1½ miles). Before we were halfway down the mountainside there was the boom of artillery and a shell whistled overhead, crashing in the valley beyond. The soldiers quickened their pace. Shell after shell came: "boom, ch-ch-ch-ch-ch-ch-ch-plump!" but the nearest fell a quarter mile behind us.

As we emerged on the tracks, I dropped to my knees in the darkness and touched the cold rails; they seemed to symbolize the Japanese invasion. I dimly saw a squad of our troops thrown out to left and right of the crossing point. Then somebody grabbed my arm and hustled me across the rails and down the river bank. Some troops were already crossing in squads of six, holding to each other to help resist the current, the water coming up to their hips. Guns and swords were held high in the air. I rode a horse led by a soldier who was holding a grenade in his hand. Once across the river we hurried up the opposite hillside for half a mile and sat down to await the others. An hour later the last soldier arrived to report that the mules had disappeared. The peasant mule drivers had run away when the firing began. I was carrying camera film in my belt bag and travel notes inside my shirt, but my typewriter was back with the mules.

The scene that followed was a demonstration of the Eighth Route Army discipline. A unit leader had been ordered to remain on the tracks till all the animals had crossed, but he had retreated when a lantern appeared down the tracks. The soft-spoken commander upbraided the guilty one in front of all the soldiers, pointing out that he had violated one of the basic principles of the Red Army. Finally the commander said, "There are two things we can do: either we all go back across the river and look for the animals, or part goes back and the rest march on." A call was made for volunteers to go back. One company commander spoke up: "Come on, men. Second Squad, Fourth Squad, we're going back." Then they were off. There was no grumbling, just silent acceptance. They knew they had another 12 miles of night marching ahead, but they turned back.

The rest of us started on: up, up, up. The first ridge was over 3,000 feet. We descended only half as far, and then started up a second ridge over 4,500 feet. The last 1200 feet of this range we crawled on hands and knees at a steep grade. I was exhausted and dropped at the top. There the whole party rested for half an hour—it was 2 A.M.—and then to my discouragement, we started up again. We reached a rolling plateau. Brown was ahead of me, muttering every time he slipped off the path into an irrigated field. By then I was walking like a robot, numb from the shoulders down. My eyes seemed to steer my feet mechanically, but for a half hour at a time I could remember nothing. The whole column had slowed to perhaps three miles an hour, but the march was relentless.

At 3:30 A.M. we reached a watershed and paused for a brief rest before a fast descent. We had to cross a Japanese motor road before dawn if we were to avoid the last danger of an ambush. Slipping and tumbling, we came down that 4,600 feet as fast as our stiffened muscles could carry us. The sky was growing gray in the east. A village ahead, through which the motor road ran, grew nearer. The advance group trotted ahead to look for Japanese. Like stiff-kneed cattle we ran as fast as we could through the village, across the motor road, and up a mountain pathway on the other side. We still had to walk another 20 *li* (7 miles) to reach Eighth Route Army territory. Men threw down their rifles at 7 A.M. that morning after 14 hours on the march.

I had no appetite, despite the night without food. Brown and I lay down on a stone bed in a farmhouse and slept till 1 P.M. Most soldiers were already up and talking, and the mule train had arrived safely. We got some food inside us and by 4 P.M. were again on the road, this time for another 36 *li* (12 miles) to the army headquarters, arriving after dark.

I typed my notes August 13, 1938 on a table in a Goddess of Mercy temple, surrounded by staring peasants who had not previously seen a typewriter. We had difficulty finding this space to sleep because the Japanese had recently burned most buildings in this town of 4,000. There was almost no food. We opened a tin of beef that the Eighth Route Army had captured from the Japanese.

That day we abandoned Brown's Japanese cavalry horse, which I had named *Showa*, after the Japanese "Era of Conquest." The horse had been captured by the Eighth Route Army in a battle near Wutai, and had been given to Brown for his journey to the Yellow River. Chinese mountain grass had proved inadequate for the Japanese animal and it had steadily lost weight. By contrast our Chinese mules and donkeys retained full flesh. The Japanese horse had finally refused to move further. I gave the animal a farewell pat on the forehead, removed the blankets from the saddle, and donated the horse to a local farmer. Poor Showa, a Japanese immigrant.

In the mountains of south Shanxi a radio transmitter sent nightly instructions to the guerilla forces of north China. These coded messages were written by military leaders of the Eighth Route Army. To find the mountain lair of this headquarters was no easy task; every three days the transmitter and its generators were strapped on bamboo poles, shouldered by a crew of soldiers, and transported 15 or 20 miles to a new hideout.

At Liaozhou Brown and I were told to go to a village near Qinzhou. There we were sent to Siting, a town 50 *li* away. At Siting we were told to go another 45 *li* south. Finally we found an officer who offered to take us to headquarters, which proved to be a village of 50 families. We were escorted to a courtyard where two young officers spoke English. After an hour's chat, we learned we were not yet at military headquarters. This was the political department. After supper we went by horse to call on General Peng Dehuai, deputy commander of the Eighth Route Army. Our horses passed through a village and up a steep slope to a lonely house, in front of which stood a single sentry. After a whispered consultation among secretaries, we entered a room lighted by a single candle where Peng Dehuai bent over a pile of papers. A stocky, deep-chested man, Peng was slow and reflective. He wore a foreign-style shirt with collar open and sleeves rolled back. His head was shaved.*

As he talked, Peng sat motionless, and he paused before answering. Despite a minimum early education, he was known as a scholar within the Eighth Route Army. He said he spent half his day reading on foreign affairs. He had been married before he entered the Red Army but had not seen his wife and children for 11 years. He now had few close friends. He spent two hours during this first interview asking about the attitudes of the United States, Britain, and Germany toward the present Chinese struggle. I had no recent news from the outside world, but I gave him my guess that communist leaders were much too hopeful about western intervention in support of China.

For three days Brown and I remained at headquarters while I interviewed the department heads, including those for village education, propaganda against Japanese troops, and the search for Chinese traitors. Before we left, General Peng gave me permission to send two interviews in his name over the Eighth Route Army radio to Hong Kong, one on American foreign policy, the other on a recent Chinese victory over the Japanese in south Shanxi.

We also attended several mass meetings sponsored by the Eighth Route Army that had a fast-paced program of songs and dramas, interspersed with brief speeches by General Peng and General Deng Xiaoping. Throughout the program the crowd was kept in high spirits by a master of ceremonies who shouted: *"Hao bu hao?"* ("Good, not good?"). The crowd shouted back: *"Hao!"* Then a soldier cried: *"Zai lai yi ge!"* ("Bring another one!") and the crowd whistled.

General Zhu De, commander-in-chief of the Eighth Route Army, was not at headquarters at the time of our visit, but we heard stories about him that suggested his military qualities. The general's orderly told us this episode: Zhu De was moving his headquarters through the mountains, accompanied by some raw recruits, when scouts reported a Japanese infantry brigade approaching along the same valley. General Zhu moved his small force into a side valley, and the long Japanese column marched by—apparently headed for an engagement on the railroad. All night Zhu De paced up and down in a nearby farmhouse. A soldier finally asked him how great was the danger. General Zhu replied, "The question is not danger, but how can I win a

---

*This same General Peng led Chinese armies in 1950 into South Korea against the American troops of General MacArthur. Peng became one of the ten marshals of the Chinese army, served as minister of war under the Peoples Republic, but was disgraced by Chairman Mao because Peng favored modernization of the Chinese military forces rather than preserving the characteristics of a peasant army. Peng died during the Cultural Revolution, still in disfavor, but was rehabilitated by Mao's successors. He is now accepted as one of the heroes of the Chinese revolution.

victory with only 200 recruits?" Next day when the tail of the Japanese column approached, Zhu De led his men in an attack on the Japanese rear guard and captured the brigade headquarters, including battle records and radio codes. When I met Zhu De a few days later in Xi'an, he confirmed the story with a grin.

Although nicknamed the "Chinese Napoleon," Zhu De was a quiet, courteous, and modest officer with a face like a bulldog. When his horn-rimmed glasses slipped down his nose, he resembled an elderly school teacher. Of all the communist officers I interviewed, he was the least talkative; he answered every question with a single word or a nod of the head. He offered no predictions. For this man, dead or alive, Chiang Kai-shek had offered a reward of 100,000 Chinese dollars.

From Peng Dehuai's headquarters we walked without incident the last 100 miles to the Yellow River, passing many central government troops. What a sight it was when we aproached the walled city of Yuanchiu, situated near the north bank of the Yellow River. Though the Japanese had burned 1,200 homes inside the walls, this was still the headquarters for General Wei Lihuang, the nationalist commander of south Shanxi. The general was a trim, jolly, uncultured peasant who had risen in the warlord armies, had won the confidence of Chiang Kai-shek, and now held one of the five key posts in the nationalist resistance to the Japanese. The general invited Brown and me to a dinner—I would call it a feast- of finer quality than any food we had seen in communist areas—tinned beef, stewed chicken, and Peking-style fish with vegetables and rice.

Next day the general's English-speaking secretary assisted with our passports and arranged for our crossing the Yellow River in an army sailboat. We took a four-hour truck ride across the mountains to the Longhai railroad—a thrill to race 200 *li* in a few hours after crawling along at 100 *li* a day for many weeks—and we finally arrived by night express in Xi'an. In the two months and eight days since I had left Peking, I had covered 1200 miles.

> *There is practically no record of any western visitor to Red China from 1936 to 1945 who came away disenchanted or hostile.*
>
> Kenneth E. Shewmaker, 1971

CHAPTER 11

# Interview with Mao Zedong in His Yan'an Cave

Dawn was breaking on September 13, 1938, when our seven trucks loaded with cotton bales departed from Xi'an. About 100 travellers were assigned their "seats" on top of the freight. The leading truck carried armed soldiers, not because of Japanese danger, but because the truce between Chiang Kai-shek and the communists was coming apart. I was riding a truck with 15 other passengers including 2 men I had met previously in Shanxi—Generals Peng Dehuai and Deng Xiaoping. Peng was a somber traveller throughout the three-day trip. Deng Xiaoping was a gnome-like man at the age of 34 with the bubbling spirit of a teenager; he was always the first to climb on top of the truck, offering a hand to others, and the first to descend at stops. (Forty years later Deng would become successor to Mao Zedong as paramount leader of the Peoples Republic of China.)

Before our departure I visited the white-haired Lin Boqu, oldest among the Long March veterans, who then headed the Eighth Route Army headquarters in Xi'an. He told me that my visit to Yan'an as a foreign correspondent would be governed by the following procedures: I would travel by truck and furnish my own bedroll; the border (communist) government would provide transport, lodging, and meals and assign an interpreter at Yan'an to arrange interviews and decide what photographs were permissible. That seemed reasonable under wartime security.

The truck trip took three days. The road to Yan'an was rutted for 180 miles. There were no bridges. At the river crossings passengers hauled the trucks across with long tow lines while the motors roared and the wheels threw up gobs of mud on the people pushing in the rear. Two hours was considered fast time for getting seven trucks across a stream.

Between rivers the trucks twisted and climbed around loess cliffs,* sometimes crawling up ridges so steep that passengers dismounted to reduce the motor strain. There were few villages. Millet and sorghum crops along the streams were turning brown in the chill autumn winds. Crops were thinly planted. There was no irrigation except on the river banks.

The road approached Yan'an at an elevation of 2,500 feet through a valley about one-half mile wide. The city walls of Yan'an hugged the west hillside and the Yan River flowed outside the city walls on the east. The nine-story pagoda dating from the Tang dynasty (618–907 A.D.) towered over the river bank. The pagoda had looked down on many rebellions and revolutions in its 1000 years.

Pockmarks ran in rows along the face of the Yan'an cliffs. These were the cave houses in which most of the people lived. "Cave" usually connotes darkness and dampness, but these caves usually had a generous-sized room, typically 12 by 30 feet, with vaulted ceiling, whitewashed walls, and a floor of brick or pounded earth. The cave-houses were illuminated at the front by daylight filtering through windows covered with white rice paper instead of glass. Yan'an at the time of my visit had no electricity or running water. When a cave dweller wanted a bucket of water, he or she climbed down the hill to the wells below.

Our truck caravan drove under a medieval gate tower in the city wall and headed for a large parade ground where uniformed soldiers sat on the ground, listening to General Zhu De speak from a raised platform.

For three weeks I interviewed military leaders and wrote press profiles. I was escorted around "Resist Japan University" by its commanding officer, General Lin Biao. In my story about street sights of Yan'an, I estimated that Yan'an was undergoing more new construction than any other town in China.

Mao Zedong's secretary came to my guest house room one evening at 8 o'clock to say Mao was ready to see me. I had previously

---

*About loess: During the glacial era several hundred thousand years ago, winds of gale force swept across the Gobi Desert (now part of Inner Mongolia Autonomous Region) and the Ordos Desert (now in Ninghsia Hui Autonomous Region), lifting vast clouds of dust into the sky and depositing this silt over seven Chinese provinces. The dust built up a blanket of earth covering 10,000 square miles, reaching a depth in some places of 300 feet. It was in this peculiar soil region that the Red Army arrived at the end of its Long March. Rainfall in the loess region averages 15 inches, barely enough to grow a crop. Striking features of the loess environment are: (1) vertical walls of earth, (2) sunken roads, and (3) cave homes dug into the loess.

submitted some written questions, more than 50 in all. The secretary and I walked through the darkening main street, turned down a narrow lane, then into a courtyard on Phoenix Hill. Mao's residence was half-house, half-cave. Through the paper window of one room we could make out a figure standing with a candle in his hand. That was Mao. He was dressed in padded peasant clothing with a jacket thrown loosely over his shoulders against the evening chill. His cave bedroom had the usual vaulted ceiling and whitewashed walls, which threw into relief his high forehead, protruding cheekbones, fluffy hair and square chin with the conspicuous mole. The room was furnished only with a brick bed (*kang*), a small wooden table that Mao used as a writing desk, one chair, and two stools.

After his words of welcome, Mao faced me with his back to the candle for a time that seemed half a minute, his shoulders slightly stooped, arms folded on his chest, peering at me as though trying to analyze his visitor's mind. When he spoke, his voice was low and resonant. He asked about my journey from Peking with the guerillas. Whom did I meet? What were my impressions? How did I travel from Xi'an to Yan'an? Were my accommodations in Yan'an satisfactory?

We sat down. After another pause he turned to current affairs in the United States. He wanted to know about the labor movement and about Roosevelt's attitude toward labor unions. (In 1938 Roosevelt was halfway through his second term.) Mao questioned me about John L. Lewis, leader of the United Mine Workers' Union. Did I think he would make a good president of the United States? I said I had been absent from the United States for four years and was not a useful source on that question. I got the impression from these inquiries that the chairman was interested in broadening his knowledge of the United States, but he did not show much understanding of U.S. political institutions.

Mao was in no hurry to start our interview. He rose, poured a cup of tea, drank it slowly, paced back and forth the width of the room, and lighted his pipe. When I called attention to the questions I had sent him, he reluctantly sat down on a stool with the candle between us, took up a bundle of Chinese notes, and began to underline Chinese words. Mao asked the secretary to check whether the marked Chinese words had been translated correctly from my questions. The chairman was known as a precise user of words, and he was checking my loose terminology.

After the secretary had revised the Chinese translation, Mao began dictating slowly, phrase by phrase, never faltering, never changing a sentence, pausing only long enough for the secretary to repeat the words in English; then he resumed. This continued for 15 minutes. He then stood up, stretched, paced the floor and asked me what was likely to happen in the 1938 elections in the United States. I earned a passing grade on this question; in Xi'an I had recently picked up a month-old copy of an American news magazine that had devoted its lead story to the elections.

Then back to dictation. He revised the order of my topics to arrive at a more logical sequence.

At the end of two hours he asked if I would join him for breakfast and requested an orderly to bring his food. He was sleeping by day and writing by night, Mao explained. His breakfast consisted of a bowl of American-style oatmeal with condensed milk and a raw egg stirred into the gruel.

Resuming his puckish conversation, Mao said, "I am more American than you are. I eat American oatmeal. I smoke an American pipe with American tobacco (gifts from visitors). I sleep when Americans sleep, and I work when Americans work. What can you say to that?"

I replied brashly, "I seem to be more of a peasant than you are. I smoke Chinese tobacco that costs 10 Chinese cents a bag in a Yan'an shop. And for breakfast I eat millet gruel, the same as your troops."

Mao smiled slowly and said, "So you think I am the capitalist and you are the revolutionary." He shook his head, deciding not to continue the gambit.

When our breakfast bowls were empty, he again lit his pipe and suggested we change the topic. He was revising two essays, one dealing with the strategy for a protracted war with Japan and the other with new democracy that would follow the Japanese war. Did I think these topics would be of interest to the Associated Press? I urged him to proceed, and he did until the early morning hours. In discussing new democracy Mao said he hoped the introduction of socialism in China would be evolutionary, not revolutionary. I protested, "There is no historical precedent for the peaceful introduction of socialism." Mao smiled as he quipped, "We are making history, not imitating it." Throughout the night Mao never seemed hurried.

Only after I returned to Xi'an from my Yan'an visit did I learn that Mao's two essays were being polished for presentation to a Politburo meeting some weeks after my interview. His long conversation on protracted war and new democracy appeared to have been a practice run. I did not grasp the extraordinary significance of Mao's thinking in September 1938, as he looked beyond Japanese defeat to the communist policies that would follow. No one but Mao was planning that far ahead.

Before we parted in the early morning, he asked if he might see my English notes on his two essays. He volunteered to revise the notes with the help of his secretary, so that the version that would reach a foreign audience would be as accurate as possible.

With traditional Chinese courtesy, Mao escorted me out of the cave and into the street before he said goodbye with a firm handshake. Two weeks later

Mao's cave at Phoenix Hill was destroyed by Japanese daylight air bombing, at a time when the chairman was absent, and Mao moved to a new location several miles outside Yan'an.

As I walked back to the foreign office guest house through deserted streets with no military guard, I thought back to other public officials I had interviewed. None had shown more precision with ideas and words.

Three qualities of Mao stood out.

First, he had the ability to put his visitor at ease, despite my feeling of awe. Second, he revealed a mind like a card catalogue, classifying everything in a logical and sequential way. Third, he had the skill of a good teacher, simplifying his ideas to the level of understanding of his audience (which in this case was me). Forty years later when I paged through Mao's *Selected Works*, I found the same qualities, and the two essays he discussed with me are included there in Volume 2.

Postscript One: This supplementary note is written 50 years after the preceding interview. Mao has been lying in his tomb in Peking for a decade. One hundred or more biographies of Mao are now on library shelves. Some rate him among history's great men; others revile him among the most contemptible. I collected phrases used to characterize Mao:

> Mao stands among the greatest leaders in 4000 years of Chinese written history —in a class with the Emperor Qin Shi Huang who unified China during 220-206 B.C. In some respects Mao is greater than Emperor Qin Shi Huang: (1) Mao unified a China larger than the Qin empire; (2) Mao overcame the nationalist armies of Chiang Kai-shek, a more formidable foe than any in the Qin period; and (3) Mao faced a Japanese invasion force employing modern weapons, not the crossbows of ancient times.

> Mao ranks among the most influential men who lived in the twentieth century.

> Mao is one of the greatest liberators of all time, in a class with Moses.

Chinese opponents of the Maoist revolution would describe Mao as one of the most ruthless killers in history: More than 10 million persons died in the Chinese civil wars (1927-1949); an estimated 800,000 landlords and their families were executed during land redistribution (1949-1952); 16 million of "excess mortality" occurred from hunger and related disease that followed the forced introduction of rural communes (1959-1962); and an estimated 1 million were persecuted to death during the Great Proletarian Cultural Revolution (1966-1976). To accusations like these Mao once replied, "A revolution is not a dinner party."

Postscript Two: For five years after Mao's death in 1976, the Chinese communist party pondered his historical role. The conclusions were issued in a 1981 pamphlet titled "Resolution on CPC History." The Great Helmsman emerged as follows:

> Comrade Mao Zedong was a great Marxist and a great proletarian revolutionary, strategist, and theorist. It is true that he made great mistakes during the 'cultural revolution,' but if we judge his activities as a whole, his contributions to the Chinese revolution far outweigh his mistakes.

Postscript Three: When I revisited Yan'an in 1983, I thought back over Mao's wartime period, and tried to find reasons for my favorable impressions of the communists. I had read nothing by Marx or Lenin at the time of my first visit and must assume that ideology played no part. The following observataions seem to have influenced me most.

- Yan'an was an impoverished community of 5000 cave-dwelling townsmen, 9000 students, and 6000 communist soldiers, living like medieval Franciscans under a code of poverty and a commitment to defeat the Japanese.
- Near equality prevailed in Yan'an. Eighth Route Army officers wore no symbol of rank. Top salaries were pegged at five Chinese dollars a month (then US$1.67). The food ration for soldiers, officers, and students was identical— 1.7 pounds of millet or sorghum per day, issued as grain.
- Students of Resist Japan University sang war songs as they walked along Yan'an streets. There was an air of gaiety.
- Yan'an was a community of primitive technology—no electricity, no running water, earthen streets, war materiel moving by oxcart. Yet the spirit prevailed that anything was possible.
- Communist leaders were avowed Marxists, but they gave higher priority in 1938 to the war against Japan.
- Communists were committed to education. They established adult literacy classes wherever they were in control.
- Yan'an policies on land reform, rent reform, and tax reform seemed moderate. Land rents in 1938, for example, were set at 25 percent of the crop.

If I were again age 26 and a reporter in wartime Yan'an, my dispatches would probably be similar to the ones I wrote.

*China was battered and blockaded, its economy ruined by enemy occupation, its government tired, corrupt, and deteriorating.*

Barbara Tuchman, 1971

CHAPTER 12

# With Stilwell at China's War Base

By the end of 1938 the Chinese government had retreated until its back was against the wall of mountains that rise to heights of 20,000 feet along the Tibetan border. China had become a landlocked country, isolated by the Japanese naval blockade. Only three backdoor access routes were still open: the rail route through Indochina, soon to be closed by the French on demand of the Japanese; the Burma road, shortly to be closed by the British, also on Japanese demand; and the central Asian highway from the Soviet Union. Only a trickle of traffic was reaching China.

In the last three months of 1938 I visited Chiang Kai-shek's war base in western China. Three news stories in that area were then important to the Associated Press. First, many coastal universities had moved to the western provinces and were receiving financial support from American charitable organizations. The AP asked me to report by cable how the universities were coping. Second, hundreds of Chinese government offices, factories, and research organizations were moving to western China. American editors were interested in their survival. Third, Chiang Kai-shek's military headquarters had settled at Guilin. There I planned to write a series of stories on the prospects for the Chinese army.

From Xi'an to Chengdu I flew in a 12-passenger plane of Eurasia Airline, my first airplane flight. Arriving at Chengdu airfield, I took a ricksha to West China Union University, a missionary school outside the city walls. The university president pressed me to talk to his students on guerilla warfare in north China. Mine was the earliest first-hand report on the Eighth Route Army that had thus far reached Chengdu, and many students asked my advice about their chances to move to Yan'an. News of Red China was generally suppressed in nationalist territory, despite the united front.

West China University enrolled 250 students before the war. Now the campus had taken in five refugee universities that had been bombed out of their buildings on the coast. These migrant schools included Nanjing University, Jinling College for Women, and three medical schools. The combined enrollment had reached 1,200.

The Chengdu campus had a surplus of professors, many of them scientists doing research that they hoped would benefit the war base. I spent a day with a group of chemistry professors who were developing byproducts from the Sichuan salt wells. They were producing iodine, caustic soda, bromine, potassium, and Epsom salts. On the basis of this work the Chinese government was establishing local factories for soap, paper, medicines, and photographic film.

The agricultural faculties were managing a dairy herd and lending some staff members to the NARB (National Agricultural Research Bureau). The bureau had been located in Nanjing but had lost its research facilities when the Japanese occupied the capital. Instead of establishing a single research center in west China, the bureau scattered its staff in half a dozen locations. Of these, Chengdu was the strongest.

Later I visited additional universities and research stations in Chongqing, Guiyang, and Guilin, all busy with wartime activity. Near Guiyang I encountered Yale-in-China Medical School; it was newly settled in a Buddhist temple and monastery. Here 40 faculty and 120 medical students with 20 truckloads of teaching equipment had started a new academic life. Nanjing Central Hospital had settled nearby. In Guilin I visited the new campus of Central China University. I sent cables or mail stories on each of these migrant institutions. The professors hoped that a favorable news story might bring more financial help from private organizations in the United States.

At Chongqing, China's temporary capital, I spent two weeks. There I visited Dr. H. H. Kung, Chiang Kai-shek's brother-in-law and finance minister. Kung was living in a 20-room suburban mansion about three miles north of the city. A heavy-set man in his fifties, he spoke poor English despite six years of American education at Oberlin and Yale. He showed no interest in the guerilla areas and referred me to his English-speaking assistants for the statistics I sought on national finances. I could not avoid comparing Kung's comfortable life with the frugal guerilla cave life I had observed in Yan'an.

The new industrial base in western China was headed by Dr. Wong Wenhao, a Belgian-educated geologist, organizer of China's geological survey. When I met him, his title was secretary to Chiang Kai-shek and chairman of the Economic Resources Commission. He was supervising the movement of 341 factories from the coast to the western provinces, about a quarter already in production. He gave greatest urgency to metal working shops for the army, but there were also chemical, electrical, textile, and food industries.

Dr. Wong was the first nationalist Chinese to caution me against overoptimism. These industrial projects, he said, could provide only a small share of China's needs. For a week I visited factories with Wong's staff and described them for the Associated Press.

I was offered a correspondent's post in Chongqing but decided against it. Government censorship made effective reporting impossible.

In December 1938, the military club at Guilin, capital of Guangxi province, had the signs of high rank—scores of staff cars with Nanjing license plates, secret service agents with drawn revolvers, and a few uniformed Russians without insignia. The 200-room club-hotel had been built to accommodate official guests of the Guangxi capital; recently it had been converted for use by Chiang Kai-shek's staff. The desk clerk told me all rooms were occupied but the club manager, a friendly American-born Chinese, offered me a cot in the room of another American already registered. Luckily, that American was Colonel Joe Stilwell, the military attache from the United States embassy in Chongqing and an old friend of mine from Peking. "Move right in," Stilwell said, and I did. Joe had often traded information with American correspondents in Peking. On this visit I could tell him about communist fighting in north China and Joe could help me with judgments on the nationalist armies.*

I had first met Stilwell three years earlier when he asked me to be scoutmaster at the Peking American School. Joe spoke Chinese and was well informed about Chinese affairs of the preceding quarter century. Now 55, he was a wiry man of medium height weighing no more than 160 pounds, and his lean cheeks and short crewcut made him look scrawny. His rimless glasses suggested a scholar. His military uniform from World War I—jodpurs,

---

*General Joseph Stilwell's name became familiar to most Americans only after the United States entered World War II, and Stilwell became a four star general—then equal in rank to Generals Marshall, Eisenhower, MacArthur, and Arnold. At the United States Military Academy Stilwell finished in the top third of his class. As Barbara Tuchman pointed out, Stilwell lacked the classroom superiority of Robert E. Lee, John J. Pershing, and Douglas MacArthur, each of whom led his academy classmates in military aptitude, but Stilwell was top in language study (French and later Chinese), a champion miler, and a letterman in football despite his small size.

leggings, and stiff-brimmed campaign hat—resembled an historic exhibit in the Smithsonian.

Japanese air raids gave us much time to talk. There was an air raid daily by some 20 Japanese planes, and the warning siren generally sounded about half an hour in advance. Joe disliked the official air raid shelters behind the club; he preferred to walk half a mile to one of Guilin's scenic humpback hills 400 or 500 feet high where we could watch the bombing from the hilltop. This gave us several hours together each day.

In our conversations I thought Joe betrayed one weakness: he was contemptuous of Japanese soldiers, whom he called "bowlegged cockroaches." Joe had characterized the Japanese bombing of Shanghai in January 1938: "Those Japanese pilots couldn't hit a thing; our American air force could drive them from the skies in a couple of days." That statement was made in December 1938, three years before Pearl Harbor. Stilwell also held an exaggerated opinion about the toughness of Americans. Once he remarked, "Any good American doughboy could lick ten Japanese in a fist fight." Three years later the Japanese army chased Stilwell and his combined Chinese-American forces out of Burma. Stilwell told the press, "We took a helluva beating." Stilwell was nevertheless a dogged fighter; he returned to Burma and stayed until the Japanese had been driven out.

One day Stilwell and I talked about Russian aid to China. I told him I found no evidence of Russian aid to the Chinese communists. He said Russian help to Chiang Kai-shek was also meager. Over the Central Asian highway from the Soviet Union, he estimated 1,000 Russian trucks had delivered no more than 2,000 tons of freight a month, or a maximum of 24,000 tons a year. That was insignificant in the Japanese war. Altogether, we guessed that Russian personnel in China numbered fewer than 1,000. The Russians at Guilin Club, he said, were infantry trainers for Russian weapons.

Stilwell speculated on Russian strategy. The Russians, he said, would enter the war in Asia only at the tail end of the conflict and under two conditions: first, that the fight was "finishable" in a few months; and second, that Russia could claim an important role in the victory. This foresight—seven years in advance—proved correct.

We also discussed Japanese prisoners. Stilwell said the Japanese army had lost fewer soldiers through surrender than any other army of equal strength in modern history. The German army in World War I, he said, had lost 60,000 soldiers through surrender in the first year of fighting. I estimated there were 550 Japanese and Korean prisoners in China in 1938, and half of them were noncombatants. The communist-led guerillas in north China had thus far taken 275 prisoners. Prisoners held by Chiang Kai-shek's armies were mostly Japanese pilots whose planes had been shot down or Korean camp followers.

I asked why so few Japanese surrendered. Stilwell thought because their army imposed the unique rule that any soldier who surrenders to the enemy in battle must commit suicide when he returns to Japan.

Stilwell admired the Chinese infantryman. In one of our conversations Joe said: "The Chinese soldier, if given competent leadership, is equal to the finest in the world. He can outwalk any other army. His courage is unexcelled. This Chinese soldier is a peasant who has suffered flood, drought, and bandits in peacetime, and war to him is no worse than peace."

As 1938 drew to a close, I decided it was time to write a China book. The Japanese lines of occupation appeared to have stabilized. I was weary from wartime travel. I had lost 25 pounds since I left Peking. I returned to the United States in January 1939 by a series of travel adventures that ended 4½ years in China.

I was sitting in the coffee shop of the Guilin Officers Club one afternon, about Christmas 1938, when an unfamiliar American wearing a leather jacket walked into the room. I introduced myself and learned he was a China National Aviation Corporation pilot leaving immediately for Hong Kong. When I told him I had been trying to fly out, he said his DC-3 plane was already fully booked, but he would take me if I sat on a stool in the galley without seatbelt, and would leave the club in 15 minutes. Most of my clothes were at the laundry and my only leather shoes were at a cobbler's shop, but I abandoned these personal effects and went to the airfield wearing Chinese cloth shoes.

The plane took off at sunset, flew without lights over territory occupied by the Japanese army, reached the south China coast at 9 P.M., and flew 20 minutes out to sea to shake off any possible Japanese pursuit planes. As we approached British Hong Kong from the south, searchlights from neutral warships in the harbor picked up our wings at 12,000 feet and followed our downward gyrations to Kaitak airport.

A doorman in evening dress at the Peninsula Hotel frowned at the entry of a westerner in military breeches and frayed red sweater, carrying a bedroll. The reception clerk said, "I shall have to ask the manager whether we have an available room." I explained that my Associated Press office was in the hotel and was admitted. I called our correspondent on the house phone and found he was the well-known reporter, Elmer Peterson, a Scandinavian-American who had grown up near my home in Duluth. I put on one of Pete's suits with pants cuffs six inches above my shoes, and the two of us stepped out to see how quickly we could forget the China war. Street lights were blinding after years of blackout.

Having restocked my wardrobe at Hong Kong, I sailed to Japanese-occupied Shanghai on an Italian passenger ship that carried 900 Jewish refugees from Austria. They reminded me that the German and Japanese crises were interlocked.

At Shanghai I submitted my resignation to Morris Harris, the AP manager who had kept me supplied with travel money for six months and had trusted my judgment on cable stories. I wrote my last war cables in Shanghai.

Next stop, Tokyo. At the suggestion of Colonel Stilwell, I planned to see the U.S. military attache's office in Japan. I sailed from Shanghai by Filipino freighter, left the ship at the southern Japanese port of Nagasaki, and took a train to Tokyo. I remained here only a few days and later caught the same ship at Yokohama when it continued to San Diego.

Captain Maxwell Taylor whom I had met earlier in Peking was in charge of the military attache's office at Tokyo. Handsome and well informed, Taylor spent two days debriefing me on what I could tell him about the China war, and in return he answered my questions on Japan. Taylor expressed greater respect for the fighting qualities of Japanese soldiers than Stilwell had. (It was difficult in 1939 to foresee that within a few years this same Captain Maxwell Taylor would rise to Lieutenant General Taylor and become Chairman of the U.S. Joint Chiefs of Staff.)

Educated Japanese whom I interviewed in Tokyo knew surprisingly little about the situation in China. The principal of the Christian high school who had praised conditions in Manchuria under Japanese rule in 1934 was now equally enthusiastic about Japan's "co-prosperity sphere" in China. He said he had never heard of the burning of Chinese villages, the raping of Chinese women, or the corruption in Japanese-occupied China. Such problems did not appear in the Japanese press.

I went shopping in Tokyo. The markets were well stocked with consumer goods and were crowded with customers. The country was experiencing a war boom. Some goods previously made with iron or rubber were now produced with synthetics, but that was no hardship.

I called at the home of my student friend Asada; he had been drafted by the army and was somewhere in training camp. The dinner I shared with his father and mother was less pretentious than the meals we had enjoyed five years earlier. Our meal was limited to rice, fish and pickles. The toast and jam, milk, fruit and chocolate bars that they had purchased for my benefit in 1934 were now prohibitive in cost. To a traveller looking for war strain, there were clues but no startling evidence.

Throughout that 1939 visit, I concealed several reporter's notebooks under my shirt, fearing that Japanese police would seize the book materials I had gathered. But (as far as I could see) my hotel room was never searched, and I left Japan with my notes and photographs intact.

Crossing the Pacific by freighter, I experienced a remarkable coincidence. Two days out of Yokohama our ship was struck by a violent storm and tossed by exceptionally high waves. At the height of the storm our ship's radio picked up a distress signal from another vessel not far away; it was a large Chinese junk sailing to the United States. The voyage of this junk proved to be the last adventure of Richard Halliburton, whose travel books had helped inspire me to go to China. The junk returned to Hong Kong for repairs, then made a second attempt and sank. All the crew—including Halliburton—were lost. I was fortunate, I concluded, to have spent my years in China with no greater disaster than an occasional bout with dysentery.

Many things in the United States in 1939 made a traveller from China glad to be home—commodious bathrooms, running hot water, telephones, the *New York Times*, fresh salads, whole wheat bread, and chocolate ice cream. There were also things I left behind in China and would miss: exciting work, rickshas, street chatter, bargaining with merchants, the patience and kindliness of people, dumplings dipped in vinegar, and fresh *lychees* (a Chinese fruit).

In California I visited relatives who taught me a useful lesson. If I talked about China more than 15 minutes in answer to their polite questions, their eyes glazed and someone changed the subject. From this I gathered that events outside the United States were then of limited interest to those on the home front.

I took the train from Los Angeles to Chicago, where I was reunited with Berni. Adhering to the time schedule we had made in Peking, we were married March 29, 1939—the third anniversary of our China parting.

I closed my China files with a series of magazine articles in *Readers Digest, Asia, Pacific Affairs,* and *Amerasia*; with lectures before audiences that included the New York Foreign Policy Association and the Chicago Council on Foreign Relations. And in 1939 Farrar and Rinehart published my book, *Humane Endeavor: Story of the China War.* The book got good reviews but did not sell well. It was published two months after Hitler invaded Poland and world attention had shifted to the European conflict. That, at least, was my rationalization. Years later the book came back to haunt me.

*To tell the truth, never, in China or abroad, has there been a revolutionary party as decrepit and degenerate as we (the Guomindang) are today; nor one as lacking in spirit, lacking discipline, and even more, lacking standards of right and wrong as we are today. This kind of party should long ago have been destroyed and swept away.*

Chiang Kai-shek speech, 1948

CHAPTER 13

# Why Mao's Men Won the War

Chinese communists were victorious in their revolution for reasons that are now widely accepted.

- Mao was correct to rely on the peasants. Mao is quoted: "He who wins the peasants controls China." The fighting strength of an aroused peasantry proved stronger than Chiang Kai-shek's reliance on the Shanghai bankers and the military hardware of the United States.
- Communist soldiers were armed with the dynamic doctrine of mobile warfare, which enabled a small military body to attack a larger enemy force and achieve superiority *at the point of contact*. Under the circumstances of the Chinese revolution, Mao was a military genius.
- Mao's armies were led by dedicated officers, convinced of the rightness of their cause. The numbers of nationalist troops that eventually surrendered to Mao's armies exceeded the total strength of the communists.
- Press interviews with Mao Zedong and other communist leaders drew opinions that were clear and candid. The communists acknowledged their shortcomings and built confidence in their cause. They made sense.
- The Chinese communists won without foreign aid. They were beholden to no one. Despite an initial American belief that Soviet Russia and the Chinese communists were partners, history proved in the end that the Chinese were not tools of Moscow.

A study in 1945 by the U.S. War Department (now the Department of Defense) summarized the reasons for communist superiority. It said:

Practically all impartial observers emphasized that the Chinese communists comprise the most efficient, politically well-organized, disciplined and constructive group in China today. It is largely because of their political and military skill, superior organization and progressive attitude, which has won for them a popular support no other party or group in China can equal, that they have been expanding their influence. . . . *

---

*Lyman Van Slycke, ed., *The Chinese Communist Movement: a Report of the U.S. War Department*, July 1945.

*Every great war is accompanied by social revolution.*
William Manchester, 1973

PART THREE

# WARTIME AMERICA

On September 1, 1939, I was standing near the middle of the Associated Press newsroom in Chicago. Suddenly someone watching the A-wire began shouting, and the staff rushed to the teletype machine. The FLASH (a signal for news of overriding importance) reported Hitler's armies were invading Poland. Teletyped copies were torn from the machine and passed among the newswriters. We stood in awed silence, probably all of us speculating what would happen to the European democracies.

Similarly I recall other events of the war period: where I was at the moment, with whom I shared the experience, and what was said. On December 7, 1941, Berni and I were sitting in our apartment at the DeWitt Hotel in Chicago reading the Sunday paper; it must have been about 2 P.M., Chicago time, when a neighbor rushed in and cried "Hey, is your radio on? The Japs are attacking Pearl Harbor!"

Lafayette Square opposite the White House in Washington is another place that remains fixed in my mind. VE Day—Victory in Europe—had been announced by radio on May 8, 1945, and at least 10,000 people congregated after dark on the grass of the park, excitedly milling about, looking across Pennsylvania Avenue, hoping to catch a glimpse of President Truman in the window. Amidst the joy there was an undertone of sadness. Almost everyone in the crowd had a relative or a friend who had died in the war, and the Japanese conflict was still to be finished.

The ten years of the 1940s were the most gripping years of my life. American democracy was operating at its best. The presidency had cast aside timidity; the Congress performed beyond its usual partisanship; and the American people responded to leadership with remarkable unity. This was the decade in which Great Britain handed world leadership to the United States, and America accepted its international responsibilities.

The new outlook was long overdue. The United States had emerged from World War I as a great power, yet it refused at that time to help maintain world order through collective security. We declined to join the League of Nations. Though we were a great industrial leader and the world's greatest creditor nation, our policies were more appropriate to a weak debtor nation.

In World War II by contrast, we became a full belligerent, and our generous use of Lend-Lease was something to be proud of. After the fighting we joined the United Nations and made massive appropriations for relief and recovery. (We learned, also, the limitations of the U.N. as an administrator of large-scale United States aid abroad.)

In 1946 our wartime cordiality with the Soviet Union waned. Some Americans warned that a Russian threat was as great as that of Hitler; others withheld judgment, unwilling to accept the possibility of a still more horrifying war in the atomic age. Official American policy toward the Russians gradually hardened as the Russians clamped their controls over Eastern Europe and infiltrated the western democracies. Communists demonstrated new forms of aggression: radio propaganda, subversion, a war of nerves, and aid to rebel groups.

After Pearl Harbor, Berni and I moved to Washington, where I was employed by the State Department. The wartime capital raised the adrenalin juices and generated two contradictory moods. The first, patriotism, was exhilarating; it generated pride in government agencies, it made people respond to the appeals of national leaders. As government workers we bought war bonds, we carpooled to save gasoline, we planted a victory garden, we wore clothing a second year to conserve textiles, we locked our office files to guard state secrets. We took pride in the "E" for excellence flag that flew over many establishments.

In a second, quite different mood, we jockeyed for increases of status—not so much for money as for power. Those of my age group (25-35) were surrounded by older men in government who had passed the age of military service, men who had been professors, magazine editors, advertising agency heads, or vice presidents of big banks. They all strove for recognition.

My 11 years in Washington served as my introduction to America as a world power and the yeasty spirit that a war and postwar period generated. But first I benefited from a period as a reporter in the American heartland—at Chicago—observing Americans at work, and how they got their news.

*In 1900 the Associated Press of America began to deliver its news report as a non-profit cooperative.*

Oliver Gramling, 1940

CHAPTER 14

# Chicago: Newsman for the Associated Press

My first workday as a reporter for the Associated Press in Chicago was in September 1939. I rode the elevated train from Garfield Park station—where I was living on the west side—to the Randolph and Wells station in the loop. I walked down the long iron stairway of the "El" and found the AP office on Randolph facing the Bismarck Hotel. Our office was half a mile from Lake Michigan, one block from city hall and—more important—two blocks from Harding's cafeteria where AP staffers could get a platter of rare roast beef with potatoes, vegetables, bread, and coffee for 35 cents without tip. That was not the cheapest meal in the loop, but it was the best quality for the money within a short walk.

I knew nothing about the Chicago daily papers or the city news bureau, which supplied raw materials for the AP. I had never heard of the Illinois downstate dailies that exchanged news with us. I was ignorant of Illinois politics. I had never followed professional baseball or football in this area. But my biggest deficiency was how little I knew about the AP itself: its emphasis on speed to beat the opposition, mainly United Press; its hatred of mistakes on the news wire that had to be corrected; its horror of a "kill"—withdrawing a news item that was potentially libelous or in poor taste. The communications system of AP was also new to me: the teletype machines with their cross-country wires; the compressed air tubes that linked the AP office to the Chicago papers, permitting news copy to zip across the loop; the motorcycle messengers at the AP street door ready to deliver photo prints to Chicago papers in minutes. Working for this organization in 1939 was like running a 100-yard dash with an upright typewriter tied around your waist.

Abbreviations for the AP bureaus were part of this mania for speed. Chicago was CX, New York AP, Washington WX, Kansas City KX and San

Francisco FX. If our bureau (CX) wished to send a service message (MSG) to New York (AP), there were standard abbreviations that the receiver could scan faster than reading English: today became TDY, yesterday YA, tomorrow TMW, correct was CQ, budget BJT. There were scores of other bits of teletype jargon. A reporter who learned teletype language was hooked for life. These abbreviations still appear in my interview notes half a century later.

Salary information was readily available. A new man coming in 1939 from a downstate paper with five years' experience was likely to draw the Newspaper Guild minimum of $35 a week, and if he proved himself, would receive a raise of $5 a week annually for the next three years. Most veteran reporters or wire editors—men who had been around the AP office five or ten years—were on the salary plateau of about $60–80 a week, and our top rewrite man (the writer who wrote the lead stories carried over from the P.M. to the A.M. papers) made $90. I started at $50, was raised to $55 and $60 in two years, and didn't stay long enough to see what my plateau would be.

That first day I introduced myself to the bureau chief, Victor Hackler. He gave me a quick handshake, a big smile, and two minutes of welcome. He knew my China background from Byron Price in the New York office and had no need to discuss employment. I learned later that Hackler prided himself on brevity; the staff said he had never written a letter longer than one paragraph.

Hackler turned me over to the day city editor, a short, cigar-chewing Milwaukeean named Marvin Tonkin. Tonkin's city desk consisted of a group of tables pushed into one large rectangle providing space for about ten reporters, all facing the city editor, each with his typewriter (the old manual model), telephone and ashtray. When a big story was in progress—a national political convention, for example—there might be half a dozen reporters writing related stories, all within a few feet of each other and each able to check details with the others.

Reporters on the day city desk followed a routine. On arrival at 9 A.M. each man read the "news file," a clipboard of stories written in the Chicago office during the preceding 24 hours. Next he paged through the final edition of the morning *Chicago Tribune* and the early editions of the afternoon papers—the *Chicago Daily News* and the *Chicago Sun-Times*. Then he checked the A-wire "budget" for a list of stories from New York that would tell him how congested the news would be for afternoon papers that day. These preliminaries took no more than half an hour. By that time the city editor (Tonkin) had made initial writing assignments. The reporters continued to scan every edition of the Chicago papers plus the city news bureau printouts that covered the fire department, police headquarters, and government offices.

Tonkin, still chomping on a cigar, gave me a quick tour. The news room was an open floor about 100 feet by 150 feet. Beyond the city desk was the man covering Chicago livestock and grain markets, a specialty requiring years of experience. Next came the two-man sports department, headed by Charlie Dunkley, a short, mustached, gregarious man whose greatest exploit was his annual trip to the Kentucky Derby for the sole purpose of snapping one picture of horses at the finish. His shot appeared on the front page of most dailies.

In the center of the news room was the desk of the AP radio wire, that tedious producer of a five-minute news summary every hour. The radio writer read all the incoming tickers and decided when to shift his hourly lead. It was not a very inspiring assignment.

On the far wall of the news room were the teletype printers, teletype "punchers" (men who prepared tapes like player piano rolls for outgoing stories), and the wire editors—the most senior newsmen in the office—who decided when to send out Chicago bureau stories.

The only part of the AP staff with a walled enclosure for privacy was the photo section. I don't know why. The photo men had their wirephoto sending and receiving machines, desks for photo editors, a waiting table for photographers, the dark room, and extensive photo files. I gained respect for the photo caption writers. Previously I thought a ten-word caption was the snap job of the office, but I learned photo men labored long over their captions, compressing words, punning, always reinforcing the visual message.

The clatter of six teletype printers, six punchers, and up to 20 manual typewriters was at first deafening, but the racket soon became a drone in which the mind could concentrate on the news story in the typewriter.

My breaking in at AP in September 1939 coincided with a drastic change in the world "news budget." I arrived the day the European war began. Obviously this demanded a major increase in news from Europe and Washington and a cutback in domestic news. This was difficult for the wire editors to accomplish because sports pages still asked the same coverage on football, the business pages still wanted full stock market reports, and downstate dailies still asked full coverage of the legislature. Eventually everything had to be written more concisely. I watched this adjustment first from the city desk and later as a wire editor.

I was successful in getting feature-writing assignments outside the office. The International Livestock Exposition was one. This was the largest cattle show in the United States, a week-long event at the Chicago stockyards where I wandered in ankle-deep sawdust, digging up feature stories, aiming for one each day. One feature concerned the names that ranchers give their famous bulls—like Hillcrest Larry and Colorado Domino. I compiled a list of names from the show catalog and hunted down the cattlemen to learn the source of names. My top story that week was a profile of a 17-year-old, 4-H Club boy whose fat steer won the grand championship. Interviewing the boy was easy, but everyone connected with the winning animal asked to get his name in the news. That included the rancher who bred the winning steer, the 4-H Club leader who supervised the boy, the suppliers of mineral supplements, and even the governor of the state.

The auto strike at the Ford Motor Company in Detroit was my longest assignment off the city desk—about two weeks. It was the most vicious strike of 1939, a year of conflicts as industrial labor recovered from frozen wages during the depression. Our Detroit office called for reinforcements; fighting had broken out at many Ford factory gates. My reporting in Detroit on bloody noses and clubbings (no gunfire) added little to the story. But over beers in the evening I learned much from the specialized labor reporters sent by the New York and Chicago papers; they were pros. I think most reporters sided with the battered strikers, but our wire editors chopped out any perceived bias toward labor or management.

Within a year I moved to the night city desk where working hours were 5 P.M. to 1 A.M. Family men despised this schedule. The night city editor was a fast and careful writer named Al Orton, and I was his only reporter. Most of the time Orton needed no help, and he sent me out of the office on any potential feature story. During the 1940 political campaign President Roosevelt was running for his third term against Wendell Willkie, the "one world" enthusiast.

One night Orton assigned me to cover the president's wife, Eleanor, who was speaking to a full house at the Chicago Auditorium. The speech was expected to be routine, but it turned out otherwise. Shortly after Mrs. Roosevelt began to speak, a bearded man in the balcony rose and shouted his disagreement with something she said. Mrs. Roosevelt stood motionless, looked at the floor, made no reply, and resumed her speech. Again the man shouted and again she made no reply. When the heckler interrupted a third time, Mrs. Roosevelt folded her arms on her chest and—looking straight at the heckler in the balcony—she said, "Young man, my mother taught me as a child that at our dinner table, we speak one at a time. That is simple courtesy. If you will let me finish what I have to say, I shall listen to what you have to say." There were no more interruptions, and the little event appeared next morning in a box on the front page of many newspapers.

My favorite assignment on the night city desk now seems incredible: I was tapped to write about the Chicago Civic Opera Company and the Chicago

Ballet. Berni and I received a pair of orchestra seats for every performance. I was not expected to be a music or dance critic; instead, my job was to write profiles of new stars, new choreographers, new opera composers, new ballet themes. There was always help from the press agents, and they made life pleasant by sending letters of appreciation to my AP superiors.

I remember one amusing little episode at the opera: A new Polish tenor received a terrible panning from the Chicago critics, but I followed with a redeeming profile. The punch line was the singer's own statement: "I may be a ham but at least I am a Polish ham."

Another assignment at AP-Chicago was my stint as editor of the Illinois-Indiana state wire, the news service to daily newspapers in about 20 smaller towns of the two states. The state wire was a test of nerves. As wire editor, I sat at a desk with three teletype printers spewing out news—the A-wire carrying top domestic and foreign news as selected in New York, the B-wire carrying market reports and other business news, and the C-wire with regional news and dozens of two-line messages addressed from one AP bureau to another.

This state wire editor's job was to read the three incoming teleprinters, each running at 60 words a minute, and select enough news for one outgoing wire, also running at 60 words a minute. The editor accomplished this compression by chopping long stories into shorter ones, or eliminating many stories altogether. Selection was greatly simplified by the "news budget" that the New York office provided when the wire opened. The budget listed the best stories for A.M. newspapers as of 3 P.M. the day before publication. This news priority would change while the wire was operating, but it enabled both the wire editor and the downstate papers to get started on their work.

Despite the hectic pace, the wire editor was expected to maintain a balanced file that would fill the front page, satisfy the sports editor, and serve the business page. When pressure became really tough—as on those maddening Saturdays in early October when college football overlapped with baseball's world series—all three wires carried urgent items. The wire editor was driven up the wall.

As I made each selection for the state wire, I slapped the copy on a spindle beside my "puncher," a tall, silent Yugoslav named Benny. Benny rocked his shoulders from side to side like a pianist as he typed at twice the speed of the outgoing teletype, his tape accumulating on the floor. When he thought he spotted an error in my copy, he could scoop up a tangle of tape beside his machine, run it through his fingers, and read the punched holes faster than I could read the original typescript. His punching got so far ahead of the outgoing wire that he could take an hour for dinner without stopping the outflow.

My biggest goof on the state wire was an error of judgment on one of those Saturday baseball-football overlaps. In the midst of all the sports, we received a long news report of a speech by President Roosevelt. It was dull, and I laid it aside to work in later in the evening. But the pressure of top news never let up, and at 10 P.M. I was still holding the story. Then hell broke loose. Some downstate paper telephoned that it had been scooped by its opposition on that FDR story, and what was wrong with AP? I gave them the story immediately, but that did not spare our bureau manager from explaining to New York who the chump was who made the error.

There were no more complaints, but by late 1941 I was getting ready to leave. Berni and I had spent our first three years of married life in Chicago. We were studying French and German at the Berlitz School because I hoped to become an AP war correspondent in Europe. Unfortunately, New York was surfeited with AP veterans. The week after Pearl Harbor, I had covered a meeting of the American Historical Association in Chicago. A Peking friend, John Fairbank of Harvard, had sought me out and urged that I join the war effort in Washington; there, he said, agencies were searching for persons with China experience. Qualified candidates would have their choice of many agencies.

I visited Washington. The excitement of wartime was everywhere. I talked to friends I had known in China—some embassy staff from Peking, now in the State Department; some reporters, now in army intelligence or the agency called Office of Facts and Figures; and one American gymnastics coach who had been recruited into the agency for economic warfare. His was not the most extreme example of career switching. I was sorely tempted. But I was reluctant to give up eight years of experience in magazine and newspaper writing. That was my life work, I thought. In the end, promising myself that this was only a temporary departure from journalism, I joined the State Department.

*The United States was the last of the major powers to take official cognizance of the great international tide of ideas.*

Wilma Fairbank, 1976

CHAPTER 15

# Washington: A State Department Program in China

We travelled from Chicago to Washington in February 1942. Our train was one of the popular diesels; air travel was not yet common. The smart new Pullman car was furnished with compartments, each with two berths, a toilet concealed beneath a dressing chair, and a midget washbowl. Other Pullman cars on the same train were of the older style with upper and lower berths on each side of a center aisle, enclosed by green curtains. Travellers on the older cars had to line up for toilets and lavatories at the end of the car.

Train travel in 1942 still had many distinctive features. The diner offered a varied menu served on starched linen table cloths by waiters in black suits, white shirts, and black bow ties. The Pullman porter carried bags without being asked. He shined shoes during the night and said "thank you" for a 25-cent tip. There were plenty of redcaps at the station, but this changed shortly, when most redcaps joined the army or navy. A large sign in the station read, IS THIS TRIP NECESSARY?

I came for a State Department interview and Berni came to hunt for housing, assuming I was hired. We picked up a *Washington Post* to read in the taxi enroute to the Annapolis Hotel ($6.00 a night double, five blocks from the White House). We arrived just two months after Pearl Harbor, and the front page stories explained why Washington suffered war fever. On the Pacific front the Japanese General Tojo was outblitzing Hitler, having occupied French Indochina, British Hong Kong and Singapore, and the American Philippines; he had landed troops on Borneo and seemed unstoppable in his drive toward Australia. In Europe German armies threatened Stalingrad and still pointed toward Moscow. In North Africa

Field Marshal Rommel was approaching Cairo. One pessimistic columnist speculated that Rommel would meet Tojo in India. On the Atlantic Ocean the disastrous German U-boat campaign was destroying Allied ships daily some along the American East Coast within sight of coastal cities.

Our taxi driver gave a more cheerful description of Washington. The city was fully lighted at night—there were no blackouts until a few months later. Auto traffic on Constitution Avenue was still jammed in rush hours; there was no gas rationing—yet. Stores were full of food and clothing. Bars were crowded after 5 P.M. Liquor stores were well stocked. The only indication of wartime shortage was the telephone service; government phones gave busy signals hour after hour.

That day I walked along Pennsylvania Avenue from the hotel to the State Department, pausing at Lafayette Square to stare at the White House (Roosevelt was in residence in the middle of his third term). I surveyed the two massive buildings that flank the White House on Pennsylvania Avenue—the five-story State Department on the right and the Grecian-pillared Treasury on the left. This juxtaposition reminded me of the acronym ST. WAPNIACL that I had memorized in high school to identify the order of succession by cabinet members if both the president and vice-president were incapacitated. The acronym stood for State, Treasury, War, Attorney General, Post Office, Navy, Interior, Agriculture, Commerce and Labor. Later legistation in the Nixon era cancelled the ST. WAPNIACL sequence and substituted a succession by legislative leaders that made more sense.

I was overly impressed that the State Department was number one. Only later did I learn that President Roosevelt was creating war agencies to conduct most emergency work, leaving old line agencies like the State Department in a quiet backwater. The most powerful war agencies became the War Production Board, War Food Board, Office of Strategic Services, Office of Price Administration, Office of War Information, War Labor Board, and Lend Lease Administration.

My State Department interview took place in an aging residence on the southwest corner of 17th and F Streets, across the street from "Main State." A spillover for the State Department staff, the house was called the Grant Building after General Ulysses S. Grant, who once had his Civil War headquarters here. A sign at the door read, DEPARTMENT OF STATE, DIVISION OF CULTURAL RELATIONS. That didn't sound like a war service center and, in fact, the peaceful-sounding title proved a handicap in getting money from Congress.

A receptionist directed me to a basement room where faded linoleum covered the brick floor and two small, high windows gave limited daylight. Here I found the three-person planning group for the newest China program in Washington. Its head was a 40-year old foreign service officer—a stiff New Englander named Stuart Grummon who had spent three years of his diplomatic service stationed in China. His assistant was Wilma Fairbank.* One secretary completed this work force.

The basement room certainly did not fit my image of the State Department as the president's number one agency. I was also put off by the term "cultural relations." But as I listened to a three-hour briefing, I substituted my own term—"technical and educational exchanges." I also saw ways that this new program could contribute practical services to wartime China. At the end of the day I was offered a position with a P-5 rating, subject to security clearance, and I accepted.

That first day's briefing revolved around one question: What would be the nature of the China program? Several bits of history should be cited here. France was the pioneer in establishing government-financed overseas schools and cultural centers. By 1933, 10 percent of the French foreign office budget was devoted to cultural activities, and the term *Alliance Francaise* became familiar in major capitals of the world. The British government followed with its British Council program, which specialized in teaching English in foreign cities and drew praise for its movie shows, amateur theater groups, and reading rooms. The Axis powers—Germany and Italy—also financed lavish cultural programs, especially in Latin America. The United States was a latecomer in the field, taking the initiative only after the 1936 Inter-American Conference produced a Convention for the Promotion of Cultural Relations. In response, the State Department created its Division of Cultural Relations and established in major Latin American cities a program of libraries, language classes, exchange fellowships for university students, and travel grants for distinguished leaders.

By mid-1941 China had been at war for four years, measured from the Marco Polo Bridge incident. Its university facultites had made the arduous 1500-mile trek from the coast to west China—some on foot, some in crowded trucks—and universities settled in clusters around Kunming, Guiyang, Chongqing, and Chengdu. Many of the Chinese professors and scientific researchers were graduates of American universities and had friends on American campuses. Not surprisingly, the State Department received appeals to extend the cultural relations program from Latin America to

---

*Wilma was a Cambridge artist and archeologist with an encyclopedic knowledge of American private organizations engaged in education, health and other civilian activities in China. She is now the author of a 230-page book, *America's Cultural Experiment in China: 1942–1949*, published by the State Department.

China. This idea was logical, but China's needs in 1942 were very different from countries at peace in the western hemisphere. The Japanese navy blockaded the China coast and the Japanese army had closed the Indochina railroad and the Burma road; China was thus isolated except for the military flights from Burma into west China. Any assistance that required heavy air freight or travel of many people was impossible.

After half a year of discussion, the State Department obtained a grant from the president's Emergency Fund, and a program of cultural assistance to China took shape around three activities: first, scientific and scholarly journal articles shipped to China by microfilm; second, emergency aid to Chinese students stranded in the United States; and third, American technicians and professors sent to China to help maintain Chinese morale.

My assignment was to select the technicians, and I recruited 27 Americans for wartime service. They included engineers, health specialists, agriculturalists, educators, and industrial experts. Each was requested by a Chinese ministry. Some produced benefits that may still continue.

The first technician to reach China under this program was a former China resident, Dr. Walter Lowdermilk, previously a forestry professor at Nanking University. Walter travelled by munitions ship down the west coast of South America, across the South Atlantic to Capetown; then flew via Cairo and Delhi to Chongqing. Like some who followed him, Lowdermilk made a greater contribution to postwar planning than to the fight against Japan. With eight Chinese assistants, Lowdermilk designed a method to reforest the eroded loess-lands of northwest China by dropping from airplanes mud pellets containing tree seeds. Many years later I heard that this method was adopted by the Peoples Republic of China.

One of the health recruits was Dr. John Tripp, a specialist in manufacture of serums and vaccines. In peacetime he was associate director at the Michigan State Health Department. His assignment? To set up a vaccine laboratory and to supervise China's blood plasma units. His laconic reports understated his initiative, such as: "7000 beer bottles, U.S. Army empties, secured for use in intravenous injections." Some called him an alchemist because he could mix medicinal alcohol with tinctures that gave forth the flavor of Scotch, bourbon, or rum. This achievement was considered a top war service by some American GIs in China.

The agriculturalists we sent to China were among the world's best. Dr. Ralph Phillips, a specialist in artificial insemination of animals, offered his skills to the Chinese cavalry and camel corps.

I thought all the men we sent to China were adventurous, but one was my favorite. He was a potato breeder named Theodore Dykstra, a USDA employee on the Madison campus of the University of Wisconsin. His baggage included seven sacks of potatoes. Dykstra was the only man among our travellers whose ship was torpedoed, but he transferred the potatoes to a lifeboat, reached South Africa safely, and was flown with his cargo to China.

Within six months Dykstra produced in western China a crop of disease-free seed potatoes that were distributed to hill farmers around Chengdu. Forty years later I visited a research station outside Chengdu and was shown some unusual potatoes that the local scientists could not identify. I told them the story of Dykstra's visit during World War II. I cannot be sure, but I think Dykstra's work lives on.

There were also failures. We made a colossal mistake by responding to a request for four American newsmen to produce news items about China for release in the United States. Shortly after they reached China, their work drew protests on two counts. One, they were competing with private American press and radio representatives. Two, the technicians themselves protested against being asked to write propaganda about the Chinese government. Three of the four asked to be released at the end of their one-year assignments. Only the photographer remained.*

One other controversy arose near the end of the war. I recruited an American specialist on industrial standards, requested by the Chinese Ministry of Economic Affairs, to help in planning. That meant choosing between the metric standard and the foot-pound system. The American expert, whose name was Dickson Reck, recommended the metric system. When Reck's recommendation reached the ears of Ambassador Patrick Hurley, he called Reck on the carpet for recommending a standard that was not tailor-made for the promotion of American exports. Reck argued that this was in the best interest of China. (Later, the Peoples Republic of China did adopt the metric system.)

As a newcomer to the State Department I tried to adjust to the State Department's long-established ways of doing things—and none more frustrating than its handling of official cables and letters. To send a cable to the U.S. embassy in Chongqing, I found, could take one week or even two, and to mail an official letter addressed to another agency in Washington

---

*The State Department was told that this request originated with President Roosevelt and was endorsed by Chiang Kai-shek. According to one version, Roosevelt complained to Hollington Tong, the Chinese minister of information, that China was getting a poor press in the United States and the minister should find ways to distribute favorable news on the China war. The minister shifted the responsibility by requesting the State Department to recruit the four Americans—two newswriters, one radio broadcaster, and one photographer—to work in his ministry.

could take a month. Such sluggishness was incredible to me. In the newspaper world the speed of communications was measured in minutes, not weeks.

There was, of course, a logical explanation. Slowness was imposed by the State Department clearance procedure. The department wanted no mistakes, and errors were less likely to occur if everyone concerned with the subject were consulted. A cable or letter became a historic document carrying the initials of all who approved.

Take one hypothetical example. Say I had drafted a 100-word message describing an engineer who was available for two years' service in China. The embassy at Chongqing was being asked to inform the Chinese government and cable back its acceptance. The clearance procedure in Washington went like this:

1. The drafting officer (myself) put his name at the bottom of the typewritten cable and initialed it.

2. The cable was then initialled by the drafter's section chief, division chief, or office chief, and sometimes all three.

3. State Department cables were sent in the name of the secretary of state. In 1942 that meant HULL (Cordell Hull, secretary of state, 1933–44). Hull, of course, did not actually see the cables that bore his name. After all, the secretary in 1942 had 5,000 employees. By the armistice in 1945, he had 10,000; and by 1950, 15,000. Many officers in the department had authority to serve as proxy signers for the secretary. They wrote HULL and placed their initials in parentheses below his name. But this draft with Hull's proxy signature still had a distance to go before it reached the cable room.

4. The drafting officer (myself) had written at the bottom of the typewritten text the symbols for the minimum number of offices that he thought had relevant jurisdiction, such as:

CA (Division of Chinese Affairs)
FE (Office of Far Eastern Affairs)
PA-H (Political Advisor, Hornbeck)
DP (Division of Personnel)
DB (Division of Budget)

The cable moved by the safe hand of a messenger from the out-box of one office to the in-box of another. Each move might require a day. In extreme cases these clearances could take weeks.

5. CR was next. The Office of Correspondence and Review had been created to ensure that all responsible parties had seen the cable and that the

United States government was not giving contradictory information through two or more offices. The reviewers in CR had been selected from among the veteran secretaries in the department because they were familiar with the responsibilities of all the higher officers. Their basic rule: In case of doubt, ask for more initials. When CR was satisfied, the cable was sent.

I won't retrace this process for a letter; initialling was the same but with even more pitfalls. If the State Department were asking another government agency to release one of its employees for service in China, the standard procedure required the letter to travel "the double pyramid route." This meant the letter had to climb the hierarchy in the State Department, be signed by the secretary of state or an assistant secretary, be carried across the city by messenger to the head of the other agency, and then descend to the responsible office. Returning some time later, the letter would again climb up and down the appropriate pyramid.

I devised shortcuts (as I'm sure others did). If my recruit were an agriculturalist, I telephoned the candidate in the Department of Agriculture, talked to his superior, and worked out the salary. Then I hand-carried the letter of agreement for all initials in the State Department and sent copies by messenger to the candidate. Success! I recruited 27 specialists in 30 months.

The procedures of the State Department were not designed to win a war against Germany or Japan. That is probably why many wartime responsibilities were assigned to special war agencies that were not so fastidious about coordination. Admittedly, other departments of government had similar controls over correspondence, but they could not compete with the State Department in the fine points of bureaucracy.

*Don't you know there's a war on?*
Popular saying

CHAPTER 16

# Family in the Wartime Capital

Life in Washington was a constant reminder of the war. An air raid warden called on us during the first evening in our Connecticut Avenue apartment to explain the sirens and shelters. The shelters were merely hallways on the lower floors of the eight-story building, the idea being to stay away from the top floors and the outer windows. I am glad we never tested the concept with live ammunition. Within a week our first air raid drill was signalled by wailing sirens at 9 P.M., and with much joking the building occupants trooped to the designated shelter areas. Here we remained 15 minutes until the all-clear sounded. Washington was never bombed during World War II, but the civil defense drill was intended to make us more conscious of the war effort. By mid-1942 the government had ordered a continuous blackout of Washington; this meant street lights were extinguished, automobiles drove with dimmed lights, and our air raid warden patrolled the dark streets, blowing a whistle whenever he or she could see residential lights through the draperies. These precautions continued for three years.

Many people planted "victory gardens" that augmented the local food supply. Berni and I planted a garden in an adjoining vacant lot that the management staked off into plots. We prepared our seedbed with mattock and shovel, digging up in the process various archeological objects such as old shoes and beer cans. In this unpromising soil we planted radishes, onions, lettuce and tomatoes, the last being braced by stakes from Sears Roebuck on Wisconsin Avenue. The gardeners showed competitive pride resembling the rivalry among lawn-keepers in postwar suburbia. Our gardens did not add much to the gross domestic product, but the effort made us feel less guilty about not being in the front lines against Nazis and Japanese.

The government required us to use ration books when we shopped for meat, cooking oil, and sugar. President Roosevelt told us over the radio that rationing was the fair way to share the burden, so that America could ship more food to the war fronts. We heard little grumbling.

At social gatherings military gossip approached indiscretion. We had a neighbor—a man of 60 who represented a large corporation—who often stopped by for a drink and talk. In a lowered voice he would report progress on "the thing," which we understood to be a secret weapon already in production but not yet seen in battle. One night he reported excitedly that "the thing" had at last gone into action; it was the hush-hush rocket cannon that knocked out hundreds of German tanks in the Egyptian western desert. We felt we had shared a secret though we did not understand the technology.

Another hush-hush topic was the air transport route across the South Atlantic from the bulge of Brazil to the bulge of west Africa. The airfields at each end were supposed to be secret. One of the landing places in Africa was said to be Fisherman's Lake, so if a man at a cocktail party dropped the term "Fishlake," he was recognized as one with inside information.

The air route over the hump from Burma to southwest China was another guarded topic. The takeoff and landing fields were classified information, but since all personnel and supplies entering China were flying over this air space, the route was known to many agencies and there was much talk. I lost one of my most admired college classmates—Bill Watson of the Army Medical Service—on a flight over the hump. These losses were usually caused by motor trouble rather than by enemy action. For many nights after Bill's death, I fantasized how Bill spent his last five minutes after the plane motors went dead: The pilot was probably gliding in search of a safe haven, but finally crashed into thick green jungle cover. To my knowledge the wreckage was never found.

Berni's father and mother came from Chicago to visit us by train. Invariably they saved enough meat ration stamps to bring us a pound of bacon and some steaks frozen in dry ice. No gift was more appealing in war days, although it is hard to explain now. When bacon and steaks are readily available in peacetime, they seem routine. But when you have gone without them and they are difficult or impossible to get, they seem mouth-watering.

During one visit Berni's father used the men's room at the Washington railroad station and returned with a grin. He said, "I was in the Army Medical Corps during World War I and never saw an officer of rank higher than a colonel. Just now I saw six generals lined up, urinating."

> The adequacy with which the United States as a society is portrayed to the other peoples of the world is a matter of concern to the American people and their government.

Arthur W. Macmahon, 1945

CHAPTER 17

# Lobbyist

At the beginning of 1945, my State Department duties took a new direction. To start, I left China work. President Roosevelt had created a new post called assistant secretary of state for public affairs and he appointed Archibald MacLeish as the first incumbent. Having served the previous five years as librarian of Congress, MacLeish was one of America's best-known literary figures—a kindly, generous man in personal relations. The State Department transferred me to be MacLeish's executive assistant. I drafted replies to MacLeish's public mail, received some of his visitors, and prepared recommendations on many problems that came to him. My office was on the first floor of "Main State," with a window looking across West Executive Avenue to the White House only 100 yards away. At 33 I felt close to the center of American power, although only as an observer.

I shared my office with a 45-year-old Chicago lawyer named Adlai E. Stevenson, who advised MacLeish on plans for the United Nations preparatory conference scheduled at San Francisco in June 1945. As an officemate Adlai displayed two characteristics: he had irrepressible wit that invaded even his most serious writings; and he was indecisive and procrastinating in his recommendations, which we usually discussed before he submitted a paper to MacLeish. Adlai was living alone in Georgetown not far from our home. The two of us sometimes stopped at his place in the evening for a drink and a sandwich and continued our conversations at his kitchen table. Three years later I had opportunity to vote for Adlai, then the Democratic candidate for governor of Illinois (he was elected) and twice for president of the United States (the 1952 and 1956 defeats). With hindsight, I believe this man of charm, because of his indecisiveness, would have made a disappointing president.

Upon the death of President Roosevelt in April 1945 and the swearing-in of Harry Truman as thirty-third president, tradition required high federal officers to submit their resignations. But on this occasion, Truman requested the entire State Department leadership to remain on the job until after the San Francisco conference—a sensible decision. But one change affecting our office did occur. MacLeish ceased to be a presidential speech writer; his style was too literary for Truman's taste. One of MacLeish's draft speeches lay on the president's White House desk on the day Roosevelt died. Truman sent the draft to his new speech writer, a Kansas City newspaper reporter, and said, "Put this in Missouri English." A few months later, James Byrnes, ex-senator, ex-governor, ex-Supreme Court justice, became the new secretary of state under Truman, and MacLeish was replaced by William Benton, cofounder of the advertising firm of Benton and Bowles.

Benton was a brilliant, brash, hard-driving man who told me in our first conversation that he had earned a million dollars before he was 30, retired from advertising at 36, become vice-president of the University of Chicago at 37, president of Encyclopedia Britannica at 43, and now assistant secretary of state at 45. He worked 16 hours a day and drove his staff likewise. I received messages from Benton dictated at his summer residence in Arizona that read:

> Dear Hal,
>
> I am sitting on the edge of the pool with my feet in the water, thinking of you. Please look after the following matters.

Instructions followed on a number of chores. The message would be delivered by Benton's chauffeur to my farm in Virginia on a Saturday afternoon (we did not have a telephone there), and Benton would follow up with a long distance telephone call to the State Department on Monday morning at 9 A.M. asking if the work had been completed. My feelings about Benton alternated between admiration and despair.

During the five-year period 1945–49, I felt close to the making of history. In that brief period the State Department obtained congressional approval for three important postwar programs: first, the activities now administered by the U.S. Information Agency; second, the worldwide educational exchange program; and third, President Truman's Point Four (or technical assistance) Program and a sister operation, the United Nations Expanded Program of Technical Assistance. I served as legislative drafting officer on all three. As a novice lobbyist for the State Department, I shared in the congressional battles to obtain approval for these activities.

The Voice of America in wartime acquired the largest radio listening audience the world had known. At the end of the war our principal American transmitters were located in Eritrea (now part of Ethiopia), Ceylon (now Sri Lanka), and the Philippines. Scripts for these radio voices poured out of the Office of War Information (OWI) on West 57th Street in New York and on Independence Avenue in Washington. As the downfall of the Nazis approached, the policy question for the State Department was, Should a powerful instrument for international persuasion be disbanded or should there be a smaller, carefully defined government information service in peacetime? State Department officers were groping toward a decision to continue the Voice of America and a U.S. Information Agency.

For the Truman administration these discussions held political dangers. The major American news agencies—Associated Press and United Press—and the broadcasting corporations opposed a continuation of government news service in peacetime, fearing government control of the press and competition in marketing their products. Hollywood corporations that had shared patriotically in the production of wartime films for distribution overseas were also less than enthusiastic about a government film service after the war. On the affirmative side, the cold war was heating up in 1945, and no private organization had the resources or motivation to provide a flow of news beyond the Iron Curtain.

John Dickey, a State Department officer and later president of Dartmouth College, suggested a fresh approach. The State Department should call on a noted Columbia University political scientist, Dr. Arthur W. Macmahon, to consult all interested parties and submit recommendations to the State Department and the White House. This was done, and I was assigned as Macmahon's assistant.

Fortunately, we found within OWI some distinguished newsmen who now had experience on both the private and public side of the news and whose views proved influential. One was James Linen, age 33, who had been an executive in *Time-Life-Fortune* before the war and had directed the government's wartime news file. Another was Edward Barrett, age 35, who had served before the war as associate editor of *Newsweek* and had spent the war years as deputy director of OWI. Another strong voice was Ferdinand Kuhn, age 40, a veteran foreign correspondent for the *New York Times* in prewar days and European director of OWI in wartime.

Professor Macmahon interviewed these men and many others. The report he distilled favored a peacetime role for a government information service overseas, but kept the government out of self-supporting activities that could be performed by private enterprise. This concept was accepted by the State Department, by the White House, and eventually by Congress.

After the German surrender, the State Department decided that educational exchanges were needed as a normal part of American diplomatic relations. This meant that the cultural relations program in the western hemisphere would be expanded to the rest of the world. The best-known aspects of the program abroad were the U.S. libraries, English language classes, and exchanges of university professors and students. Yet there was no consensus in Congress for this expansion. Senator Robert Taft raised his familiar cry, "Where is the money coming from?"

Assistant Secretary Benton assigned me to draft the legislation and assist the campaign for approval by Congress. This turned out to be a two-year task. The House Foreign Affairs Committee was the logical starting place, and the chairman of that committee, Rep. Sol Bloom (Democrat, New York) was the obvious sponsor of the legislation because he had been a New York music publisher. He was a crotchety veteran of Congress, then age 76, not popular with his own committee, and I needed consensus among the 25 committee members.

The committee that year was a remarkable mix. Two women members were both named Douglas, both Democrats, both former actresses, both very smart. They were Helen Gahagan Douglas (Democrat-Calif.) and Emily Taft Douglas (Democrat-Ill.). Karl Mundt, a conservative South Dakota Republican, was a fellow Carleton alumnus and ex-debater. John Vorys, Ohio Republican, became a grudging supporter of the Democratic bill; in his younger days he had been an English instructor at Yale-in-China. Walter Judd and Mike Mansfield were both old China residents: Judd had spent 11 years there as a medical missionary, and Mansfield had served two years in the American infantry at Tianjin.

I helped Bill Benton organize working dinners for congressmen at Benton's home, one of the palatial mansions of Washington. Benton gave his sales pitch on the legislation before the food was served. In the committee Bloom left the choice of witnesses entirely to the State Department, and I lined up the heads of voluntary organizations like the National Education Association and the American Association of University Professors.

The legislation passed in the House, but Senator Taft—as I had feared—blocked the bill in the Senate. That meant we had to start over again in the Republican 80th Congress—the body that President Truman later labelled a "do-nothing Congress."

On the second time around we were fortunate to have the bill sponsored by two conservative Republicans, Rep. Mundt and Senator H. Alexander Smith of New Jersey. Mundt had his own ideas about witnesses: he called General Eisenhower, then army chief-of-staff and General George C. Marshall, then secretary of state. Mundt asked me to ride in the government limousine with each of the witnesses enroute to testify and to give them a few key points they would remember.

The bill sailed through the 80th Congress, and the world soon learned about "Smith-Mundt exchanges." The cold war had helped the vote.

Senator William Fulbright (Democrat, Arkansas), previously a Rhodes scholar and president of the University of Arkansas, suggested an additional source of funding for educational exchanges. The United States was holding billions of dollars in foreign currency credits as a result of Lend Lease and other aid programs. Use of these funds had not yet been decided, except for the purchase of new embassy buildings. Sen. Fulbright's suggestion: Why not use the currency for educational exchanges? Scholars visiting the United States could use local currency to pay international air fares. American scholars going to teach or study abroad could use foreign currency to pay local living costs. I worked with Fulbright on a bill that shortly became law, thanks to the pressure applied by nearly all the American universities. Fulbright became the most widely known member of Congress as the sponsor of "Fulbright scholars" in countries around the world.

*It is declared to be the policy of the United States to aid the efforts of economically underdeveloped countries to develop their resources and improve their working and living conditions by encouraging the exchange of technical knowledge and skills and the flow of investment capital....*

Act for International Development, 1950

CHAPTER 18

# Truman's Point Four

After President Truman was reelected in November 1948—by a near miracle—he set to work preparing the two traditional messages to Congress: a State of the Union address for January 5, 1949 and the Inaugural Address for January 20. The union message was to discuss domestic affairs and the inaugural would look abroad. Clark Clifford, a presidential assistant, has reported: "We were having a real problem during late December 1948 in putting the inaugural speech together. All of us thought that when the president stood up to take the oath of office on January 20, he should have something big and new and challenging to present to the country." The difficulty was that the pillars of the Truman foreign policy had already been presented to the public during the president's first term. What could be new? Clifford recalled: "A State Department memorandum had crossed my desk a few weeks or months earlier. A technical assistance program had been tried on a very modest scale in Latin America, and this memo raised the question whether it might be adapted to the Far East as a sort of substitute for the ERP (European Recovery Program)." Clifford suggested it to the president, who said after a moment of reflection, "That looks good. We'll use it. We can work out the operating details later."*

The audience at Truman's Inaugural Address was thus to be told that in dealing with other nations the United States would depend on the United Nations, the Marshall Plan, and the North Atlantic Alliance. He then added a fourth point—technical aid to developing countries. The final version of the speech read:

> Fourth, we must embark on a bold new program for making benefits of our scientific advances and industrial progress available for the improvement and growth of underdeveloped areas....

---

*William Manchester, *The Glory and the Dream*, 1974. This version of the Point Four origin was unknown to me before I read Manchester's excellent narrative.

Point Four raised the spirits of a world still exhausted by war. It offered the hope that technical skills could modernize backward agriculture; improve health conditions; and raise the level of incomes in Asia, Africa and Latin America.

I can speculate on the memo that crossed Clark Clifford's desk. In the summer of 1948 my assignment in the State Department had again changed. This time I became director of a little-known technical assistance program for Latin America. My office was called "Interdepartmental Committee on Scientific and Cultural Cooperation with Latin America." We distributed congressional funds to federal agencies engaged in joint projects with Latin American republics. Our committee financed agricultural research in Mexico, El Salvador, Costa Rica and Peru; it supported nurses' training by the U.S. Public Health Service in Ecuador; and it sponsored an archeological dig in Mexico through the Smithsonian Institution. The program cost only five million dollars a year at that time but generated substantial publicity and good will from the participating Latin American governments.

No sooner had I taken over these duties than I saw two major deficiencies: Why were American specialists recruited only from federal agencies? By broadening our selections to include universities and industries, we could recruit a greater range of skills. And why was this successful program limited to Latin America? I wrote a memorandum to the assistant secretary of state in charge of my work—a career minister named George V. Allen, one of the most thoughtful and creative persons I met in government. I recommended that the program be broadened to Asia and gave examples. Allen sent copies of the note to the secretary of state and to friends in the White House. Allen may have added the useful thought that technical assistance to developing countries could serve as a substitute for the Marshall Plan in poorer areas. Congress delayed 17 months, but finally approved the Point Four legislation, which was signed into law by President Truman in June 1950.

The Truman administration was already busy in another direction: It sponsored before the United Nations a technical assistance program that would be administered by the UN, parallel to the United States program. Again the State Department assigned me to the campaign.

In the summer of 1949 the U.S. delegation to the United Nations Economic and Social Council (familiarly known as ECOSOC) had offices in the Palace of Nations in Geneva, Switzerland. This was the old headquarters of the League of Nations. The head of our 20-person delegation was Dr. Willard Thorp, assistant secretary of state for economic affairs. Thorp had to deal with a dozen economic topics on the ECOSOC agenda, and he assigned members of his delegation to speak for the United States on subcommittees. As the only delegation member who had directed a technical aid program, I was assigned to sit on a subcommittee of eight nations to discuss President Truman's Point Four.

When I met the subcommittee members from the other governments, I was overwhelmed. Great Britain was represented by its vice minister of colonies, Sir Gerard Clausen; France by its under secretary of foreign affairs, Dr. Phillipe DeSeigne; and the Soviet Union by its vice minister of agriculture. Brazil sent Dr. Roberto Campos, later Brazilian minister of finance; Australia, a career ambassador; India, a professor of economics; and Chile, its former minister of foreign affairs. Since the president of the United States had proposed Point Four, everyone assumed that a spokesman for the United States would explain the program—a large order for me.

We discussed the nature of "backwardness." Britain and France spoke for their development methods in the colonies, and I described American experience in assigning technicians to Latin America and China. We also invited representatives of the UN specialized agencies to present their ideas. We spent a confusing week debating how to apportion funds. Not surprisingly, each UN agency considered its field to be the most important. To resolve the debate, we asked the eight national representatives on our subcommittee to write confidentially what percentage of funds they would allocate to the various development fields (such as agriculture, health, and education); then we averaged the answers. This was not a very analytic approach, but those percentages remained unchanged through the ECOSOC session and the UN General Assembly.

ECOSOC's debate on Point Four was repeated six months later when the UN General Assembly held its fourth session at Flushing Meadows, New York. There the U.S. delegation, headed by Sen. Warren Austin, numbered more than 60.

I was fascinated—and distressed—by the pressures that the United States delegation was able to apply to other nations in the assembly. At a typical staff meeting our delegation leader would raise the question: How do we ensure support for our resolution that is up for approval? The United States had a staff large enough to cover all other delegations—some for a drink, some for a meal, some for a chat in the corridor. These were pressure techniques adapted from lobbying in Congress and they generally attained results, although occasionally the pressure antagonized everyone, even our friends.

When the General Assembly voted unanimously to support a UN technical assistance program, my brief career at the United Nations was completed.

In Washington President Truman created a new agency to administer the Point Four program, called the Technical Cooperation Administration or TCA. He chose as administrator the head of one of the great land grant universities—Dr. Henry Bennett of Oklahoma State. This was an appropriate symbol. In the latter part of the nineteenth century, the land grant institutions had been pioneers of the Point Four idea, serving underdeveloped regions of the United States. Henry Bennett died in an airplane crash in Iran a few months after his appointment, but in his short service he accomplished much: He charmed a hostile Congress, he helped recruit top university administrators for the Point Four organization, and he persuaded the emperor of Ethiopia to establish an agricultural university that—with some American support—became one of the major agricultural institutions of Africa. Bennett's successor was Stanley Andrews, previously head of the Office of Foreign Agricultural Relations in the Department of Agriculture.

I was named assistant administrator under both Bennett and Andrews, with responsibility for the aid programs to India and other countries of Asia. My first task was to propose technical cooperation directors who would be attached to the United States embassies in all the countries of my area. That step had to be completed quickly; if we did not show progress in the first year of the program, we would have difficulty getting appropriations for the following year. I proposed Clifford Willson as director for India; Willson had supervised the largest flood control dams in the United States. For Pakistan I recruited an economist who had been vice president of Oklahoma State University. For Afghanistan I went to Tennessee Valley Authority to recruit one of the top river basin developers. The director for Nepal was a Virginian, the director of 4-H Clubs for his state.

My Washington office needed a small group of economists to appraise the grants. Few people in the United States had this kind of experience in international development. For this task I obtained three classmates with Ph.D.s in economics from Harvard, all in their early thirties, each of whom later had a distinguished career. They were Charles Wolf, Gustav Papanek, and Jack Bennett.

My role was to energize this young and enthusiastic staff. I also formulated a regional explanation of our program that won from the Bureau of the Budget and the Congress steadily rising appropriations. The early 1950s were a heady period for those of us in Point Four.

Our first Asian grants included the drilling of irrigation tubewells in India and Pakistan, the completion of irrigation canals for two hydroelectric dams in Afghanistan, a technical training school in Burma, and a fisheries development project in Indonesia. These were cautious, well-conceived projects financed by an initial Asian budget of $25 million. By the time our

Asian program exceeded $300 million, in the third year, it was more difficult to maintain the same prudence.

From the start two American groups pressed us to follow their program ideas. One was the postwar generation of American college students who were idealistic and wanted to work alongside our Point Four technicians. This was the Peace Corps concept, which was approved by Congress ten years later. Looking back, I think we were slow to recognize an overseas role for young people. The other pressure group was composed of American missionaries. They thought we should bypass Asian governments, which they regarded as ineffective and corrupt, and deliver aid directly to villagers. It was an appealing notion, but because our program in each country required sponsorship by the host government, we could not ignore our sponsor.

My own career in government service came to an abrupt end during the McCarthy era.

> *Joe McCarthy was an opportunist who happened to stumble upon an idea. He climbed on a political horse and rode it to death, his own included.*
>
> Brig. Gen. Ralph W. Zwicker, 1982

CHAPTER 19

# An Encounter with Senator McCarthy

It was noon on March 13, 1950. I was attending a meeting in the office of Willard Thorp, assistant secretary of state for economic affairs, when the hall door opened and in came Mike McDermott, the plump grey-haired press officer for the department. He pointed at me, smiled, and beckoned me into the corridor. Senator Joseph McCarthy (Republican, Wisconsin), Mike said, had testified in Congress that morning that Haldore Hanson was "a man with a mission to communize the world." Reporters were waiting to interview me.

My mind froze. To be called a communist in those cold war days was no different from being called a Russian spy. McCarthy made this charge less than two months after Alger Hiss had been convicted of perjury and only ten days after Klaus Fuchs, the atomic scientist, had been arrested for stealing bomb secrets from the Los Alamos project. There was fear across the nation.

In the pressroom 20 reporters began calling questions. I asked if anyone had a transcript of what the senator had said. None did. They had only a wire service bulletin quoting McCarthy on my "mission." The reporters demanded: Are you a communist? Are you a spy? Are you disloyal to the United States? I don't remember how I phrased my denials. The senator, I said, was quoting from a book I had written in China 11 years earlier when I had been 27 years old. I was not ashamed of the book, but if I were writing it now—during the cold war—I would say some things differently. Next day the Scripps Howard columnist, Peter Edson, had a helpful column in the *Washington Daily News*, entitled "About Haldore Hanson." Edson wrote in part: "Hanson's book *Humane Endeavor: Story of the China War*, from which Senator McCarthy quoted passages, is just what the title implies. It is a reporter's book. It tells what he saw, good and bad, on the Japanese, Chinese,

An Encounter with Senator McCarthy / 113

and communist guerilla fronts." Edson must have been one of the few who read the book when it appeared in 1939.

At the beginning of 1950 Joseph McCarthy was a little-known senator. His first three years in Washington had been undistinguished, and he was looking for a political issue that would assure his reelection in 1952. The Republican Party asked McCarthy to make five speeches during the week of Lincoln's birthday—February 1950—in obscure places starting with Wheeling, West Virginia and ending at Huron, South Dakota. The prospect for publicity was slight. McCarthy's office handed the senator a draft speech on communists in government, prepared by a group of Washington newsmen. There was nothing new in the cold war rhetoric about traitors in high places, but the speech writers caught the headlines with one paragraph in McCarthy's Wheeling text:

> While I cannot take the time to name all the men in the State Department who have been named as active members of the Communist party and members of a spy ring, I have here in my hand a list of 205—a list of names that were made known to the Secretary of State as being members of the Communist party and who nevertheless are still working and shaping policy in the State Department.

To McCarthy's surprise the speech received front page treatment. By the time he had varied the text in four more cities, he was a national figure. He closed the week with a five-hour speech in the Senate on February 20, which drew so much publicity that the Truman administration felt compelled to sponsor a special Senate investigative body—the Tydings subcommittee—to take testimony on McCarthy's charges.

The Tydings subcommittee was formed from within the Senate Foreign Relations Committee and authorized to "investigate whether there are employees in the State Department who are disloyal to the United States." The subcommittee was composed of three Democrats and two Republicans, reflecting the democratic majority in the Senate. McCarthy was not a member of the subcommittee but he was invited to be the first witness. Under oath McCarthy was pressed to make good on his charges—to provide a list of 205 communists and Russian spies in the State Department or to name 57 persons in the State Department who "would appear to be card carrying communists and certainly loyal to the communist party," his statement in the senate speech. During the first two days of wrangling, McCarthy gave no names but repeated his charges of disloyalty in the Truman administration. This set the partisan tone, which continued throughout the life of the subcommittee. On March 13, McCarthy began a rambling two-day presentation describing nine persons whom he considered security risks. Of the nine named, four were then employed by the State Department and five had served the department as occasional consultants, lecturers, or United Nations Commission members. The accused?

*Dr. Esther Caulkin Brunauer, age 48*:
Liaison officer between the U.S. government and UNESCO (United Nations Educational, Scientific and Cultural Organization)

*Gustavo Duran, about age 40*:
Former State Department civil servant and now a United Nations international civil servant

*Haldore Hanson, age 37*:
Point Four program administrator in the State Department

*Dr. Philip C. Jessup, age 53*:
Ambassador at large, State Department

*Judge Dorothy Kenyon, age 62*:
New York attorney and judge, serving on the United Nations Commission on Status of Women

*Dr. Owen Lattimore, age 50:*
Director, Walter Hines Page School of International Relations, Johns Hopkins University, and occasional consultant to the State Department

*Prof. Frederick L. Schuman, age 46:*
Faculty member of Williams College, occasional lecturer in the State Department's Foreign Service Institute

*John S. Service, age 40:*
Consul General, U.S. Consulate, Calcutta, India

*Dr. Harlow Shapely, age 65:*
Harvard University astronomer; member of the U.S. National Commission for UNESCO, representing the American Association for the Advancement of Science

Senator McCarthy was a latecomer in the communist search. A hunt for Russian spies had been going on in Washington since the end of World War II. The leader of the hunt was HUAC (House UnAmerican Activities Committee). By 1947 President Truman had decided the government needed a more formal loyalty-security review. He ordered the FBI to gather fingerprints and biographic data on civilian government employees—all 2 million of them. Wherever the FBI found "disloyal evidence," the bureau was authorized to conduct a "full field investigation." This involved interviews with past schoolmates, neighbors, employers, police, banks, and credit agencies. The evaluation of these interviews—that is, determining whether a person was loyal and secure—was entrusted to a new Loyalty-Security Board in each government agency.

The State Department board was headed by Brigadier General Conrad Snow from Army Intelligence, and the hearing panels under General Snow were composed partly of State Department employees who were passing judgment on their peers. If the Loyalty Board recommended dismissing an employee, the action went to the secretary of state for his review. To ensure equal treatment among agencies, the president created in 1947 a Loyalty Review Board under the Civil Service Commission that would review all decisions by the lower boards. It was a slow process that did not satisfy the right-wing members of Congress, including Senator McCarthy.

One tool in this hunt for subversives was the attorney general's list. This was a compilation of public organizations that the justice department had determined to be subversive—a secret determination that permitted no court appeal. The list was considered to be a counter-move against the American communist party, which was said to have infiltrated labor unions and to have created hundreds of "communist front" organizations with appealing liberal names and impressive sponsoring committees. To be a member of any organization on the attorney general's list was considered a communist affiliation.

I was one of 15,000 employees under the secretary of state who were fingerprinted in 1948 for the loyalty-security program. The FBI conducted a full field investigation on me because of my China writings. For months I received letters from former classmates, employers, and neighbors reporting that the FBI had asked information about me. It must have been a thorough process; even the press correspondents with whom I worked in China were questioned. Eventually the FBI submitted my file to the State Department, and I was summoned to a half-day hearing before the loyalty-security board. The verdict? I was cleared for "top secret" work. Several hundred State Department employees were fired as a result of this type of investigation, according to published reports. These screenings preceded by several years the first accusations by Senator McCarthy.

The day McCarthy called me "procommunist," Jack Peurifoy came to see me. Jack was the deputy under secretary of state for administration—the number four officer in the department—but he came as a warm, smiling friend. We had attended baseball games at Griffith Stadium together and pulled off our shirts in the centerfield bleachers to soak up sunshine while our big league team, the Washington Senators, usually took a beating. Jack had served in the Marine Corps in the 1930s, been a congressional clerk, spent most of World War II in the Board of Economic Warfare controlling strategic war materials, and later had risen rapidly in the State Department. Now 43, he had been designated by Secretary Dean Acheson to give official replies to Senator McCarthy.

I asked if he wanted me to resign. He countered: Is there any reason why you should resign? I said I didn't want to be a burden to the department when cold war legislation in Congress was awaiting passage. From my work on Capitol Hill I knew there were only so many problems the congressional liaison officers of the department could cope with at one time.

Jack replied, "If you appear publicly before the Tydings subcommittee and rebut McCarthy, you will be dealing with Republican party politics. For that you will have any help this administration can provide."

I asked Senator Tydings if I could appear before his group as a witness under oath, and my appearance was scheduled for March 28. That meant that two weeks elapsed between McCarthy's allegations (March 13) and my reply. It was a time of restless sleep, of embarrassment when I met acquaintances on the street. Our daughter was ridiculed at kindergarten. Some State Department officers failed to show up for meetings in my office and looked the other way when we passed in the corridor. It was the greatest emotional tension I ever experienced. My job was at stake. A reputation I had earned during eight years as a newswriter and eight years as a State Department officer seemed to be in ruins. I was 37 and unable to look ahead.

To prepare for the hearings, I reviewed Senator McCarthy's allegations. He objected only to my writing in China during 1937 and 1938, specifically,

- That my book *Humane Endeavor* had included favorable dispatches about communist guerilllas fighting against the Japanese.
- That the magazines *Pacific Affairs* and *Amerasia* had republished chapters from my book. McCarthy called these magazines procommunist.
- That a magazine called *Democracy* with which I was associated in June-July 1937 at Peking was communist.

To refresh my memory, I reread my freelance articles written in China before the Japanese invasion, my war dispatches for the Associated Press, and the 62-page diary I had kept while travelling with the communists. I asked the State Department security office to read these papers.

Next came the group drafting of my testimony that Jack Peurifoy had offered. I remember with special appreciation the contributions of Carlisle Humelsine and Adrian Fisher. Working from my first draft of 20 typewritten pages, the three of us improved the rhetoric, added bright quotations, but tried to show a respect for McCarthy's charges by responding with statements of fact. One evening we worked from 5 P.M. to midnight trying to solve a dilemma: If McCarthy won national headlines with bombastic allegations, could a witness reach the same national audience by making counter-challenges against McCarthy? We decided on three deliberate news-catchers.

First, I would challenge McCarthy to repeat outside the Senate, without congressional immunity, the charges he had made against me. If he did, I promised a libel suit. (McCarthy never repeated the charges without hiding behind his immunity.)

Second, I would cite the factual misquotations that McCarthy had made in referring to my writings and conclude thus: If Senator McCarthy were a reporter and made these mistakes in a news story, he would be fired by his employer.

Third, I would insert a quotation from Winston Churchill. If I were a man of "procommunist proclivities" because I wrote favorably about the fighting of the Chinese communists against Japan, then Winston Churchill was also a "man with procommunist proclivities." Churchill had written in 1943, "That monstrous juggernaut engine of German might and tyranny has been beaten and broken, outfought, and outmaneuvered by Russian valor, generalship and science."

These three bits of color made the front pages of the national press on the day after my testimony.

The Senate caucus room was jammed with 500 people on March 28 when I took the oath as a witness. My only companion at the witness table was my legal counsel, David Louisell, a former debating partner in Duluth. His main job was to keep me from getting angry and exploding at a senator. He succeeded. At the start I was blinded by the klieg lights of six newsreel cameras, and the heat from their lights made me dizzy. The men with still cameras were jockeying for position in front of me while they popped their flashbulbs.

Five members of the Tydings subcommittee sat at a raised table covered with green felt. I sat facing them at a lower table about ten feet away. Chairman Millard Tydings (Democrat, Maryland) was in the center of his group; Theodore Greene (Democrat, Rhode Island) and Brian McMahon (Democrat, Connecticut) completed the majority. Bourke Hickenlooper (Republican, Iowa) and Henry Cabot Lodge (Republican, Massachusetts) were the minority. Sen. McCarthy was not present, probably piqued because he had been denied permission to cross-examine the witness.

After the oath the chairman invited me to proceed in my own way, and I read my 17-page statement, which had been distributed in advance. The only interruptions were friendly requests by the chairman that I repeat my testimony that directly refuted Senator McCarthy.

I was able to introduce in this testimony some facts that McCarthy had failed to give: that I had been a war correspondent carrying press credentials from both the Chinese government and the U.S. Embassy; that Chiang Kai-shek and the communists had negotiated a united front at the time of my reporting; that my book devoted 13 chapters to the Japanese army, 9 chapters to the communists, and 9 chapters to the central government area where Chiang Kai-shek had his headquarters; that my reporting in China had been praised for its objectivity by my superiors in the Associated Press and by book reviewers in many newspapers, including the *Chicago Tribune*.

My statement closed with this appeal:

> I am a loyal American and I believe I am entitled to have this committee say so. . . . But the corrective action of this committee cannot attain the same headlines, reach the same people, or fully counteract the suspicions and hatreds which Senator McCarthy's charges have unleashed. Congressional immunity may protect him from lawsuit, but it will not save him from moral accountability.

I thought it was a strong flourish, but I now realize that an unknown civil servant could not win the same headlines as McCarthy did in 1950.

The question period took an hour, and the questions came mainly from the slow, poorly informed Senator Hickenlooper, who served as proxy for the absent Senator McCarthy. Hickenlooper worked from a paper containing 14 questions that McCarthy's staff had apparently supplied to him. Senator Hickenlooper had never seen my book, which he was attempting to quote, often incorrectly; he did not know the page numbers of his citations; and he could not pronounce the Chinese names. Though he was courteous and apologetic, any good graduate student of modern Chinese history would have made a more effective prosecutor.

That was my only appearance before the Tydings subcommittee, but there was a secret session that I did not hear about until the Tydings documents were published four months later. Louis Budenz, a prominent ex-communist who often served as an informer for the FBI, was subpoenaed by Tydings and appeared at a closed session on April 25, 1950, about one month after my testimony. Budenz, 58, was then an assistant professor at Fordham University. He had served as a journalist in the communist party for the decade 1935–45, part of that time as managing editor of the *Daily Worker*, official organ of the party. After becoming disillusioned, he said, and breaking with the party, he returned to the Catholic Church, which arranged his professorship. According to the transcript, Budenz mentioned a list of 400 hidden communists in the United States that he was assembling for the FBI, another list of 1,000 secret communists that he said he had memorized as part of his party work, and a list of 16 writers who had contributed to *Pacific Affairs* while Owen Lattimore was editor. Budenz named me as one of the 16 and claimed all were communists. Senator McMahon (according to the transcript) said that he was surprised to hear Hanson was a communist because Hanson "made as forthright a statement as I ever heard from a witness." Under questioning by the committee counsel, Budenz said he had never seen or met me, that he knew little about my writing, and that his statement was based solely upon oral information given him at communist headquarters about 1940 or 1941 by Jack Stachel. When pressed, he acknowledged he had not given my name to the FBI until the preceding week, more than a month after Senator McCarthy's public testimony about me. The majority report of the Tydings subcommittee said that Budenz' testimony "leaves us in wonderment."

The Tydings subcommittee documents were released on July 20, 1950, approximately four months after the hearings began, and long after Senator McCarthy had shifted his attack to other people. All nine persons who had been publicly labelled subversives by McCarthy, including myself, were exonerated by the Tydings report, but this became a partisan stance when the two Republicans on the committee refused to sign the report. Perhaps that was irrelevant, since it was doubtful that anyone would read the 2,800 pages.

McCarthy's attacks, of course, did not end with the hearings. Every few weeks the senator referred in a speech to "the top radicals like Lattimore, Jessup, and Hanson." I recall one particularly painful jab. I had taken Berni and our two children to the circus in Washington, and we were driving home when our car radio brought the five o'clock news. The first item was a Senate speech by McCarthy. He said that "an ex-communist has now identified the top communist in the State Department. He is Haldore Hanson."

Ugh! I pulled onto a side street and sat stunned for several minutes, wondering what to do next. Our two children, aged five and two, seemed to recognize the seriousness of the moment and were silent in the back seat. I returned to my office and issued a press statement, though this was probably futile, since I did not have a copy of what the witness had said. Three months later I obtained the transcript of the closed testimony by Louis Budenz. He had not named anyone as the top communist in the State Department. That was McCarthy's invention. McCarthy was able to exploit secret committee sessions by rushing to the Senate floor to report what he claimed a witness had said, and no one was able to contradict him. I still think of the day of the circus as my low point with McCarthy.

> *The great fear has been a recurrent phenomenon since the French Revolution but not in exactly the same form. In France, Italy and Germany, the blood flowed; in Britain and America, mainly tears.*

David Caute, 1978

CHAPTER 20

# Fallout from Communist Hunters

In a northern Virginia community near our farm, McCarthyism caused the greatest excitement since the Civil War. Arcola was a village of 50 houses that had grown up around a crossroad 34 miles west of downtown Washington. In 1950 the village had two grocery stores, one gas pump, a post office, a Methodist church, and an eight-grade elementary school. Arcola's population was no more than 250. Men who lived in this village were mostly construction craftsmen—carpenters, plumbers, and the like—who commuted to work in the Washington suburbs. Surrounding the village were dairy and beef cattle farms ranging in size from 100 to 1,400 acres, with mailboxes displaying English names like Walker, Marshall, Pope, Barton, Harrison, Minor, Cooper, Biggers, and Hutchison. The only non-English name on a mailbox was Hanson: We had bought a beef cattle farm in 1945, two miles northwest of Arcola straddling state road 621.

In mid-March 1950, Berni and I visited the farm, as we usually did on a Saturday to look after chores. We were still living in the city and had not yet moved to the farmhouse for the summer. I first called on an elderly neighbor to ask help on some fencing. He told me that the previous day, while he was standing at his mailbox, several neighbors stopped. One said, "Could you believe that we have had a Russian spy living in our neighborhood for years and didn't know it?"

I called next on a farmer who had been feeding my Hereford cattle. He said he had been asked by people in Leesburg, the county seat, whether he intended to continue working with "that communist." From a housewife in Arcola Berni got word that a petition was being circulated calling the Hansons undesirable and asking us to leave the community. The last news we picked up concerned a meeting of the county agricultural committee at which a

Virginia state official denounced the growing number of communists in government and cited the current news about Haldore Hanson. All this had happened within five days after the McCarthy allegations and before my hearing for reply. The news spread mainly by radio.

The *New York Post* sent a reporter named John Hohenberg to interview Arcola residents. He wrote five full-page stories that ran for five days under the title "The House that McCarthy Haunts." The stories were not of national significance but served as a sociological study of McCarthyism in one rural community. The sketches below are taken from the *New York Post* interviews, but with names omitted.

> A petition telling the Hansons to "get out" was prepared by a road contractor, a workman who drove a bulldozer and road scraper, a red-faced, fast-talking man who lived near the village crossroad. He said he had four sons who were wounded in World War II, and he feels that communism threatens another war. "In a case like this, I think a man is guilty until proved innocent."
>
> A son of the road contractor was interviewed. He asserted, "I say that communist fella ought to be killed." Later he conceded that maybe he didn't mean it.
>
> A second son of the road contractor, a man about 30, said, "If Hanson is guilty, we aim to run him out of town. We don't want no communist living here."
>
> In the grocery store at the crossroad, the wife of the owner would choose no side in the community argument. Her business was at stake.
>
> In the second grocery store the owner grinned at the reporter and asserted he was neutral, a warm pleasant kind of neutrality, to which the grocer added, "If the Hansons are communists, I'll never know what to believe. They are right nice people."
>
> A man farming next to the Hansons was a former newspaper reporter. He asserted: "Good God, if Hanson could be run out of this community, it could happen to any of us. You don't know when people like McCarthy are going to make charges."
>
> A chicken farmer in his 30s told the reporter: "This petition is unjust. I don't agree with the way people have reacted."
>
> Another village resident told the reporter that he had refused to sign the petition and advised the author, "You want to go slow. Mr. Hanson doesn't look like a communist to me."

The *Washington Times-Herald*, a Hearst paper, carried a banner Sunday headline on August 16, 1953:

HALDORE HANSON OUSTED
POINT 4 AIDE HELD RED BY MCCARTHY
ORDERED TO RESIGN OR BE FIRED

The headline was correct. I declined an opportunity to resign and was fired—three years after my hearings before the Tydings subcommittee. General Eisenhower had been elected president in November 1952 and had taken office in January 1953. The Republican party had been out of power for 20 years starting with Roosevelt's first term in 1933. Most of the 2 million government employees had been appointed during the democratic years; it was not surprising, therefore, that Republicans sought to open up vacancies for their supporters, especially in posts that carried higher salaries. To consolidate foreign aid activities under a new agency outside the State Department, the new president created the Foreign Operations Administration (FOA), headed by Harold Stassen, the former governor of Minnesota. Stassen's first action was to fire more than 1,000 employees in the agency, including me.

I looked at other jobs. Bill Benton, my former chief in the State Department, arranged interviews in New York with three international oil companies and an international pharmaceutical company. I discussed with them public relations assignments in Saudi Arabia, India, and Indonesia. Nothing developed. At that time I blamed McCarthy's publicity, but a more reasonable judgment is that my years in government probably offered little of value to a private corporation.

For Berni and me the trauma of the McCarthy period was greater than we realized. For one entire year we had no personal contacts in Washington. We saw no State Department friends. We read nothing about China. Never again did I consider taking a government job. Years later, Chester Bowles asked me to become his assistant in the State Department during the Kennedy administration, and I rejected the offer without a moment's thought. Privately Berni and I recited a catechism—that we enjoyed good health, and sooner or later a new career would open up.

The McCarthy era faded in 1954 after four years in the headlines. Others have described the closing events in McCarthy's career, and they need not be repeated in detail.* In 1954 the Senate held five months of acrimonious hearings over McCarthy's charges of subversion in the U.S. Army, followed by five months of political maneuvering to censure McCarthy. The motion of condemnation, which came to a vote in December 1954, read: "Resolved:

---

*A readable account of McCarthy's downfall appears in William Manchester's popular history, *The Glory and the Dream*, 1973; and in Thomas Reeves's detailed biography, *The Life and Times of Joe McCarthy*, 1982.

that the conduct of the Senator from Wisconsin, Mr. McCarthy, is unbecoming a member of the United States Senate, is contrary to senatorial traditions and tends to bring the Senate into disrepute, and such conduct is hereby condemned." The motion was upheld 67 to 22. McCarthy retained his Senate seat and his committee chairmanship, but he held no more hearings and was often absent from the Senate. He died of alcoholism in 1957, at age 48.

## Reflections on McCarthyism

Senator Joseph McCarthy was a political guerilla who slew his victims by slander and left the bodies lying in government agencies, in the armed services, in the Hollywood movie industry, and among the leadership of the Democratic party. I was a witness only in the State Department, and my first-hand reflections below will describe only one corner of a four-year battlefield.

John S. Service, O. Edmund Clubb, John Paton Davies, John Carter Vincent—these men and a dozen other colleagues in the foreign service were accused during the McCarthy era of "losing China" by their "treasonous" reporting. All had served in China during the war. All spoke Chinese. All had been assigned to report what they saw—a task they performed with devotion and skill, often under dangerous conditions. All had concluded that unless he controlled corruption among his followers, Chiang Kai-shek was sure to lose in the power struggle against the more disciplined followers of Mao Zedong. In the inquisition in Washington that followed the 1949 communist victory, nearly all the China specialists were hounded out of the foreign service or were reassigned to obscure posts.

The loss to the United States was more than the destruction of a few brilliant careers. After this generation of Asian specialists was annihilated, the United States stumbled into two Asian wars—Korea and Vietnam; we can only guess how history might have been changed had these talented specialists on East Asia served out their government careers. The fears engendered by McCarthy may still live on; after all, what officer will risk becoming a scapegoat if he is asked to report on some corrupt, authoritarian government confronted by a popular, Marxist revolution?

*This is the farmer sowing his corn,*
*That kept the cock that crowed in the morn.*

English nursery rhyme

CHAPTER 21

# Virginia Cattle Farmer

Following my unceremonious dismissal by the State Department, I landed on my feet—so to speak—as a full-time farmer. This exposed me to the agricultural revolution that was then at its height in the United States, and proved useful when I later became an administrator of agricultural grants in the third world, and still later, when I served as director of an agricultural research center in Mexico; but that is getting ahead of the story.

Berni and I had bought a 270-acre grazing farm in 1945, originally as a weekend place. The farm was in Loudoun county, Virginia, about one hour commuting distance from Washington. At first I managed the farm in partnership with a neighbor, Ferne Marshall, a tall, lean, sober Virginian, in mid-40s, who was raising five children on an adjoining farm. Under this arrangement I supplied land, buildings, and fences; Ferne provided machinery and labor, and we divided the cost of seed, fertilizer, and cattle. The profits were split 50-50.

The 1940s and 1950s were a fascinating time to watch the changes in American farming. I saw some of our own practices pass into history. For example, harvesting wheat in 1946 we used a reaper and binder drawn by horses. We hauled wheat shocks by the wagonload to a rented steam-powered threshing machine. A crew of 12, including me, hand-fed the shocks into the thresher; most of the labor was obtained by exchanges among neighbors. That was the last time a "steamer" operated on our farm, ending a century-long practice. One year later we rented a self-propelled combine and 2 men replaced the services of 12.

Silo filling underwent a similar change. In 1946 and 1947 Ferne Marshall used his horse-drawn binder to cut the corn and lay the bundles in rows. Then a crew of ten loaded the bundles on wagons. A gasoline engine drove the corn chopper that blew the feed into the top of the silo. By 1948 we introduced a tractor-drawn field chopper that enabled us to cut the labor crew from ten to three, and to fill a 40-by-14-foot silo in one day.

This farming revolution took many other forms. During the depression years of the 1930s and the war years of the 1940s plant breeders had developed new seeds for higher-yielding plant varieties; animal scientists had tested faster-gaining feed mixtures; and chemists had devised new fertilizers. But the spread of these innovations had been delayed, first by the depression and then by the war. Now farming boomed. Starting in 1945 much of the wartime explosive industry was converted to the production of nitrogen fertilizer. These changes produced marvels of farm efficiency that are still the envy of the third world. They explained why half the American population was employed in farming at the time of the First World War, but only 4 percent was needed a half century later.

I shouldered full management of our farm in 1953. To learn more about the new technologies, I registered for short courses on cattle care at Virginia Polytechnic Institute at Blacksburg. I went to field days at the USDA Pasture Grass Experiment Station near Middleburg. I sought advice from the Soil Conservation Service in our county. I joined an evening discussion group among local cattle farmers.

After listening to new ideas, I discontinued cattle fattening (that is, buying 400-500 pound yearling animals and selling two-year-olds at 900 to 1000 pounds); instead I switched to a cow-calf program of 70 breeding cows, selling the calves at 300-500 pounds. I also adopted the "rate of gain testing" system. This meant I replaced a few cows each year with heifers from within the herd; the replacement heifers were selected by how fast they gained weight between birth and weaning. A scientific principle lay behind this practice. Rate of gain is highly inheritable—that is, if a heifer calf gains two to three pounds a day on its mother's milk, it is likely as a mature cow to produce calves with the potential for a similar rate of gain. Once we began using this system, the average gain of weight among our calves rose steadily.

Berni and I performed most of the routine veterinary tasks that are critically important in a breeding herd. But vet work is not for the squeamish. First I built a holding pen for the calves and an adjoining "squeeze," which holds one calf tightly in position. We passed the entire calf crop through the squeeze in October each year, performing five chores: (1) we attached a numbered aluminum tag in the calf's ear and recorded the name of its mother; (2) we dusted the animal with insecticide to kill lice; (3) we pushed a thumb-sized pill down the animal's throat to kill intestinal parasites; (4) we dehorned the animal with a long-handled cutter that scooped out the inch-long nubbins of horn; and (5) we castrated the male calves. This took an entire day. At sunset Berni and I were both ready for a stiff drink.

Animals were on our minds 24 hours a day. I often awoke at 2 or 3 A.M. to hear a cow and calf calling to each other. That meant the calf had climbed through a fence and couldn't find the way back to its mother. So I left a warm bed, put on my work clothes, picked up a flashlight in the kitchen, and headed into the night. If the bawling calf were under 100 pounds, I could lift it over the fence to its mother. But if the animal were older and heavier, I drove it along the fenceline to a gate. Invariably the calf rushed to its mother to suckle. The farm returned to silence and I returned to bed.

One night when we were returning from a farmers' meeting, our truck headlights picked up an animal standing in the road, a quarter mile from home. We recognized our biggest Hereford bull, Hillcrest Larry the 27th; weighing 2500 pounds he was ferocious looking but actually very gentle. I took a stick out of the truck and walked slowly up to the bull. He made several playful snorts at me, pawed the air with his front feet, then turned and trotted obediently toward the barn where someone had left the gate open. The bull knew the way. Inside the barnyard he made one more festive snort, then sauntered off into the darkness.

Damyankees" was a phrase we heard occasionally in conversation when we walked into an Arcola grocery store, but it was said with a smile because Berni had made a great effort—so the neighbors acknowledged—to pattern her family style after the surrounding Virginians. Berni baked her own bread, churned her own butter, cured her own hams, and sewed cothes for herself and the children. She had one steer and one hog butchered each year and kept the family meat supply at a frozen food locker plant. (Few families in those days had their own freezers.) Berni drove an aging pickup truck with cattle racks, and she pumped her own gas from our farm tank. She attended the Methodist Church with the children. Religion was for the women and children in rural Virginia; few men attended church.

In the chicken business Berni emulated her neighbors. She started the first year with 1,000 chicks to produce fertile eggs for a hatchery which supplied stock for the broiler industry in the Shenandoah Valley. The second year she was up to 2,000 layers, and the third year, to 3,000. There she levelled off. She gathered eggs twice a day, cleaned them and stored them in a cool, stone-lined basement. Several times a month she delivered a truckload of egg crates to the hatchery 20 miles away. She vaccinated her birds for fowl pox once each season. After five years she took stock of the hours she worked and found she was netting about eight cents an hour. So she quit the chicken business and took a job teaching Latin in the county high school.

The family lived on a tight budget. I manipulated bank loans to buy cows and machinery, and Berni paid the grocery bills with her teaching salary (a source of humiliation for me). Each year we thought we could see the light at the end of the tunnel, although the weather was always threatening. A small drought in 1955 gave us a scare but we survived. Another drought of 60 days in 1956 was a more serious warning, but again we paid our bills. But the drought of 1957 was different. Starting in the spring, a rainless area spread out of Texas through Tennessee, West Virginia, across our part of Virginia, and on into Maryland and eastern Pennsylvania. Farms located along rivers were installing sprinkler irrigation for the first time, but we had no river. By early June our farm had had no rain for two months and the hay crop was reduced by half. We planted our corn late, and it was parched.

The family had planned a vacation trip to visit friends in Minnesota and South Dakota—our first in ten years—and we bravely took off. All along the vacation route we read about the severe eastern drought. We dreaded to telephone home. On the return journey I remember the sinking feeling as we passed through Pennsylvania—pastures brown; then Maryland—pastures brown; and finally over the hilltop to our own farm—all brown. The temporary caretaker had started feeding hay in mid-July and the winter supply of hay would be gone by October. We ordered a trailer load of baled hay from western Pennsylvania and calculated that would be gone by Christmas. But what then?

Now something happened that again changed my career. Bob Nathan, the Washington economist, president of Robert R. Nathan Associates, telephoned to ask if I were available to take a two-year assignment in Burma as one of the economic advisors attached to the office of the prime minister. How soon could I go?

I hesitated to sell my cow herd, on which I had devoted so much care. But on the other hand, if I switched to a career as an economic advisor in the third world, I would enter an exciting aspect of twentieth-century development. So, with mixed feelings, I sold the cattle and rented the farm to a "contract producer"—a man who managed thousands of acres of corn and soybeans, adding to the U.S. grain exports. The producer used "low-till" methods: By a single pass of machinery in the spring he was able to apply corn seed, fertilizer, and weed-killing chemicals. Four months later he returned to pick and shell the corn and chop up the stalks, again with a single pass of his machinery. This was the latest step in the farming revolution, and it kept me in touch with American farming methods while I worked overseas.

> *Poverty has been the universal lot of man until our day. ...The idea that the majority could have access to a little modest affluence is wholly new.*
>
> Barbara Ward, 1962

PART FOUR

# MY WORK IN THE THIRD WORLD

Before 1960 disparaging terms were used for the third world. We talked about the "poor," or "backward," or "underdeveloped" countries. "Underdeveloped" was replaced by "less developed countries," often abbreviated LDCs. But statesmen felt the need for a more euphemistic term and someone suggested "third world."*

I have listed some common features of the third world nations, but a glance at their statistics—as published by the World Bank—reveals great differences among them. Nearly any general statement must be qualified by exceptions. For example:

- Most third world countries as everybody knows are poor, but how poor? The *World Bank Atlas 1985* found 2.2 billion people, or nearly half the world's population, had an average income per person of less than US$400 in 1982. That compared with $10,000 per person in the industrialized countries and $14,100 in the United States.

- Most third world people are engaged in farming or its services. As late as 1982 seven out of ten persons in the third world lived in rural areas.

- Most of the world's hungry people live in the third world. If the global food supply were distributed equitably, there would be

---

*Definitions for the first, second, and third worlds appear in the Prologue to this book.

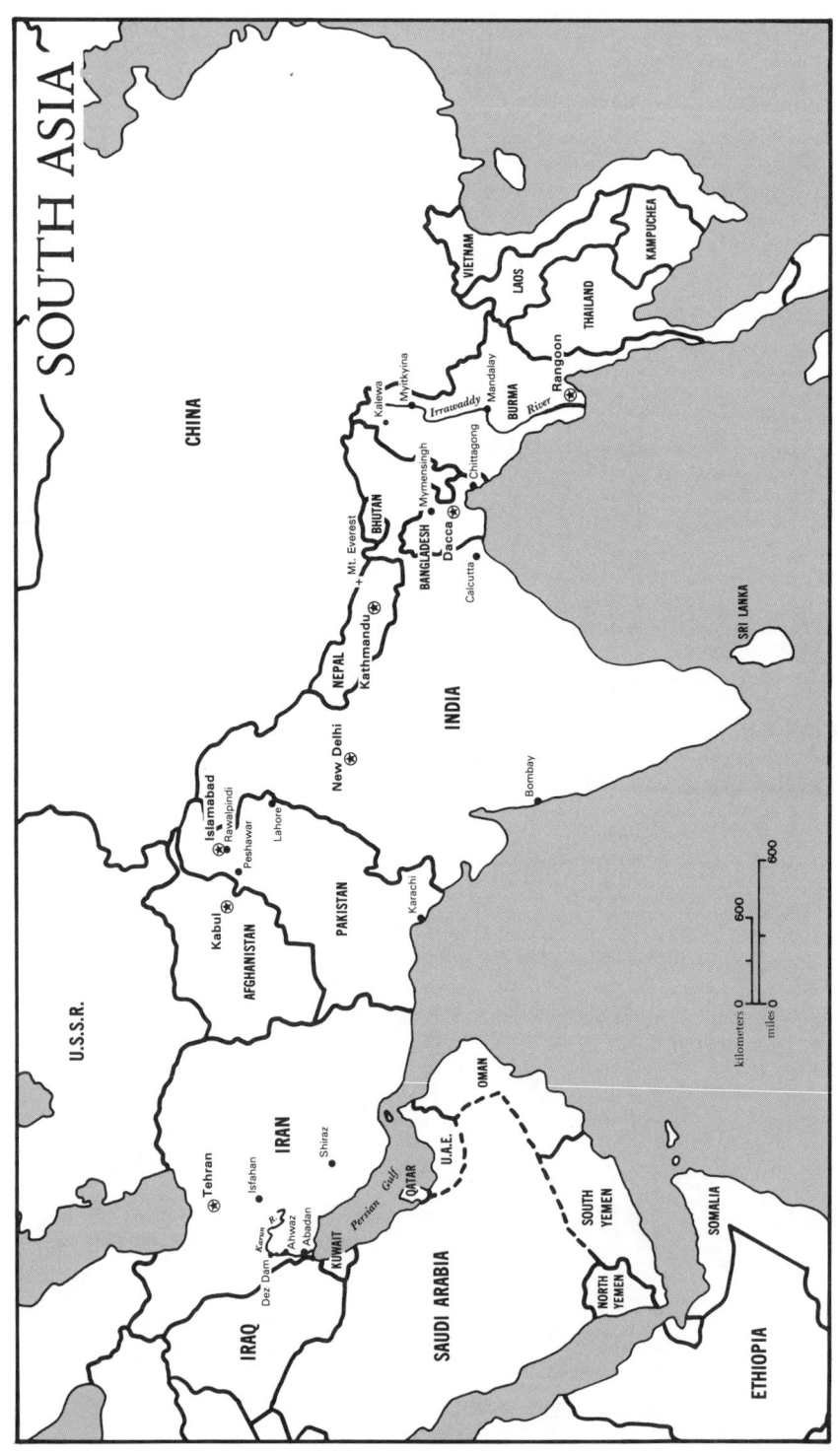

enough to go around. But it is not distributed equitably, partly because third world countries do not produce enough food for themselves, and partly because they do not have enough money to pay for needed imports. So modernization of their agriculture is a principal need.

- Population in the third world is growing at a higher rate than in industrialized countries. In 1982 the growth rate in the LDCs averaged 2.1 percent a year compared to only 0.6 percent in the more prosperous nations.
- Most third world countries are small, many smaller than individual states in the U.S.A.
- Many developing countries have suffered violent disturbances including civil wars, wars with neighbors, and army coups. More than half the developing countries have experienced army rule sometime since World War II.

Most third world countries lie in the tropics and subtropics, between latitudes 30 degrees north and 30 degrees south. By contrast, all present industrialized countries are found in the temperate zone. How does climate affect the LDCs? Environmentalists have put forward two opposing hypotheses. Some argue that if you live in the tropics, you don't need fuel to keep warm; you don't need much clothing; you need not cultivate food intensively because wild bananas, papaya, and nuts grow in the bush. The conclusion: life is easy.

Other geographers say the opposite. Development programs in the tropics, they argue, require greater effort to satisfy human needs. More capital is needed for irrigation because of extended dry periods; more funds are needed for fertilizers and for control of plant pests; more financing goes for agricultural research because tropical regions are different from cooler regions where a major part of past research has been done. A hot climate reduces the efficiency of man: manual laborers wield their tools with a feebler stroke. Erosion of soil from rain and wind is more severe. All told, the disadvantages of the tropics seem to outweigh the advantages.

What about international assistance to the third world? The United States Congress approved the Act for International Development of 1950, which began:

> It is declared to be the policy of the United States to aid the efforts of the peoples of economically underdeveloped areas to develop their resources and improve their working conditions by encouraging the exchange of technical knowledge and skills and the flow of investment capital . . . .

Other industrialized nations followed the American lead, bringing about a historic change. Previously it had not been common for nations in positions

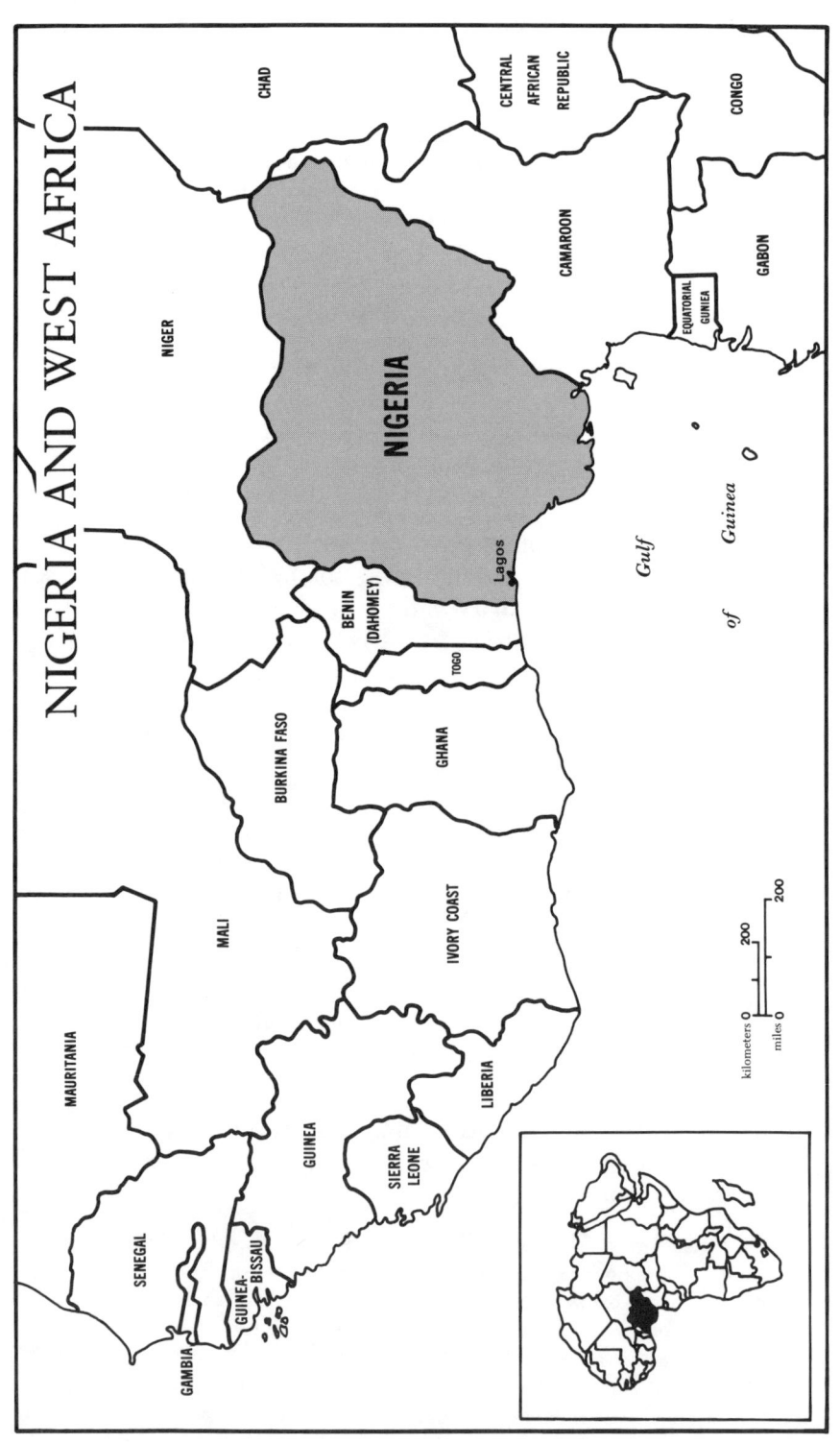

of scientific leadership to spread technical knowledge and skills abroad.

In the 1970s and 1980s, developing countries raised the cry for a mammoth increase in foreign aid—a "Marshall Plan for the third world," they called it. Under this proposal much larger official wealth transfers to the third world were asked—even demanded.

Prof. P. T. Bauer of the London School of Economics pointed out that this analogy to the Marshall Plan is mistaken. The task of the Marshall Plan in postwar Europe was not development but reconstruction. The west Europeans did not need to be modernized. The people already had the needed skills, motivations, habits, institutions, and political arrangements required to sustain material prosperity. That is why the Marshall Plan could be terminated in four years and West Germany could become an exporter of capital.

Few people are aware of the current size of the resource flow from western nations to the third world. The Organization of Economic Cooperation and Development (OECD) in Paris has been estimating and publishing the flow since 1956. In 1982—the most recent year for which we have OECD estimates—the net total of "overseas development assistance" provided directly by western nations was about US $18 billion. Multilateral development banks and agencies, supported largely by western donors, provided additional aid in 1982. OECD put that sum at US $8 billion. Western nations also provided finance capital to developing countries in many forms: bank lending, government-to-government export credits, and direct private investment. All told, OECD placed the total net transfer of financial resources in 1982 at almost US $80 billion. That was "net"—after deducting profit repatriation and loan repayments.

Now what about the years back to 1956? OECD estimates that the financial flow to developing countries between 1956 and 1982 exceeded US $670 billion. Adjusting for intervening inflation, the OECD estimate for the 27-year period would reach $1,500 billion—that is, $1.5 trillion. Even this figure ignores the transfers in the first half of the 1950s and in the years since 1982. Two trillion dollars would probably be the nearest round number to measure the net financial transfers from the west to the developing nations in the postwar era.

A sum of $2 trillion is hard to imagine. The writer Nick Eberstadt, a visiting fellow at Harvard University, tried to calculate what this sum would buy. He thought of the entire U.S. farm system and all the industries listed on the New York stock exchange. At current market value, $2 trillion would buy them all.

Where have all these resources gone? When I lived successively in Burma, Iran, Pakistan, Bangladesh, Nigeria, and Mexico, I began to gather some answers firsthand.

> *Burma is the third country in modern history to free itself completely from the British Empire.... It was preceded only by the United States of America and Eire.*

Frank N. Trager, 1954

CHAPTER 22

# Burma: With Prime Minister U Nu

Bob Nathan is a very large man with a gravelly voice, a sharp mind, and a genial personality. He has had a remarkable career: Born in Ohio in 1908, he studied economics at the University of Pennsylvania, rose rapidly in President Roosevelt's Department of Commerce in the 1930s, became chief of the National Income Division by the time he was 30, and served in World War II as chairman of the Planning Committee for the War Production Board. Why do I recite his profile? Because Nathan started me on a chain of overseas postings that continued for more than two decades.

When Harry Truman proposed in 1949 a program of technical assistance for poor nations, Bob Nathan was better equipped than most American economists to set up a private company that would perform economic planning for LDCs. That was one of Nathan's purposes when he established Robert R. Nathan Associates in 1949. One of his first overseas contracts was with the government of Burma. His eight years of experience there were followed by other contracts with Korea, Vietnam, Colombia, Afghanistan, and El Salvador—eventually 50 countries around the world.

When Nathan sent me to Burma in 1957, I was given a briefing on the country by his Washington staff. I had visited Burma a few years earlier when I was setting up the field offices for the State Department's Point Four program, and had met with the pious Buddhist prime minister, U Nu, and his cabinet.

Burma is a remote tropical country the size of Texas on the south coast of Asia, squeezed between India on the west, China on the north and east, and Thailand on the southeast. Burma's population in 1957 was then said to be 20 million, but nobody knew for sure. Great Britain had granted Burma its independence in 1948, ending 100 years of colonial rule in southern Burma and 60 years in the north. As a colony, Burma achieved economic self-sufficiency by exporting its rice surplus, petroleum products and teak logs. Some colonial railroads and roads were built, and a school system was developed, mainly to train colonial clerks. The Japanese invasion of 1942-1944 had wrecked the country, however. Under the circumstances, the self-rule that Britain bestowed in 1948 was a doubtful blessing, answering the demands of Burmese nationalists.

When I arrived as a new resident in 1957, fighting against the independent government was still going on, waged by Karen and Kachin hill tribes and by two Burmese communist factions. A nationalist Chinese army of Chiang Kai-shek was also operating in the mountains of northern Burma, harassing the border of the Peoples Republic of China. Chiang still hoped to reoccupy the mainland.

The United States tried to strengthen Burma's economy by offering money, but it soon concluded that the Burmese government could not make effective use of money without foreign planners and engineers. So in 1951 the United States gave Burma the funds to employ consultants: economists from Nathan Associates and engineers from a New York consulting firm. These planners remained in Burma for eight years, until 1959.

My colleagues at Nathan Associates came to Rangoon airport in December 1957 to greet me, a pleasant British tradition. Rangoon was then a river port of 700,000 people. We drove through stifling humidity to the British-owned Strand Hotel where I lived until my family arrived. Near the hotel was a branch of the British Lloyds Bank that I visited to cash my first check—an experience I still remember vividly. It took approximately half an hour for Burmese clerks with quill pens—straight out of Dickens—to pass my check from one to another and make entries in various account books, always under the eye of a single Englishman who finally handed me the cash. This procedure was representative of colonial-era management, by which a few Englishmen had governed millions of Asians in prepartition India, Pakistan, Burma, and Ceylon.

Our office was in the Ministry of Planning next door to the Foreign Office. Office vehicles parked outside carried the name *Moskvich*. The Russian version of Volkswagen, these cars were tinny in sound but adequate for city driving. Burma had acquired the cars under Russian barter.

A staff meeting was held the day I arrived. The leader of the Nathan group was Louis Walinsky, a balding New Yorker in his late forties. Walinsky took seriously his responsibility to steer the Burmese government toward an expanding economy. Other staff were all Americans and all in their thirties and forties.

Aside from serving as Walinsky's deputy, my assignment was to negotiate the distribution of a US$25 million low-interest loan from the U.S. Aid agency. Luckily this meant traveling with Burmese officials to discuss their proposals. I visited the teak forests near Myitkyina with the chief forester, U Hman, and watched trained elephants dragging logs that weighed several tons. I inspected the Kalewa coal mines with the industries minister, U Raschid. I travelled with U Hpu, chief of agricultural extension, to see abandoned rice fields in the Irrawaddy delta. After each trip I drafted a loan agreement for negotiation by the Burmese government with the U.S. Aid office.

Other loan projects included the Rangoon water supply, Rangoon airport, and ships for the inland waterways. One of the most important was refurbishing Rangoon General Hospital, which had 1,200 "beds," most of them only bamboo mats laid on the stone floor. By the time Nathan Associates withdrew from Burma in 1959, the loan of 25 million dollars was fully committed.

Soon after I arrived I called on the prime minister in his office. Like Pandit Nehru of India, Jinnah of Pakistan, and Sukarno of Indonesia, U Nu was regarded as one of the great nationalist leaders of Asia; each had been in the forefront of his country's struggle for independence in the 1930s and 1940s.

U Nu was of medium height, looked younger than his 50 years, and wore in the office his national dress—a *longyi* or wraparound skirt, a long-sleeved shirt, and the traditional Burmese cloth headress called a *gaungbaung*. He spoke excellent English with a British accent and often displayed a radiant smile. It was easy to like him.

On that visit to his office I had a special problem: I reminded him that on our first meeting in his office in 1951—six years earlier—I had asked his permission to establish an office in Rangoon for the U.S aid program. He had approved. It was also in his office in 1953 that Burma requested to cancel the U.S. aid program—out of anger at the United States for supporting the troops of Chiang Kai-shek in northern Burma. I said I hoped that my duties for Nathan Associates would not be confused with my earlier role for the United States government. U Nu laughingly said he understood.*

---

*Nu is the prime minister's first name, and *U Nu*—pronounced *Oo Noo*—translates Mr. Nu or Uncle Nu. Most Burmese do not use a family name. The prefix "U" varies with the relationship of the speaker to the person being addressed: *Ko Nu* = student Nu; *Maung Nu* = young man Nu; *Thakin Nu* = master Nu—a prefix used by the nationalist political party to underline their aim to become masters in their own country; *Bo Nu* = general or leader Nu; *Saya Nu* = teacher Nu. We foreigners in the prime minister's office addressed the prime minister as *U Nu*. When the prime minister addressed personal notes to us he signed himself simply *Nu*.

Prime Minister Nu was a surprising mix of a revolutionary nationalist and deeply religious Buddhist, and the two sides of his character were sometimes in conflict. Nu was born in 1907 in the Irrawaddy River delta, where his parents sold supplies needed by Buddhist monks. The boy completed high school in Rangoon and a B.A. degree in literature at Rangoon University. Most of his teachers were British. Already in high school he had become a demonstrator against colonial rule, and by his senior year at the university he was president of the student union, one of the most combative organizations for independence.

With B.A. degree in hand, he tried employment as school headmaster but found the work dull. He reentered the university to study law and was preparing for final examinations in 1936 when the British expelled him for his strike activities. That steered him into full-time politics as vice president of Burma's nationalist party, which later adopted the formidable name of Anti-Fascist People's Freedom League or AFPFL.

When World War II broke out in Europe, the British jailed many Burmese nationalists, including Nu, and he remained behind bars for two years until the invading Japanese army released him. Initially Burma greeted the Japanese as saviors who would overthrow British rule, but soon recognized the Japanese army as another form of foreign domination. Shortly after World War II the British negotiated independence for all their colonies in South Asia, and called Nu to London to sign with Prime Minister Attlee the papers for Burma's independence. On January 4, 1948—Burma's independence day—U Nu became the first prime minister, a post he held with brief interruptions during 1948-1958 and 1960-1962.

As prime minister Nu proclaimed Buddhism the state religion and established a ministry of religion. He sponsored courses on Buddhism at Rangoon University. He commuted the prison sentences of criminals who passed an examination on Buddhism.

In private life he devoted two hours every morning, from 4:30 to 6:30 A.M., to Buddhist prayers. He told me he continued this schedule even during stops at the Kremlin in Moscow, at the state guest house in Peking, and at Blair House in Washington. In 1938, at age 31, he gave up alcohol for the rest of his days, and in 1948, at age 41, he foreswore sex after 18 years of marriage during which he and his wife produced five children. To strengthen his celibacy he moved out of his family home. Occasionally he withdrew from official duties to spend days in a meditation center that he had created in Rangoon. At least once while prime minister he donned the saffron robe of a monk and begged for his food on the street.

One advisor to Nu characterized the prime minister this way: He was an inspiring leader who impressed political colleagues with his daring, energy, and sincerity. His most serious weaknesses were his lack of experience as administrator, his unwillingness to delegate authority, and his inadequate understanding of the democratic process.

When U Nu offered to introduce his foreign advisors to the purifying effects of meditation, I was one of three who went to the meditation center. We neophytes were each assigned a room without windows or furniture and we were instructed to sit crosslegged on the floor for hours facing a blank stone wall, trying to cleanse our minds of worldly thoughts. A good Buddhist, we were told, could reach a state of blankness in which pulse and breathing became slow and evil thoughts were expunged; this state of inactivity might continue like a trance for days. To reach this passivity we were instructed first to count our breaths—in-out, in-out—and then to concentrate our thoughts on a particular part of the body, like the tip of the nose. My undisciplined mind continued to receive signals about the cramps in my knees and the correspondence in the in-box at my office. I withdrew from the class after that first encounter, conceding that dedicated Buddhists might find purification that had escaped me. I am still not clear how meditation affects public administration.

As I think back over the Burma experience, I ask myself how Burma compared with other developing countries. Arriving in the third year of independence, the Nathan economists found Burma suffering from the familiar cycle of low income, low savings, and low investment, a combination shared by most LDCs. Health standards were low. Burma's tropical climate discouraged hard physical labor. There was a shortage of skilled labor and of skilled managers. The colonial background had left a leadership unschooled in self-government. Burmese leaders tended to equate colonialism with capitalism; they preferred a socialist ideology and were hostile toward private business. They thought government agencies should manage major development projects. Burma differed from most LDCs in one respect: it had an abundance of natural resources relative to its population and good prospects for export trade.

During the 1950s, Burma's progress was mixed. According to the Nathan reports, the total output of goods rose 5 percent a year and the output per person increased 3.6 percent a year. This performance was one of the best among LDCs. Agricultural cropping area increased substantially. Transportation was largely rehabilitated. School enrollment in grades 1-12 rose from 666,000 to 1,760,000. The health program created 28 new hospitals. Infant mortality dropped by one-third. The government survived four armed insurrections. Despite these significant achievements, Burma at the end of the 1950s had barely regained the level of national economy that had existed in its colonial days before the Japanese invaded.

How did we Hansons fare during our first overseas posting? Our daughter Signe was then 12 and in the sixth grade; our son Eric was 9 and in the third grade. With Berni they had travelled by air to Rangoon. Shortly after they joined me, Berni's recently widowed mother arrived. At age 68 she had a marvelous year, relishing the prestige given all white-haired people in Asia.

At Rangoon our family was able to rent a handsome, newly built house of four bedrooms on Golden Valley Road with a picture window looking on the famous Buddhist shrine—the Shwe Dagon, 400 feet high and covered with goldleaf. Our house was built by a Burmese medical professor who said he had to rent the house for a number of years before he could afford to live there himself—a common practice.

Our children enrolled in the British-founded Methodist English school, studying with 2500 Asian pupils in grades 1–12. Ethnically the pupils were about one-third Burmese, one-third Indian, and one-third Chinese, plus six western children, two of them Hansons. Teaching was in English. The Asian teachers must have been superior, especially in mathematics, because both our children skipped a grade when they returned to the United States. But there were sources for stress in the curriculum. For example, in arithmetic pupils were required to convert four kinds of money—British pounds, shillings, and pence; Indian rupees, annas, and paise; Burmese kyats and pyas; and American dollars and cents. The metric system and the English foot-pound measurements were additional pitfalls. Signe learned in a history of England that the American colonists in New England were rowdies who started a revolution, forcing England to send in troops. The following year in Virginia she was taught that the English were so unfair in their tax policies that the American colonists were driven to revolt. It was an unusual opportunity to hear both sides of history.

Since this was our first family experience in Asia, we accepted the conventional wisdom of some colleagues that we needed at least six servants, preferably drawn from different ethnic groups. We had a Bengali cook, a Karen housekeeper, a Shan driver, a Bihari Indian gardener, and two Burmese watchmen who carried vicious-looking knives and struck gongs during their night-time patrolling.

Though General Ne Win's coup of 1958 was sudden, it was nonviolent, befitting a Buddhist government. Berni and I returned from a Rangoon dinner party one night at 11 P.M. to find army tanks patrolling the streets. Driving home, we were stopped repeatedly by soldiers who carried rifles with fixed bayonets and demanded our identity. The experience was unnerving, although we heard no shooting. Shortly thereafter the army cancelled the contracts of Nathan Associates and other consultants and gave our staff 90 days to complete our business and depart.

Before our group left Rangoon in 1959, most of the staff received offers to work in other countries. Nathan Associates was able to offer employment to some in Colombia. I myself received a job inquiry from Development and Resources Corporation for work in Iran, which turned out to be my next post.

Prime Minister U Nu was reelected prime minister in 1960 but was once again overthrown by the army in 1962. This time he was imprisoned for 4 years, then went into voluntary exile for 14 years—first in Thailand, then India. He returned to Burma at the invitation of the Burmese government in 1980 and now lives quietly in Rangoon with his wife, both of them in good health. His age approaches 80.

After staging his second coup, General Ne Win abrogated the constitution, dissolved the parliament, liquidated the courts, took the title of president, and ruled by fiat from 1962 to 1981. Thereafter he continued to be the shadow chief of state who made the decisions. Under President Ne Win, Burma became a hermit-like country with little foreign trade, few tourists, and extensive black markets for smuggled goods. Local ethnic wars continued. By 1986 the Burmese population had grown to 38 million, and the former rice surplus was now consumed largely at home. Burma is one of the many third world countries that has made disappointing progress since World War II.

As I look back on the Burma experience, I conclude that economic development is a slow process for citizens of the third world. Burma increased its national income by about 75 percent during the 1950s while population rose only 25 percent, a highly creditable record as viewed by economists. But if you were a Burmese citizen, with average income, your take-home pay rose from US$50 to US$87 a year—still not enough to buy a bicycle or a sewing machine. The end of colonialism was supposed to bring instant riches. It did not.

My next look at the difficulties of development was in Iran.

*People think of Iran as being primarily an oil-producing country. But that is a mistake. For thousands of years we have been primarily an agricultural country, and we still are.*

Mohammed Reza Shah Pahlavi, 1961

CHAPTER 23

# Iran: Developing a River Valley

Mohammed Reza Shah Pahlavi was a prince of 21 when he was elevated to the throne in 1941, succeeding his father, Reza Shah Pahlavi. The upbringing of the crown prince had been elitist: He was supervised in the palace by a French governess and had attended elementary grades 1-8 at a Tehran military school, where classmates were the sons of cabinet ministers. He then transferred to a French language preparatory school in Switzerland for four years, accompanied by a personal physician and an Iranian tutor in Farsi language (the official tongue of Iran). There he had competed in skiing, soccer, and boxing and had graduated at 17 from Le Rosey, a boys' boarding school located between Lausanne and Geneva. Back in Tehran, he studied two more years at the Iranian Military Academy under French instructors from St. Cyr. By the time he was enthroned in 1941 he was trilingual in Farsi, French, and English. He was also an experienced airplane pilot and was anxious to modernize his country.

His ideas for modernization had to wait. During World War II British and Russian armies occupied Iran. The railroad and highway from the Persian Gulf to the Russian border became the principal delivery route for allied munitions moving to the Russian front. Some 5 million tons of war supplies reached Russia through Iran. The older shah was forced by the British to abdicate because they considered him pro-Nazi; he was exiled to South Africa, where he died in 1944. The younger shah signed a military alliance with the British and Russians, and declared war on Germany. After the war Iran regained its full independence.

In 1959 Berni and I moved to Iran where I worked for the New York consulting firm, Development and Resources Corporation (we called it D and R), and remained in Iran three years. This project—so different from my preceding work with Burma's prime minister—was conceived by two men who wished to develop a river valley. The men were the Persian king and his American consultant, the ex-chairman of the Tennessee Valley Authority (TVA), David E. Lilienthal. The river of their interest was the Karun and its largest tributary, the Dez.

At the time of my Iranian service, 1959 to 1962, the young king had gained respect by two courageous decisions, both of which I admired: First, he ordered the Pahlavi Foundation, the family business enterprise, to dispose of the vast agricultural lands he had inherited from his father. The land was to be distributed to the tenants in return for a nominal price that would be collected over a period of years. Second, he ordered 60 percent of Iran's oil revenues to be paid to a new government agency called the "Plan Organization," which would invest millions of dollars annually in development projects. That was the image of the shah at age 36 when he met David Lilienthal.

Lilienthal had been a little-known Wisconsin lawyer of 31 when President Roosevelt selected him in 1933 to be chairman of the newly created Tennessee Valley Authority. Under Lilienthal TVA built hydroelectric dams in the Tennessee River valley, sold electric power at low rates to stimulate industrial growth, and built fertilizer factories to spur agriculture. A backward mountainous area of mid-America gradually became a prosperous region, a transformation that many developing countries might envy. At the end of World War II President Truman selected Lilienthal to be the first chairman of the U.S. Atomic Energy Commission, which took charge of the peaceful uses of the atom. In the 1950s Lilienthal left public service. He formed a private company called Development and Resources Corporation that offered to manage major water and power projects.

One of Lilienthal's greatest accomplishments was to plan the development of the Indus River, sponsored jointly by India and Pakistan, a scheme that probably forestalled a war between Asian neighbors. The geography was this: The Indus River rises high in the Himalayas and flows 1,800 miles to the Arabian Sea. As the river travels southward, it is fed by waters of five tributary rivers—the Jhelem, Chenab, Ravi, Sutlej, and Beas. All of them supported irrigation systems during British rule. The 1947 partition of the subcontinent—the action that formed independent India and Pakistan— sliced the Indus irrigation system in two. It left in India rivers that provided waters to Pakistan; it separated major canals from their headworks; and it provoked one of the most angry disputes in the third world. It was Lilienthal who visited Asia and suggested a formula for dealing with the Indus problem. "The whole Indus system," he said, "must be developed as a unit, as the TVA system was." After years of mediation by the World Bank, Prime Minister

Nehru of India and President Ayub Khan of Pakistan agreed on an Indus plan that—with water storage—offered both countries increased water.

When Lilienthal first met the shah in 1956, the two men soon found common interest in river basin development and turned their attention to the Karun River. The Karun in southwest Iran drains an area equal to the combined states of New York and Pennsylvania. Early in the Persian Empire, starting about 500 B.C. the Karun River was the center of one of the greatest irrigation systems of ancient times, spreading water across a low rainfall region. The area became so productive that it was called in Arabic the Khuzestan or "land of sugar cane." Later, Mongol invaders in the thirteenth century destroyed the Khuzestan canals and most of southwest Iran reverted to desert. In the first half of the twentieth century the waters of the Karun flowed—largely unused—into the Shatt-al-Arab and the Persian Gulf.

The shah invited Lilienthal and his company to make surveys of the Karun basin. The resulting D and R proposals contained these elements:

- A thin arch concrete dam would be built on the Dez River over 200 meters high, tallest in Asia, with generators of 520,000 kw capacity. Geological surveys would be made for 13 more dams in the same region with estimated power capacity more than double that of TVA.

- Khuzestan Electric Company—a distributor—would introduce electricity to the towns and villages of the Khuzestan, just as TVA had done in the Tennessee Valley.

- A high-voltage transmission line 275 kilometers long would carry power from Dez dam to the industrial cities of Abadan and Khorramshahr.

- An irrigation system below Dez dam would provide canals initially for 20,000 hectares of private agricultural land (the so-called pilot project) and eventually 100,000 hectares (the greater Dez project).

- A government sugar plantation below Dez Dam would grow 10,000 hectares of sugarcane, with attached sugar mill of capacity to extract 30,000 tons of refined sugar a year.

- A fertilizer testing program would determine the best types of fertilizers to be manufactured with Dez power.

- A new Iranian agency called Khuzestan Water and Power Authority (KWPA), patterned after TVA, would be headed by an Iranian of ministerial rank and would take charge of the river valley services as they were completed.

Lilienthal considered these proposals only a beginning. They would require seven years of work and cost 250 million dollars. About one-third of the capital was proposed to come from World Bank loans and the balance from Iran's oil revenues. The plans appeared well balanced at that time, especially the emphasis on training Iranian staff for KWPA—even down to the maintenance crews for power lines and the Iranian water masters who would distribute irrigation water.

There were two possible flaws: One was the autonomous nature of Khuzestan Water and Power Authority. Like TVA, this Iranian authority was to be located in the capital of its region—the city called Ahwaz—and the KWPA leaders would bypass the ministries in Tehran, reporting directly to the Plan Organization and the shah. TVA enjoyed a similar status, bypassing the Department of Interior in Washington and reporting directly to the office of the president. This had provoked one of the classic rivalries within the United States government.

The other flaw involved regional priorities. The Khuzestan was a sparsely populated area, and the Plan Organization raised a question: Might money for this project be better spent on other provinces with larger populations? This question was brushed aside by Lilienthal but it later became a major political issue in Iran.

Dez canyon was 300 meters deep and only 20 meters wide at the streambed. During thousands of years the Dez River had cut through solid rock, leaving almost vertical canyon walls. The damsite was located in the Bakhtiari Mountains 275 kilometers north of the Persian Gulf and 25 kilometers from Dezful, the nearest town. Upstream from the damsite was an unpopulated area like a saucer, suitable for the reservoir; almost no people would need to be evacuated. Downstream the Dez River gushed out of the canyon upon a broad and potentially rich agricultural plain.

The work force to construct the dam expanded at its peak to 10,000 Iranian laborers, 1,000 Italian craftsmen, and 25 American consulting engineers. Lilienthal retained for his own company one responsibility at the damsite—"contract enforcement." This required frequent inspectors from New York.

On my visits to the damsite from our headquarters at Ahwaz, I was fascinated by the installing of cable cars across the canyon, the erection of concrete mixing plants that clung to the mountainside, and the tunneling for the powerhouse at the base of the dam. The medical department soon had an elevator to the bottom of the canyon to evacuate injured men.

The 1,000 Italian craftsmen signed one-year contracts to go to Iran without families, work 12 hours a day and six days a week, live in army-like barracks, eat army-like food, then receive vacation travel to Italy where they were offered a cash bonus to return to Iran for another year. And many did.

Dam construction is dangerous. The chief engineer calculated that for every million dollars spent on the dam, one man would lose his life. The estimate proved close. Despite the efforts of a safety office, Dez dam still killed 62 men. Most deaths occurred among Iranian laborers, caused by men falling into the canyon or construction materials falling on their heads.

My assignment was to be program and budget officer for Khuzestan Development Service. This made me a general trouble shooter. It involved me in one way or another with nearly every aspect of the large valley project.

KDS first built a residential community called Golestan on the barren bank of the Karun River, ten miles south of Ahwaz. This was headquarters for the agricultural staff, electric power company, and administrative services. Golestan contained attractive housing for 70 families, a company guesthouse, grocery store, and recreation center provided with a bar, swimming pool, and billiard hall. All our homes and offices were air-conditioned because temperatures soared above 100 degrees Fahrenheit at least a few days each month during the "cool season" and more frequently during the "hot season." Once the thermometer at Ahwaz stayed above 100 degrees day and nght for more than 30 days.

High as these temperatures may sound, Ahwaz could not compete with Dezful. If a newspaper could publish daily temperatures for the hottest places in the world, Dezful would probably head the list more days in the year than any other city, reaching 60 degrees C (130 degrees F) a few days each year. Temperatures were so high at the canyon damsite that work hours in the "hot season" were from 8 P.M. to 8 A.M.

At Ahwaz our clerical service posed a problem that I had not encountered before—we were unable to recruit Muslim women secretaries. We found a few Armenian Christian secretaries but never enough. Our solution was to hire British male secretaries in London, unmarried, mostly under age 35 and alumni of the British colonial service.

We had other challenges. At the damsite, old tribal feuds broke out within our Iranian labor force, and some workers were murdered. We hired an Iranian social scientist to sort out the warring tribes and separate them on the opposite sides of the canyon.

We employed a German-Jewish medical doctor—a refugee from Hitler in World War II—to make a health survey of the villages along the Karun; we felt we should advise the Iranian government on the preventive health services that they would need. Malaria, for example, was widespread. We also feared the new Dez reservoir might spread the dreaded disease schistosomiasis, a snail-borne malady. For that study we brought in an American public health doctor from Baltimore.

Land levelling machines at the sugar plantation were inadvertently breaking open ancient graves containing historic Elamite relics. (Elam was the name of this area in the Old Testament of the Bible.) An American archeologist identified the finds for us and recommended establishing a local museum.

After wrestling with these problems, I wrote progress reports for the World Bank, which sent loan inspectors to review our progress every six months. I had helped Gordon Clapp, Lilienthal's partner in New York, to write the original work schedule for the bank loan, so I was familiar with the pace of work that the bank expected. Some bank loan officers were difficult to cope with, but on the whole I found these inspections helpful, both to the bank as lender and to Iran as borrower.

My third and last year in Iran I transferred to Tehran as D and R company representative. Our KDS office was next door to the shah's office on Avenue Pasteur. Here I assisted the director of KWPA—an Iranian with rank of minister—to take over the completed services in the Khuzestan.

In 1976, 14 years after I completed my work in Iran, I was invited by the Iranian government to visit the Khuzestan development program. This was before the Khomeini era. I was fascinated to observe how well or how badly the old plans were turning out. As the following trip notes show, David Lilienthal's hopes for the region were only partly fulfilled.

> Dez Dam is a beauty, its reservoir filled with sparkling blue water and its generators operating at 520,000 kw. Power is selling at the recommended wholesale price. Thus the flagship of Khuzestan development is a success—so far.
>
> Khuzestan Electric Company is another success. This Iranian company has completed the rewiring of five cities—Abadan, Khorramshahr, Ahwaz, Dezful and Andimeshk, and local power lines now reach many villages on the Karun plain. Village homes generally have only a single lightbulb in the ceiling of each room, but this is progress.
>
> The sugar plantation now produces an annual cane crop on its 10,000 hectares of irrigated land and operates its own mill. Khuzestan is again calling itself the "land of sugar cane."
>
> There was bad news too. In 1962, a year before the completion of Dez Dam, the minister of agriculture decided to redistribute the land that would be irrigated by the dam. Ownership of 20,000 hectares passed from 50 landlords to 3,000 previous tenants. The new smallholders were not experienced in planning the crops, managing the irrigation, and marketing the harvest; in these matters the government provided inadequate assistance,

and the "land reform" made a disaster of previous financial plans. In frustration D and R shortly withdrew.

Bigger disasters followed. After KWPA spent $43 million on the headworks and primary canals to serve 100,000 hectares under the greater Dez irrigation project, a new minister of agriculture subleased the newly irrigated land to large corporations, using Imperial Valley, California as a model. Against the advice of the World Bank, five corporate contractors were permitted to lease 60,000 hectares. American, British and Iranian managers were involved. Within ten years all the contractors had failed financially, and the government took back the land.

## Reflections About Iran

Mohammed Reza Shah Pahlavi was a tragic figure among twentieth-century rulers. He wore the crown 38 years and accomplished many useful things for his people before he was driven into exile by the Muslim zealot, Ayatollah Khomeini. In 1981 the shah died of cancer in Egypt at age 62.

The shah contributed to his own downfall. His greatest mistake was his drive to hurry the Iranian nation into the modern age, not permitting time to win over the Muslim clergy who dominated the poorer classes. The shah himself belonged to a small minority of urban Iranians who were university educated, wealthy, cosmopolitan, and generally indifferent to the practices of the Muslim faith. The great majority of Iranians were peasants of low income and little education—men who pray toward Mecca five times a day and keep their womenfolk veiled in *purdah*. In his reign the shah's father— old Reza Shah—tried to abolish *purdah* by royal decree and directed his people to wear European-style clothes. The younger shah avoided these extremes; but by flying his own jet plane over Iran and taking skiing holidays in Switzerland, he perpetuated the image of a royal playboy—not a fair picture of his national contribution. Mohammed Reza Shah did not deserve the rejection he suffered from the western world when he became a dying refugee in the closing years of his life.

David Lilienthal—quite unintentionally—contributed to the shah's political misfortunes by advocating a TVA on the Karun River. Consider the differences between a river development in the United States and in southwest Iran. The Tennessee watershed of the 1930s was a backward mountain area surrounded by more prosperous states; it was the role of TVA—by means of hydro-electric dams, fertilizer factories and diversified industry—to help this area catch up with the prosperity of its neighbors. By contrast, the watershed of the Karun River in the 1950s was a sparsely populated semidesert. Nearly all the provinces of Iran were in need of agricultural investment. If the shah had calculated how best to gain popular support for his reign, he would probably not have spent a quarter billion dollars on the hot and arid Khuzestan, but would have scattered smaller projects in more populated areas.

Burma and Iran were my first lessons in third world development, and both were disappointments. My next assignment was in Pakistan—a very different experience.

*I have viewed problems as a Pakistani, a Muslim, and an Asian. Pakistan is my passion, my life.*

President Mohammed Ayub Khan, 1967

CHAPTER 24

# Pakistan: With President Ayub Khan

In the spring of 1962, I received in Tehran a cable from the Ford Foundation in New York, asking if I would accept appointment as the foundation representative in Pakistan. Pakistan and India at that time shared the reputation for the broadest and most imaginative development programs in Asia. I was torn. David Lilienthal and Gordon Clapp urged that I stay with D and R in Iran, but their program was slowing down to routine and no longer offered the same excitement. I made a hasty trip to New York to discuss the foundation proposal; their offer represented a cut in salary but a wider range of new experience. After weighing pros and cons, I chose the move to Pakistan because I believed an interesting assignment was more than money.

My five years in Pakistan should begin with a description of the Ford Foundation and how it gives away money constructively. The Ford Foundation was created during the depression of the 1930s by Henry Ford Sr. and his son Edsel, who wanted to benefit society and thought a professional grant-giving organization could best serve that purpose. The two Fords between them gave 93 million shares of Ford Motor Company stock. These securities were sold by the foundation over a period of years, and the proceeds reinvested in other stocks, leaving no connection between the motor company and the foundation, a separation that both sides preferred.

After settlement of the estates of the two founders—both men died in the 1940s—the foundation in 1950 entered upon a national and worldwide program of giving. Some gifts caused public controversy, but for me, the foundation's small staff of grant makers showed remarkable social imagination. For example, the Ford Foundation pioneered the support in the

United States for the College Entrance Examination Board, the National Merit Scholarship Corporation, the National Achievement Scholarships for blacks and the National Endowment for the Arts. In the 1960s the foundation became the leading private supporter of birth control research, seeking simpler and more reliable contraceptives. In another direction, the foundation promoted educational television and supported the Children's Television Workshop, including its most popular program "Sesame Street." The foundation gave massive "challenge grants" to private colleges and universities that totalled $350 million but required matching grants from other sources in various proportions. These challenges drew an additional $1 billion in contributions. Among its less-publicized activities, the foundation financed research on arms limitation that laid the groundwork for the U.S.-Russian talks.

The law requires a tax-exempt foundation in the United States to give away substantially all its current income. Between 1950 and 1984 this foundation made grants exceeding $6 billion; it gave financial assistance to more than 8,000 nonprofit or governmental institutions and to more than 100,000 individuals for research and training. Approximately $1 billion was spent in developing countries.

Naturally, large give-aways become the subject of ridicule. A *New Yorker* cartoon showed a man in an office marked FORD FOUNDATION, throwing dollar bills out the window while a stern-faced older colleague said, "No, no, John; that's not the way we do it here." A puzzled British Ford automobile dealer in London once asked me: "Do I get this straight? The Ford Motor Company pushes me to make more sales, so the company can give more money to the foundation, so that men like you can give it away in Asia?" No, I told him; it was not that simple. The foundation has no present connection with the Ford Motor Company and its profits.

The foundation's trustees are all prominent citizens with major responsibilities in universities, corporations, or other institutions. They meet several times a year and divide the foundation's annual budget into areas of public interest: for example, research on the urban and rural poor, mid-career training for government administrators, or support of business education in the United States. The foundation's professional staff, working in New York, develops proposals for grants to nonprofit organizations that will fulfill the intentions of the trustees.

Outside the United States the foundation has maintained about ten offices in places like Cairo, Delhi, and Mexico City, each headed by a representative who formulates grant proposals in consultation with local leaders. In my period these proposals were sent by the representative for approval by a foundation vice president in New York and then to the foundation president. At that time the president was Dr. Henry Heald, an engineer, previously president of Illinois Institute of Technology.

I became one of those overseas representatives. My office in Karachi was responsible for grants in Pakistan and present-day Bangladesh. There I met and worked with the remarkable national leader of Pakistan, President Ayub Khan.

Ayub was a Pathan—one of those handsome six-foot, two-inch, ramrod-straight soldiers from a fighting tribe on the Afghan frontier. His life story taught me much about modern India and Pakistan. Ayub was born in 1907 in a village 50 miles north of Rawalpindi, son of a retired army officer and landowner. After village schooling he was sent by his family to the famous Aligarh Muslim College, east of New Delhi. His classmates at Aligarh were Muslims from all the states of India and a few foreign areas such as Afghanistan, Iran, the Arab countries and North Africa. They spoke a polyglot of languages including Hindi, Urdu, Bengali, Pushtu, Farsi, and Arabic, plus Ayub's native Punjabi.

From Aligarh he went to the British Royal Military Academy at Sandhurst where he graduated 60th in a class of 123. He later wrote with delicacy that ethnic prejudice existed among the British faculty, for while he himself was rated first among the non-British cadets, there were 59 Britons ranked above him. He was the first non-British cadet in his class to be promoted to corporal, which was said to be a measure of military aptitude.

After Sandhurst Ayub was commissioned a lieutenant in the Indian army and spent his first years in barracks on the northwest frontier, India's "wild west," living the army life made famous by Rudyard Kipling.

One anecdote survives from Ayub's early military service. Each year a regiment was selected for a field exercise designed to test the leadership of the commanders. In Ayub's third year a British officer commanded the "home force" and Ayub commanded the "enemy." Twice during the exercise the "enemy" encircled the "home force" and cut up its defenses. At the end of the exercise the British brigade commander, giving his assessment, turned to Ayub and said, "I have real praise for the enemy commander." Ayub wrote in his life story that the British regimental commander in charge of the "home force" never forgave him for the humiliation and "chased me about for several years, giving me a difficult time."

When Japan invaded Burma in 1942, the British government ordered the Indian army into the Burma fight. Ayub spent two years, 1942–1944, in bloody jungle warfare against the Japanese.

At the end of World War II, the British offered independence to India, but the leading Hindu and Muslim political parties—known as the Indian National Congress and the All-India Muslim League—could not agree on a single constitution; Muslims insisted on a separate nation. After talks dragged on for more than a year, the British government finally granted dominion status to two separate nations on June 14, 1947. Pakistan was assigned the "contiguous Muslim-majority areas" which resulted in a country of two "wings," East and West, separated by more than 1,000 air miles of Indian territory. This was an unmanageable situation in which the two halves of Pakistan had little in common except their religion and resentment against Hindu India.

The British thought a British-led army could maintain order during partition, but they did not foresee the holocaust that engulfed the Punjab. Militant Hindus and Muslims fought to retain their villages, and the Sikhs waged a separate war to keep the old Punjab as a unified Sikh state. The Indian army was helpless in the massacres that followed. Ayub wrote later, "I have never seen anything so terrible. Women and children were mutilated and innocent people butchered." After many months, fighting over partition subsided.

Ayub became commander-in-chief of the Pakistan army in 1951 when the last British commander was called home to England. Ayub drew up a program to remedy the Pakistan army problems, which the British had left unsolved. He raised salaries. He set up military farms to feed the troops. He established factories to manufacture uniforms. He created an army medical service. He organized housing and schooling for army dependents.

Throughout the first decade of independence, Pakistan was in political chaos. Divisive issues separated West and East Pakistan; the two areas spoke two different languages—Urdu and Bengali—and quarrelled over the division of revenues.

Finally in 1958—the eleventh year of independence—President Iskander Mirza concluded that Pakistan could not be governed by an administration split among tens of parties, with scores of geographic units demanding benefits. Mirza favored martial law, but when Ayub was approached, he would not accept army authority unless Mirza issued a presidential decree abolishing the constitution, dissolving the National Assembly, and designating Ayub as martial law administrator. Mirza took these steps, and the army thus came to power in October 1958 without staging a military coup.

Ayub's actions in establishing a martial law administration could well be studied by other armies that find themselves responsible for national rule. The cabinet under Ayub was largely civilian, composed of senior civil servants, professional men, and business leaders from private life. The army was ordered to stay in its barracks.

Under Ayub's leadership, the country settled down. Strikes ended. Agricultural production rose. The port of Karachi was developed. A new national capital was built at Islamabad, adjacent to Rawalpindi, and a secondary capital was constructed at Dacca for East Pakistan, now capital of Bangladesh. Ayub believed in national planning; he studied the documents and gave his support. He advocated family planning and although he produced seven children, he told audiences of women with a twinkle, "Do what I say, not what I did."

Berni and I took up residence in Pakistan in 1962 during the fourth year of Ayub's administration. We remained five years. This was an era favorable for technical assistance. It was also my most successful period in the third world. At the Ford Foundation office in Karachi I learned I was responsible for about 25 "grant projects" and for the welfare of 50 expatriate families, mostly American, who served as advisors in six cities of East and West Pakistan.

My contribution to the Ford Foundation program in Pakistan was mainly in agriculture. Seventy percent of Pakistanis lived in villages, engaged either in farming or in village services such as carting and blacksmithing. The Pakistan planning commission, it seemed to me, was giving proper emphasis to this 70 percent by expanding irrigation canals and fertilizer supply, but agriculturl research had not contributed much to farmers' income. The so-called green revolution had not begun.

Traditionally wheat was the most important farm crop of West Pakistan and the largest contributor of calories to the diet. But wheat yields at the beginning of the 1960s were very low. A year before I arrived, the U.N. Food and Agricultural Organization (FAO) had sent two young Pakistani wheat scientists to Mexico to spend one cropping season with Norman Borlaug, then a little-known Rockefeller Foundation wheat scientist, and with Ignacio Narvaez, director of Mexico's national wheat program. Nothing remarkable happened. The two Pakistanis worked with Borlaug's "semidwarf wheats" and carried home to Pakistan seed for more than 100 advanced lines. Semidwarfs had many advantages; the most obvious was low plant height of 70–100 centimeters compared to 125–150 centimeters for traditional varieties. The short wheats grew to a man's waist instead of his shoulder. The semidwarfs tillered profusely (gave more stems from each seed) and had more grains per spike. Shortness gave the semidwarfs a stronger straw that resisted "lodging" or falling over before harvest. These Mexican wheats also required a change in cultivation methods; for example, the short wheats were seeded 5 centimeters deep instead of 15 centimeters (2 inches instead of 6).

I visited the two Pakistani wheat scientists at their research station in the

Punjab. They had hidden their Mexican wheats in a far corner of the station. When I asked why, they said wheat breeding in Pakistan was a profit-making business for many government breeders, who sold seed of new varieties; older scientists would resent the introduction of competing wheats from Mexico. Nevertheless, the two returnees were obviously excited. Most Mexican semidwarfs—when tested at Lyallpur—had yielded half again more grain than the best Pakistani varieties. These young men said they did not dare to publicize such remarkable results until they had performance records covering two or three crop cycles.

I wrote to Borlaug in Mexico in 1963, raising four questions: (1) Could Borlaug train five more Pakistani wheat scientists each year for the next five years? (2) Could Borlaug and Narvaez visit Pakistan the following year at wheat harvest time to decide whether Pakistan was beginning a wheat revolution? (3) If this visit confirmed what the two Pakistanis had told me, could Narvaez spend several years in Pakistan organizing the national demonstration of the short wheats? (4) Based on Narvaez's findings, should Ford Foundation finance a large shipment of wheat seed from Mexico to Pakistan?

Borlaug answered yes to all four questions. Borlaug and Narvaez made separate visits to Pakistan. They confirmed the remarkable yields in the Lyallpur trials. They interviewed young Pakistani wheat scientists who would be candidates for training in Mexico, five each year. They visited President Ayub Khan and kindled his enthusiasm for a wheat campaign.

Narvaez arrived in Pakistan in 1964 and quickly devised a national wheat testing program using a pattern he called the *microplot*. A microplot was a half hectare of private land (1.25 acres) on which 36 different varieties of wheat were planted, checkerboard fashion, receiving identical sunshine, moisture, and fertilizer. At harvest time neighboring farmers were invited to see the plots. There were 50 such microplots in West Pakistan.

Even in the first year—and continuing for two more years—the topmost wheat in the microplots was an experimental Mexican semidwarf called *Cross 8156*, which was later released in Pakistan under the name *Mexipak 66*. Cross 8156—under many different names—became the most widely grown spring wheat variety in the world after it spread across Asia, Africa and Latin America.

Pakistan's wheat program caught the imagination of President Ayub Khan and he became a close friend of the young Mexican Narvaez. The two men made field trips together and jointly recommended that 350 tons of seed for semidwarf wheat be imported from Mexico in 1965, a year in which Pakistan was short of food because of monsoon failure. The shipment arrived by sea in the midst of a short India-Pakistan war—a near disaster, but the ship landed safely. The seed germinated poorly because of excessive fumigation in Mexico; this second potential disaster was corrected by using a double rate of seeding.

How should the seed be distributed? President Ayub shared in the decision. He recommended that half the seed be distributed to 1,400 large landowners, a list that included himself. Each of the large landowners would receive enough seed for two hectares. In addition the extension service was asked to distribute 5,000 packets of seed to small landholders. They would each receive enough seed for a quarter hectare. Finally, government seed farms would multiply the balance. Each recipient of seed was instructed in the new methods of cultivation, but not all listened.

The following spring Borlaug and Narvaez joined the Pakistan researchers in measuring the harvest from the new seed. The best irrigated fields produced more than six tons per hectare, which was then a fantastic commercial yield.

President Ayub Khan called Narvaez to Flagstaff House, the president's residence at Rawalpindi and asked for the results. Nacho gave him the names of the landowners who achieved six tons, many of whom were the president's friends. The average yield from Cross 8156 was 2.5 to 3.0 tons, compared to Pakistan's national average of 0.8 tons from older varieties. When Nacho mentioned some failures, the president asked for names. Narvaez shuffled his feet, but the president insisted. Well, Nacho said, the men who are failures are well known to you. The first failure was the secretary of agriculture, Malik Khuda Baksh. Why? Because he failed to instruct his farm manager about the new cultivation methods. The president shook his head slowly. And the second failure? That was the governor of West Pakistan, the Nawab of Kala Bagh. Same reason. And the third? Nacho looked at the floor, then pointing a finger hesitantly at the president, he said: "The third, sir, was you. Same reason." The president grimaced.

Excellent publicity received from the widespread planting of new wheats should have assured the rapid spread of the seed, but xenophobic government employees, including many senior scientists, protested the use of foreign wheats. They complained that Mexican wheats did not taste as good when made into *chapatis* (flat whole wheat cakes). The governor of West Pakistan demanded that the protesters take a blindfold test; it proved that none of them could tell the difference in taste between chapatis made with Mexican and Pakistani flour. The civil servants then protested that Mexican wheats were reddish in color, whereas Pakistani consumers preferred amber-colored or yellowish brown chapatis. The governor replied that until Pakistan achieved self-sufficiency in wheat, it should grow whatever color wheat would give the biggest harvest. Finally, Pakistani scientists protested that the short wheats would give less *bhoosa* (straw) causing a shortage of feed for the farmers' bullocks. This proved untrue. When short wheats were planted with higher plant population—more plants per square meter—the semidwarf wheats provided a surplus of bhoosa.

These protests died down, and Pakistan in 1967 was able to import 32,000 tons of Mexican wheat seed, which at that time was the largest shipment of seed for any crop ever moved between two countries. That assured the rapid spread of semidwarf wheats in Pakistan and stimulated the expanding use of fertilizer, tubewell irrigation, and machinery.

What were the benefits? An annual report of the Pakistan accelerated wheat program showed a steady rise in production for more than 20 years, as given in Table 1. Another way to express the results was this: Pakistan's wheat harvest during 1980-83 was 7.6 million tons greater than in the early 1960s before the short wheats. This wheat increase was worth US$1.5 billion a year at a world price of $200 a ton. The increased wheat provided the recommended carbohydrates for about 50 million additional people. That was a measure of Pakistan's green revolution, which still goes on.

TABLE 1. Yearly Wheat Production in Pakistan, 1960–1983

| Years | Average wheat area in million hectares | Average wheat production in million tons | Average wheat yield in tons per hectare |
| --- | --- | --- | --- |
| 1960–65 | 5.0 | 4.1 | 0.82 |
| 1965–70 | 5.8 | 5.7 | 0.98 |
| 1970–75 | 5.9 | 7.2 | 1.2 |
| 1975–80 | 6.5 | 9.4 | 1.4 |
| 1980–83 | 7.2 | 11.7 | 1.6 |

President Ayub Khan expressed his gratitude for the wheat campaign by awarding Pakistan's distinguished service medal to Norman Borlaug, the breeder and promoter; to Nacho Narvaez, the field demonstrator; and to myself, a nonscientist, for organizing the financial support. A dozen Pakistani scientists deserved to have their names added at the top of that list.

Through Ford Foundation in New York I arranged a series of agricultural grants that further bolstered the wheat revolution program. We assigned an American curriculum advisor to the training schools for agricultural extension workers. We trained private farm machinery drivers and mechanics. We provided a Norwegian agricultural economist named Oddvar Aresvik who sat in the office of the secretary of agriculture at Lahore and helped to calculate government incentive prices for wheat. By the time Ford Foundation advisors to Pakistan were withdrawn in 1981, the wheat revolution was secure.

Postscript: After Ayub retired in 1969 Pakistan was buffeted during the 1970s by disruptive political and military events, so different from the Ayub era. For me four events had greatest impact in that decade.

• In 1971 East Pakistan proclaimed its independence as the People's Republic of Bangladesh. In a brief civil war the East Pakistan "liberation army," assisted by the Indian government, overwhelmed the Pakistan army. Thereafter the two wings of Pakistan were recognized as separate nations.

• In 1973 the OPEC revolution in oil prices created high prosperity in the Persian Gulf states, as well as a need for imported labor. An estimated 2 million Pakistani men signed contracts as guest workers in the Arab countries. Overseas Pakistanis sent back funds to their families for more than a decade, and their remittances were estimated as high as U.S. $7.5 billion a year, sometimes approaching 25 percent of Pakistan's gross national product. This windfall in hard currency was, of course, unstable—it depended on the continued prosperity of OPEC.

• In 1977 the Pakistan army again seized power, installing the army commander, General Mohammed Zia ul Haq, as president in place of the previously elected president, Zulfikar Ali Bhutto. General Zia arrested his predecessor, tried him in a military court on charges of having been accessory to the murder of a political opponent, and hanged him. General Zia was a curious mixture of a western-trained military commander and a religious zealot. He was a graduate of the United States Command and General Staff College at Fort Leavenworth, Kansas, yet his administration banned liquor, introduced public flogging, prohibited interest payments by banks, and abolished political parties and civil courts.

Perhaps because of its authoritarian style, Zia's administration brought stability to Pakistan. The economy surged forward at more than 6 percent a year during Zia's first seven years in office—the highest growth rate in south Asia. In 1984 Zia conducted a referendum that confirmed himself as president for another five years, thus extending military rule—barring violence—to 1989. President Zia's Koranic policies are sometimes compared to those of his Iranian neighbor, Ayatollah Khomeini, but the Zia regime is actually closer to those of Egypt and Morocco, both Muslim countries but not Islamic. (*Muslim* is used here to describe believers in Allah, and *Islamic* describes a government that enforces as national law the *sharia* or code of conduct laid down by the Koran. Pakistan has applied Koranic law selectively, whereas Iran has gone much further in making all aspects of life—politics, law, economics, and family—conform to Islam as described in the Koran.)

• The Soviet invasion of Afghanistan in 1979 caused some 3 million Afghanis to move as refugees into Pakistan. A formidable relief operation was organized, financed by international agencies with full cooperation from Zia's administration. Pakistan became the third ranking recipient of United States aid after Israel and Egypt.

One other significant development: President Zia brought home from the World Bank the brilliant Pakistani economist, Dr. Mabub ul Huq, who had learned his trade as an economic planner under the planning commission of Ayub Khan. Dr. Huq later spent 12 years at the World Bank in Washington, rising to be the bank's director of program planning before returning to Pakistan to serve under Zia as minister of planning. Pakistan may be 50 years behind the west, Minister Huq told the press, but it doesn't take 50 years nowadays to catch up.

In 1967 the Ford Foundation notified me that, under a five-year rotation policy, I would be transferred to another country. The foundation offered to send me to West Africa, with residence at Lagos, Nigeria, or to South America, at Rio de Janeiro, Brazil. Those were the foundation's largest programs in Africa and Latin America. I protested. By remaining in Pakistan I could draw upon five years of contacts that I would lack in Africa or South America, but the foundation stood firm in its decision for transfer.

I chose Nigeria. Black Africa was passing through interesting changes.

*People in developing countries seek assistance, but on the basis of mutual respect; they want to have friends, not masters.*

President Mohammed Ayub Khan, 1967

CHAPTER 25

# Family Matters in Asia

Recently, while looking through dust-covered letters in a closet at our Virginia farmhouse, I came upon a "family letter" written by Berni almost 20 years earlier, reporting to friends about life in South Asia. The year was 1966. Some family letters can be dull, including ours. But I found this one fresh, bringing back the flavor of events long forgotten. The letter describes some events of the India-Pakistan war in September 1965; it gives contemporary impressions of Pakistan's development program; and it recounts a visit by the Hanson family to the Soviet Union. So without editing, I add this narrative.

The Ford Foundation
P.O. Box 7282
Karachi, Pakistan
April 12, 1966

Dear Friends,

This letter will doubtless be so long that I shall use sub-titles, and you can skip the topics outside your interest.

Last spring Hal flew to Mexico to negotiate an exciting agricultural project (more below). In August he attended a world conference in Switzerland on family planning (much more below) and returned to Karachi the day the Indian-Pakistani fighting broke out (much, much more below).

I was visiting my mother in Virginia when I heard the news of the fighting over the radio. As soon as I realized that it was more than the weekly border skirmishing that we had had for years, I caught a flight to London from Dulles Airport, 20 miles from our farm and made connections with a Pakistan International Airlines flight for Karachi. This turned out to be the last international plane for the duration of the emergency. Pakistan had no fuel for commercial airlines, consequently no flights.

People thought I was out of my mind to be rushing back to Pakistan when most of the embassies in Karachi were attempting to evacuate their dependents. My only thought was how would Hal hold the collective hands of 50 Ford Foundation wives and their 100 children!

I started to draft this letter on October 5, 1965, just after the hostilities ceased. I didn't finish it at that time. But maybe you'd like to hear what we sounded like then.

*The emergency*

I am typing this behind blackout curtains in my bedroom. The ceasefire is two weeks old but Indians and Pakistanis are still shooting at each other along the 500-mile line. An armed policeman is patrolling the dark street outside our house because of anti-American feeling (still no street lights for fear of new air raids). A shortwave radio sits on our dining table at every meal, because that is the only reliable outside news we can get; cables take ten days and mail from the United States one month. Half the wives and children of our Ford families are sitting in Tehran and Manila—evacuated by the U.S. Air Force from West and East Pakistan. The censor will read this letter before you do.

Trying to maintain emotional stability during hostilities is a problem. Hal had been through two years in China with the armies of the communists, the nationalists, and the Japanese. I had fled before the invading Chinese communists from my teaching job in Shanxi. In Burma in 1959 our advisors in the prime minister's office had been caught unaware when the army overthrew the U Nu government (first time). In Tehran in 1961 Hal's office was adjacent to the shah's palace which was the many-times target for rioting students. We have learned that no matter how badly shaken the city is, the danger to any individual foreigner is probably not great.

None of these episodes, however, could reassure the Ford Foundation families in Lahore who heard Indian artillery for 17 days, only eight miles away. They headed for the hall closet when Indian planes came over. One man told me he and his wife spent the first two nights on the rooftop, watching the flashes of artillery shells, and timing the sound to see if the Indians were getting closer. (They weren't. The front had stabilized.)

Two Ford families who lived at the edge of Peshawar airfield had their windows blown in by the first Indian air raid. Next day they evacuated by car through the Khyber Pass to Kabul. It took us two weeks to find them because international cables were jammed with official messages.

In East Pakistan, 1500 miles from the fighting, there was great anxiety among the Ford families, because an Indian invasion was expected momentarily, communal rioting was feared (Muslims 80 percent, Hindus 20 percent), and all civilian air service was grounded. Our Karachi office lost contact with that group. The U.S. Air Force finally evacuated 600 people to Manila, including some Ford personnel.

Karachi reached an emotional crisis on September 22. Student mobs, raised to hysteria by the press, took control of Karachi streets for eight hours, burned down the USIS library and the British Information Service (along with about 50 foreign firms including Pan American and Aeroflot), and painted signs through out the business district, 'Damn Imperialists, Go Home!'

It took India and Pakistan 18 years of shouting over Kashmir to start a war. It is going to take more than a few months of tight government controls on both sides to quiet things down.

Amen. That is as far as I got.

The Tashkent Conference (India-Pakistan-USSR, 1966) didn't settle Kashmir, but it got the two armies to withdraw from their eyeball-to-eyeball positions. Premier Kosygin did an effective job of helping coax onto paper an Indian-Pakistan declaration to live and let live. Both governments are now struggling against political opposition that prefers fighting to eating (so it seems), and peace is not yet assured.

We got all our Ford families reunited in Pakistan by Christmas. No casualties.

Hal and his Norwegian economic advisor, Oddvar Aresvik, were teargassed at Lahore in January when their car was caught in a riot on the Mall. About 40 police fired teargas shells at a student mob. One canister overshot the target, struck Hal's car and rolled under the front wheels where it spewed out its white fumes.

*To the USSR with our children as interpreters*

Summer 1965: Before the fighting, we had one of our most successful family vacations. Signe and Eric (our two children) flew out to Karachi from their schools, one at Grinnell College, the other at Peddie School in New Jersey. They were both employed at the Karachi American School for the summer vacation: Signe as a drama instructor, Eric as tennis coach.

In August all four Hansons set off for Afghanistan and three weeks in the Soviet Union. Eric had studied Russian in Rosenberg Academy in Switzerland, and Signe had learned some of the language at college. The two of them got us successfully into subways (yes, they are immaculate), buses, workers' cafeterias (very low cost), sightseeing with taxi drivers, and just poking around. The two Hanson interpreters proved observant and sensitive. It was a delight to see them operate a few days in Tashkent, a week on the Black Sea beach at Sochi, and then a week in Moscow.

Hal and I had spent two weeks in the Soviet Union the year before, mainly following the footsteps of Genghiz Khan and Tamurlane in Uzbekistan (Tashkent, Bokhara, Samarkand and the old Silk Route to China). We carried with us the average stock of American preconceptions.

The USSR for a tourist is a continuous paradox. Its scientific and educational advance is to be seen everywhere. The department stores have entire floors of television sets, radios, Hi-fis and cameras, but the prices are beyond the purchasing power of all Soviets but a few. Most men's suits at the state department store are above $150, and ladies shoes $30–35. But the people on the street seem adequately dressed, if not stylish, and certainly calorically replete. (Don't try to find a low-carbohydrate diet in a Moscow restaurant.) But one college-graduate Intourist guide in Moscow told us she lived in a two-room apartment with her engineer husband, one son, and two parents-in-law; she considered herself luckier than most.

The skyline of Moscow is lined with 10-story apartment houses—one city block square—for miles and miles and miles. The horizon seems covered with construction cranes putting up more.

During two visits covering five Soviet republics in two successive summers we never saw a soldier on duty; we never had a policeman ask to see any paper (except on first arrival at the international airport); we never saw any discourtesy toward foreigners, nothing but wide-eyed curiosity toward Americans (and a few appreciative whistles for Signe, age 19).

But Lord protect the Soviet citizens (and tourists) from the rude waitresses in the restaurants and the insufficient and incompetent salesgirls in the state department stores. As foreigners we were escorted to the heads of many lines, ahead of Russians who had been waiting for hours, much to our embarrassment.

But LIFE IS REAL AND EARNEST! The 135,000 Soviets with whom we shared the Sochi beach were there as state guests, a month's free vacation as a reward from their trade unions. At 6 A.M., as the sun came up, they were striding purposefully down all the hilly streets to stake out their places on the gravelly shoreline, beachbag over one shoulder, a loaf of bread and some sausage in a paper. Coffee and ice cream were available at beach stands. They would lie there all day until sunset, men and women, some reading, some playing cards, some just dozing, some body-building with calisthenics. (I had the questionable distinction of being the only woman on the beach over age 40 and under 140 pounds.)

After dark a Russian version of a combo took up its place on a concrete platform at the beach and hundreds of young Russians came to dance, many of them trying twisting, frugging and watusi-ing. Signe and a pick-up Russian partner stopped the show with an Iowa version of college dancing.

We went to cultural performances for 14 nights—opera, ballet, symphony, vaudeville (with Cole Porter tunes), circus—and there wasn't a mediocre evening, nor an empty seat. Prices were very low ($1.00–1.50). but we were told that local residents have difficulty getting tickets. Most of the audience were Soviet tourists.

We didn't meet any Soviet writers, but we did have one curious encounter with artists on our earlier trip. After days of pressing to see some artists at work in Samarkand, we were taken to an apartment where ten artists lived and maintained their studios. They had the usual doctrinaire portraits of Lenin at the barricades. But they also had some excellent street scenes from the old city of Samarkand, including the Bibi Khanum Mosque that Timur built for his favorite wife. It was an oil.

Could we buy it? Certainly not! All Soviet artists work only for the state; and all their works belong to the state. If they are superior in quality, they go to the National Museum in Moscow. If a shade less good, they go to the State Museum. If they are mediocre, they go to the Workers' Hall of Rest and Culture in a provincial park or factory. But they are all state property.

Seeing my obvious disappointment, one artist said, "You know I can't let you take a finished painting, but before I do an oil, I always start with a charcoal drawing of the scene. These I keep. I will give you your choice." After inspection, we chose two, which he autographed, and they are now framed in the hall of our Karachi home.

He declined payment. And then we asked if there was anything we could send him.

Finally, he said the government did not encourage impressionistic painting. But he admired it. Could we send him an illustrated catalogue from the Museum of Modern Art in New York? We did. But we will never know if he got it.

We left feeling our image of the USSR had been ten years out of date. The changes we saw help explain why the communist bloc is no longer monolithic.

## Hal, the promoter (hard-sell!)

During four years in Pakistan Hal has negotiated $3-5 million in grants annually, and he has begun to reshape the Ford program to fit the changing priorities of Pakistan.

Pakistan achieved economic growth of 30 percent during its last Five Year Plan, 1960-1965, and its population rose about 14 percent in that period. Among all developing countries that is a creditable performance and gave Pakistan the reputation among aid agencies that it generally achieves what it sets out to do. But Pakistan feels it must still accomplish four things to stand on its own feet without foreign aid:

1. Double its grain production.
2. Cut in half the number of babies born each year.
3. Train more managers for industry and government departments, fast.
4. Export enough Pakistani products to pay for all imports.

The Ford program, therefore, is shifting from an earlier pattern of general education to the new objectives.

## Food grain

Grain for Pakistan means wheat for 50 million in West Pakistan and rice for 50 million in East Pakistan.

The trouble with Pakistani wheat is that when fertilizer is added, the plant gets taller, up to six feet, adds almost no grain, and falls over before harvest. The Mexicans with Rockefeller Foundation help have developed a semi-dwarf wheat that is only three feet high. When fertilizer is added, the plants will produce 30 pounds more grain for every pound of nitrogen.

So Hal went to Mexico last year, arranged a large shipment of seed and talked the Mexican government into releasing their No. 1 wheat breeder, who is now assisting the Pakistan program.

Doubling the rice crop in East Pakistan has been approached in the same manner. Here again the problem has been genetic. Monsoon rice in South Asia is highly vegetative—that is, when fertilized, it puts most of its energy into more leaves and very little into more grain.

Now the International Rice Research Institute in the Philippines (IRRI, pronounced "Erie"), supported by Ford and Rockefeller Foundations, has come up with new rice varieties that behave like Mexican wheat. The scientists crossed tall

South Asia rice with several varieties from mainland China that have a recessive gene for shortness. By selecting the short offspring from the cross, the scientists found they had a variety that could tolerate high fertilizer and outyield any previously known variety in South Asia by 2 to 1.

Hal visited the Philippines institute in 1964, got the director to come to Pakistan in 1965 and prepare an action plan for introducing the new short rice. The first planting of more than 300 test varieties went into the ground this month (March 1966). By July Hal hopes to have some exciting news.

The big push on both wheat and rice in Pakistan is not merely to import new seed, but to retrain the entire Pakistan research staff. Pakistani scientists can then carry forward the improvement of these two crops.

## Hal, the contraceptive-wallah

Reducing the number of babies in Pakistan is a different story. Ford Foundation financed most of the research in Pakistan (along with the Swedish government) on the IUD—or intra-uterine device—which resulted in launching a mass government program in July 1965. The government pledged U.S.$62 million of its own money for a five-year drive and hired 8000 staff, including lady doctors to do the insertions and both high school and college graduates to do the "motivating" (house-to-house canvassing, publicity and mass meetings). The Ford Foundation has ten medical and health education advisors helping on continued research, evaluation and training.

For anyone who hasn't heard the spiel before, this IUD gimmick is a one-inch plastic coil or loop that costs one cent, takes five minutes to insert, is 99 percent effective in stopping pregnancies, and can be removed whenever a family wants to have more children. So the doctors call it safe, cheap and reversible. And it works just as well on illiterate village women as on urban college graduates.

Out of 15 million fertile married couples, the government hopes to introduce contraception among 1 million the first year, 6 million by the end of the five-year plan and drop the birth rate 20 percent in that five-year period. If Pakistan succeeds, it will be the first country of large population to drop its birth rate significantly by a government program in the 1960s.

Many of our dinner guests in Karachi are now medical and propaganda people working on this program. Tourists from the U.S. find themselves embarrassed by the heated arguments that go on in mixed company, over what is the average consumption of condoms per fertile couple per year (the current answer is 100).

## More administrators

Pakistan's industrial growth rate has averaged 20 percent a year, compounded, for the last seven years since President Ayub took over leadership in 1958. That isn't as big as it sounds, considering the low starting base, but it explains why the country is pinched for managers. The country is creating new factories faster than it has men to manage them.

Ford Foundation is now helping organize the first school of business administration in East Pakistan, the area in which the government is investing U.S.$700 million in new industrial capital during 1965-1970.

Indiana School of Business is providing the leadership on this project, including several men now writing case studies on business management in East Pakistan, to be used when the first classes are scheduled to open in September 1966.

This is one of the half-dozen training institutions for businessmen and civil servants that Ford is helping. The most senior civil service school—the Administrative Staff College—has been drawing help from Maxwell School at Syracuse on a Ford grant since 1960. Harvard Business School offers advanced management courses in Pakistan for top business executives—at Ford expense.

## More exports

Partly as a result of good management, Pakistan raised its annual exports from $350 to $600 million a year during the 1960-65 plan. To make itself independent of U.S. or any other aid, Pakistan has set a target of $1 billion a year in exports by 1970, and they are already ahead of target during the first year of the Five Year Plan.

The Pakistan government has asked Ford Foundation to help create a school for training businessmen in export techniques and the consultants are here now devising the scheme.

(See next year's letter for the results.)

## Berni's life

During four World War II years in Washington, I groused that I never even travelled across the Potomac River. I'm now making up for lost time.

One religious holiday here—the Muslim Eid-ul-Fitr, comparable to our Easter—is usually about one week long. Hal and I managed to spend two of these holidays in successive years at opposite ends of the country: one year in Chitral, the farthest northwest valley where Afghanistan, USSR, and communist China meet. The valley is inhabited by blue-eyed, blond-haired non-Muslims who claim to be descendants of Alexander's Greek soldiers. On a snowy field in March, with the towering Himalayas in the background, we watched a polo game between the Chitral Scouts (local militia) and valley tribesmen. The tribesmen won.

The next year's Eid we were 2500 miles away at the southern tip of East Pakistan on a 60-mile sand beach called Cox's Bazaar, over against Burma. I never found out who Mr. Cox was, but the March sunshine was balmy over the deep-blue Bay of Bengal, and the miles of sand dunes permitted long, solitary barefoot walks along the water's edge.

At our home in Karachi, we have a stream of guests, mostly professors from U.S. universities that assist the 20-odd Ford projects in Pakistan. With professional servants, I find it unnecessary to plan meals, or shop, or even check whether the beds are made in the guest room. (My culture shock is yet to come—back in Virginia.)

Since this letter goes to old friends, some dating back several decades, I can't resist closing with the story of a new friend who turned out to be an old enemy. Recently in

Dacca, capital of East Pakistan, I sat at lunch with a Jordanian, an ex-Palestinian Arab who now represents the United Nations.

Talking of fighting in Pakistan, I said this did not scare me as much as a riot in Jerusalem in 1936 when a rock was thrown through the windshield of my taxi. He asked what month. I told him. He asked what street. I described the location as best I could. There was a long pause. Then he said, "I threw that rock."

*Khoda hafiz.* May we meet soon.

Berni Hanson

## Pakistan Reflections

The 1960s were an interesting time to watch a pioneer effort for introducing contraceptives in Asia. Pakistan never came close to cutting its birth rate in half, though that was one target of the population program under the Ayub Khan government. Pakistan then had nearly 100 million people, including East Pakistan (now Bangladesh). The most common contraceptives in use were the IUD and the condom.

Ford Foundation experimented with grants for family planning, and from this work I came to three conclusions: First, it is possible to introduce contraceptives successfully among poor, illiterate village women—if the program has active support from a popular chief of state. Second, such a program can be separated from a costly hospital or clinical investment. Third, Muslim clergy or mullahs need not be an obstacle.

The starting point in Pakistan was our KAP surveys (Knowledge-Attitude-Practice) introduced by researchers from the Population Council in New York, the Johns Hopkins School of Public Health in Baltimore, and the Berkeley School of Public Health in California. These American specialists trained hundreds of Pakistani women to interview other Pakistani women with three questions: Do you know about contraceptives (knowledge)? Do you favor using contraceptives to discontinue child bearing or to space your children (attitude)? And, have you tried it (practice)? A surprising number answered in this pattern: No, I have no knowledge; Yes, I would like to try; and No, I have not practiced. Illiterate village women, over age 30, with two or more children, were most numerous candidates. The government concluded that little publicity should be used; the program should provide contraceptive services to those who already wanted them. Medical and paramedical workers were trained to insert loops, and government workers established door-to-door contact with women who asked for contraceptives. Within a year the family planning program was inserting 50,000 loops a month in East Pakistan and 25,000 in West Pakistan.

The ten foundation specialists on my staff limited their work to classroom teaching and gathering statistics. The foundation gave numerous fellowships for Pakistanis seeking Master's degrees in public health at foreign universities, and I arranged travel for Pakistanis to observe family planning work in South Korea, Taiwan, Thailand, and India. In the 1960s this was a successful beginning.

A word about clinics. Many medical doctors outside Pakistan argued that family planning was a subordinate activity in maternal and child health (MCH) and should proceed only as rapidly as a comprehensive MCH program could be developed. I could see the desirable relationship, but for most third world countries, to delay family planning while awaiting MCH clinics would have meant postponing a population program until the twenty-first century, and by then the population could double. Pakistan was willing to pursue family planning as a separate program, and that is what our grants supported.

About mullahs: Pakistan has always had its share of conservative Muslim clergy. But it also had a counterforce in East Pakistan—a remarkable retired civil servant named Akhtar Hameed Khan, alumnus of the famous Indian Civil Service (ICS). After he retired from government Akhtar Hameed's main interest was support of rural cooperatives, which he organized from a Rural Development Academy in Comilla (a Ford-supported project). He was also interested in family planning. As soon as this charismatic leader heard a mullah say that family planning was contrary to the *Koran*, Akhtar Hameed gathered a number of quotations from the *Koran* and himself visited some of the great Muslim research centers such as Al Azhar University in Cairo. He then prepared a pamphlet arguing that the Muslim religion endorses family planning and persuaded leading mullahs in Pakistan to pronounce this conclusion. There was no further opposition from the mosques.

Unfortunately this story does not have a happy ending. After President Ayub retired in 1969, the family planning program declined. Ayub's successors lost interest. In 1986 Bangladesh had a population of 102 million and a birthrate of 45 per 1000, one of the highest in the world. Pakistan in 1986 counted 99 million residents and a birthrate of 43. Military governments in the two countries give no effective support to birth control. Bangladesh has a per-capita income of only $130 a year, the lowest in the World Bank's 1985 *Atlas*. It could have been different.

*Nigeria was once a funnel through which as many as 100,000 slaves a year were shipped to the new world.*

National Geographic *Atlas, 1980*

CHAPTER 26

# Africa's Green Revolution Falters

In October 1967 our air route from the United States to Nigeria was circuitous. Berni and I were starting a Ford Foundation assignment in black Africa, and we needed a fix on African geography. We crossed the Atlantic by the nonstop flight from New York to Casablanca in Morocco, where we put down overnight. North African weather was chilly from an Atlantic breeze. Next we flew Air Afrique—an airline owned by a consortium of West African countries—from Morocco to Senegal on the hump of west Africa and again paused overnight. At the Senegalese capital of Dakar the temperature was in the 70s, although the map said we were in the tropics at 15 degrees north latitude. We had now entered black Africa because Senegal is one of 45 African countries with black population and black rulers. From Senegal we booked the Nigerian Airways "milk run"—a route that overflew or stopped at eleven countries in a single day. We spread out an airline map on our laps and checked off the countries we passed at the rate of one per hour: Senegal, Gambia, Guinea, Sierra Leone, Liberia, Ivory Coast, Ghana, Guinea-Bissau, Togo, Dahomey (later renamed *Benin*), and Nigeria. By the time we reached Lagos on the coast of Nigeria, we were at five degrees north latitude and the airport lying 10 miles from the coast was blistering hot.

The 11 countries we saw from the air that day had smaller populations than many American states, ranging in size from 400,000 for Gambia to 8 million for Ghana. The exception was Nigeria, the most populous country in Africa, then with 54 million people. Ten of the 11 countries were new to self-government, having gained independence between 1957 and 1960. They were split in official language, six francophone (French-speaking) and five anglophone (English-speaking). Berni and I speculated about the impact of these circumstances on Ford Foundation work. New nations meant weak governments. Small populations meant small revenues and small investment.

The decade of the 1960s was a confusing time for two Americans to take up residence in west Africa. From this region 10 million African slaves were kidnapped during the fifteenth to nineteenth centuries, many to become chattels and later second-class citizens in the United States. A great upheaval was then shaking the black community of the United States—the civil rights movement of the 1950s and 1960s. Its landmarks included the Supreme Court's 1954 decision on school desegregation; the Montgomery, Alabama, bus boycott of 1956; the sit-ins that desegregated restaurants in 1960; the "freedom riders" that desegregated railroad and bus stations in 1961; and Martin Luther King's March on Washington in 1963.

In the same two decades—the 1950s and 1960s—an upheaval was shaking the blacks of Africa. Freedom came to more than 40 poor and black nations; it subjected them to a new challenge—could they manage their own affairs with peace and equity? Already there had been one civil war in the old Belgian Congo—now Zaire—and a civil war raged in Nigeria's eastern region as we arrived. Could the Ford Foundation help to solve West Africa's problems? Years later we would conclude that the problems of Africa were more intractable than we realized when we reached Lagos in an optimistic mood.

The Ford Foundation office in a six-story building looked out over the blue tropical waters of the Lagos harbor on the Atlantic, an area cooled by sea breezes, but most of the city population of 1.5 million was crammed into shanty neighborhoods that made Lagos "the Calcutta of west Africa." Berni and I were lucky to rent from the University of Lagos a house that jutted out over the inner lagoon, where fascinating boat life passed near our screened veranda.

When I made my first call on the Nigerian chief of state, I found General Yakubu Gowon to be a slender, shy, and handsome six-foot soldier; he spoke the musical English of west Africans and was able to discuss Nigerian problems with a maturity much beyond his 33 years. Gowon had been born in 1934 in a minority Christian tribe in Plateau State, part of the middle belt of Nigeria. He had studied at Government College, Zaria, in the Muslim north, and like President Ayub Khan of Pakistan, he had graduated from Britain's Royal Military Academy at Sandhurst. He neither smoked nor used alcohol. He had served three years in the United Nations peace keeping force in Zaire before he became Nigeria's army chief of staff in 1966 and was selected by his fellow army officers to head the federal military government in 1967. A remarkable climb.

I brought General Gowon a small gift, and he gave me a token in return. I carried from Ayub Khan a copy of Ayub's autobiography inscribed to Gowon and calling his attention to a chapter on Pakistan's population policies. Both Gowon and Ayub were heads of governments in the British Commonwealth, which established a fraternal relationship. Gowon gave me a wall poster with his own portrait appearing above his wartime slogan: TO KEEP NIGERIA ONE IS A TASK THAT MUST BE DONE. That poster still hangs in my study in Virginia. Gowon's greatest accomplishment was in terminating the civil war and healing the national wounds (more in the next chapter).

I developed a warm friendship with General Gowon. He invited Berni and me to a small church wedding when he married a Nigerian army nurse and asked us to call at his home in the military barracks after their first child was born.

Gowon managed a peaceful but very cautious government until 1975 when he was forced out of office by other military officers—they thought he wasn't tough enough against ex-rebels. He was permitted to leave the country unharmed. He enrolled at Warwick University in England, first as a graduate student and later as visiting lecturer on the faculty. Yakubu (meaning Jacob) is still widely admired in Africa.

The Ford Foundation office in Lagos was responsible for a program that embraced 23 countries, but gave its principal attention to Nigeria and Ghana, two of the largest. My predecessors had sponsored grants dealing mainly with university development, social science research, and the training of African civil servants who would replace the European colonial officers. One Ford representative had been an enthusiast for Africanization and had helped establish public administration institutes in Nigeria, Ghana, and Zaire. Another Ford predecessor had sponsored grants totalling $4 million to the University of Ibadan, thus helping make that university the Rolls Royce of African institutions. The grants for social science research had concentrated on the Nigerian Institute for Social and Economic Research (NISER), which engaged in economic planning for Nigeria. In those heady days of the 1960s, every newly independent African country needed almost everything, so it was not difficult to identify worthy proposals.

I was keenly interested in west African problems of population and agriculture, but quickly learned that Africa moves more slowly than Asia. For example, not a single national government in black Africa in the mid-1960s supported a family planning program. I found only three African doctors who conducted local family planning clinics, all in English-speaking countries. I arranged small grants for them. The only population effort of mine that may have struck a spark was the visit by international consultants who talked about population with chiefs of state. Their discussions—like the products of Johnny Appleseed—might have borne later fruit, but I have no evidence of it.

My largest effort in West Africa was in agricultural research and even that activity might take decades to show results. Seven families out of ten in black Africa were farmers, but our Lagos office had not yet taken interest in agriculture. When I inquired about foodcrop research, I found that colonial governments in all countries of black Africa had conducted some agricultural research, but trained African scientists were scarce. There was little cooperation between English-speaking and French-speaking countries.

The Ford and Rockefeller foundations decided to sponsor jointly a new agricultural research center for tropical Africa to be located in Nigeria and called International Institute of Tropical Agriculture (IITA). The government of Nigeria contributed 2400 acres of land a few miles north of Ibadan. Ford agreed to finance the buildings and land development, which eventually cost more than $25 million. The two foundations also paid the initial operating costs, which were later underwritten by a consortium of foreign aid agencies.

Construction of IITA had just begun when I arrived in Nigeria. The American director was Dr. Herbert Albrecht, a leading agronomist and former president of North Dakota State University. He had to develop the IITA campus during a civil war and to recruit the initial scientific staff during a period of wartime anxieties.

How could the Ford Foundation office in Lagos be useful to IITA? I asked Dr. Albrecht. Our joint answer was that someone needed to assemble the existing state of knowledge on African foodcrop production. That was an immense task. The information was scattered among 45 African governments and in archives or universities of the former colonial powers—Britain, France, and Belgium. How could the study be organized? We decided to sponsor a week-long seminar every two months for two years. Each seminar would deal with one research topic and bring together the scientists of tropical Africa with the best-known tropical experts from Europe, the United States, Asia, and Latin America.

Twelve conferences were held in 1970 and 1971 and involved in all about 600 scientists. Some of the seminars were devoted to individual crops such as rice, maize, sorghum, and tubers; others dealt with irrigation, pesticides, and machinery.*

---

*At the end of the seminars a book was published by Oxford University Press titled *Food Crops of the Lowland Tropics*, edited by C. L. A. Leakey and J. B. Wells. It remains a classic for agricultural researchers in Africa.

As the foundation representative I gave the opening lecture at the first seminar on January 26, 1970. Fifty participants were seated in the Ibadan University conference center—agricultural research directors from London, Paris, Brussels, and Washington and black scientists from more than 30 African governments. I decided to shake up the audience by challenging these researchers to bring about—within ten years—a green revolution in Africa similar to the changes already spreading in Asia. I found more skeptics than believers in that gathering, and history has proved their judgments more realistic than mine. But the following dare was useful:

> I suggest that the agricultural scientists in this room and their colleagues can be a key factor in launching a green revolution in tropical Africa during the 1970s. Unless this green revolution begins soon, there will develop gradually, during the next 30 years, political unrest accompanied by more military governments, more civil wars, more conflicts between African nations, and disruption of economic growth. In short, agricultural scientists hold a special responsibility to decide whether black Africa can remain at peace.

Why, I asked the audience, was there no green revoluton in Africa? My own answer, which I now recognize was incomplete, cited several obstacles: (1) Many Africans used shifting cultivation (also called slash and burn). (2) Tropical Africa lacked irrigation. (3) Most Africans cultivated with a hoe and not with animals. (4) African land was often owned by the community, not by the individual. (5) The price of agricultural chemicals in Africa was prohibitively high. (6) Marketing arrangements were inadequate.

This analysis in 1970 omitted some important African handicaps. The governments of Africa were inexperienced. These were small nations, averaging less than 7 million people, with low tax revenues and a dearth of investment capital. They suffered from a harsh environment (heat, drought, pests, plant diseases, soil erosion and leaching of nutrients). The governments were divided by language. They had few trained scientists. For these reasons a revolution in agriculture within ten years was unlikely to occur.

Early in the 1970s IITA launched its research efforts, training young African scientists as it moved forward. By 1980 (the end of my one-decade challenge) IITA had made substantial progress with new farming systems based on minimum tillage, requiring no plowing but control of weeds by chemicals. IITA had also gained the confidence of a few black African governments and received the cooperation of both francophone and anglophone researchers. On the debit side few African governments could afford the foreign exchange to import chemicals for weed control. And there had been famines in sub-Sahara Africa that had caused governments to be overthrown.

## Reflections on Africa

Much has been learned and written since my four years in black Africa, and better answers are now available to the question: Why does Africa suffer food shortages more often than any other continent?*

I now believe there are three reasons for the recurring African hunger: First, population is multiplying at the fastest annual rate of any continent in history (birth rate 46 per thousand, death rate 16 per thousand, net growth rate 30 per thousand in the 1980s). Second, Africa suffers soil erosion in most regions from the Mediterranean in the north to the Republic of South Africa. Third, many African governments have discriminated against agriculture in their investment programs. They have imposed low food prices to benefit city dwellers and failed to give incentives to farmers.

Africa's production of grain per person peaked in 1967—the year I arrived in Nigeria—at about one pound per person per day—and it has been falling ever since. Hunger is the result of population growing 3 percent a year and food output growing less than 2 percent. A population growing 3 percent a year will multiply its numbers twentyfold in a century—yes, twentyfold. That means Africa's half billion people in the 1980s could theoretically become 10 billion in a century—more than the present total world population. But long before that level is reached, either massive starvation would cut the numbers or governments would make effective changes in their agriculture.

But something even more frightening may be happening: population growth may be causing a change in the African climate. Here is how that works. A growing population cuts down more trees for fuel and converts old forests to cropland. Greater population causes overgrazing of grasslands. Both changes increase the runoff of rain water and reduce the evaporation of water that recharges the rain clouds. This not only reduces moisture for crops; the dry soil turns to dust and blows away, thus increasing soil erosion. More and more rainfall in Africa is believed to be flowing directly into the oceans.

What will it take to reverse this circle of deterioration? A realistic answer sounds alarmist. Africa needs massive reforestation, massive soil conservation, massive water storage, and massive family planning—all on a continental scale, larger than anything that Africa has known. The Peoples Republic of China is the only precedent for such massive agricultural reversal that comes to mind, and Africans have so far not shown discipline of the Chinese sort.

---

*One of the best brief analyses appears in the Worldwatch Society's pamphlet, *Reversing Africa's Decline* by Lester R. Brown and Edward C. Wolf, 1985.

The African situation is not hopeless, nor is it irreversible. Achievements in food production in Asia during the 1960s and 1970s offer encouragement that something can be done in Africa during the 1980s and 1990s. But the African program must be designed for Africa, not copied from Asia. It must give attention to these points:

• Technological breakthroughs are less likely in Africa than in Asia because Asia had better soils, better prospect for water control, and better labor productivity.

• Asia found it necessary to focus research on problems and regions where payoffs were most likely to occur. The same will be needed in Africa. That means favoring some areas and neglecting others.

• Fertilizer will be more important in Africa than in Asia because African soils are extremely low in nutrients.

• African crop research decisions will be more difficult than earlier choices in Asia, but there is no question that food production can be greatly accelerated. Research is still the key to success.

*International assistance involves risks and risks involve mistakes. If you have not made mistakes, you are not doing the job I sent you to do.*

Personal letter from F. F. Hill,
vice-president, the Ford Foundation, 1964

CHAPTER 27

# Nigeria: Biafrans

While we lived in Nigeria the biggest news was the Biafran war. The war lasted 30 months, from July 1967 to January 1970. At Lagos we felt the shock waves that struck the federal military government, but the fighting was far away. It was as though we observed the American Civil War (1861–1865) from New York City while the battle field was in faraway Mississippi. Despite the distance we were reminded daily of the Nigerian struggle—50 to 100 ships were anchored in Lagos harbor below my office window, waiting to unload war materials.

The Biafran war was a tribal catharsis. It was fought between the federal government and a minority tribe, the Ibos. The key issue was whether a tribal group should be allowed to secede from its nation; there were passionate Nigerian believers on each side. If Ibos were successful in seceding, it was widely predicted that other tribal wars would erupt throughout Africa, and decades would be lost in pacifying the continent.

I won't recount the Nigerian coups and counter-coups that preceded the Biafran war but will cite the flash point. On May 30, 1967 the military governor of the Eastern (Ibo) Region, Lt. Col. E. O. Ojukwu, proclaimed the independence of the "Republic of Biafra." General Gowon, as chief of state in Lagos, declared this a rebellion and sent armies into the field to reunify the country. Within one year the federal forces reduced the rebel area to one-quarter its original size, and Biafra became a landlocked enclave. The federal troops then paused for one year to await Biafra's collapse. This was the period when the world heard much about Biafran starvation. A final federal offensive in late 1969 produced a breakthrough and Biafra surrendered.

I had three involvements in the Biafran war. First, the Ford Foundation allotted me a discretionary sum of $25,000 a year for small grants of my own choosing. I devoted part of these funds to a mediation effort in the civil war. I had encountered in Lagos a Quaker group that was engaged in secret conciliation efforts between the federal government and Biafra. Even before the war started, the Quakers had interviewed General Gowon and Colonel Ojukwu and had reported the views of each side to the other. After fighting erupted, the mediators risked their lives flying chartered planes or planes loaded with illicit arms from the Portuguese island of Sao Tome to a secret airfield in Biafra. On each trip they talked with General Ojukwu, sometimes in his underground air raid shelter: on return they talked with General Gowon. They carried written messages between the two sides and eventually satisfied the Biafran leaders that General Gowon was sincere in offering total amnesty to Biafran rebels. Ford Foundation paid for these mediation trips, which were costly because the planes were insured against wartime loss. The mediation proved sufficiently useful that I would recommend a similar effort to any other Ford representative who is confronted by a civil war. Postscript: General Gowon fulfilled his promise of total amnesty to Biafrans.

My second involvement in the civil war failed. This was a proposal I worked out with the chief justice of the Nigerian Supreme Court, a 64-year-old, British-trained barrister named Adetokunbo Ademola. He was a law graduate of Cambridge University. What kind of constitutional conference in Nigeria, I asked him, might produce fresh ideas for restructuring the government at the end of the civil war, giving acceptable protection to minority tribes? The chief justice offered his own judgment: Call a conference of the chief justices from the major federal governments of the world—Great Britain, India, Pakistan, Australia, Canada, and the United States. These six men are familiar with most of the world's experience for protecting states' rights while maintaining effective federal unity.

Chief justice Ademola agreed to obtain approval for the conference from his own government and issued invitations to the chief justices from other governments. I calculated the cost at $50,000 and obtained approval for a Ford Foundation grant that was to be deposited in a Nigerian bank under control of chief justice Ademola. He said he obtained approval from General Gowon, but for reasons not known to me, the plan was not initially revealed to the military governors of the 12 Nigerian states. Justice Ademola had already received messages agreeing to participation by the six chief justices from outside Nigeria, including Chief Justice Earl Warren of the United States, when the 12 military governors rejected the plan. The idea was dropped.*

My third experience with Biafra occurred at the conclusion of fighting. Two days after the cease fire but before the signing of the armistice, Berni and I were invited to dinner in a Nigerian home in Lagos. Our host was head of the federal motion picture office, a man I knew well, and the hostess was the assistant curator of the Nigerian National Museum, a friend of Berni's. We were not warned that this would be an unusual evening.

When we arrived, the other guests were three Nigerian men in civilian clothes, unaccompanied by wives. We were the only foreigners. Nobody was introduced, which seemed odd. During drinks, the conversation indicated that the Nigerians in the room had known each other in newspaper work before the war but had not been together for some time. They asked about former colleagues.

Berni made some small talk and then speculated what would happen when the first Ibos arrived in Lagos. Would their presence provoke violence? One of the guests exploded, "What do you mean? Is our presence causing any violence?" Another guest asserted, "You talk like a British colonial, stirring up trouble between Nigerians."

Only then did the hostess intervene apologetically to explain that the guests were Biafran army officers, a colonel and two majors. They had left the fighting lines two days earlier, commandeered a taxi at Benin and arrived in Lagos before the armistice. No federal road guards had stopped them. Here they were in the federal capital—not yet pardoned for their role in the rebellion but enjoying the hospitality of old friends. We were incredulous at the instant reconciliation.

I tried to imagine a similar situation in Washington, D.C. at the end of the American Civil War. Three officers set out in 1865 from Richmond, the rebel capital, before the armistice; they drive by horse-drawn carriage into Washington without being stopped and are invited to dinner by old friends on the Union side. Was it possible? I doubt it. But here in Nigeria the chief of state, General Yakubu Gowon, had promised total amnesty, and he was trusted.

---

*When I recounted this story to a Nigerian official, his comment was "Wawa." That is a common acronym in west Africa from the English expression "West Africa wins again." Frustrated residents say "Wawa" when appointments fall through, or the telephone line goes dead, or an airline flight is cancelled. This is a cynical indication that plans in west Africa are often unsuccessful.

*Above:* Cultivating rice in China, 1935. *Below:* Farmers helped to feed the guerillas.

Two foreign school teachers in Shansi Province in 1935: Bernice Brown (Hanson), left, and Josephine Hamilton. *Below*: Wheelbarrows moved the grain supply in 1936.

Foreign technicians at the University of Nanking (*above*) testing a hand-propelled fanning machine to save peasants' harvest time, 1936. *Below:* Spiked guard on a river boat prevented pirates from climbing from steerage to first class.

*Above:* A third-class rail coach, 1936. *Below:* Marco Polo Bridge, where the Japanese-Chinese War began in 1937.

The author with General
Wei Li-huang, commander
in Shansi for Chiang
Kai-shek, 1938. *Below:*
Students of "Resist Japan
University" gather below
the Yenan pagoda, 1938.

*Above:* "Little devils," the Red Army orderlies. *Below:* A schoolboy reads my passport for the guerillas. *Opposite:* A mass meeting of thousands, 1938.

*Above:* Women organizers from Peking universities supporting the guerillas. *Below:* Red Army generals and one administrator, 1938.

Yenan: Mao Zedong after his cave interview, 1938. *Below:* The guerilla theater displayed both communist and nationalist flags.

Canadian doctors Richard Brown (left) and Norman Bethune (right) provided surgical services to guerillas in Wutai. *Below:* This ferryman and his barge carried our horses and Eighth Route Army escort across the flooded Hu To River in Hungtsetien.

*Above:* Arcola Corner, Virginia, where Senator McCarthy stirred up fear of communists, 1950. *Right:* The Hanson farmhouse near Arcola, Virginia.

Courtesy of *New York Post*

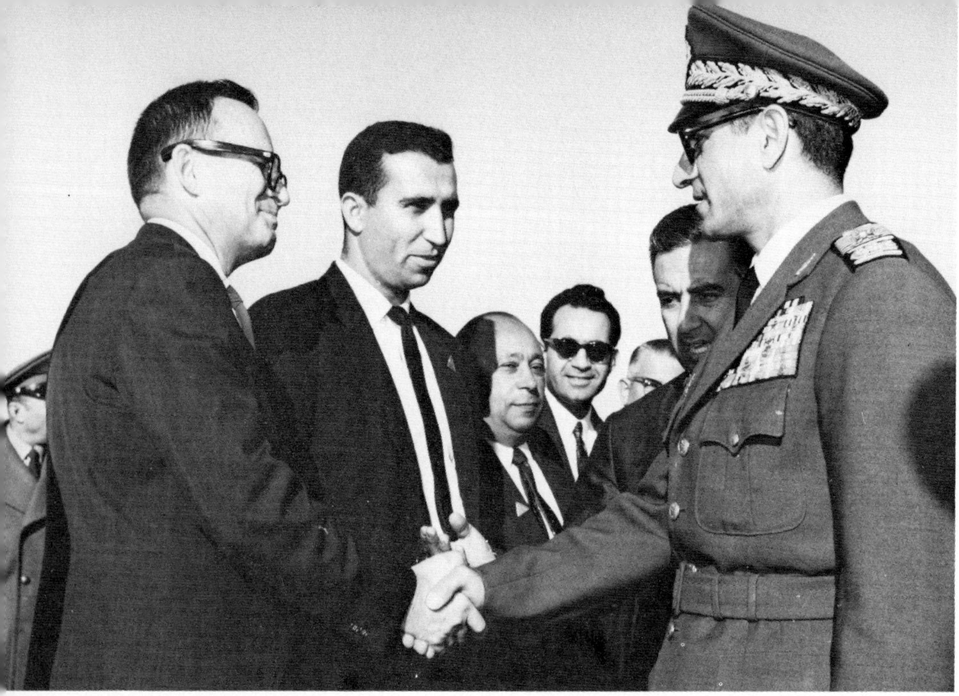

Courtesy of Resources and Development Corporation

*Above:* The author with the king of Iran (1941–1979), Mohammed Reza Shah Pahlavi, 1960. *Below:* Dez Dam in Khuzestan Province, Iran, highest in Asia.

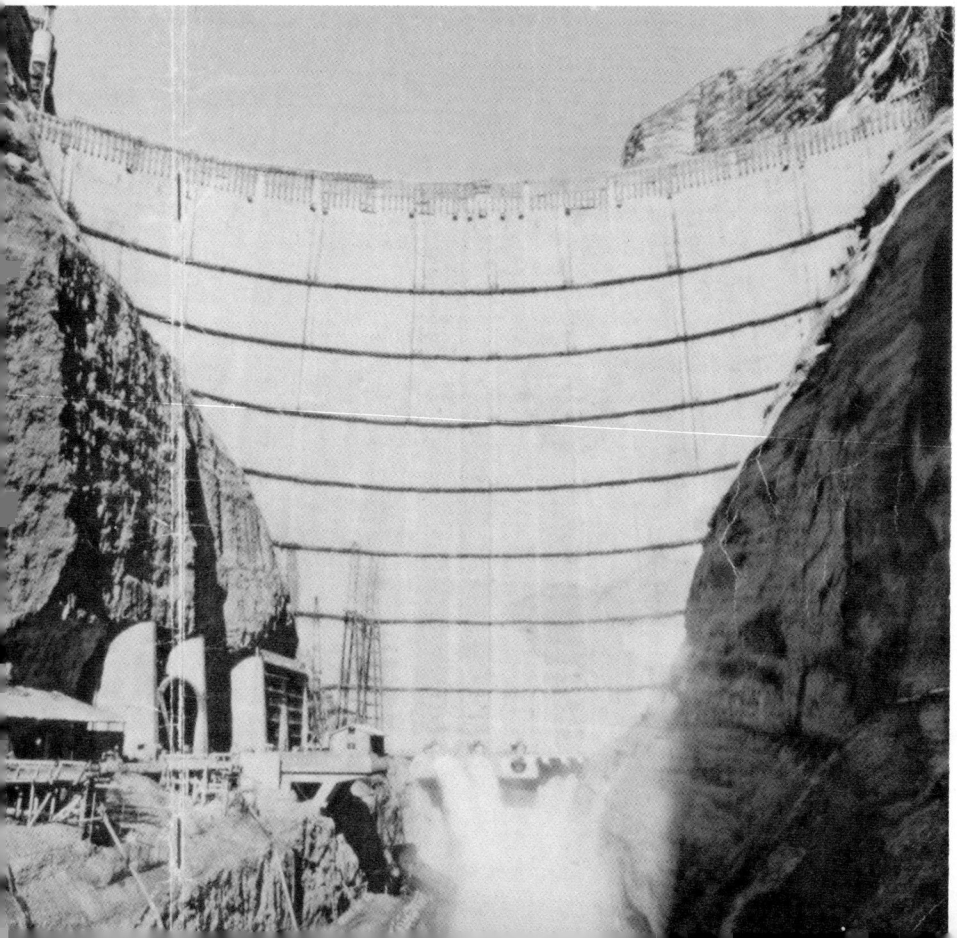

Courtesy of Resources and Development Corporation

President Ayub Khan of Pakistan in 1966, at the height of his success. *Below:* CIMMYT Research Center, 30 miles northeast of Mexico City.

Courtesy of CIMMYT, Mexico

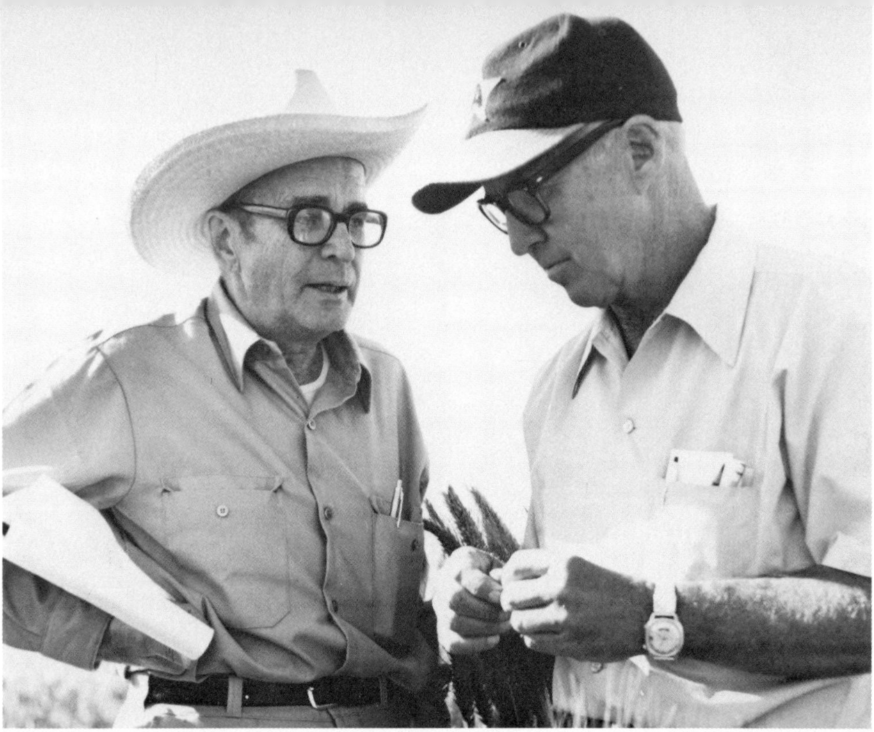

*Above:* The author (left) discussing wheat research with Norman Borlaug, 1973.
*Below:* Elmer Johnson, CIMMYT maize breeder, examines his short maize plant with third world training fellows.

Courtesy of CIMMYT, Me

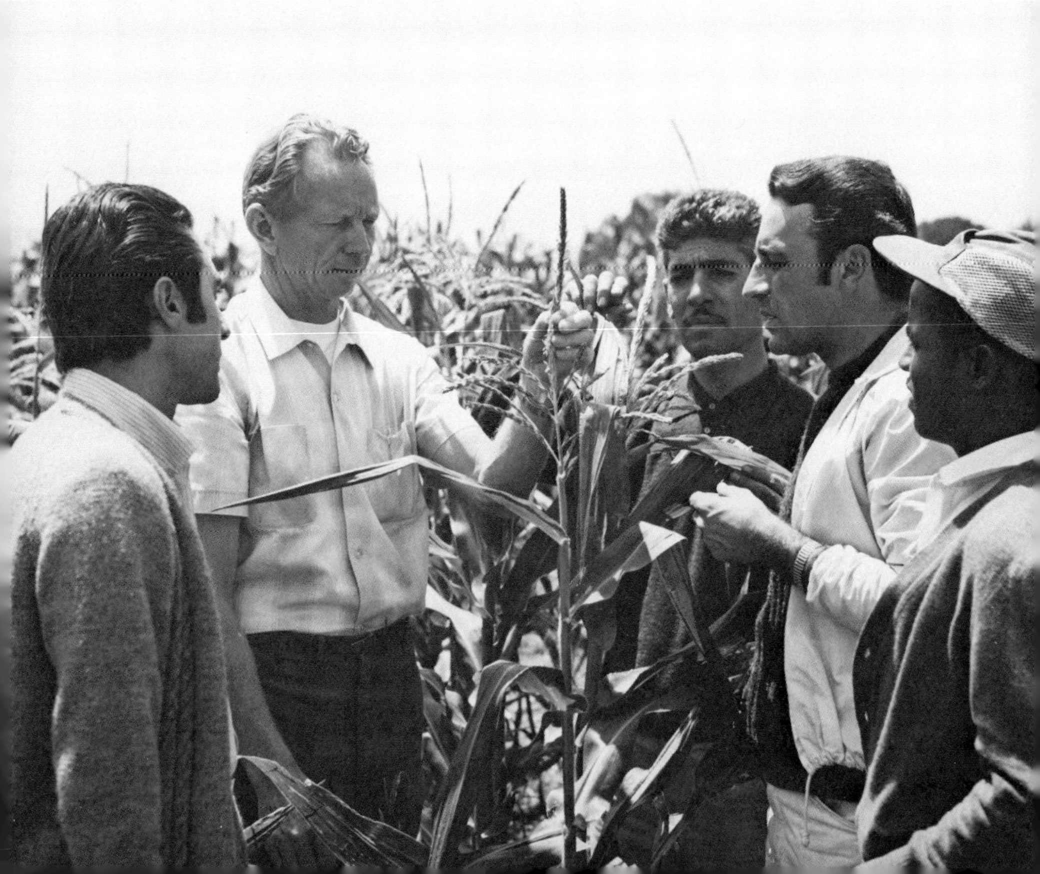

Another who "got rich": This Guizhou peasant woman paid for a new house in four years running a dumpling restaurant. *Below:* A peasant-contructed aquaduct doubled the income of 400 villages (both Chapter 45).

*Above:* The author revisiting Yenan in 1983. *Right:* Gazelle carvings in the author's African art collection.

> *Our coinage system was among the earliest, and the* **golden** *daric and* **silver** *siglos of Darius the Great, corresponding almost exactly in weight with the modern English sovereign and shilling, were the standard of the ancient world.*
>
> Mohammed Reza Shah Pahlavi, 1961

CHAPTER 28

# A Compulsive Collector

My favorite diversion during four years in west Africa was collecting tribal art, especially wood carvings. And in south Asia my passion was ancient coins. I had been an avid collector all my life, and now directed my gatherer's instinct toward the most remarkable collector's items at hand—African carvings.

Our wood carvings—which eventually numbered 400—included face masks and head masks from the harvest dances; family ancestor figures, generally a grandfather-grandmother pair; Yoruba twin statues, called *Ibeji*; and chief's stools from Cameroon with the seat upheld by a leopard carved from a single block.

Our largest carving is installed in our home in Mexico. This is a carved door from a house in the middle belt of Nigeria, acquired in a town called Agaie. According to its owner, the door carried a fascinating folk history. When the Arab armies marched across North Africa in the eighth century and conquered Spain, a splinter army of Arabs turned south in Algeria, crossed the territory of modern Mali and Niger and reached the middle belt of Nigeria. Here a great battle took place between Arabs and Africans, and the Arabs were defeated. Instead of going home, many Arabs settled down and intermarried with blacks. To commemorate this merger of two cultures, we were told, a special door was designed: half the door was covered with African animist carvings of animals, birds, and humans and the other half with Muslim symbols like the dagger, powder horn, water flask, and fly whisk of Arab troops. In the 1960s, more than 1000 years after the battle, almost every home in Agaie had one of these doors. I rapped on the door of a home and with interpreter's help from my Nigerian driver, I asked the lady of the house if she would sell me her door. She pointed to the bottom of the door where termites had already eaten away an inch or two. Yes, she said, if I paid her a few pounds, she could get a new door from the woodcarver, and I could take the old one.

African art is connected with the spirit world. At Lagos we had a Cameroonian cook named Philip who was familiar with the practices for appeasing village spirits. When I brought home from Cameroon a wooden statue of a monkey spirit about one meter high and set it in the dining room, Philip said it was very powerful and we should take great care with it. Thereafter he kept a peanut in the monkey god's mouth and walked past it only on the opposite side of the room.

In the state of Western Nigeria we visited the sacred grove of the Yoruba animist religion at Oshogbo by invitation of Susanne Wenger, an Austrian artist. She had taken up residence in Nigeria and had become a high priestess of the Oshun cult. She asked a ten-year-old boy to guide us across a bridge over the river Oshun near the sacred grove. But when the boy was halfway across the bridge, he froze, turned abruptly and—abandoning us—ran as fast as he could back to his house. He later explained he feared an encounter with the spirits near the grove.

At the same grove we saw small stone figures of women, about half a meter high, placed beside the river. If a village woman comes to collect a bucket of water, we were told, she is likely to be attacked by an evil spirit from the water. The stone statues would protect her. We purchased two of the stone figures, and they now guard our home in Mexico. Berni is sometimes asked if she believes in African spirits. "No," she replies, "but I play both sides."

One of the fringe benefits of the Ford Foundation assignment in Nigeria was that distinguished visitors stopped to see us.

On a Sunday afternoon in 1970 our phone rang about 6 P.M. Our caller said, "This is Bob McNamara of the World Bank. Can you and your wife join us at the hotel for dinner?" He was a Ford Foundation trustee and President Bundy had suggested he discuss the foundation grants in west Africa. Over dinner McNamara said he admired African art and that he had just acquired a rare grave carving from Gabon, the French-speaking republic on the African coast a little south of Nigeria. We went to his hotel room to inspect the piece. When I told him I had recently returned from Cameroon with a trunkful of art objects that I had not yet unpacked, he asked to see them. We spent the rest of the evening in our basement, carefully unpacking spirit figures. I admired his interest in African art.

In the Iranian Khuzestan, as mentioned earlier, our land-levelling machines inadvertently tore open ancient graves that contained relics, including clay pots of coins. Most coins were Elamite—2,000 to 2,500 years old, a quarter inch in diameter, usually depicting a bewhiskered Elamite king with a star and crescent over his crown. No one else in our organization was interested in coins, so our laborers gladly accepted from me a few modern rials for each handful of old coppers. In two years I collected 3,000 specimens.

Later in Tehran, I found jewelry shops with silver coins of Alexander the Great—the *drachma*, size of an American dime, and the *tetradrachma*, the size of an American half-dollar. (Alexander lived from 356 to 323 B.C.) Tehrani jewellers melted down these Alexandrians to make modern jewelry for Iranian women, so it was possible to buy coins by the ounce for the current price of silver bullion. I bought about 100 silver pieces at prices that ranged from US$.10 to US$1.00 each. Their true value has no doubt by now been discovered.

In Pakistan my coin collecting was again stimulated when I visited Taxila. Taxila is an old capital of Alexander the Great, located about 20 miles northwest of modern Islamabad. It is now a ruin of foundations a quarter mile square, located on a slight rise. There is a small museum there, but something more important to me—farmers who till the surrounding fields constantly discover coins in the soil. If a visitor were to stand for a few minutes on the front steps of this ancient site, a farmer would walk from the fields, draw from his pocket a folded rag and display a small collection of ancient coins, usually a mixture of silver and copper. I never saw a gold coin here although gold coins existed in Alexander's day.

In Pakistani jewelry stores at Peshawar and Lahore I found collections of Alexandrian *drachma*, all green with patina and looking truly ancient. But when I cleaned some of them with acid, I discovered they were reproductions, cast by the same jewellers who sold them. I asked one jeweler how he produced the green oxidation. Easy, he said. He had pushed the dime-size coin down the throat of a chicken; when the coin came out with the droppings, the acid of the intestinal tract had caused the green color.

On my last visit to Taxila—just before the end of my Pakistan assignment—a village boy showed me some exciting silver coins, and I offered to buy them all. Then it occurred to me to ask if he had others. Yes, he said, he had a hoard at his home. We drove to his village a few miles distant, and there he produced a lump of coins, the size of a grapefruit, mostly coppers stuck together. We had no time to break them apart and count them because my plane was about to depart from Rawalpindi. How much did he want? He said 10,000 rupees which was probably the largest sum he could imagine. I gave him a one thousand rupee note (US$140), and he jumped with joy. That hoard still sits in a closet drawer awaiting my retirement and an appraisal of their value. I don't think they are fakes, but they may be.

> *When an individual enters a strange culture, he or she is like a fish out of water. A series of props have been knocked out from under the person; this causes a feeling of frustration and anxiety.*

Dr. Kalervo Oberg, 1962

CHAPTER 29

# Culture Shock and the Ten Commandments

Technical assistance is an ancient occupation. My illustrious predecessors included Joseph of Egypt in the *Old Testament*, the Israelite who organized a 14-year famine relief scheme for an Egyptian king; the Greek architects who built a palace for Cyrus the Great at Shush in Elam, now southwest Iran; Marco Polo, employed as counsellor and negotiator for the Mongol warrior, Kublai Khan; and the Dutch craftsmen who constructed industries in Russia for Peter the Great.

Those of us who continue this ancient occupation in the twentieth century have no illusion that we can match our predecessors, but we experience the same frustrations that those earlier foreign advisors must have encountered. A few of our accomplishments, I like to think, compare favorably with the achievements of the earlier men—for example, the introduction of semidwarf wheat into Pakistan and India.

Culture shock is a common affliction among Americans who work overseas—an occupational disease, a state of depression triggered by anxiety from losing most familiar symbols of communication. These symbols include the hundreds of ways in which we orient ourselves: how we greet people, how we give orders or make suggestions, how we recognize whether statements are true or not. The cues may be gestures, facial expressions, or customs acquired in the course of growing up; they are as much a part of us as the language we speak. Our peace of mind depends on them.

When one enters a strange culture, these cues change. One feels anxious. The reaction of most persons to this frustration is similar. First, he or she blames the surroundings that cause the discomfort: the host country must be bad because it makes the newcomer feel bad. So he grouses. Second, one's memories of American life become glorified. One forgets all the shortcomings of home, and remembers only the good things. The person in culture shock becomes a superpatriot.

Some symptoms of culture shock are excessive washing of hands, excessive worry about food and drinking water, fits of anger over minor frustrations, great concern about little pains and, finally, a terrible longing to be back home, to get a "real" cup of coffee and to talk to people who "really make sense."

Individuals differ in their passage through shock, but those of us who have watched many new arrivals abroad have come to recognize some common stages. I like the diagnosis of the American anthropologist, Dr. Kalervo Oberg, whom I met in Brazil. During the first few weeks after arrival in a strange culture, Oberg observed, most individuals are fascinated by their surroundings. They associate with local nationals who speak English and are gracious. This honeymoon stage may last several weeks.

The second stage is characterized by a hostile and aggressive attitude toward the host country. The antagonism grows out of difficulties in adjustment—language trouble, housing trouble, transport trouble, shopping trouble, school trouble, servant trouble. Nationals of the host country seem largely indifferent; therefore they must be unsympathetic. The conclusion: "I just don't like them." The newcomer becomes aggressive. He joins his fellow countrymen at cocktail parties where much of the conversation is critical of the host country. This is the crisis stage of the disease.

In the third stage the newcomer regains his sense of humor. He jokes about his own difficulties. He is now on the way to recovery. He discovers other poor devils who are worse off than himself.

In the fourth stage, one's recovery is complete. The newcomer accepts the customs of the host country as a normal way of living. He participates in this new environment without a feeling of anxiety. He not only accepts the food, drink, habits and customs; he begins to enjoy them.

A story is told about adjustment to culture shock. A coffee drinker in a third world restaurant finds a fly in his coffee. In the first month, he calls the waiter and indignantly orders a second cup. In the second month, he removes the fly with a spoon and drinks the coffee. (Moral: Learn to accept the inevitable.)

This description of the stages of shock is oversimplified. Some difficulties for the individual are not fantasy; they are very real. Most newcomers suffer some intestinal disturbance. The change of food and water may upset people. The bureaucracy of government is irritating when the newcomer presents himself for the first time at the police station for a driver's permit, or at the immigration office for a residence permit, or at the health ministry for a dog license. When these irritations are added to those arising from not knowing how to communicate, anxieties are understandable.

Problems of the husbands in shock apply equally to their wives—in fact some anthropologists believe culture shock affects wives even more. The husband's duties may not differ greatly from his previous work at home. The wife, on the other hand, must operate in a third world environment (read kitchen and market) that differs much more from her home community; hence the strain of her adjustment is greater.

In my office the question often arose: What can the newcomer do to speed recovery from culture shock? The answer is to get to know the people of the host country—but one cannot do this in many places without learning the language. Some shortcuts are possible. Going shopping with an English-speaking national gets the newcomer started. Reading is a help. Entertaining English-speaking nationals has its value. Local sightseeing is refreshing. Those in shock gradually learn to cope.

Describing culture shock will not remove the pain, but knowing the source of pain is useful. The newcomer can be assured that the passage of time will set things right.

In Pakistan I became a strong believer in Orientation Week, which I later introduced in west Africa. This started as an annual gathering of our 50 Ford Foundation families—husbands, wives, and teen-age children—at an isolated hotel like Swat in the Himalayas. Here the group discussed why we were in Pakistan, the progress we were enjoying in our programs, and the mistakes we had made. We diagnosed culture shock. We invited Pakistani officials to tell the group how they viewed Pakistani development problems. Then we asked our foreign technicians to describe their work. Richard Gilbert, the leader in Pakistan of the Harvard Development Advisory Service, was especially good at presenting the government's budget limitations and how they affected our assignments. Some staff wives described how they coped with household problems. Orientation Week revitalized the work of the staff. It enabled us foreigners to step back from our assignments once a year and to rethink what we were doing.

I recall the half-day staff discussion I organized each year on the subject, "Ten Commandments for Foreign Technicians." The idea came from a book I had read in college titled, *Ten Marks of an Educated Man*. If we had a dependable scale for weighing the effectiveness of Americans abroad, I suggested, we might find that 10 percent of our staff were makers of history, another 10 percent were outright failures, and the remaining 80 percent were distributed in between. Since we had no such scale for determining effectiveness, I proposed ten commandments, and each participant in the gathering could score himself or herself. The ten commandments that follow evolved gradually over the years I led this discussion in Asia and Africa.

*Commandment No. 1. Don't criticize the third world. Don't argue.* You are a foreign guest in the third world and you should conduct yourself with the manners you expect from a guest in your own home. Don't comment critically on local religion. Be sensitive to local attitudes. Wives and daughters should not wear miniskirts or sunback dresses in a country where local women wear skirts to their ankles and veil their faces. Observe local laws scrupulously. Foreigners are held more accountable than local citizens. Drive your car according to posted speed limit. Avoid black market currency.

*Commandment No. 2. Learn about your third world post.* Read its history and the local press. Travel about the country of assignment. Listen to all kinds of people, from the mighty in the power structure down to your household gardener.

*Commandment No. 3. Identify with your third world country.* Cultivate an enthusiasm for some local foods. Wear some local clothing (perhaps western sportshirts tailored from local fabrics). Mix words from the local language with your English, even though you probably don't have time to acquire full fluency in a local tongue. Attend some local festivals and sporting events. Say "we" when you wish to associate yourself with the local people. These gestures are appreciated.

*Commandment No. 4. Accept with tolerance the behavior in the third world that is irritating to a westerner.* A local man will crowd in front of you in the queue for the bank teller. A pedestrian will clear his throat noisily and spit on the ground, missing your shoe by inches. A Muslim night watchman may pray loudly beneath your bedroom window in the middle of the night. A high official will ask you at a dinner party how much you paid for your suit.

*Commandment No. 5. Speak slowly and clearly when you converse with a person for whom English is a second language.* Avoid slang; it is confusing to local people. This is a courtesy.

*Commandment No. 6. Avoid discussion of unpleasant weather.* Dry heat in western Asia and humid heat in southeast Asia or west Africa can exasperate anyone; but the person who complains about the weather increases his own discomfort.

*Commandment No. 7. Safeguard your health against local hazards.* Take the inoculations recommended by your office. Protect yourself against hepatitis and malaria where these are local problems. Use boiled drinking water in the home if local water is of doubtful purity.

*Commandment No. 8. Make your private life in the third world even more circumspect than you would at home.* Use alcohol moderately. Avoid ostentation in housing and spending. The foreigner who remains inconspicuous is less likely to be a victim of public comment.

*Commandment No. 9. Learn to accomplish things through a slow-moving bureaucracy.* That requires familiarity with the government structure, the budget process and the procedures for appointing and promoting local employees.

*Commandment No. 10. Modify your western judgments to fit the needs of a third world government.* Be cautious, for example, about pushing labor-saving equipment in a country with high unemployment. Avoid sophisticated plans in a country that lacks trained administrators. Forget the cliché, "In Peoria, we do it this way."

I carried these commandments to my next assignment—in Mexico.

*If you don't know the five grains,
you don't know anything.*

Confucius

PART FIVE

# PLANT BREEDING FOR THE THIRD WORLD

Most Americans have never heard of CIMMYT (pronounced Sim'-it), the Spanish acronym for International Maize and Wheat Improvement Center. CIMMYT is a research institute located 30 miles northeast of Mexico City airport, near the town of Texcoco. A passing motorist on the highway to Vera Cruz would see only 200 acres of green research crops, an office building standing well back from the road, some 50 apartments occupied by visiting scientists from many countries and a two-story dormitory that houses 60 foreign trainees. Even if we add CIMMYT's five other research sites in Mexico, the combined area is only 1100 acres—less than two square miles.

In 1971 I received a cable in Nigeria inviting me to become director general of CIMMYT. I had previously worked with CIMMYT scientists in Pakistan, and I admired their practical, dirty-hands approach. There was no other organization working for the third world that I would rather have joined. If I show pride in the stories that follow, it is because the worldwide achievements of CIMMYT's 80 scientists seem incredible when compared to their modest resources. Since 1962, governments around the world have released to their farmers more than 300 semidwarf spring wheat varieties based on CIMMYT breeding. In the mid-1980s the increased annual harvest from the CIMMYT-related wheats was estimated conservatively at 65 million tons a year, valued at more than 10 billion dollars. These achievements earned CIMMYT the controversial title "home of the green revolution."

I accepted the CIMMYT offer, and took up my duties January 1, 1972. But first Ford Foundation granted me three months to wind up my responsibilities in west Africa. The foundation also approved an additional three months to read up on my new duties. The latter included a month of intensive Spanish language study. (I previously had had no Spanish.) The language preparation proved inadequate and remained a handicap throughout my years at CIMMYT.*

The CIMMYT story began in 1940, when President Roosevelt sent his newly elected vice president, Henry A. Wallace, to Mexico to represent the United States at the inauguration of a new Mexican president. Wallace was identified with the agricultural revolution in the United States through his farm journal, *Wallace's Farmer*, and his seed company, which grew into Pioneer Inc., the nation's largest producer of agricultural seed. Wallace told the Mexicans that he hoped the United States would help Mexico establish agricultural research stations. But on returning to the United States, he found Congress took no interest in his proposal in the midst of World War II. So Wallace approached the president of the Rockefeller Foundation, Raymond Fosdick, knowing that the foundation was already assisting Mexico in public health.

Responding, the foundation sent to Mexico in 1941 a survey mission of three prominent American scientists. The group concluded that Rockefeller could do much to improve Mexican food production.

In 1943, as a second step, the foundation chose 35-year-old J. George Harrar, a plant pathologist from Washington State University, to organize within Mexico's ministry of agriculture a research operation called the Office of Special Studies. Here Harrar surrounded himself with a group of young American plant scientists—about 20 of them in their early thirties. What this group and their Mexican associates accomplished over a period of two decades not only changed Mexico but also altered world agriculture and probably caused Harrar to be chosen president of the foundation.

By the mid-1960s, having developed new crop technology that more than doubled Mexico's food output and trained some 500 Mexican scientists to

---

*CIMMYT experience with language study indicates that scientists engaged in agricultural field research, supervising Spanish-speaking laborers, will acquire their needed language skills with a minimum of classroom study because their language is in daily use. By contrast, CIMMYT officers who engage mainly in desk work have difficulty in acquiring the professional Spanish appropriate to their contacts with the Mexican government because their correspondence, phone calls, and visitors nearly all use English; their secretaries are bilingual and their travel outside Mexico is principally in areas where English is required.

carry on the work, the Rockefeller group had essentially worked itself out of a Mexican job. Their research activity was thereafter converted into a worldwide center—called the International Maize and Wheat Improvement Center (CIMMYT) to serve the wheat and maize crops in developing countries.

At the time I arrived, CIMMYT had a strong directing staff of scientists, including:

*Norman Borlaug*, age 57, an American plant pathologist trained at Minnesota, heading CIMMYT's 25 wheat scientists.

*Glenn Anderson*, age 48, a Canadian plant breeder trained at the University of Saskatchewan, associate director of CIMMYT's wheat scientists. He had served as joint coordinator of wheat improvement in India for seven years.

*Ernest Sprague*, age 47, an American plant breeder trained at Cornell, leader of CIMMYT's 25 maize scientists.

*Don Winklemann*, age 40, an American agricultural economist trained at Iowa State, head of the economics staff. He had been a professor for five years at Mexico's Postgraduate School of Agriculture.

*Robert Osler*, age 47, an American maize breeder trained at Minnesota; he was deputy director and treasurer of CIMMYT.

*Keith Finley*, age 47, an Australian barley breeder, deputy director of CIMMYT.

The combined professional experience of the six leaders amounted to 140 man-years, more than half that time spent in Mexico or other third world countries. They had firsthand experience in farming, forestry, university teaching, plant breeding, and supervision of government research and extension. I could be confident that CIMMYT's research and training work were well supervised.

My two deputy directors, one for research and one for administration, took off my desk most of the problems connected with 600 employees in Mexico, with the testing of crops on about 1000 acres, and with training courses for about 120 foreign trainees. The senior scientists needed no instructions from me on what to do. But I soon learned that I had residual duties that a Chinese might call the "six outsides." These were CIMMYT's relations to trustees, to donors, to the Mexican government, to visitors and the press, to sister research institutes, and to the "CG" secretariat (explained later).

1. The trustees were 15 distinguished persons who served collectively as the boss of the CIMMYT director. The CIMMYT board of trustees was a

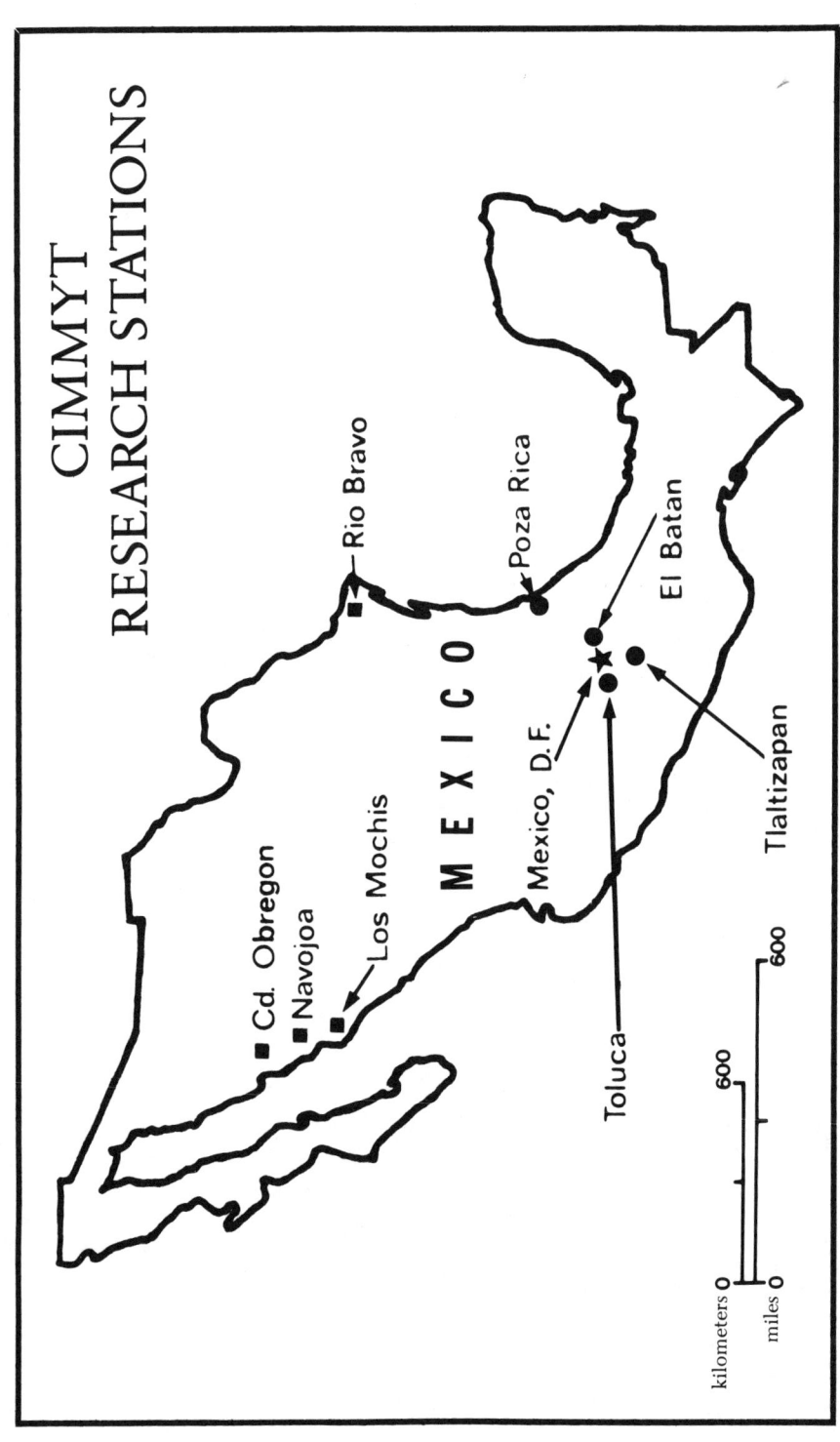

self-perpetuating body that elected its own replacement members. The trustees have included persons of such world prominence as the presidents of Colombia and Ecuador; the foreign ministers of India, Thailand, and the Philippines; and the agricultural ministers of Mexico, India, Sudan, Egypt, Brazil and Argintina. The trustees met twice a year to pass judgment on CIMMYT's program and budget.

2. Donors who supported CIMMYT included about 15 national and international agencies. To get money, CIMMYT had to justify its needs. The donor agencies, on their side, had to explain to their congress or their governing body what benefits they expected to achieve by giving money to CIMMYT. The soliciting of grants was an annual affair. CIMMYT started with less than $1 million a year from a single donor—the Rockefeller Foundation. In my period the budget rose to $12 million and the additional donors included the World Bank, the Inter-American Development Bank, the United Nations Development Program, and the national governments of the United States, Canada, Great Britain and about ten others.

3. The government of Mexico posed a delicate relationship. We used Mexican research stations, and they used our germ plasm for wheat and maize. That sounds like an easy swap. But if you happened to be a middle-level Mexican scientist in a Mexican research agency that could not offer the same salary and perquisites, or the same equipment, or gain the same publicity as the international center down the road, you might feel some grievance. Genuine diplomacy was needed on the part of CIMMYT. This relationship was eased partially by the appointment of the Mexican minister of agriculture and his director of research as CIMMYT trustees.

4. Sister research centers included 12 institutions financed by many of the same donors. There was a rice research center in the Philippines, a sorghum center in India, and ten others. Yet the sister-like relationship concealed many problems. Donors asked why sister organizations did not adopt a common salary scale. The answer was that the centers were located in countries with different national economies. Sisters can sometimes be competitive; three of these centers worked on rice, two on maize, and two on wheat. The sisters borrowed facilities from each other: for example, CIMMYT placed several of its staff at the headquarters of centers in Colombia, Nigeria, and Kenya. These arrangements were not convenient when a center was short of space.

5. Visitors and the press were a continuing responsibility. CIMMYT received over 3000 visitors a year, including trustees, donor representatives, Mexican officials, press and magazine journalists, researchers from other research centers, hundreds of university professors and their students from all over the world, and—you wouldn't guess it—busloads of American farmers. In my first year at CIMMYT, I organized a visitors office that steered arrivals

to the appropriate staff members. Many of these visitors asked to meet the director, and they were of such importance to CIMMYT that the director ought to see them, no matter how tight his schedule. So one of my most time-consuming functions was to give briefings on world hunger, population growth, plant breeding, and the experiences of CIMMYT staff in assisting more than 100 governments in the third world.

6. The "CG" relationship was our relationship with a group of our donors called the Consultative Group for International Agricultural Research, or CGIAR. The secretariat for this body was located in the World Bank in Washington. One of its important functions was to gather from the 13 centers their annual budget requests and to present these budgets in consolidated form to the donors at their funding meeting. By a series of negotiations, donors indicated how much they would contribute to each center. The secretariat helped allocate the funds so that each center received—if possible—the budget recommended by its trustees. Even though the total pledges of the donors have risen from $20 million (1971) to about $200 million (mid-1980s), there still is rivalry for increased funding. (I will say more about the CG in Chapter 31.)

I travelled four months each year for CIMMYT and Berni often accompanied me. This may seem a lot, but some of our directing staff were on international airlines six to nine months a year.

Our travel began with visits to donors—to the World Bank in Washington, the UNDP in New York, and national capitals such as London, Bonn, and Berne. The next trips took us to interview future trustee candidates or to learn about sister research institutes. The greatest number of trips—and some of the most fascinating—were to third world agricultural research centers in remote places unfamiliar to the hardiest American tourist. What tourist has visited Karaj, a wheat research center in Iran, west of Tehran, or Darul Aman, a wheat center in Afghanistan, or Pirzabak, a maize station in Pakistan? In Africa we stopped at Kenyan stations for wheat (Njoro) and maize (Kitale). In Zaire we spent a week at a maize station near Lubumbashi, called Elizabethville by the Belgians in colonial days.

At each of these stops we followed a similar routine. We called on the ministry of agriculture. We walked through the research plots, most often under a tropical sun, taking notes on a briefing by the national research director. We talked about CIMMYT's work with the local press. We received (or gave) a farewell dinner attended by the local research staff, many of whom were friends because they had received training in Mexico.

Occasionally we accompanied CIMMYT scientists on their travel rounds.

Norman Borlaug shared his wheat travels in Argentina; Ernie Sprague accompanied us through a maize review of India and Pakistan; Alex Violic, the CIMMYT training officer for maize, showed us through his native Chile; and Art Klatt, wheat breeder, travelled with us in Colombia and Ecuador.

We sharpened our impressions by attending week-long workshops for scientists: once for six maize-growing countries of Central America, another time for the wheat-growing countries of northern Africa and the mideast.

Then I would return to Mexico to a desk piled high with unanswered correspondence and unopened agricultural journals. Observations from these travels found a place in my annual report to donors, or in press interviews with visiting journalists in Mexico. There was no slack season.

## *Reflections*

In 1978 I completed seven years as director general of CIMMYT at age 66 and handed over leadership to an American successor, Robert Havener, age 48, an Ohio State graduate who had worked 17 years on problems of the third world, mostly in Pakistan and the mideast.

The most significant measurement of CIMMYT's effectiveness in my opinion was the rising production of wheat and maize in the third world. During the decade from the mid-1960s to the mid-1970s, population in the third world rose 30 percent, while wheat production in the third world rose 50 percent and maize production 38 percent—both well ahead of population.

I predicted to the trustees that if governments gave adequate attention to agriculture, the world grain supply could stay ahead of population growth—even if the numbers of people in the world doubled in 45 years from 4 billion to 8 billion between 1975 and 2020. I was using the current projection of demographers based on growth rates of the 1970s.

But averages conceal great differences between countries. The biggest problem of the 1980s and 1990s is to help lagging countries—especially in tropical Africa—to raise their food production at a rate faster than their population increases.

A precarious balance between food and population is the best that we can expect until a demographic equilibrium is reached—and even then the uncertainties of weather will remain. The contribution that CIMMYT scientists can make to solving this problem is best illustrated by our experience with wheat—a story that comes next.

*The greatest service that can be rendered any country is to add a useful plant to its culture—especially a bread grain.*

Thomas Jefferson, 1821

CHAPTER 30

# Dr. Borlaug Receives a Nobel Peace Prize

In 1944, a 30-year-old American named Norman Borlaug arrived in Mexico to join the group of Rockefeller Foundation scientists. Borlaug was an Iowan of medium height, erect, lean, from Norwegian immigrant stock. He had studied forestry at the University of Minnesota to become a forest ranger, but his professors persuaded him to switch to a doctorate in plant pathology, which he completed in 1941. Borlaug's chief professor was Charles Stakman, a world authority on diseases of wheat, especially the rusts. Stakman recommended Borlaug for the Mexico assignment because the area was a "hot spot" for wheat rust, and he thought Borlaug had the stubborness to cope with one of the world's most difficult agricultural problems.*

On arrival Borlaug found a Mexican economy that was primarily agricultural, but food production was stagnant and the country was importing half its wheat and 20 percent of its total cereals. Fields had been cultivated for hundreds of years with virtually no replenishment of soil nutrients. Crops were ravaged by almost every known disease and insect. Most farmers were illiterate. The Mexican population was increasing at a rate that would double it in 25 years. Under these circumstances what could a plant researcher do?

To gain perspective, let's look at the development of plant improvement and how breeders produce new varieties today. Until 12,000 years ago man was a wild grain gatherer. Dr. Jack Harlan, professor of plant genetics at the University of Illinois, told me this story. On a mountainside in southeastern Turkey he located a good stand of wild einkorn wheat, a primitive ancestor of

---

*Most of the information in this chapter was told me by Dr. Borlaug when we served as coauthors of a book, *Wheat in the Third World* by Hanson, Borlaug, and Anderson, 1982.

the modern bread cereal. Using first his bare hands and then a flint-blade sickle, he harvested two kilograms of grain an hour (4.4 pounds). From this he calculated that a Stone Age family, working slowly up this same slope, could have harvested in three weeks more grain than the family could eat in a year. Professor Harlan's Stone Age yield was not very different from that of many developing countries in the twentieth century—that is, a harvest of 500 to 800 kilograms a hectare (or 8 to 13 bushels an acre).

Roughly 12,000 years ago there appeared in different regions of the world the most successful plant and animal breeders the world has ever known—the Neolithic domesticators. Within a geological period of 20 to 30 centuries, Neolithic man and woman domesticated all the major cereals, grain legumes, root crops and animal species that remain our principal sources of food. Archeological evidence suggests that wheat and barley were first planted in western Asia between the Himalayas and the Mediterranean, millet in northwestern China, rice in southern China, sorghum in northeastern Africa, and maize in middle America—probably in Mexico. Cultivation spread rapidly from the various points of origin across vast areas of Asia, Africa, and the Americas.

From the time plants were domesticated until the nineteenth century, farmers were in charge of crop improvement; they saved their own seeds from preferred plant types.

Now enter the scientists. Most genetic improvement of plants is based on the writings of Charles Darwin describing the variation of species, published in 1859, and Gregor Mendel's discovery of the laws of inheritance, reported in 1865. Mendel was a Catholic priest whose home was in an area now part of Czechoslovakia. For 14 years he experimented in a monastery garden with one species of plant, the pea. He found that when he crossed two plants of the same species—for example, a taller and shorter pea plant—one-fourth of the progeny resembled the taller parent, one-fourth resembled the shorter parent, and the remaining one-half were intermediate. Mendel's findings enabled the plant breeder to make deliberate matings—transferring male pollen from one plant to the female flower of another—and then select among the progeny for specific changes. If he discarded, for example, all the taller plants and retained only the shorter progeny for the next generation, he was able to develop a very different plant, one that was sometimes shorter even than the original short parent.

Mendel's laws of inheritance, Borlaug told me, were neglected until 1900 when their rediscovery aroused great interest in plant sciences. Researchers applied Mendel's principles to three types of plants: *self-pollinated* like wheat, *open-pollinated* like maize, and those that are propagated from their *vegetative* parts (the potato). To each plant group the researchers applied

Mendel's two basic procedures: First, they made deliberate matings between selected plants with desired characteristics; and second, they selected and recrossed the progeny until stable characteristics were reached. When a new line of plants significantly outperformed existing farm varieties, the new seed was multiplied and released to farmers.

Major breakthroughs from this research appeared in Europe and North America before World War I. But the greatest progress took place between 1940 and 1980; for example, the combined production of 17 major crops in the United States more than doubled—from 252 to 610 million metric tons. This jump was achieved with an increase of planted cropland of only 3 percent. Better cultivation practices were also developed in this period and played their role. This was a "green revolution," although that term was only applied later in the third world.

Now back to our story. On arrival in Mexico, Dr. Borlaug—always an impatient man—drove immediately to Chapingo to see the wheat fields. No research was needed, he told his Mexican escort, to identify three of Mexico's wheat problems: First, the wheat was deathly sick with rust. Second, the wheat was starving in Mexico's wornout soils. Third, after fertilizer was applied, the spindly wheat stems *lodged*—that is, they fell over before harvest. Lodging causes plants to stop growing and the kernels to shrivel. Of these three problems, Borlaug decided, he had to attack the rust disease first. Without control of disease, nothing else would help. The three rusts—stem, leaf, and stripe—are caused by moldlike fungi. Carriers of the disease, Borlaug explained, are spores transported by the wind. When spores land on a susceptible wheat variety under moisture and temperature conditions favorable to them, they bore into the stem, leaf, or head of the plant. There they cause *pustules*—blisterlike swellings—that become little factories for further multiplication of spores. Pustules interfere with the reception of sunlight, slow the plant growth, cause drying out, and in extreme cases kill the plant.

Through centuries of evolution, Borlaug said, a few of the oldest wheat races (varieties) developed resistance to some strains of rust, but this resistance was generally narrow: that is, one gene in the wheat plant seemed to guard against only one race of rust. Borlaug hoped to achieve broad, stable resistance to rust, but his task was made difficult by hundreds of rust spore types that looked alike but differed in disease virulence. And the races were constantly changing through mutation and sexual mating. One way to achieve a broad spectrum of resistance was to incorporate many resistance genes into a few wheat varieties, then intercross the varieties that carried different kinds of resistance. That is the approach that Borlaug chose in Mexico.

In 1944—when Borlaug arrived—Mexico had no wheat breeding program. It had no collection of wheat varieties to be used for breeding. So Borlaug and his coworkers gathered mixtures of old Spanish wheats from Mexican farmers—altogether some 8,500 head selections—but the Spanish wheats proved to be poor yielding and extremely susceptible to disease. The collectors then turned to other countries. During the first year their imported "seed bank" consisted of 38 varieties. Borlaug's team found four of these varieties to be substantially better than any commercial variety in Mexico. Two came from Kenya in east Africa and two from the United States. The Mexican government released seeds of the four varieties to farmers. These wheats were not high yielding compared to later varieties but they were a step forward.

By 1949 Borlaug had grown the collection of 30,000 worldwide wheats that he had obtained from the U.S. Department of Agriculture. He exposed each plant to the Mexican rust spores. Among the 30,000 only a few entries showed resistance, and those were not desirable plant types. So Borlaug and his Mexican colleagues set out to cross a few disease-resistant plants with others with better plant architecture.

Making a cross between two wheat plants is exceedingly tedious, as I saw from the methods of Borlaug and his colleagues. The wheat plant is normally self-pollinating. That means the plant has both male and female organs, and pollen from the anthers (male) will be shed upon the pistils (female). To cross two plants, the breeder must remove the anthers from one plant before it sheds pollen. The breeder sits on a three-legged stool under the tropical sun, crouching over the plant, straining his eyes as he uses tweezers to pluck out the anthers, almost 200 of them in every wheat head. This step is called *emasculation*. To fertilize the plant at flowering time, the breeder shakes pollen from another plant chosen as the male parent over the female ovaries of the emasculated plant. No substitute for emasculation and hand pollination in the research plot has been found for this breeding operation. And this Mexican research team now performs 10,000 crosses every season—more crosses than any other wheat center in the world.

Seed produced by a cross carries genes from both parents. Subsequent generations planted from this seed are numbered $F1$, $F2$, $F3$, and so on. $F$ stands for filial generation. The early generations following the $F1$ may exhibit great variation in plant height, number of days to maturity, disease resistance and other characteristics resulting from recombination of genes.

No two plants produced by sexual crossing are ever alike. Only after reselection of offspring for six or seven generations are the genes stabilized into a "pure" line—a seed that reproduces with considerable uniformity.

In the 1940s, Borlaug said, conventional wheat breeders required nine or ten years to develop a new wheat. This included one season for the crossing of the two parents, five or six additional selection cycles to choose the best offspring (more than 80 percent of the progeny were discarded), then two to five seasons for yield testing and seed multiplication. Ordinarily only one cycle was completed in a year.

The impatient Borlaug and his Mexican coworkers began growing two cycles a year. A winter cycle, November to April, was grown in Sonora state of northwest Mexico at 28° north latitude near sea level. The summer cycle, May to October, was grown at Chapingo in central Mexico at 18° north latitude and an elevation of 2200 meters. Other scientists ridiculed Borlaug, arguing his system would not work, but he persisted. One of Borlaug's former teachers at Minnesota, so Borlaug told me, even said Norman had not learned the first thing about plant breeding. But the speedup permitted the Mexican government to release five new wheat varieties in 1948 from crosses made in 1944—five years faster than the conventional timetable. Between 1948 and 1960 this breeding group completed 20 new wheats, all more resistant to diseases than previous Mexican varieties and higher yielding. By 1957 Borlaug had the rust problem under control. These new wheats also had wider adaptation across latitudes and they were good enough, when combined with improved cultivation practices, to double Mexico's national average wheat yield from 750 to 1700 kilograms per hectare. Mexico temporarily became self-sufficient in wheat.

Still, the new varieties, Borlaug said, had one serious flaw: they had tall, spindly straw that lodged when well fertilized and watered. The highest yielding of the Mexican wheats rarely reached 4.5 tons per hectare, even when carefully tended in the research station, and lodging discouraged application of more than 50 kilograms of nutrients.

The solution to lodging was found in Japan, Borlaug told me. One of General MacArthur's agricultural staff had identified unusual Japanese wheats during the American administration of Japan. Japanese farmers were then using dwarflike wheats less than one meter tall with sturdy stems that resisted lodging. The Japanese also fertilized their wheats heavily with manures. One of these winter wheats was called *Norin 10* (Norin means "ministry of agriculture and forestry.") The Norin wheats were derived earlier from *Daruma*, a traditional Japanese wheat. (How and where *Daruma* originated remains a mystery.) Seeds for Norin 10 reached Dr. Orville Vogel of the U.S. Department of Agriculture stationed at Washington State

University. Vogel tried crossing Norin 10 (the Japanese immigrant) with some of his tall American winter wheats, but at first he obtained only shrivelled grain. After eight years he developed a new winter semidwarf that he named *Gaines*; this variety later set the American record for yield of a winter wheat at 14.1 metric tons per hectare (207 bushels per acre).

To Borlaug in Mexico Vogel sent an envelope containing 60 seeds of the Japanese-American cross, *Norin 10-Brevor* (one of the predecessors of Gaines). Borlaug grew these seeds in a Mexican research field and crossed the plants with his best Mexican spring wheats. Like Vogel, he first found the progenies produced shrivelled grain and were very susceptible to disease. But Borlaug persisted and finally produced a hybrid between the Japanese-American and his Mexican plants. The Mexican government released Borlaug's first spring wheat semidwarfs in 1962 under the names *Pitic 62* and *Penjamo 62*.

These semidwarfs, Borlaug told me, could tolerate heavy fertilization without falling over. They tillered more profusely (gave extra stems from the same roots), thus producing more heads per square meter. They could move north and south across latitudes (since they combined genetic adaptation from Japanese winter wheat, Washington State winter wheat, and Mexican spring wheat). They were more efficient in using water and nutrients. Up to this time farmers had always believed that taller plants were better. Now Mexican wheats proved this idea wrong. Borlaug's new spring wheats were about three feet tall, compared to traditional varieties that often reached five feet. The semidwarfs had a higher yield because the plant put less energy into its foliage and more into grain. Scientists would say that the short plants had a higher "harvest index" or a greater "grain-stover ratio."

Only three years after release of the semidwarfs, 95 percent of Mexican wheatland was planted with the new short varieties, and the best Mexican wheat farmers achieved seven tons per hectare, an increase of nearly 100 percent.

Borlaug sent seeds of the new Mexican wheats to south Asia where they were found adaptable. In Pakistan (see chapters 24–25), Mexican seeds doubled the wheat yield. In India, the short wheats did even better, quadrupling wheat harvest by the 1980s. Many other countries made notable gains in wheat production, using seeds with Mexican parentage and improved production practices.

From my post in Pakistan I watched Borlaug as he made three more contributions to wheat improvement: (1) he developed a change of cultivation practices for the semidwarf wheats; (2) he created a worldwide team of wheat scientists who tested the new wheats; and (3) he exerted great influence over ministers of agriculture, gaining their confidence and support for introducing the semidwarfs.

Scientists from the developing world began to visit Mexico in the mid-1960s to study under Borlaug. More than 400 made the pilgrimage from Asia, Africa, and Latin America. They worked in mud and dust, heat, and cold and absorbed Borlaug's enthusiasm. He trained each one for six months, long enough to perform every stage of wheat production in the research fields. He sent them home with new knowledge and bags of seed for testing under their own environments.

In the following years Borlaug sent out samples of successive varieties of Mexican seed for testing by his former trainees, and he himself travelled six months each year to consult with this network and encourage their work. Countries active in the network rose from 50 to 120, and the locations performing trials each year increased from 700 to 1600. It was this vast testing organization that triggered the revolution in wheat and guided the annual crossing program.

Borlaug impressed on his trainees his own intensive work habits. He was in the research plots at first daylight and rarely home before dark. He observed no weekends. He preached a concept of interdisciplinary team research that was spread by hundreds of his trainees. He urged national wheat programs to grow two cycles a year, preferably in different climatic zones, to put breeding materials under diverse selection pressure. He resisted paperwork and rejected sophisticated laboratory research, insisting that the surest indicator of success was the improved wheat plants growing in the field. Above all, he preached confidence in the wisdom of farmers. He believed that those who planted wheat in India, Egypt, or Argentina were shrewd men, no matter what their education, and that the scientist who aimed to serve them must produce a plant that grew better in the cultivator's field.

Borlaug's influence with ministers of agriculture became legendary, and tales are told about his vehement arguments emphasizing the importance of fertilizer, farm credit and support prices.

Borlaug was touring the Indian Punjab in March 1967, a time when the new semidwarf wheats were being introduced. Farmers were excited by the change. Borlaug stopped at a tractor factory and spoke to thousands of farmers gathered for a field day. He told the audience,

> During the last month I have seen the wheat revolution in your fields. If the government gives full support, India can replace famine with plenty. If I were a member of your parliament, I would leap from my seat every 15 minutes and

shout, 'Fertilizers!' No matter what the subject of debate, I would shout, 'Fertilizers! Give the farmers fertilizers!' Fertilizers will give India more food. And if there is no more food a volcano will erupt under the political leaders of this land.

The next day New Delhi was in ferment. The Indian Congress party had suffered a setback in elections. Borlaug arrived in the capital and went immediately to see the minister of agriculture, Mr. C. Subramanium. Borlaug made a dramatic entrance, pointing out the window and asking, "Do you know what is going on out there? A revolution is building up. You must take action. Farmers are demanding more support. You must tear up your five-year-plan. Start again; double and treble everything—fertilizer, water, credit."

"Dr. Borlaug," the minister cried, "you don't have to persuade me." He held up a fistful of newspaper clippings and shouted, "I know what you said yesterday, but it is already too late for me. I have just been removed from office. From tonight, I am out. But before you leave India, please go see the head of the planning commission, Mr. Ashok Mehta, who is also minister of chemicals. He is chairman of the commission whose plans you are criticizing."

An appointment was fixed for 7 P.M. that night. As Borlaug was leaving, Subramanium called after him, "Dr. Borlaug, speak bluntly. Hit him hard, as hard as you hit me."

That evening Mr. Mehta gave Borlaug polite greetings, but Borlaug interrupted him with a torrent of words: "Mr. Minister, I have no time to beat about the bush. I leave on a night flight within two hours. I must say some things that you will not like." Leaning across the desk and looking into the minister's astonished eyes, Borlaug commanded, "Tear up those five-year-plans. Start again and multiply everything three or four times. Increase your fertilizer, increase your support prices, increase your loan funds. Then you will be closer to what is needed."

The minister raised his voice to quiet Borlaug, but the visitor went on, "Your planning is atrocious. It is based on the stagnant past. You have a new situation, new seeds that outgrow all others. You have a chance to feed your own people for the first time. You must keep faith with millions of farmers. Give them fertilizer and credit. If you do not do these things, then I tell you, your government will not be in office a year from today."

In all of India Borlaug was probably the only man who could have talked to the chairman of the planning commission like that. "Imagine your country free of famine," he said. "It is within your grasp." He hammered at the fertilizer question, at support prices, at loan funds.

Borlaug left for the airport to catch his night flight to Pakistan. Next day the Indian newspapers announced that Mr. Ashok Mehta had decided to reopen negotiations with foreign chemical companies for the construction of fertilizer factories in India. Since the night of that stormy interview in 1967 India has been building more fertilizer factories—even into the 1980s.

On October 20, 1970, Mrs. Margaret Borlaug was already up at 7 A.M. in her apartment in Mexico City, as she later related the story to me. The telephone rang. The operator said the call was from Norway. A man with Norwegian accent identified himself as a reporter for the Oslo *Post* and asked to speak to Dr. Borlaug. Margaret told him that Borlaug had left two hours earlier for his wheat plots in the mountains near Toluca and could not be reached by telephone. The reporter informed her that the Norwegian Parliament had awarded the Nobel Peace Prize to Norman Borlaug. The award—with its prize of $78,000—would be announced within a few hours*.

Margaret was both flabbergasted and skeptical. Could it be a mistake? How, she asked the reporter, did he know this before the official announcement? "It will be announced, all right, at 5 P.M., Oslo time," he assured her. She thanked him and hung up. Immediately the phone rang again, and another reporter gave her the same message. When the phone rang a third time, she let it ring.

Margaret wanted to be the first to tell Norman the news. She called Dr. Robert Osler, top administrative officer at CIMMYT, who agreed to send a car and driver to carry Margaret into the mountains near Toluca. It was nearly 10 A.M. as the car jounced over the rutted road to the wheat plots where Norman was working with a group of foreign trainees. As he saw the car approach, his first emotion was alarm. He ran to the car and asked, "What's wrong?" But Margaret was smiling. "Nothing is wrong, Norm. You have won the Nobel Peace Prize!" He did not believe the news. "Who says so?" he asked. She described the phone calls. "It doesn't sound very official to me," he said. She wanted him to come back to the city immediately with her, but he looked back at the wheat plots and shook his head. "Best thing is for you to go back to the city, and I will continue the harvest. We will see what happens."

Within 40 minutes an American television crew arrived. "Which one of you guys is Borlaug?" a cameraman shouted. Borlaug identified himself and told the crew that since he had not yet been informed officially of the prize, he could not make a statement. "You better believe it," a cameraman shot back.

---

*Recipients of the Nobel Peace Prize are chosen by a committee of five Norwegians named by the Norwegian Parliament.

"It's on the world news wires." More crews arrived and argued among themselves over priority of interviews. Two hours later Robert Osler came racing through the wheat and told Borlaug there was no way to escape the demands for a statement. A press conference had been scheduled for 5 P.M. in Mexico City with live television hookups to follow.

Borlaug decided to drive home and change his muddy field clothes, but when he neared his apartment he saw it was surrounded by men with recording equipment. Without stopping he headed for the nearby home of Ed Wellhausen, the CIMMYT director general.

"I suppose it's true, Ed," Borlaug said as the two men shook hands. "If it is, the prize is for all of us, for you and me and the Rockefeller Foundation—our whole bunch." When Borlaug faced the newsmen, he still wore his muddy boots and held his baseball cap in his hand until Osler took it from him. This was the beginning of Borlaug's new life—a conflict between his research in the field and his role as spokesman for the hungry people of the third world. Next day he was back in the wheat fields near Toluca, continuing the harvest. But the demands on his time for speeches and interviews had already begun.

Borlaug remained head of the wheat research group in Mexico until his retirement in 1979, a span of 35 years, and he still serves as a program consultant.

Norman Borlaug is one of the most creative, productive, inspiring, and intense persons I have ever worked with. He is also a difficult person to meld into an organization.

Borlaug hates paperwork and bureaucracy. When the CGIAR, our donors' organization, requested a five-year budget projection, Borlaug said it could not and would not be done. He argued that his annual budgeting incorporated the research findings of the previous year and therefore a five-year projection was out of the question. Once Borlaug denounced me heatedly in front of a CIMMYT gathering of international scientists for trying—as he put it—to make bureaucrats of his wheat staff.

Borlaug cherishes the memory of the early days at his research plots near Ciudad Obregon, where he slept in a tent, worked seven days a week, and stayed away from his office in Mexico City for four or five months at a time. Later he tried to convert married staff members to this same devotion to the wheat plots, but times had changed. Today some CIMMYT wives accompany their husbands to Obregon, and no one sleeps in a tent.

Borlaug has mellowed in his early seventies. We reminisce about the days when I set up his appointments with President Ayub Khan of Pakistan, and the president gave CIMMYT one of its early wheat triumphs. Like the great race horse that he is, Borlaug will never slow down to the pace of ordinary men.

Today there are 13 international research centers and institutes like CIMMYT, loosely affiliated, conducting research on major food crops and other key factors in the hunger problem. In varying degrees, they follow the pattern established by Borlaug. How these centers came into being is the next part of this story.

*Few scientists think of agriculture as the chief, or the model, science. Many, indeed, do not consider it a science at all. Yet it was the first science—the mother of all sciences. It remains the science which makes life possible.*

Andre and Jean Mayer, 1981

CHAPTER 31

# The Cloning of Research Centers

The explosive success of Dr. Borlaug with wheat raised the question in the Rockefeller and Ford Foundations at New York: Can this strategy be repeated for other crops? The successful ingredients of the Mexico experience seemed to be:

1. Create a research center for a single crop or a few related crops with narrow enough focus to make possible a "center of excellence."

2. Gather seed samples of that crop from all over the world.

3. Breed improved varieties with wide adaptation—that is, plants that can move across latitudes and around the world.

4. Bring scientists from developing countries to study at this center of excellence.

5. Organize a testing program so that seeds can be demonstrated every year in a large number of countries.

The two foundations experimented with this strategy. The first new start was in the Philippines in 1960—the International Rice Research Institute (IRRI). Within five years the IRRI staff of about 20 scientists had developed semidwarf rice varieties that doubled and tripled the previous potential yields. The new varieties used plant nutrients and irrigation water more efficiently and resisted diseases and pests better; therefore they yielded more.

The IRRI experience produced some important guidelines on how to organize new centers. As I learned the story from McGeorge Bundy, president of the Ford Foundation, there were two key men in these developments: George Harrar, the first leader of the Rockefeller-Mexico program, and F.F. (Frosty) Hill of the Ford Foundation. A professor at Cornell who had sent forth a whole generation of agricultural leaders for many countries, Hill came to the foundation in 1955 to head overseas development grants. With a few colleagues they began to organize new international agricultural research institutes by applying the following principles:

First, locate each new institute in a third world country that is a "hot spot" for the problems that would be researched, thus making the host country a motivated participant.

Second, give control of each institute to an independent, nonprofit, self-perpetuating, multinational board of trustees. The autonomous board has been a device so familiar in the American nonprofit world that it was easy to forget how valuable it could be when extended to the international scene.

Third, provide a physical setting for each new institute that fulfills the needs of first-class scientists: experimental cropland, laboratories, suitable family housing, and access to worldwide travel.

Fourth, assure long-term financial support.

Without the spectacular successes with wheat and rice, the rest of this story would not have unfolded so rapidly. By 1969 the two foundations had launched four research institutes at a cost of $43 million. and it was clear that further expansion would require additional donors.

Foreign aid involves complicated motives. Most donor agencies think like politicians; they look for prestige and credit for themselves that they can report to their governing bodies. It was not easy for donor agencies, each accountable to a different government or private body, to join in supporting agricultural research institutes—especially when the added contributions might be misinterpreted as "bailing out some rich American foundations." It was remarkable then that a group of 20 different donors held meetings from 1969 through 1971, often at Bellagio, Italy, to discuss joint action on agricultural research. Credit goes to all of them, but especially to the leaders of three organizations: Paul Hoffman of the United Nations Development Program, Adekko Boerma of the United Nations Food and Agriculture Organization, and Robert McNamara of the World Bank. From their labors emerged an informal association of development assistance agencies, officially named the Consultative Group on International Agricultural Research, but known informally as the Consultative Group or the "CG."

Participants at Bellagio agreed that they would not pool their funds and set policies collectively. Instead, each donor would make separate contributions to the research institutes of its choice and negotiate conditions for the use of those funds directly with each recipient. It sounds simple, but it took two years to reach a formula that gained the approval of industrialized countries like Britain, West Germany, Japan, and the United States; of private organizations like the American foundations; and of international bodies like the World Bank and the United Nations Development Program. Initial pledges in 1971 totalled US$20 million. That support grew steadily to about US$200 million in the mid-1980s. The presence of the World Bank gave donors confidence that financial management would be responsible.

Meanwhile nine more research institutes were added to the four originally established by the U.S. foundations. These institutes carried out crop research for the potato, cassava, sorghum, and legumes; attacked animal diseases in Africa; and provided specialized services such as germplasm banks, studies on world food problems, and counselling third world governments on strengthening the management of their research systems. To increase its own capacity for research judgment, the Consultative Group established a Technical Advisory Committee (TAC) composed of 15 distinguished agricultural scientists and research administrators.

By 1985 the 13 institutes employed over 900 scientists from more than 50 countries. They had established strong connections with the research organizations in third world nations, and this joint network of professional men and women was consciously evolving into a worldwide scientific enterprise.

With what results? The increased wheat crop in India is often used as an indicator. The Indian wheat harvest grew from 11 million tons in the mid-1960s to 46 million tons in the early 1980s. The value of the increased wheat in India reached almost 7 billion American dollars a year. And the greater number of Indian adults receiving carbohydrate requirements reached 260 million people.

These figures for India encouraged the Consultative Group to believe that the third world had reached a technological turning point, and that the international centers could justify—many times over—the funds they received.

The Consultative Group and the international centers have evolved so quickly—in less than a quarter century—that there are many unanswered questions.

Will the centers be needed indefinitely? I believe a group of agricultural centers will continue to serve the world's farmers for the next 100 years, at least until population growth grinds slowly toward a stable world late in the twenty-first century. But great changes in these centers can be anticipated. Some research will be shifted from the international centers to national research institutes in third world nations. This is a logical step as the LDCs acquire more scientists trained to the doctoral level. Also, third world research leaders like Brazil, India, and China will participate in the worldwide consulting work of the centers, thus establishing a partnership that arouses less national sensitivity than at present.

As for the centers, their subject matter will change. Some centers may be eliminated and others take their place. Like the plants they study, these centers will mutate. Some activities of the present centers probably will be needed indefinitely, either because they are too costly for individual third world countries or because they can be performed best at one location for the entire world. These long-term functions include: (1) managing world seed collections, (2) distributing worldwide nurseries and publishing results, and (3) training scientists for the low-income countries. The need for these activities may diminish during the twenty-first century, but it will not disappear.

*The struggle for fairness in the countryside is a hard one almost everywhere.*

McGeorge Bundy, 1977

CHAPTER 32

# A Donnybrook over the Green Revolution

In the 1970s, during one of the oddest intellectual clashes of the twentieth century—CIMMYT became a center of controversy over the green revolution. The storm began when overenthusiastic newswriters claimed that "miracle seeds" of wheat and rice had triggered a "green revolution" in Asia that would "solve forever" the world's hunger problem. These writers described CIMMYT as the home of the green revolution, Norman Borlaug as the father of the green revolution, and agricultural changes in Asia as "miraculous."

Such excessive claims prompted retorts by university social scientists that many peasant problems remained to be solved. The green revolution, they said, was not a scientific term; the phrase suggested greater results than had yet occurred. CIMMYT received scornful visitors—some from the media, some from universities, some from our donors—who pressed for evidence of provable progress. In the mid-1970s, one quarter of my time, and that of our directing staff, was spent dealing with this controversy.

Like most phrases popularized in the press, the term *green revolution* was probably here to stay. Rather than fight it, our CIMMYT staff decided to define it more carefully, removing some of its imprecision. The agricultural changes in India and Pakistan, we pointed out, were a continuation of a process of agricultural modernization that had begun in Europe in the nineteenth century. Scientific methods in the temperate region were gradually being adapted to the subtropics and tropics. The first results in the warmer climates were remarkable but they were not miraculous—at least no more miraculous than the results achieved in Europe, North America, Australia, and Japan, where yields of food crops had doubled and tripled in the previous 100 years.

I gave to our visitors the CIMMYT opinion that the green revolution had four ingredients, and that only when all four elements were combined did the full benefits appear. The elements were:

1. New seeds for wheat and rice that gave higher yield potential.
2. New "packages of practices," including a change in seeding depth, increased fertilizer, better weed control, and revised irrigation practices.
3. More government services to peasants, including technical advice, sale of chemicals at reasonable prices, increased farm credit, and support prices for crops at harvest.
4. Continuous research to solve new problems as they arose.

There was nothing miraculous about any of these elements. But the storm of criticism continued, passing through the following stages as we witnessed them from Mexico.

Stage one: In 1972 exceptional droughts occurred in wheat areas of the Soviet Union, China, and Australia; in the rice region of southeast Asia; and in the sorghum region of Africa, south of the Sahara. Critics then called the green revolution a lie, a myth and a dead slogan. They said it was too late to save countries like India and Bangladesh because of overpopulation. Our factual reply? Drought had reduced world grain production by 4 percent in 1972, but this small change was enough to raise food prices in the areas of shortage, and many poor people suffered. Obviously the green revolution had not overcome the weather cycle, but it showed what could be done; it reversed centuries of agricultural standstill in the subtropics and tropics.

Stage two: Social scientists attacked the injustices that they perceived in the green revolution. They claimed that rich farmers were getting richer and poor farmers poorer; that rich farmers could better afford increased fertilizer and irrigation, and therefore gained more; that rich farmers could buy more machinery and thus reduce employment of hand labor; and that semidwarf wheats were driving out *pulses*—the bean family—and impoverishing the peasant diet. These claims, generally advanced without supporting evidence, were a mixture of emotion and ideology.

In 1979 the World Bank employed an economic consultant to survey the literature on the green revolution. His conclusions were of great interest to the CIMMYT staff. Among them were these:

- The income of the large and small farmers who grew the new wheat and rice went up in approximately the same proportion. In West Bengal, India, for example, farmers with less than one hectare gained 24 percent in income and the largest farmers with four to six hectares gained 18 percent.

- Neither farm size nor farm tenure (ownership or rental) was a major impediment to a farmer's adopting the new varieties.

- The new varieties required more farm labor to cope with increased fertilizer and irrigation, better weed control, and greater harvest. One study showed that labor on the fields planted to the new wheat and rice increased 23 man-days per hectare. So landless laborers benefited.

- The nutritional impact of the new wheats was beneficial. Studies in India showed that production of protein, calories and essential amino acids were all higher than they would have been if the new cereals had not been planted.

- Low-income consumers were the greatest beneficiaries from the new cereals. Increased food output drove down prices and, since low-income consumers spent a higher proportion of their income on food, the decline in food prices gave them a disproportionate benefit.

Stage three: There was a lull in the controversy, then the attack shifted to ecology. The critics now conceived modern technology to be bad for developing countries. Critics described the traditional peasant life in the third world as an idyllic scene in which millions of peasant families lived peacefully with nature. This harmony between man and environment was now presumably jeopardized by misguided scientists who were encouraging the peasant to use energy-intensive technology. The introduction of chemical fertilizers, pump irrigation, and mechanization were all viewed as evil for the third world. In effect the critics accepted scientific progress for the industrialized countries but advocated a standstill for the third world.

I share the conclusion of William Tucker who wrote in *Promise and Privilege* in 1982:

> The overwhelming fact is that the green revolution has been successful, and as a result, people in tropical countries have been eating better and continue to eat better. Total per-capita grain production for people in third world countries has been rising ½ percent per year since 1950, so that people are now eating—on average—15 percent better than they were at midcentury.

As I look back, it seems to me that those who castigated the green revolution were more interested in advancing an ideology than in securing an adequate food supply for the third world. The green revolution, in my opinion, continues to be a process whereby third world peoples are able to grow more food for themselves. It is a practical example of the Chinese proverb: "Give a man a fish to eat and he is hungry tomorrow. Teach him to fish and he will never be hungry."

*In parts of Central America, corn grows 20 feet tall and is harvested on horseback.*

E. J. Kahn, Jr., 1984

CHAPTER 33

# Maize: A Potential Supercereal in the Third World

During most of the 1970s I was concerned about CIMMYT's maize program. We were not getting the same results in maize as in wheat, at least not in farmers' fields. Our donors were aware of this and asked me why. The research budgets for the two crops were about the same, and the number of scientists working on the two crops was similar. Yet the Rockefeller scientists who had long preceded my arrival in Mexico had achieved less success with maize. Between 1940 and 1980 Mexico's average wheat yield rose almost fivefold—from 700 kilograms per hectare to 3400 (that is, about 10 to 50 bushels an acre). But maize yields in the same period rose from 750 kilograms per hectare to 1500 (that is, 12 to 24 bushels per acre). This slower progress for maize seemed strange because in the years 1940 to 1980 the maize crop in the United States was demonstrating an agricultural revolution—some would say the greatest food revolution the world had seen since cereal plants were domesticated in prehistoric times. So why was maize slower in Mexico?

I will describe what I learned from the staff about the maize plant, the problems in Mexico, and why I think maize—despite its slow start—may still demonstrate the greatest production gains in the remainder of the twentieth century—greater than wheat, greater than rice, greater than any other cereal crop.

The word *maize*, I was told, is the name scientists give to the species *Zea mays*, a plant that most North Americans call *corn*. The word *corn* is used in the Bible and in most European languages to mean cereals in general; it does not refer specifically to the maize plant, since maize did not exist in the eastern hemisphere in Biblical times, nor east of the Atlantic before Columbus. I will use the word *maize* here.

Three cereal plants—wheat, maize and rice—provide approximately half the human calories. According to the U.N. Food and Agriculture Organization (FAO) here is the average annual worldwide production of these supercereals during the period 1980 to 1983:

   Wheat—471 million tons
   Maize—411 million tons
   Rice (without husk)—328 million tons

CIMMYT works primarily with low-income countries of the third world, so it is useful to know how much of these champion cereals the countries of Asia, Africa, and Latin America produce. Again from FAO we find for 1980-1983 the following yearly averages:

   Rice (without husk)—309 million tons
   Wheat—173 million tons
   Maize—154 million tons

Rice is thus the leading foodcrop of the third world, followed by wheat and maize.

I learned from the staff that the maize plant is unique in several ways.

1. Maize holds the world's yield record among grain crops at 21.22 tons per hectare compared to wheat and rice at 14.52 and 14.40 tons. World records are not expected from ordinary farmers, but the maize record confirms the yield potential under ideal conditions of maize compared to other cereals.

2. Maize is the leading animal feed of the world, used for beef and milk animals, hogs and poultry. As incomes around the world rise and people can afford more meat products, the demand for maize expands.

3. The maize crop in the United States has become the most valuable national cash crop in history, in one year reaching $25 billion.

4. More than 70 countries in the world grow 100,000 or more hectares of maize a year (250,000 acres). That makes maize the most widely distributed grain crop.

5. Four hundred million to 500 million people mostly in Latin America and Africa south of the Sahara, eat maize as their primary food. There are

more wheat-eaters and rice-eaters than maize-eaters, but those who eat maize are the world's poorest people and thus represent a hunger problem.

The CIMMYT staff also gave me some sex education about the maize plant to explain the breeder's technique. Maize is a promiscuous, open-pollinated plant. The male sex organ is the conspicuous erect tassel at the top of the plant, waving publicly in the sunshine. The tassel produces the pollen—a fine yellow dust that is airborne to maize plants growing within 100 or 200 yards. The female organ that receives the pollen is the *ear shoot*, or future ear, located about halfway down the maize stalk, wrapped tightly in green leaves with fine silklike fibers protruding from the tip of the shoot. Each silky fiber that snares a grain of pollen will transport the male sperm to the female ovary. There it becomes a kernel of grain on the ear. Though this process appears haphazard, it is made more reliable by the fact that each tassel releases up to 25 million grains of pollen and the sexual rite continues for many days.

A cross-pollinated grain like maize offers several methods for developing higher yielding plants. *Recurrent selection* is one common procedure. This method was used for centuries by early maize farmers who picked ears from the best plants and saved them for seed the following season. The modern breeder has more efficient ways to find superior individual ears within a population, but the idea of choosing the best ears—year after year—is the same. After many generations of reselection by the breeder, the plants improve and become more uniform for the characteristics that the breeder has chosen. A name is then given to the new variety, and the seed is made available to farmers.

A very different procedure is used to develop hybrid maize, which justifies some historical explanation. By the late nineteenth century botanists had identified an unusual characteristic of *Zea mays*. If the maize plant is "selfed" for several generations—that is, if pollen from the tassel of a plant is applied to the female silks of the same plant—the progenies lose vigor: the stalk grows shorter and the amount of grain on each ear declines. This is called *inbreeding depression*, and the weakened plant is called an *inbred*. If inbreeding continues for several reproductive cycles, the inbreds become nearly identical in appearance.

Now the payoff: When two selected inbreds—unrelated to each other—are crossed, their progenies often display an explosive recovery of vigor. Charles Darwin described this phenomenon in his book *The Vegetable*

*Kingdom,* published in 1876. This vigor was later given the Greek name *heterosis,* defined in the dictionary as "a marked vigor or capacity for growth shown by crossbred animals and plants."

For almost half a century no one succeeded in applying Darwin's observation to the genetic improvement of maize, although many able plant breeders were studying it. Finally a geneticist named Donald Jones, working at Connecticut Experiment Station from 1915 to 1918, demonstrated how seed that exploited hybrid vigor could be produced economically, increasing the grain yield by 20 to 30 percent over the original parents.

Hybrid maize began to spread slowly in the United States after Henry A. Wallace (see Part V opening) established his seed company in 1926, but changes in agriculture were held back by the disastrous depression of the 1930s. Then the maize revolution took off. Within the ten years from 1936 to 1945, the planting of hybrid maize in the corn belt—the ten states surrounding Iowa in the American midwest—increased from 5 percent to over 90 percent.

The average yield of maize in the United States had been about 1.5 tons per hectare (about 26 bushels per acre) for more than a century, from 1800 to 1940. Then national average yields rose to 2 tons in 1945, to 3 tons in the 1950s, to 4 tons in the 1960s, to 5 tons in the 1970s, and in 1984 reached a record 7.3 tons. This sensational progress was not accomplished by seed alone but also by increased mechanization, denser planting, larger application of chemical fertilizer, better control of pests, and market prices that made farming profitable most years.

Among the North American scientists recruited in 1943 for the Rockefeller-Mexico group was Edwin J. Wellhausen, a 35-year-old, Oklahoma-born maize geneticist. He was placed in charge of maize research. Ed soon added to his team tens of Mexican agricultural graduates who were given local in-service training. The most promising were also sent abroad for advanced study.

One of Wellhausen's greatest accomplishments was to collect maize seeds representing the different types of maize plants that had evolved since the prehistoric domestication of the crop. He gathered seeds from all parts of Mexico and Guatemala, from the mountains and jungles of Central and South America, and then the varieties used by the North American Indians. Wellhausen's plant explorers fanned out over the back roads of Mexico, then by foot over mountain trails; they finally reached isolated forest clearings where farmers had planted maize seeds handed down from antiquity. The maize they collected varied in kernel texture from floury to dent to flint; in seed colors, with white and yellow predominant; in geographic environments spread from the equator to 50 degrees north and 40 degrees south and from sea level up to elevations of 3000 meters. Sweet corn and popcorn were included. This *maize bank*, as it was called, eventually contained more than 10,000 entries. It is now regarded as the world collection and serves breeders in all countries.

Drawing on his seed collection for parent materials, Wellhausen became one of the pioneer developers of maize hybrids and synthetic varieties for the third world. By the early 1960s the government of Mexico was able to release to farmers hybrids and synthetics developed by Wellhausen and the Rockefeller group that were much better than anything grown in Mexico up to that time.

Strangely, local farmers were slow to plant the hybrids. There were unexpected Mexican problems that we now see clearly by hindsight.

First, maize land in Mexico is not the same as wheat land. The wheat land is uniform; it is mainly the flat, irrigated desert area along the northwest Pacific coast—in an area where the government has invested millions of dollars in irrigation storage dams wedged into the nearby mountains. Maize by contrast is grown as a rainfed subsistence crop in all the Mexican states, scattered over the mountains and valleys, in good soil and bad. Some 90 percent of the wheat harvest is irrigated. Less than 10 percent of the maize crop is.

Second, maize growers are not the same as wheat farmers. Wheat growers are "large" operators by local standards; maize farmers are smallholders. The average wheat planting is 28 hectares; the average maize planting is less than 5 hectares, and many of the maize fields are less than 1 hectare. Wheat farmers sell their harvest to flour mills for cash, have better access to credit, and make larger use of fertilizer. Maize farmers grow mainly for the home dinner table; they begrudge cash expenditures. Wheat farmers are better educated.

Third, there are now 40 times more maize farmers than wheat growers in Mexico—some 2 million farmers produce maize, while about 80,000 grow wheat. So new technology spreads less rapidly among the maize farmers.

In 1966 the Rockefeller Foundation's agricultural operation in Mexico became the International Maize and Wheat Improvement Center (CIMMYT), and Ed Wellhausen became the first director general.

CIMMYT acquired research stations at different elevations in Mexico— the lowest at tropical sea level near Poza Rica, not far from the Gulf of

Mexico; a second near Cuernavaca, at an elevation of 940 meters (about 2900 feet); a third at CIMMYT's headquarters at El Batan, outside Mexico City at an elevation of 2240 meters (7000 feet); and the highest near Toluca at 2660 meters (8200 feet). CIMMYT maize researchers were thus able to test breeding materials under different environments common to large regions of Latin America, Africa, and Asia.

Three other developments in the 1960s and 1970s generally established CIMMYT as a worldwide leader of maize research. The first was a method for shortening the tropical maize plant, accomplished by Dr. Elmer Johnson, who improved the harvest index (explained shortly). The second was the worldwide selection and testing program for maize, conceived and organized by Dr. Ernest Sprague. The third was the improvement of maize protein by incorporating a high-lysine gene, an achievement led by Dr. S. K. Vasal. These developments have probably set the stage for a maize revolution in the third world. I was a witness to each of these developments and had to explain them to the donors and the press.

Elmer Johnson, an Oregonian geneticist, was 38 when he joined Ed Wellhausen in Mexico. Johnson had his doctorate from Minnesota and had travelled for seven years as a seed extension agent in Oregon. His research strategy was to shorten the height of the tropical Mexican maize plant and to observe the impact on grain yield. The maize population he studied most intensely was a widely adapted Mexican maize called *Tuxpeno*. The results were so startling that they have been cited in college textbooks.

Johnson grew a crop of Tuxpeno 20 times in 20 seasons. After each cycle he selected seeds from the shorter plants to use for his next planting. There was no crossing with other populations. In 20 cycles he reduced the average height of Tuxpeno by approximately 50 percent—from 273 to 143 centimeters (that is, from nine feet to four feet seven inches). The side effects were surprising. When the crop was sowed at optimum plant density, the grain yield went up from about four tons a hectare to almost seven tons (63 to 110 bushels an acre). The length of growing period from planting to maturity was reduced by eight days. And the *harvest index* rose from 0.30 to 0.49. Harvest index, you will recall, is a measure of plant efficiency that gives the weight of the grain as a percent of the weight of the whole plant. The shortened Tuxpeno now had about the same efficiency in producing grain as high-yielding hybrids in the U.S. corn belt. Johnson's research procedure for shortening the maize plant was soon repeated on most leading maize populations, and the shortened maize has spread across the third world.

Ernest Sprague was 47 when he became leader of the CIMMYT maize program in 1970. He was a lean, hard-driving Kansan—a coffee-drinker who consumed one or two cups an hour from his rising to bedtime. His credentials included a doctorate in plant breeding from Cornell and 12 years as a leader of maize research in India and Thailand. Sprague introduced a series of program changes at CIMMYT that later had a major impact on many countries of the third world.

First, Sprague divided the materials in the maize seed bank into 33 *pools* suitable for different geographic conditions, for example, tropical, subtropical, and temperate. These pools were grown every year in Mexico and the best ears from each pool were saved.

Next, a worldwide network of cooperators, organized by Sprague, tested the seed from each pool in its appropriate climate, either annually or biennially. Ratings given by the cooperators were used by CIMMYT to form experimental varieties (that is, mixtures of the best seed selected from the trials).

By 1983, developing countries had released to their farmers more than 100 new open-pollinated varieties from this process. The new varieties surpassed the best traditional third world varieties by 20 to 35 percent. The increased maize harvest from the new varieties was estimated to be worth more than 1.5 billion dollars a year (1983).

CIMMYT breeders in Mexico continue to improve the experimental varieties in the most important characteristics—for drought tolerance, for early maturity, for insect and disease resistance, and for better protein. These improvements are fed into the pools. Sprague's worldwide testing procedure is expected to give continued gains in yield for the rest of the twentieth century and beyond.

The enrichment of protein in CIMMYT maize was described in an article in *Reader's Digest* for January 1975, titled, "The Corn that Could Change the Lives of Millions." Paul Friggins, the science writer, used reports on CIMMYT's protein work. I will summarize the materials here.

Scientists had known since 1913 that maize grain contains poor-quality protein; it is low in two essential amino acids that the human body cannot manufacture—lysine and tryptophan. But not until 1963 did agricultural scientists at Purdue University—studying a recessive gene in maize that produces soft, chalky kernels instead of the shiny ones—discover that these odd kernels contained about twice as much lysine and tryptophan as normal maize. The news excited plant breeders around the world. For the first time scientists thought they saw a way to raise the quality of protein in grain to approximate the protein value in animal products.

A Rockefeller scientist working in Colombia, an animal nutritionist named Jerome Maner, fed the Purdue maize to swine with remarkable results. He found that young pigs without protein supplement gained weight twice as fast on *Opaque-2*—as the Purdue maize was called—as on traditional maize. He also fed piglets on a diet limited to traditional maize. These animals developed a protein-deficiency disease similar to kwashiorkor, which afflicts millions of humans. After 110 days, the pigs restricted to "normal" maize began to die. The first group of pigs, fed only on opaque maize, remained healthy.

This experience intrigued a Colombian pediatrician, Dr. Alberto Pradilla, who began feeding opaque maize to seven children suffering from advanced stages of kwashiorkor. In two weeks their diarrhea had ceased and they began to gain weight. Within 100 days they were fully recovered.

With such dramatic results, CIMMYT began to promote high-lysine maize. But it soon became apparent that the task of transferring the Opaque-2 gene was not simple. The gene was associated with a soft-textured endosperm (the starchy filling of the kernel). When the gene was transferred to a high-yielding maize variety, it gave adverse side effects. For example, people accustomed to eating a shiny maize kernel didn't like the unappetizing look of the lustreless opaque type. Worse still the new soft maize was more vulnerable to plant diseases and insects and yielded 15-20 percent less than normal maize varieties.

In 1970 the United Nations Development Program in New York decided to finance a worldwide effort to modify Opaque-2. They selected CIMMYT as the breeder.

The first breakthough was the discovery that the grain of "normal" maize populations contained minor modifier genes that could gradually change the soft starch of the opaques without loss of protein quality. But it was necessary to accumulate a large number of modifier genes to convert the soft-textured opaque to hard kernels. The chief CIMMYT maize breeder for this assignment was Dr. S. K. Vasal, a 32-year-old Indian from the Indian Agricultural Research Insititute outside New Delhi. As soon as modifier genes began to transform the opaque appearance, Vasal could no longer see if the protein quality was still there. He enlisted the help of a Mexican colleague, Dr. Evangelina Villegas, who held a doctorate in cereal chemistry. For each generation of Vasal's breeding, Dr. Villegas analyzed the lysine and tryptophan in thousands of laboratory samples.

By 1984, after 14 years and 28 generations of pooling the genes, the

Vasal-Villegas team finally produced high-lysine composites in which the grains appeared normal, yet retained high protein quality and were adapted to a range of tropical and subtropical environments. The early problems of low acceptability, lower yield, and insect damage in storage were almost completely resolved.

Today just one more step will ensure the permanence of the high-lysine work—the incorporation of the hard Opaque-2 character into a high-yielding hybrid. This ultimate step is likely to occur first in China. Vasal delivered some of his Opaque-2 seed to China in 1983, and breeders there are busy creating the necessary inbred lines for future hybrids.

I believe that maize production in the third world could well outgain all other cereals in the remainder of the twentieth century. Here's why. First, as I stated earlier, maize has the highest genetic yield potential of all the cereals. Second, in many third world countries where incomes are rising and people are eating more meat, the demand for maize as animal feed is steadily increasing. Third, population growth in the next few years will be greatest in sub-Saharan Africa, where maize is a principal cereal crop. Fourth, farmer access to good hybrid seed in developing countries should no longer be an obstacle. Fifth, more farmers will adopt superior, open-pollinated varieties for which seed can be saved from season to season.

*The lives of the villagers are not dull.*
Oscar Lewis, 1961

CHAPTER 34

# Neighbors to an Aztec King

On our arrival at CIMMYT in 1971, Berni and I decided to buy land and build a home. The plain surrounding Mexico City is like an oval saucer 40 to 50 miles in diameter with Lake Texcoco in the center. The lake elevation is 7000 feet and the hills at the rim of the saucer rise in some places to 14,000 feet. Our research center is at the edge of the plain, northeast of Mexico City, close to the hills. A lucky house builder might find a site with dramatic views of the snow-capped volcanoes, but of course he would also want a location with an access road, a source of safe drinking water, and a power line.

In 1971 we selected the village of San Nicolas Tlaminca in the foothills, six miles from CIMMYT. The village then had about 80 adobe houses, a population of 500, and the usual inventory of an elementary school, a whitewashed church (seating 50 worshippers), two general stores, a soccer field, a bandstand, one *pulqueria* (a bar that sells *pulque*—the Mexican fermented cactus juice), and a cemetery. The village drinking water came by pipeline from a spring higher in the mountains. Most of the houses were "electrified"—they had one light bulb in the ceiling of each room. The streets were unpaved. The animal population of the village—made up of cows, horses, donkeys, sheep, goats, pigs, flocks of chickens, turkeys, and pigeons—approximately matched the number of humans.

At the highest point of the village was an orchard for sale. Its three hectares (eight acres) were spread over eight Aztec terraces, half of them irrigated. The terraces supported 1000 fruit trees, mostly crabapple (which the Aztecs called *tejocote*), with some apricots, apples, peaches, and avocadoes. The price of the land seemed high at seven pesos a square meter (roughly US$5500 a hectare or US$2200 an acre), but our inquiries at Texcoco indicated that by local standards the price was reasonable. We made the down payment.

Some Americans cautioned us that Mexico prohibits ownership of land by foreigners, but we learned that the restriction applied only within 50 miles of the seacoast or within that distance of a foreign border.

We needed an architect. One day when we visited the National Museum of Anthropology and History—one of the most stunning museum buildings we had seen anywhere—Berni spotted on a plaque the name of the architect, Dr. Pedro Ramirez Vasquez. He had designed several Mexico City landmarks as well as the Aztec Stadium for the 1968 Olympic Games. He also headed a private architectural firm. In response to Berni's letter his firm agreed to undertake our house design, which fell to the 45-year-old partner, Dr. Rafael Mijares.

Our encounters with Mexican builders (not architects) were painful. Probably our lack of familiarity with construction practices and our inadequate Spanish language contributed. We negotiated first with an English-speaking builder in Lomas Chapultepec, an upper-income suburb of Mexico City. We ended those talks after the builder admitted that he had doubled the budget estimates because his city-based workmen demanded a bonus to work in a rural area. Next we talked to a builder who lived in Mexico City but was willing to employ craftsmen at rural wages. A crew of stone masons immediately appeared on the job from villages around Pachuca, a town 60 miles to the north. The labor crew slept in our orchard and ate meals with families in the village. The *maestro*—or master mason—was a wiry 25-year-old named Alberto, a primary school graduate. He had taught himself to read architectural plans and had supervised construction of one house before he came to us. He commanded the respect of the other crew members because most of them were his illiterate relatives.

Small troubles with the builder-contractor began immediately. He had promised to inspect the work three days a week but rarely appeared. He failed to deliver construction materials, causing idle periods for the crew. The bills he submitted for reimbursement were probably correct but rarely receipted. Finally he failed to pay the workmen on a Saturday, and they threatened to quit. Berni then paid the wages and asked the *maestro* why we needed the contractor. If Alberto could read the architect's plans and Berni could purchase the building materials, why use a contractor? So we fired the builder when the house was less than half completed.

Alberto spoke no English, and Berni had reached only Book Three in *Beginner's Spanish*. But within days she was ordering from a building supply house in Texcoco truckloads of *arena* (sand), *grava* (gravel), *ladrillos* (bricks), *piedra* (stone), *varillas* (steel reinforcing rods), *losetas de barro* (floor tiles), and *azulejos* (decorative wall tiles).

We moved into the house 36 months after selecting the land. Of that time, half was required for title papers under Mexico's complicated legal system and half for construction.

We were the only foreigners in San Nicolas. In fact we were the only nonrelatives in a village where most families were named Reyes, Flores, and Olivares. But slowly the villagers accepted us.

We dealt with the village water master who controlled the irrigation water for our orchard. We bought from a neighbor half a dozen sheep to be fattened on grass under the fruit trees. A village grocer contracted to pick and sell our crabapples, and the mother of our orchard worker asked to market our apricots on her weekly sales trips to Mexico City. Berni became the godmother for a neighbor's baby and the godmother for a wedding, which meant supplying the cake. Young people in the village asked for job recommendations at CIMMYT; Berni gave them directions to see the personnel director and cautioned that jobs were scarce. Our Protestant family constructed at our front gate a lighted shrine to the Virgin of Guadalupe, patron saint of Mexico, and our neighbors helped keep the shrine decorated with flowers.

Shortly after we moved to the village, a committee of three women appeared at our door one evening to request our contribution for a festival. Naturally we asked many questions.

How many fiestas, we asked, did San Nicolas celebrate in a year? Five, they explained (some of our neighboring villages observed twelve). Ours were:

1. Easter

2. June 13—feast day of San Antonio, patron saint of Texcoco, our municipal seat.

3. August 15—Day of Asuncion, feast day of the original Indian village on this site, which was nearly wiped out more than 100 years earlier by a cholera epidemic and merged with the nearby settlement of San Nicolas.

4. December 6—feast day of San Nicolas, principal celebration of the village.

5. December 12—feast day of the Virgin of Guadalupe, patron saint of Mexico.

How much should we contribute? we asked. The leader of the solicitors said the committee recommended a uniform contribution for the village. On this occasion they asked 100 pesos, about US$8 at current exchange. Future fiesta committees would ask from 100 to 300 pesos, and the cumulative fiesta cost for one family in a year might be US$50.

Did everyone contribute? we asked. Old residents, we learned, including elderly widows and widowers, generally give the recommended amount. But some newcomers to the village did not participate; they felt the fiesta was an old-fashioned idea, not productive for the village. The treasurer among our solicitors opened a large account book and showed where villagers had written the amounts of their contributions and signed their names. This was public accounting in its simplest form.

What do you use the money for? we asked. The term *feast day*, it seemed, was misleading. The village gave no feast. Private families might bring together their extended members for a midday meal, but the public observance usually involved:

Decorating the church with banks of flowers

Paying the priest to conduct special services

Hiring a 20-piece band to play in the village churchyard from 7 A.M. to 6 P.M. The band was entitled to three meals.

Purchasing fireworks, mostly explosive rockets

School children formed a procession through the village, carrying a religious statue. And once in a while a commercial carnival agreed to set up its rides and games in our village. The larger neighboring villages were more successful in attracting carnivals.

A friend tells this revealing story: A Canadian businessman with a Mexican wife lived in a village near Cuernavaca. The man offered his community a major gift. Since the villagers had to travel 25 miles to a city bathhouse (*bano*), he suggested building a bathing facility in the village with the proviso that the village would maintain it. A committee of elders pondered the proposal and decided the village would prefer musical instruments and colorful uniforms for a band that would march in local parades. The businessman accepted this judgment. When he returns from Canada, he is now met officially by the band. (I have known villages in Burma, Pakistan and Nigeria where the priorities would probably be the same. They would prefer the pomp of a marching band over the sanitary merits of a bathhouse.)

San Nicolas is today a prosperous village, but when we moved here in 1974 its economy was stagnant. The 100 households then supported themselves with four principal livelihoods. For example, about 40 women were selling flowers, fruit, and herbs in the Mexico City markets. These women boarded a bus at 4 or 5 A.M., each carrying a large basket of home-grown fruits and herbs, arrived at a city market by 7 A.M., and staked out floor space for display of their wares. Having earned a few pesos, they returned home by bus in the afternoon. They also carried city ideas back to the village.

Some 20 husbands were commuter-laborers, employed by CIMMYT, or by the agricultural university at Chapingo or by small industries at Texcoco.

Seventy-two village families were *ejidatarios*—members of the Mexican agricultural cooperative system established after the revolution of 1910, which broke up large estates and placed most agricultural land under joint ownership of the villages called *ejidos*. In our village each *ejido* member was assigned one hectare of land on which he was able to grow enough maize to feed the family one year. The maize crop was not high yielding, the main problem being insufficient irrigation water. Few villagers were full-time farmers.

Finally, a dozen women or more were self-employed in their village homes. Some cooked Mexican barbecue that they sold to picnickers on Sunday. Some took in village laundry. Some made handcraft articles that they sold in Texcoco. One woman specialized in lampshades which she sold in Mexico City.

Since 1975 two remarkable developments have raised the income of San Nicolas: One was the opening of a sand and gravel mine, operated by our village cooperative; the other was the wholesale production of flowers in plastic greenhouses, built by many village families.

The cooperative mine, near a riverbed half a mile from the village, contains millions of cubic feet of sand and gravel suitable for making concrete. Every day from earliest daylight to dark a stream of trucks hauls sand and gravel from the mine to various construction projects. Sales from the mine have risen rapidly to the level of US$1 million a year, and the mine now pays dividends to each cooperative member—about US$1000 per family per year. The mine also employs a dozen villagers as machinery operators and enables several village women to earn their living selling hot lunches at the mine. The mine manager is himself a villager in his fifties.

The production of flowers in plastic greenhouses is built around one product—the giant white chrysanthemum, which is the favorite Mexican blossom for weddings, funerals, and anniversaries. A typical plastic greenhouse in the village is 120 feet long, 20 feet wide, and may cost US$1500. It produces 15,000 blossoms in each 120-day growing cycle, and the crop can be repeated two or three times a year, depending on whether the producer installs a heater for the coldest season. San Nicolas growers now sell about 1 million blossoms a year.

The greenhouse industry also supports several sidelines of employment: builders who erect the plastic houses, gardeners who raise the seedlings, merchandisers of fertilizer, sprayers, and pesticides, truckers who deliver the flowers to Mexico City and, of course, the retail florists.

Between 1975 and 1985 about a quarter of the families in San Nicolas, 38 out of 156, have become involved in the greenhouse business, either as owners or as laborers who participate on shares.

I have no accurate data on family incomes, but here are two personal observations. First, when we became residents of the village in 1974, there were four automobiles owned by 100 households. Now there are between 75 and 100 pickups and sedans, mostly ancient, owned by 156 households. Second, almost every adobe house has at its doorstep piles of sand and gravel and bags of cement. These residents are busy expanding their living space with their own labor. Better housing is a top priority of villagers whose income is rising. Most villagers have been sleeping on the floor because they have not had enough room for beds. As soon as they build an addition, they also install beds.

San Nicolas is mentioned in Mexico's pre-Columbian history. Just behind our village rises a cone-shaped hill about 500 feet high. Near the top of the hill an Aztec poet-king named Nezahualcoyotl (translated "Hungry Coyote") built a summer retreat—a pleasure garden. That was during the century before the Spaniards arrived in 1519. The poet-king (he lived 1402-1472) terraced the hillside and brought irrigation water from a neighboring hill over an earthen aqueduct. The water splashed down the hillside from pool to pool. The king also assembled a botanical garden of rare fruit trees and flowers and collected singing birds in cages. On a neighboring hill he grew 1000 cypress trees and fenced in a game park stocked with deer that he hunted with bow and arrow. This was probably the finest royal retreat in the western hemisphere, rivalling the pleasure gardens of the Chinese emperors near Peking and the Mogul emperors in Kashmir.

Little remains today of those Aztec gardens except for stone stairways cut into the hillside, stone basins that are called *Aztec baths*, and a fine circular pathway near the top of the hill, three-quarters of a mile long, affording splendid views of the Mexico City plain. The first Spanish bishop of Mexico, Fray Juan de Zumarraga, ordered destruction of all the buildings on this hill, thinking they must contain idols.

I feel possessive about the hill, which is called *Tezcotzinco*, because I climb it almost every afternoon at sundown. I follow the circular pathway three times around and return home in approximately one hour. It is a private exercise club, a wonderful place to be alone and to retrace the footsteps of the Aztec kings.

A story is taught to Mexican school children about this hill. When Nezahualcoyotl was a prince of 15 and living in his father's palace in Texcoco, part of the army rebelled and killed the king. The lad was whisked by his tutor to this hill at San Nicolas and hidden in a cave for 14 days until the revolt was put down. The prince survived to rule for almost half a century. I have found three caves on the hillside, each of which might be the site of this story.

There is one more link to Aztec days. Among the rare trees that Hungry Coyote collected in his pleasure garden was a flowering species called the *manita* ("little hand") because it produces a brilliant scarlet flower the size of an infant's hand, two inches in diameter, with five baby-like fingers. Mexican physicians know that the flower can be converted into a tea and drunk as a remedy for hypertension. We have three manita trees growing in our orchard and are able to pick as many as 1000 blossoms a week during a three-month harvest. The blossoms are sold at the Sonora market in Mexico City.

Before the revolution of 1910, San Nicolas was part of a great *hacienda*, or estate, called *Molino de Flores* (translated "mill of the Flores family"). The family had many buildings along a stream, surrounded by a small forest in which they operated a flour mill with water power. Their agricultural land, including that of San Nicolas, was devoted to wheat, which fed the mill. Violence of the Mexican revolution is still evident in the Flores family buildings—the roofs destroyed by fire and the family chapel pockmarked with bullet holes. Today Molino de Flores is a national park, crowded on Sundays by Mexico City families taking picnics in the wooded area. The ruins of this great hacienda are occasionally used as the setting for Mexican motion pictures, recalling the lavish wealth that existed on the feudal estates before 1910.

The Mexican village of San Nicolas Tlaminca, with a present population of about 800, manages its affairs as well as any village we have observed closely in the third world. Every three years a meeting of all the villagers elects a *delegado*, an unpaid official who represents our village before the municipality, the next higher tier of government. The delegado also performs many of the services of a local headman. When village cattle stray on another's property, the delegado will adjudicate. If heavy rains wash gullies in the dirt streets, the delegado will arrange repairs. Each public expense must be covered by a *faena*, or special fee, approved by a majority vote of the villagers. This village manages its own pipeline for drinking water and a network of irrigation canals. It provides its own elementary school building. It sees that all school-age children are in school. It installed street lights at village expense. It arranged for a private busline to connect the village with the municipal city. Crime is unknown, except for occasional drunkenness in public, which is regarded as an illness, not a breach of law. Not all village services are performed promptly or well, but in a community with rising income, there is little complaining.

Mexican government services to this village are minimal. The national ministry of education employs the teachers in the village school, which charges no tuition. Children who continue beyond elementary grades have access to a secondary school in a neighboring village—a one-mile walk. A public health nurse from the national ministry of health visits San Nicolas once a week. The national telephone company maintains one telephone at a village grocery store. There is no registration of births and deaths in the village. All in all, the Mexican government services are no worse than those we have observed in other third world countries and are probably better than most.

The ability of our village to manage a mining enterprise with revenues of US$1 million a year is remarkable—on a par with some of the small industries we have observed in the Peoples Republic of China and in South Korea. Likewise, the rapid growth of the greenhouse business must be credited to the aggressive business instincts of the Mexican villagers, most of whom have only elementary-level schooling.

Our village population has increased approximately 50 percent in ten years, largely from a high birth rate rather than from migration of new families. Mexico has an active family planning program—at least in the cities—but its results in the villages cannot compare with the more effective population programs in the third world, especially in China.

When I retired as director general of CIMMYT, Berni and I faced a choice between spending our retirement years in San Nicolas or on our farm in Loudoun County, Virginia. For the present we have chosen to stay in San Nicolas. Why?

1. A village on Mexico's central plateau provides a healthy tropical climate at 18 degrees north latitude and an elevation of 7000 feet. Temperatures reach into the 60s and 70s almost every day, winter and summer.

2. Climbing the hills rising at the edge of our village provides us with exercise that is pleasant and near at hand.

3. CIMMYT's international scientific community is 15 minutes from the village; it affords stimulating social contact. Other CIMMYT benefits include international telephone service, a post office, a bank teller, and a library.

4. We are an hour's drive from Mexico City's bookstores (they are admirable), first-run U.S. movies (we seldom go), a talented amateur theater group (we rarely miss), great museums, and a range of restaurants comparable to a large American city.

As Oscar Lewis wrote, the lives of the villagers are not dull.

> *Today China is a rapidly developing country that has been freed of the worst afflictions suffered by its people over the centuries.*
>
> Professor John G. Gurley, 1975

PART SIX

# RETURN TO PEOPLES CHINA

After an absence of almost 40 years Berni and I returned to Peking in October 1975. I had left China as a newspaper correspondent, age 26; I returned as director of an agricultural research institute, age 62. In the 1930s my attention focused on wars and peasant turmoil. Now, after living 18 years in the third world, I viewed China as another developing country—the largest and perhaps the most creative. I hoped to compare China with other third world nations.

The opportunity to return to China arose in this manner. The United States Academy of Sciences in 1974 sent a 12-member Plant Studies Delegation to observe Chinese agriculture. The group was headed by Dr. Sterling Wortman, a CIMMYT trustee, and included Norman Borlaug, leader of the CIMMYT wheat program. The report of this group was the best general description of Chinese agriculture then available. I read it several times. It aroused my hope that CIMMYT might help in China's development.

Also in 1974 a team of scientists from the Chinese Academy of Agricultural Sciences (CAAS) visited Mexico. I gave them a tour of CIMMYT and learned from them that China had already imported through the Mexican government 19 tons of seed for semidwarf wheats. The leader of the Chinese group was Xu Yuntian, a wheat breeder about age 55, then secretary of the Chinese academy.

During our day-long conversation Xu said he would propose that his academy invite Berni and me for a visit to Chinese

231

agricultural institutions. No invitation arrived for almost a year, but during that period we found time to do some reading on developments in China during the first 25 years of communist rule. China was still a partially closed country, and we did not have access in Mexico to good Chinese source materials, so our calendar of recent Chinese history was skimpy, looking like this.

*A Calendar of Chinese Events: 1949-1974*

| | |
|---|---|
| 1. Liberation Day | October 1, 1949 |
| 2. Economic reconstruction and land reform | 1949-1952 |
| 3. The first five-year plan | 1952-1957 |
| 4. The Great Leap Forward | 1958-1959 |
| 5. The Russians depart | 1960 |
| 6. Turmoil and near disaster | 1959-1962 |
| 7. The Cultural Revolution | 1966-1969 |
| 8. Recovery | 1970+ |
| 9. Twenty-fifth anniversary of PRC | October 1, 1974 |

Here are the notes we wrote on each of these events.

1. *Liberation: October 1, 1949.* When Mao Zedong proclaimed the Peoples Republic of China on October 1, 1949—a date that Chinese call *liberation*—China was already freed of the unequal treaties; the provincial warlords had already been pushed aside by the civil war; and the struggle to wipe out the landlords was already in full cry, with the outcome hardly in doubt. So victory over the three evils that the communists pledged to eliminate was in sight. The principal objective of the next 25 years, according to Mao, was to build a socialist society. That sounded simple for a revolutionary party that was already victorious in its civil war. But from our reading we concluded that conflicts within China in the next 25 years included struggles of communists against communists over the nature of the revolution.

2. *Reconstruction and land reform: 1949-1952.* After the communist takeover, the government focused on reconstruction of the country, which had been severely damaged during the preceding 12 years of fighting. By 1952 the country had been essentially restored to its prewar level of economic activity.

The land reform program during 1949-1952 confiscated farmland from landlords and rich peasants and gave it to middle and poor peasants. China was still at a stage that Mao called *new democracy* (the concept that Mao had described to me in his cave in 1938). The land distributed became private property for those who received it. In theory the power of the landlords could be eliminated without killing any of them, but the peasants often took the law into their own hands in dealing with their former masters. Mao contended that the peasants had to liberate themselves, so land reform was not carried out by the government—from above—but by a violent peasant movement in which 800,000 landlords and their families were estimated to have died.

I found it difficult to obtain impartial judgment on the results of land reform, but one useful study was a 1974 doctoral dissertation of C. R. Roll at Harvard. After comparing survey data from the 1930s and 1950s, he concluded that the average income of the poorest 20 percent of the Chinese rural population rose in the 1950s nearly 90 percent in real terms, while that of the next 40 percent rose by perhaps 15 percent. Landlords, who constituted only 3 percent of the population, had been virtually wiped out.

Later in the 1950s, the communist party changed the basic land-holding unit from peasant households (170 million) to communes (50,000). It appeared to me that the first stage of land reform created incentives for farm production, but the later collectivization wiped out most of that stimulus and triggered a food shortage.

3. *The first five-year plan: 1952–1957.* China's first five-year plan was regarded as highly successful at the time, and later experience confirmed this to be the most successful period under Mao Zedong's leadership. The USSR provided loans for China to buy about 200 complete industrial factories. Over 10,000 soviet experts went to China during the 1950s to train Chinese in industrial skills, and China sent more than 13,000 students to the Soviet Union for advanced study. By the end of the 1950s China was able to produce high grade steel, motor vehicles, jet aircraft, and power-generating equipment.

4. *The Great Leap Forward: 1958–1959.* Toward the end of the first five-year plan Mao Zedong grew restless under the soviet-imposed development plan, which stressed tight centralization, neglected local initiative, and gave heavy industry priority over agriculture. Mao wished to replace the soviet model with one more closely resembling China's successful guerilla tradition. The result was the Great Leap Forward. This was an attempt in 1958–1959 to use guerilla tactics for economic development in the countryside. The tactics emphasized local initiative, heroic deeds, and nonmaterial incentives. The upsurge of small industries, new roads, irrigation schemes, and reforestation projects was remarkable initially, but

was soon brought to a halt by overambitious plans and lack of technology.

The most publicized feat of the Great Leap was the drive for backyard steel smelters. More than a million small smelters were reportedly set up by villagers during 1958 and over 100 million people gained some experience in small industry, but their product proved largely unusable.

5. *The Russian departure: 1960.* Russian technicians working in China were called home, taking with them the blueprints for factories on which they were working. This collapse of Chinese-Russian relations was provoked by many irritations, including Krushchev's ridicule of Mao's Great Leap and the question whether China was to be a subordinate or leading member of the soviet bloc. (An old maxim says: Two kings can't live in the same palace or sleep under the same blanket.)

6. *Turmoil: 1959-1962.* PRC encountered near disaster during 1959-1962. The crisis was reflected in reduced grain harvest, a severe drop in industrial production and abandonment of the second five-year plan. When demographers were able to study the population data for that period they found "excess deaths" and "reduced births" (both compared to the previous trendlines) totalling 16 million during the three years. The effects equalled a traditional Chinese famine, although the government avoided that word.

7. *The Great Proletarian Cultural Revolution: 1966-1969.* The economic setback of 1959-62 gave Mao's opponents in the communist party (leaders who considered production more important than class struggle) the opportunity to restore individual rewards—for example, peasants again received individual kitchen gardens and public markets were reopened where peasants could sell produce directly to city customers at open market prices. Mao looked on with dismay.

The Cultural Revolution was Mao's dramatic attempt to cleanse China of bourgeois values, as he called them. This was a power struggle to determine which course China would follow—the path toward socialism or back toward capitalism. Mao said, "Our objective is to struggle and overthrow those persons in authority who are taking the capitalist road." His two principal targets were Liu Shaoqi, the chief of state, and Deng Xiaoping, the secretary general of the party. Unlike Stalin and his secret executions, Mao conducted his struggle mainly with public humiliation.

Mao called on millions of students to form themselves into Red Guard units, backed by the Peoples Liberation Army. They filled the streets with parades, mass meetings, and propaganda banners. In 1966 some 13 million Red Guards assembled in Peking for a series of national rallies, then were sent forth by Mao to attack the "four olds"—old thoughts, old habits, old customs, and old ideologies. Many victims were found among the educated classes who possessed foreign books and foreign-style clothing. Their homes were ransacked. Victims were hauled through the streets wearing dunce caps. Some committed suicide. A wave of hysteria gripped the cities. Violence erupted at universities in Shanghai and Peking, and the army had to be called out to restore order.

As wild emotions died down in 1968-1969, millions of Red Guards were sent to rural communes where their labor on agricultural production was expected to give them a better understanding of socialism.

Some elements of the cultural revolution continued into the 1970s. First, revolutionary committees took charge of most government agencies and educational institutions. These three-part committees consisted of one army officer, one communist party member, and one Red Guard. This was a step backward in management.

Second, many communist leaders attended *May 7 schools* where they spent six months or a year studying Marxism, separated from their offices and families.

Third, many city *ganbus* (civil servants) spent part of every month laboring as farmhands or factoryhands, becoming familiar with the problems of the peasants or workers, but slowing their office work to a halt.

8. *Recovery: 1970+*. After the Cultural Revolution, PRC entered a period of surging economic growth. Small industries in rural communes reemerged on a sounder basis. In this same period, Mao was increasingly feeble. He made his last official appearance at the party congress in 1973. Thereafter he withdrew to his study and confined himself to brief meetings with foreign dignitaries.*

9. *Twenty-fifth anniversary of PRC: October 1, 1974*. Despite its disruptions, China counted many achievements in its first 25 years under the PRC. It had more than doubled its agricultural production, greatly reduced illiteracy, and virtually eliminated the threat of pestilences such as smallpox, cholera, and plague. Its economic progress is summarized in Table 2, prepared from data of the Joint Economic Committee of the U.S. Congress, 1975.

Despite our 25-year survey, Berni and I were unprepared for the startling changes in Peoples China. And some of the Chinese we met were unprepared for us. Once when I mentioned to a Chinese youth that I had shared a midnight supper with Mao Zedong in his cave at Yan'an, the youth looked at

---

*Mao died September 9, 1976 at the age of 82.

TABLE 2. China: Major Economic Indicators, 1949–1974

| Year | Grain | Millions of metric tons Crude steel | Crude oil | GNP billions US$ | GNP per capita US$ | Population (millions) |
|---|---|---|---|---|---|---|
| 1949 | 108 | * | * | 40 | 74 | 530 |
| 1952 | 154 | 1 | * | 67 | 117 | 564 |
| 1957 | 185 | 5 | 1 | 94 | 147 | 626 |
| 1962 | 180 | 8 | 6 | 93 | 133 | 686 |
| 1965 | 210 | 13 | 11 | 134 | 179 | 723 |
| 1969 | 240 | 16 | 20 | 157 | 192 | 774 |
| 1974 | 259 | 24 | 65 | 223 | 243 | 838 |

Source: Joint Economic Committee, U.S. Congress, *China: A Reassessment of the Economy,* 1975
*Less than ½ million tons

me through narrowed eyes, as though I had said I camped with George Washington at Valley Forge. For younger Chinese, Yan'an and the Long March belonged to ancient history.

> *Peking was not only much cleaner, more orderly, more disciplined; it was somehow much quieter . . . Everything was more subdued than I remembered.*

Edgar Snow, 1961

CHAPTER 35

# What the Beijing Airport Road Tells Us

When our Japanese Air Lines plane taxied to Beijing's air terminal in September 1975, we passed row on row of planes flown by China Airline—the Russian AN24, similar to a Fokker Friendship with 52 seats, used for short internal flights; the British Trident, flown on longer internal flights; and the Boeing 707, used internationally. By the end of the 1970s, CAAC added Boeing 737s and 747s, the former for domestic routes and the latter on schedules to Europe and North America. In the mid-1980s, China did not yet manufacture its own commercial passenger planes.

Beijing's airport road in the 1970s and 1980s would astonish the traveler who knew this area before the Peoples Republic. In the 1930s, Peking had no modern airport, just a grass field south of the city at Nanyuan. Even at the end of World War II there was only a small Japanese military airfield near the Summer Palace. Now the commercial airport, situated east of the capital, is of world class.

Our drive on the airport road revealed impressive changes:

• The one-lane wagon tracks on which I had bicycled in the 1930s were then sunk in the ground because oxcarts churned up the earth and wind would blow the dust away. In the mid-1970s, the airport road was four lanes wide, raised three meters above the surrounding farmland, and asphalted.

• No trees grew in this area in the 1930s. All had been cut for fuel. Now the airport road was lined on each side by 30 meters of trees (locusts and acacias), giving shade and greenery. A new civic discipline protected these trees from the axe.

• Almost no irrigation existed in this region in the 1930s. Now all fields along the airport road were irrigated.

- The skyline of each village in the 1930s was a silhouette of one-story, mud-block houses. Now villages had at least one tall smokestack, and factory buildings rose above nearby housing—part of rural industry that Mao Zedong called "walking on two legs," meaning that villages should develop both agriculture and industry.

- There were few schools in the countryside in the 1930s, and those were attended mainly by children of landowners. Now every village appeared to have a school or at least access to a neighboring school. We saw school pupils marching on the airport road in the uniform of the Young Pioneers, recognizable by their red neckerchiefs. They carried farm implements.

Changes inside Beijing were equally conspicuous. The 1.4 million population of the 1930s had increased to 9 million in 1975, and the city had spilled over into the countryside, mainly in bedroom suburbs of five-story apartment houses. There was a major industrial complex in the western suburbs producing steel, motor vehicles, and chemicals.

My return was marred by one great disappointment: the fifteenth-century city walls had been torn down. This was said to have purged China of outdated symbols and ideas. I share Professor John Fairbank's lament that if ample traffic lanes had been cut through the Beijing walls, and each double gate tower had been retained as the center of a traffic circle, Beijing would now be the architectural envy of London, Washington and Moscow. But when the walls came down in the 1960s, such imaginative planning did not fit the ideology.

On our arrival in the city we were invited on a three-hour drive with a Chinese wheat scientist who had been our guest in Mexico. He asked what we would like to see first. We named four favorites among Beijing's historic sights: a panoramic view of the palaces from the Coal Hill; a walk through North Sea Park where long ago we had spent hours in the tea houses beside the lake eating melon seeds (the tea houses are still open, and they still serve melon seeds); the Temple of Heaven, whose blue roof line we consider one of the most graceful structures in the world; and finally the Summer Palace, the pleasure garden of the last Qing rulers. This drive confirmed that Beijing is still one of the loveliest capitals in the world, though its former clear sky is darkened by a pall of smog from burning soft coal.

We also drove past the monumental buildings constructed in the capital since 1949. Most of the new landmarks can be seen on a drive along *Changan Jie* (Everlasting Peace Boulevard), starting at the railroad station on the east, then the cluster of massive structures around the central square, *Tian An Men*; next a series of towered government buildings west of the Palace Museum, and finally the Military Museum. To drive along Changan Boulevard is like a walk down Pennsylvania Avenue in Washington from the Capitol to the White House. To our western taste, Beijing's new buildings are more grandiose and less graceful than China's historic architecture. Even Mao's mausoleum, with its stately pillared design, seems strangely un-Chinese in its surroundings, which include *Qian Men*, the somber fortresslike front gate, and the well-proportioned *Tian An Men*. Perhaps when Mao's mausoleum has stood for centuries, as it probably will, it will acquire the architectural legitimacy of age. (Each time we passed the Tian An Men Square we noted the four giant photographs of the "international Gang of Four"—Marx, Engels, Lenin, and Stalin.)

Having completed this flyby of the sights normally shown to tourists, we visited places of personal interest. We rode the subway from the Military Museum to the railroad station, following the route of the old city wall. Subway stations were free of graffiti, more like Washington than New York. The subway engineer riding in a glassed cab was a young woman in a green uniform with beret tilted over one ear. This called our attention to the changing role of Chinese women.

We walked through the art shops on Liulichang, and through the crowded No.1 Department Store on Wangfujing. The goods in both places were more interesting than in the Friendship Store for foreigners.

We noticed the traffic—brigades of bicycles and a variety of motor vehicles, all obedient to traffic lights (a civic virtue we find lacking in Mexico). There were automobiles made in China: the Jeep-like green vehicle; the heavy Russian-type, flat-bed truck; the light grey sedan resembling a 1950 Plymouth, and the pretentious Red Star limousine, strangely conflicting with the socialist ethic. We saw the bicycle taxis at the railroad station with their two-passenger trailers that dated from before the revolution. We observed a few motorcycle taxis with trailer, so common in South Asia, where they carry two riders. The motorcycle taxi seemed to be a logical step up from the man-propelled bicycle cab. On the main streets away from the center of Beijing we encountered scores of horsecarts, donkey carts, and handcarts carrying loads of bricks and cabbages.

Pedestrians appeared uniformly well dressed, well fed, and in good health. No beggars were in sight.

Unlike the old hospitality we remembered among Chinese friends in the 1930s, we were not invited to a private home in 1975 (a time when Mao and the Gang of Four were still in charge), nor were we on our next trip in 1977 when Mao was dead and the Gang of Four in jail, but people were still not sure that the Cultural Revolution was finished. The government discouraged social contact with foreigners, and most Chinese housing units were cramped. Nevertheless, during our third visit in 1981, two scientists were brave enough to entertain us for dinner in their apartments. (The Chinese consider a meal in the home to be a much more hospitable gesture than a meal in a public restaurant.)

The first invitation was from a Nanjing family in which both husband and wife worked. They had an apartment of 47 square meters (about 470 square feet) that housed six people: husband, wife, 24-year-old son (unmarried), 20-year-old daughter (unmarried), 94-year-old grandmother, and the husband's unmarried sister, who cared for the grandmother. In one room that served as parlor, bedroom, and dining room, a card table had been set for six. Eight Chinese center dishes and a soup had all been placed on the table before we sat down. Space was tight. There was no servant and no apologizing. This family had recently moved from an apartment of 40 square meters and felt upwardly mobile.

Our second invitation came from a family in Beijing whose 40-square-meter apartment housed three people: husband, wife and 23-year-old son (unmarried). Again husband and wife worked; this was the common pattern for university educated families. They invited four neighbors besides us and prepared ten Chinese dishes on a two-burner gas stove in a kitchen resembling a closet—no more than 2 by 1.5 meters (about 6 by 4 feet). The food included a fish cooked whole and *jiaozi* (dumplings). Around a table for nine, three sat on a bed, two on end tables, and two on stools. A neighbor was so impressed at the hostess's courage in entertaining foreigners that he sent in a dessert of "eight precious sweets." A male guest (scientist) did most of the cooking. The conversation in English was sparkling.

This home entertaining gave us several insights not granted to tourists. In the Nanjing home, the 20-year-old daughter was a high school graduate who had been waiting two years for a job assignment. In the Beijing family, the 23-year-old son worked in a factory 20 kilometers from home. He commuted by bicycle—two hours each way. We asked why he did not change to a job nearer home. He said the ministry of labor at that time must approve job changes (for 200 million urban residents!). This man had been waiting two years for approval of his petition, which was granted the following year.

Housing was obviously very much on the minds of city dwellers in Peoples China. It occurred to me that a visit to my five former residences in Beijing might supply a valuable flavor of the city.

> At least 35 percent of families in China's cities have housing problems. . . . The average floor space per person falls below 20 square feet per person, the basic minimum supposedly guaranteed everyone in China.

Jay and Linda Mathews, 1983

CHAPTER 36

# I Learn from My Former Beijing Residences

In Beijing I set out one afternoon in October 1975 to find the five residences where I had lived in the 1930s. I did not anticipate how dismal the picture would be. Leaving the Beijing Hotel I strode up the main shopping street, Wangfujing, turned east into a narrow *hutung* and found myself facing the entrance of the Peking Union Medical College, referred to in old days as PUMC. The bright red pillars on the hospital entrance were freshly painted, and the green roof tiles added a splash of color to the city, but the walls of the college were grimy with coal soot, an appearance made shabbier by personal laundry flapping from the hospital windows. PUMC had been the pride of the Rockefeller Foundation health program in the old days, rightly claiming the best medical faculty on the continent of Asia. The college and hospital were still operating in 1975 under the Peoples government, now flying a Chinese flag.

Continuing through lanes that circled the hospital, I emerged on Hadamen Street. There, across the avenue, I spotted the house where I lived in a walled residential enclosure formerly called *PUMC North Compound.* I tried to enter the compound through the north gate and found the access blocked by brick shacks constructed in the passageway. Such construction in other countries would be called squatters' huts, but these undoubtedly had been approved by a neighborhood committee, which in the Peoples China was responsible for knowing about anyone sleeping within the neighborhood.

I entered the compound through an alternate gate on the south and walked slowly among the 15 residences originally built as four-bedroom single family dwellings. Now they were occupied by four families or more in each house, as indicated by name plates. The lawns formerly kept tidy by Rockefeller gardeners were now bare of grass. The house I had once shared with one of the U.S. diplomatic officers, Jack Service, was losing its roof tiles and, like most preliberation houses in Beijing, needed paint.

Continuing at a rapid pace up Hadamen Street, past the American Bible Society (boarded up), past the Chinese YMCA (boarded up), I stopped at the intersection of Hadamen and Dongshikou where the guest house of American-supported Yanjing University had formerly stood on the southwest corner. I found no building there, just a weedy lot. Like many other sites in the inner city, this building had been torn down and nothing built in its place. I had memories of the pleasant tree-shaded courtyard when I was a 1935 summer resident. With Beijing's housing shortage it was surprising that no agency had constructed housing facilities here.

Still walking north on Hadamen Street, I headed for the College of Chinese Studies where a residential dormitory had been my last abode when the city was occupied by the Japanese. The school had been located just a short distance from the East Four Archways (*Dongsi Pailou*). The archways had disappeared from the middle of the street, which was an improvement for the flow of traffic but a loss of color for those who remembered the red, green and white memorial arches.

The lane where the college had stood, I found, was completely blocked by new construction, which linked the old language school on the north to a new ministry building on the south. It was logical that a former two-story dormitory should become a government office building but a landmark in my memories of the 1930s was gone. I recalled the manicured lawns of the school where some California chauvinist had erected the sign: LOS ANGELES CITY LIMITS.

Having exhausted the two hours available for my first walk, I set out on another day to look for the home of Mrs. Ruth Yang. Her place, I remembered, stood at number one, Yellow Earth Big Garden (*Huang Tu Da Yuan*), a branch of East Biao Bei Lane.

The interpreter who accompanied me found East Biao Bei Lane without difficulty. Houses along this lane were old-style grey-walled compounds, no windows in the outer walls, but with heavy wooden doors the size of garage entrances standing ajar in the daytime. They gave a glimpse of the courtyards. Trees that formerly stood in these sunlit compounds had been chopped down and the space filled with brick huts that provided crowded shelter for more people. The asphalted lane, replacing the muddy roadway of older times, was alive with activity. Bicycles whizzed by. A man pulled a handcart loaded with furniture. A public toilet 30 feet long was identifiable by the two doorways labelled with the Chinese characters for "Man" and "Woman"; there was no odor. Steel barrels stood at intervals along the lane for deposit of family trash.

## I Learn from My Former Beijing Residences / 243

We found a street sign for Yellow Earth Big Garden but there was no number 1, my old address. A house that resembled Mrs. Yang's displayed number 37. Two grey-haired women with bound feet were sitting on the stoop between two stone lions. Could they direct us to number 1? A shrug. Did they know whether this house had been occupied 50 years earlier by Mrs. Ruth Yang? A shake of the head. A small crowd gathered. Bicyclists stopped. Twenty people discussed our problem. House numbers were changed during the Cultural Revolution, they said. I asked who was the oldest resident in the neighborhood and they directed me around the corner to Mrs. Chen. At her door a teenage boy was inflating a bicycle tire with a hand pump. Was his name Chen? Yes. Was his family at home? Only his grandmother. We asked to see her and he led us through a narrow passageway that had once been part of a courtyard. A wrinkled old woman stood in the doorway of a low-ceilinged shack, stir-frying some vegetables. Was she Mrs. Chen? Yes. How long had she lived here? Since 1923. Did she remember a neighbor, Mrs. Ruth Yang? Oh yes, Mrs. Yang lived at the intersection only 30 meters away. Did Mrs. Yang have children? Of course, two sons. Then I was sure. Where were the Yangs now? They had moved to America after liberation.

I asked the young man to point out the Yang's house. It was indeed number 37 where we had previously drawn a crowd. The two women with bound feet still sat on the stoop. This time we asked the name of the occupants at number 37 and were told the Hu family. So I rang the bell. The door was opened cautiously by a girl of about 12, holding a baby. She looked frightened on confronting a foreigner, and planted herself squarely in the middle of the doorway. Were the Hus at home? No, they worked. You are of the Hu family? No, I am a small auntie who cares for their baby. I asked how many members were in the Hu family; she said father, mother, son, daughter-in-law and baby, plus two aunties, total seven.

My interpreter explained I was an American visitor who had lived in this house 50 years before and was interested to see my former residence. The girl looked doubtful. Without awaiting an invitation I stepped into the courtyard. On the left, walnut trees that I had known as saplings in the 1930s had grown into a canopy 30 feet high, casting a deep shadow. On the right, the former garden was filled with two ugly brick shacks without windows that probably contained two rooms. I asked who lived there. It was another family of seven, assigned by the street committee. No one was home there. By quick census this residence, which had formerly housed Mrs. Yang, her retired husband and two American bachelors, now contained 14 people. I stepped onto the veranda of the main house and was engulfed by memories. I could fantasize the slippered footsteps of Feng Lin, our manservant, bringing dinner on a tray from the basement kitchen.

After thanking the auntie, I returned to Mrs. Chen with one more question: Did she remember whether Mrs. Yang took in foreign guests? Oh yes, for many years that house was known as the house with American visitors. I told her I was one of them. At that she clutched my arm and asked if I would share her dinner of stir-fried vegetables. She was serious. I put my arm around her shoulders, returned her squeeze, and made a hurried exit.

My last goal that day was the Chang family residence on Eight Great Men Lane. We went by car up Hadamen Street, turned right at the East Four Archways (still standing there in my mind's eye) and left the car near the site of the former city gate called *Qihuamen*. It was a hot day but we proceeded on foot through the *hutungs*. When we came to an old lady sweeping her stoop, we asked if she remembered Ba Da Ren Lane. No, she didn't, but she called to her neighbor, and as before we quickly attracted a crowd. They suggested we go on further.

Another inquiry of an old lady. Another call to the neighbors. Another crowd. No definite information, but they suggested we try the alley to the right.

To my joy we found a short stretch of lane labelled "Eight Great Men Hutung," but there was no number 26. The houses resembled our old neighborhood—big compounds, stone lions at the gates. Again we were told that house numbers had changed, and if we went two more blocks there was an isolated section of Ba Da Ren Lane. Sure enough, this was our neighborhood, but in place of the Chang's residence there stood a five-story building called Golden Star Fountain Pen Factory. The driveway entering this factory was flanked by two stone lions, indicating a residence had stood there. We entered the parking lot. There we saw two mulberry trees that resembled those that had stood in the Chang's garden, but no longer with bird cages hanging from the branches, or wind chimes giving out clacking sounds.

We spoke to a middle-aged man with crewcut who appeared to be a factory supervisor, asking what happened to the residence that formerly stood on this property. He said he had been there less than 10 years, but he had a friend who had joined this factory immediately after liberation. He would telephone him. In a few minutes Crewcut returned with news: the Chang family home where I had lived had been nationalized in the early 1950s and a paint factory had been assigned to use a part of the house. As the factory expanded one room after another was torn down. My college classmate had continued to live in part of the house until 1966. Then during the Cultural Revolution the family had moved elsewhere in Beijing. Nobody knew where.

I rode back to my hotel curious to learn what had happened to my college classmate. Eventually I obtained a reassuring answer through a newspaper advertisement: my friend had become an English professor at a technical institute where he was assigned a modern apartment closer to his work.

I toted up the score on my visits to five former residences. Only two were still used as residential housing, and each of them contained three to five times the number of people they had held in the 1930s. The municipal government of Beijing has tried valiantly to provide new housing for the 9 million people now living in the metropolitan area by constructing five-story apartment buildings and offering 25 square meters (250 square feet) for most families. That housing supply in 1975 still fell short—and it does in 1986. Even by 2000 at the current construction rate, the supply will not catch up with housing needs.

> *I can talk to the wheat plant. And it talks back to me in a low voice that cannot be heard in an office. It tells me if it's happy, healthy, or if it is just asi, asi (so, so).*

Norman Borlaug, briefing trainees, 1972

CHAPTER 37

# Dr. Borlaug Examines Chinese Wheat

In 1977 the Chinese Academy of Agricultural Sciences invited our CIMMYT scientists in Mexico to inspect Chinese wheat research and production. China was then the third largest wheat producer in the world after the Soviet Union and the United States, and it would shortly become number one. We expected our tour to give us a picture of how Chinese agriculture had changed since 1949, and we were not disappointed.

The leader of our visiting party was Norman Borlaug, Nobel laureate. A second scientist was Borlaug's Canadian deputy, Glenn Anderson. Glenn could walk into a wheat field, look carefully at the plant population (number of heads per square meter), wrap one hand around a few heads to gauge their plumpness, and estimate what the harvest would be. He had been doing this for years, and the Chinese found him surprisingly accurate. At first he gave his forecast in western style—that is, metric tons per hectare—but since the Chinese measure their yields in *jin* per *mu*, Anderson pulled out a pocket calculator and repeated his estimate in Chinese terms. (A *jin* is half a kilogram; a *mu* is a fifteenth of a hectare.)

Glenn Anderson had another skill that mystified the Chinese. Without labels, he could identify in the research plots most western spring wheats. He was like a mother spotting her children in a nursery school. Anderson would call out to Borlaug: "Here's a row of the Chilean variety Orofen White." Or, "Here is the Italian variety Ardito." When the Chinese checked their plot books, they confirmed his call.

A third member of our CIMMYT group—besides myself—was Gene Saari, a Minnesota-trained pathologist then stationed in Turkey where he was mapping the movement of Asian wheat epidemics. Saari could circle through a Chinese wheat field and estimate the presence of individual diseases. He would call to Anderson: "Stripe rust five, stem rust zero, bunt ten." The numbers represented Saari's estimate of the percentage of plants infected by each of the wheat diseases.

The Chinese Academy of Agricultural Sciences (CAAS)—a division of the ministry of agriculture at Beijing—had proposed the exchange of four groups of scientists between Mexico and China in 1977, two missions from the academy and two from CIMMYT. Each four-person group would study either wheat or maize. Each visit would last one month, and each team would return home with seed samples that they had selected in the research plots. Each side paid its own international travel, and the receiving institution paid living expenses. This made an even split.

Mao Zedong had been dead only nine months when the exchanges began, and Mao's widow and her colleagues, the so-called Gang of Four, were in prison. The Cultural Revolution was presumed ended, but revolutionary committees still controlled research, and the Chinese scientists were cautious about what they told foreigners.

We went first to a northwest suburb of Beijing where the academy had its offices and 47 hectares of research plots. The academy had then arranged for us to visit seven provinces that produce half the wheat in China. We stopped at research institutes and universities where the head of each institution gave a briefing on local research; then we spent four to eight hours in the research plots, asking questions about introduction nurseries (wheats on trial from other countries); the local breeding program; and cultivation practices such as seeding rates, fertilizer rates, and the schedule of irrigation water. Our visit took place at the season of grain filling (about the last 30 days before harvest), which gave us the best opportunity to estimate yields and to observe damage from diseases, insects, and winter kill.

From the research plots we moved to neighboring communes where wheat was being grown for food. Again we walked in the fields, made our own estimates of yield, and calculated disease damage. Here we were introduced to a unique Chinese practice. Each research institute had established a working relationship with a few communes where farmers tested the institute recommendations. This collaboration was speeding the transfer of new technology from the research institutes to the farm fields. In fact, some visitors have called this the most successful extension service in the world.

To broaden our impressions beyond wheat, we asked to talk also with some teachers in commune primary schools, to visit patients in hospitals, and to see some farm wives who were living in new commune housing. I recall one Shandong woman who complained about her new housing that the planners had failed to provide space for a pig in her front yard, but she did find room for a chicken coop containing ten laying hens.

We were taken to factories in the communes. There were small cement factories, flour and feed mills, wineries, iron foundries, and machine shops producing farm tools and machinery—some making even complex industrial lathes. We saw the much-publicized small fertilizer factories producing 5,000 to 10,000 tons a year. We toured six of them. Some were producing low-concentrate nitrogen fertilizer from coal, a product called *ammonium bicarbonate*; other factories were making single superphosphate from local phosphate rock. These fertilizer plants put very little burden on the transport system because their products were delivered to farmers within a few kilometers of the factory.

At each research academy we presented a seminar for the Chinese staff. The chairman of the meeting invariably asked to hear the criticisms of our visiting group so that, as he put it, "we can learn from each other's experiences."

The Chinese Academy of Agricultural Sciences, CAAS, was established in the 1950s; it nearly perished during the Cultural Revolution when its staff was scattered to communes and its research equipment and data were partially destroyed by Red Guards. Most unfortunate, its germ plasm (seed collection) deteriorated when the seed could not be grown periodically. One Chinese scientist estimated that the academy lost a quarter of the entries in its seed bank. By the early 1980s the academy again stood tall under the leadership of a new director, Lu Liangshu, a 1953 Nanjing University graduate, and the number two officer, Ren Zhi, a Shanxi-born guerilla fighter who had attended after liberation the People's University in Beijing.

What else did we learn? Here are some trip notes.

*Mexican wheats in China*: The Chinese received their first experimental lines of Mexican wheat seed from Pakistan in the early 1960s. After good initial results China imported from Mexico in the 1970s 19 tons of additional seed to be used for wider testing. These Mexican varieties were found to be superior for short stems and high yield potential, but they also caused problems. In south China the most serious difficulty was that the grain sprouted in the field when warm rains fell before harvest. The Mexican wheats were also susceptible to several diseases prevalent in China— especially scab and *helminthosporium*, both fungus diseases. To remedy these defects the Chinese scientists crossed the Mexican wheats with outstanding Chinese varieties. By the time of our visit in 1977, Chinese-Mexican crosses were growing in every research institute.

*Wheat yields*: Every Chinese research institute showed us maximum yield trials of wheat covering two or three hectares. Their best yields were over seven tons, approximately equal at that time to our best research trials in Mexico. The better communes showed us wheat crops of more than 100 hectares (250 acres) with yields of three to four tons per hectare, and a few of five to six tons. Again that equalled the best in Mexico.

*Irrigation*: Every commune wanted us to inspect its new irrigation system. China had increased its irrigated land from 15 million hectares in 1949 to 45 million hectares in the late 1970s. China then had the largest irrigated area in the world, covering about 48 percent of Chinese cropland.

*Chemical fertilizer*: Communes were increasing their use of chemical fertilizer, supplementing their previous reliance on manures. The Chinese government was constructing 13 of the world's largest ammonia-urea complexes with rated capacity to push China's annual fertilizer production to 15 million tons of nutrients. The new fertilizer was expected to boost China's grain production in the 1980s, and it did.

*Grain storage*: In the communes each family stored its grain reserve in large household pottery crocks about one meter high and one meter across, each crock holding 300 to 400 kilograms of grain. The families we visited had up to six crocks, which they said would hold a year's supply of rice or wheat. After household storage, we visited silos in the production brigades (serving 10 to 15 villages). Each silo held nine tons. We saw as many as a dozen silos standing together in a brigade. Finally, we were taken to a state-owned grain storage center at the town of Weifang in Shandong province, where six warehouses in a railroad yard had a capacity of 25,000 tons of grain. We visited these warehouses during wheat harvest and saw the floors had been cleaned with the tidiness of a good housewife. Storage was in bulk—that is, no bagging—but the floors, walls, and tops of grain piles were sealed with sheets of plastic into which was fed an insecticide gas. This was an impressive picture compared to the food-short China before the revolution—the same country that had suffered 1800 recorded famines between 100 B.C. and 1910 A.D.

*Pigs*: Mao Zedong called the pig "a fertilizer factory on four legs," and he urged villages to raise more pigs to provide more organic fertilizer. Various targets were set, such as one pig per rural household, or one per person in the commune, or one per *mu* of cropland. (A *mu* equals a sixth of an acre.) Wherever we went, the commune leaders boasted about the number of their pigs.

At the end of our visit, the academy in Beijing asked the CIMMYT scientists to submit oral suggestions for improved research. Dr. Borlaug agreed, but began his response with this caution: "China faces many problems with which we are not familiar, and our brief observations could therefore be wrong. If you will accept our comments as first impressions, I will give you my reactions." Some of his proposals were too technical for this narrative, but here are three examples.

1. China's spring wheat crops in 1977 often developed short heads, with fewer than normal kernels per head, and lower than normal weight per 1,000 kernels. These symptoms suggested inadequate plant food in the first 30 days of growth, and indicated that farmers had not added enough fertilizer to compensate for multiple cropping (growing more than one crop on the same land in the same year). For centuries Chinese farmers had grown only one crop a year, with low plant population. The rapid spread of irrigation under the Peoples Republic had stimulated multiple cropping, higher plant population, and higher nutritional requirements. Fertilizer practices had not always kept pace. Other third world countries have encountered the same problem. The Chinese Academy, we suggested, needed to conduct fertilizer trials using a wider range of doses to find the best application in each climatic zone.

2. In the Yangtze valley, 12-month cropping had caused a buildup of insects and plant diseases. The farmers were trying to cope with this problem by chemical sprays. In every commune we saw spraying of wheat. The Chinese Academy, we suggested, needed to redouble its efforts to breed wheat varieties with resistance to disease. This would require a larger number of wheat crosses each year. We asked the breeders we met how many crosses they were making; the usual answer was 300. That was not enough. In Mexico we made 10,000 crosses a year of bread wheat and 5,000 of durum wheat. Wheat breeding is like a game of roulette; the greater the number of crosses, the greater the likelihood that a few progeny will be found with the desired disease resistance. Then the breeder needs to "pyramid the genes"; that means to cross plants that show some disease resistance, until the available resistance has been concentrated in a few superior varieties. Achieving disease resistance through breeding is a slow process, but after it is successful the farmer can reduce his expensive spraying.

3. Chinese wheat in the Yangtze valley suffered from a disease that in English is called *scab* and in Latin *Fusarium*. This head infection was destroying 5 to 10 percent of the Yangtze valley wheat crop every year, and up to 25 percent during epidemics that occurred about two years out of ten. No

absolute resistance to scab had been found anywhere in the world, but Brazil and Argentina each had found local wheat varieties that showed limited resistance. So CIMMYT had entered into an arrangement with Brazil and Argentina that we called *shuttle breeding*. Each year we took seeds from Brazil and Argentina and crossed them in Mexico to our best spring wheats. In the following year we sent seeds from the best plants harvested in Mexico to Brazil and Argentina for them to regrow and select the best progeny under their disease conditions; those selections in turn were shuttled back to Mexico. After repeating the process for ten years, we had gradually combined stem rust, leaf rust, and modest scab resistance with high yield.

We suggested adding China to this procedure. Chinese wheats would be crossed in Mexico to the best combinations of Brazil-Argentina-Mexico wheats. The resulting seed would then be returned to China for reselection of the best progeny under Chinese conditions. (This China-Mexico collaboration actually began in 1981. Another ten years beyond the mid-1980s may be needed to develop wheats that are strong enough to resist a Chinese scab epidemic.)

Those three observations indicated to us that Chinese wheat research could continue to produce higher yields during the 1980s and 1990s.

At a seminar at Cornell University in 1981 I was asked to evaluate Chinese wheat research. Since I knew of no objective rating system by which to compare researchers in different countries, I described a few achievements of Chinese wheat scientists. Here are four.

- Breeders in Shandong province released in the early 1970s two winter wheat varieties called *Taishan 4* and *Taishan 5* that possess a yield potential of nine tons per hectare. That equals the best Mexican wheats. (*Yield potential* is the yield when grown under supervision of scientists at the research station with near ideal conditions.)

- Nanjing wheat breeders doubled the yield potential of new wheat varieties released in Jiangsu province during 1960-1974 (from 3.8 tons per hectare to 7.5 tons). That was a remarkable jump.

- Beijing breeders were more successful than researchers elsewhere in developing wheat varieties with earliness (fewer days from seeding to maturity). The best winter wheats in the Beijing area now ripen by June 10, thus permitting harvest before the rains and enabling the farmer to plant summer maize on time. In Heilongjiang province—up against the Russian border—spring wheats now ripen in 70 days, among the earliest in the world.

- China's highest wheat yield in a "maximum yield trial" has been 15 tons per hectare, grown in Qinghai province in 1977, and repeated in several subsequent years. This China record exceeds the 14.1 tons recognized as the national record in the United States (grown by a private farmer in Washington State in 1964–1965 winter season, using the winter wheat variety Gaines). The Chinese record was attributed to a high-yielding spring wheat variety, full irrigation, optimum fertilizer, total absence of disease and ideal climate.

Judged by their accomplishments, Chinese wheat researchers are among the best in the third world, and they are closing the gap with researchers in industrialized countries of North America and Europe. Nevertheless, important problems await Chinese progress in the late 1980s and 1990s—improvements that will include greater disease resistance, greater kernel plumpness, stiffer straw, and greater moisture conservation in the dryland areas of China's northwest.

After our China trip in 1977, I reported at the World Bank on what we had seen. I closed with two observations. First was a quotation from Norman Borlaug: "The people we saw in the communes were adequately fed and clothed. They had medical services down to the village level. The children were in school. Everyone was employed, although part of the work is on rural works that maximize hand labor in development of irrigation, roads, and reforestation. The people showed a dignity in their status and a pride in their community. As far as I could observe, they were happy."

The second observation: "China is a country where farmers are feeding 22 percent of the world population on less than 7 percent of the world's cropland. There must be things we can learn from them."

*We have had few great agricultural travellers and few books that describe the real and significant rural conditions . . . . The spirit of scientific inquiry must now be taken into this field.*

Dr. L. H. Bailey, U.S. Department
of Agriculture, 1911

CHAPTER 38

# Briefing Travellers to China

This chapter will not be easy going. It gives an agricultural picture of China that tourist guides are not able to provide during the usual 20-day China itinerary. This is part of the briefing I have given our scientists in Mexico when they make their first visit to China. I think this picture is more important to an understanding of China than mere sightseeing.

By 1981 our maize and wheat center in Mexico was sending scientists to consult in China every year. I created a briefing notebook that answered three interesting questions:

1. Why is Chinese agriculture important to the rest of the world?
2. How does Chinese food production compare to that of a leading third world country like India?
3. What has China found useful in its exchange of information with world research centers?

China's agriculture is important to the outside world for five reasons.

First, China is the world's largest producer of grain. China surpassed the United States in total grain harvest for the first time in 1983, and the United States is unlikely ever again to move ahead of China. China leads the world in rice and wheat production and is second in maize after the United States. When we recall that China was known—less than 50 years ago—as the land of famines, these Chinese harvests in the 1980s are all the more significant.

Second, the PRC is one of the historic storehouses of plant germ plasm, or seeds. In neolithic times, China became one of the eight world centers for domestication of crops—for example, rice, millet, soybean, and scores of vegetables and fruits—and China remains the center of diversity for many species. Major seed banks elsewhere still lack adequate samples of the genetic diversity available in China, and both PRC and its foreign collaborators would benefit from more seed exchanges.

Third, China has the widest range of environments for foodcrops found in any single country—from subarctic to subtropical—and for this reason China can play an important role in testing improved plant types.

Fourth, Peoples China has set up new forms of management for rural development and new incentives for peasants. Some third world countries are studying Chinese methods to determine whether aspects of PRC rural strategy are transferable.

Fifth, Peoples China plays a role in world grain trade that is sometimes helpful and sometimes disruptive. Regularly China exports to other countries a part of its rice crop at $300–400 a ton and imports part of its wheat needs at $150–200 a ton; thus for every ton of grain that China exchanges in this manner, it makes a profit. Since the exported rice helps to meet a deficit in South Asia and the imported wheat provds sales opportunities for the world's principal wheat exporters (USA, Canada, Australia, France, and Argentina), everyone benefited.

The disruptive side of China's grain trade emerges when bad weather reduces Chinese grain production. Then China enters the grain marketplace with enough clout to outbid smaller importers; this can cause hardship to LDCs that are regular importers. Therefore it is useful both to PRC and the third world if international scientists help China to maintain its grain production at a steady or rising level.

Comparing China and India in agricultural production should reveal how China ranks among third world countries. India has been the recognized leader in the green revolution. Has China now displaced India?

Travellers who visit the two countries make several familiar observations: (1) China uses its animal manures as fertilizer, while India burns most of its cow dung for cooking fuel. This difference gives Chinese agriculture a major advantage. (2) The distribution of rivers in the two countries has favored irrigation in China, with the result that PRC irrigates half its cropland and India only a quarter. Again, the difference favors China. And (3) China has been more aggressive than India in rural development, especially in land-levelling, drainage, reforestation, and manufacture of chemical fertilizers. Each of these developments has stimulated food production. Might China now surpass India in food production? By what measures? Could one make a statistical table that would give an objective comparison?

Such a statistical table was assembled in 1977 by an American scholar, Dr. Benedict Stavis, then of Cornell University, who presented it as a research paper at Sussex University in England. I have copied the method of Dr. Stavis but have substituted more recent data through 1984. And I caution my Indian friends that the conclusions are startling:

*Peoples China in 1983 produced approximately double the basic foodstuffs of India, on 40 percent less cropland, at yields more than double those of India. Or: China produced 40 percent more basic foodstuff per person, almost three times more animal protein products per person, and more than twice the amount of cotton per person for clothing.*

When I quote these findings to scholars who specialize in research on India, someone always shakes his head and declares there must be something wrong. I then give my supporting evidence and invite corrections. My evidence is organized in ten numbered points below. (If you are bored by statistics, you can skip the next two pages, but for me the table tells a fascinating story.)

BASIC DATA
COMPARING FARM PRODUCTIVITY
OF CHINA AND INDIA

1. *Population*:
   China–1023 million in mid-1983
   India–730 million in mid-1983
   Source: *World Population Data Sheet*, Population Reference Bureau, Washington, D.C., 1983

2. *Total staple foods produced* (cereals, tubers, pulses, oilseeds):
   China–377 million metric tons, 1983
   India–195 million metric tons, 1983
   Source: *FAO Production Yearbook 1983*,
   (Tubers are included at 20 percent of fresh weight).

3. *Staple foods produced per person per year*:
   China–368 kilograms, 1983
   India–267 kilograms, 1983
   Source: calculated from 1 and 2 above

4. *Animal products produced* (meat, eggs, milk solids, fish):
   China–26.3 million metric tons, 1983
   India–5.9 million metric tons, 1983
   (Milk solids are calculated at 12.5 percent of whole milk) Sources: *FAO Production Yearbook 1983*; *FAO Fisheries Yearbook 1983*

5. *Animal products produced per person per year*:
   China–25.7 kilograms, 1983
   India–8.0 kilograms, 1983
   Source: calculated from 1 and 4 above

6. *Cotton production and per person supply*:
   China – 4.6 million tons of cotton lint produced, equalling 4.5 kilograms of cotton per person, 1983
   India–1.4 million tons of cotton lint produced equalling 1.9 kilograms of cotton per person, 1983
   Source: *FAO Production Yearbook 1983*

INPUTS

7. *Cropland in use*:
   China–99.3 million hectares, 1983
   India–169.6 million hectares, 1983
   Source: *FAO Production Yearbook 1983*

8. *Chemical fertilizer applied, nutrient weight*:
   China–15.3 million metric tons, 1981
   India–5.2 million metric tons, 1981
   Source: *FAO Fertilizer Yearbook 1981*

CONCLUSIONS

9. *How does China achieve its higher productivity?*
   China irrigates about 50 percent of its cropland, and India 25 percent.
   China had a cropping intensity of 1.5 compared to 1.2 for India. This means China grows an average of 1.5 crops on its land each year, and India 1.2.
   China applies five times more chemical fertilizer to each hectare of cropland. (China uses 153 kilograms of chemical fertilizer, nutrient weight, for each hectare, compared to 30 kilograms used in India.)

10. *Gross national product per person*:
    China–US$310 in 1982, increasing at 5 percent a year during 1960–1982.
    India–US$260 in 1982, increasing at 1.7 percent a year during 1960–1982.
    Source: *IBRD World Development Report 1984*, page 218

What do we learn from this comparison? Overall, Peoples China *has* surpassed India as leader of the green revolution. And if we repeat this China-India exercise for all the larger third world countries—say, all the countries with populations larger than 50 million—we find that China now leads the third world in agricultural growth.

What exchange of information with international research centers has China found useful? As we sat in Beijing Airport awaiting a plane I put that question to Fang Cuinong. A man from Zhejiang province in his fifties, Fang was a scientist who had spent 30 years in agricultural development.

Before answering my question, Fang sketched the PRC's experience with foreign agricultural exchanges. During the 1950s, China relied on the Soviet Union and the socialist countries of eastern Europe. These countries exchanged seeds and visiting scientists, and a number of Chinese plant breeders earned their doctorates at Moscow (among others, Xu Yuntian, Liu Dajong, Shen Jingpu).

After the breakdown of relations between China and the USSR in 1960, Peoples China invited agricultural missions from Commonwealth countries including Canada, Australia and Great Britain. Through these visits China broadened its exchange of germ plasm.

Not until the mid-1970s did China begin to establish working relations with the newly formed International Agricultural Research Centers, and then—within a few years—China received visiting scientists from the Rice Research Institute (IRRI), from CIMMYT, and from six other centers. The other six were the Germ Plasm Board at Rome, the sorghum and groundnut scientists from ICRISAT in India, the barley researchers in Syria (ICARDA), the potato center in Peru (CIP), the tropical pasture research center in Colombia (CIAT) and the sweet potato and bean research scientists in Nigeria (IITA).

"OK," I said to Fang, "you have 8,000 employees in your academy and related institutes, including scores of well-trained Chinese plant breeders. What are you getting from outside China that you haven't already done for yourselves?"

He thought for a moment. "Your international centers are doing four things for us that are important," he replied. "First, you give us access to the world collections of germ plasm. Your centers have searched the world for seeds and you save us time if you let us draw on your world collections.

"Second, your consultants tell us what is new in the world of research. You keep in touch with everyone. And we are constantly hearing about new things through your visitors.

"Third, and this is very important: your centers have become world leaders in genetic control of insects and plant diseases. When we add your advanced lines to our breeding work, we find the best available materials for genetic control of pests.

"Fourth, your international centers have trained a few of our younger scientists and have received some of our old-timers for refresher experience. This supplements our PRC graduate schools. China needs thousands of new scientists and we cannot afford to rely primarily on foreign universities. But we find that our scientists who go to your centers bring back specialized knowledge that adds a further dimension to our training work."

At this point my plane arrived. I thanked Old Fang for his judgments and added his information to our CIMMYT briefing book.

*There is not much snow in the Himalaya—very little below 17,000 feet and none in Kathmandu.*

Joel Bernstein, 1986

CHAPTER 39

# My Trek to the Mountain Called Chomolungma

The Chinese claim that their mountain *Chomolungma* is the highest peak in the world (29,028 feet or 8,870 meters), and they are correct. *Chomo* is the Tibetan name for Mount Everest, sometimes translated "Mother Goddess of the Snows." The mountain stands on the common border between China (Tibet) and Nepal, and climbing parties have scaled the mountain from both directions. When a climber stands on the peak, he can plant one foot in China and one in Nepal.

I made a trip to the base of Chomo in 1981. This four-week walking trip revealed to me the kind of exhaustion that Long Marchers suffered and their danger from altitude sickness when crossing parts of the eastern Tibetan plateau.

China shares common borders with eleven countries. If you run your finger over the map of Asia along the China boundary, starting in the south China Sea and moving clockwise, the eleven neighbors are Vietnam, Laos, Burma, Bhutan, Nepal, India, Pakistan, Afghanistan, USSR, Mongolia, and North Korea. Six neighbors are landlocked and therefore remote and somewhat mysterious. Of those, the most intriguing for me is Nepal—a hermit kingdom that closed its borders until 1950. I made my first visit to Nepal in 1951 to discuss the United States technical assistance program with the king and prime minister. Subsequently I made five or six more visits. Whenever I looked up at the snowy peaks, I resolved some day to make a trek to Chomo; but not until 1981 when I was 69 did I fulfill that wish.

Our son Eric (then 33) and I planned an easy trek in Nepal in the fall of 1981—possibly two weeks walking a level route around the base of Annapurna. But Eric saw an announcement for an Everest trek in the catalog of a California travel agency. The leader of the Everest group was a medical doctor who lived in Burlington, Vermont—just a few city blocks from Eric's home. So Eric talked to Dr. Charles Houston, the noted mountain climber and medical researcher; Eric got Everest fever, and I agreed to join them.

Dr. Houston's group planned to walk from Kathmandu, capital of Nepal, to the base camp on Everest or Chomo, a distance on the map of 125 miles, not counting uphills and downhills that probably double the distance. The trek would begin at 5,000 feet and end at 19,000 feet on a glacier that comes off Everest. The party numbered 19 people—11 men and 8 women, ages ranging 19 to 69. More than half had medical degrees. Some were superb athletes, including several of the women.

On an afternoon in September 1981 we were at the Malla Hotel in Kathmandu, packing our equipment to start next day. The duffle bag, limited to 40 pounds, contained sleeping bag for 20 degrees below zero, double-thick long underwear, heavy woolen pants, pile sweater, down jacket, hiking boots, woolen face mask, sunburn cream for snow glare, and other things that strained the zipper on the bag. The duffle would be toted by a porter. The day pack, with suggested limit of 15 pounds, we were to carry ourselves. It contained camera supplies, snacks for the trail (mixed nuts and raisins), and space for warm clothes that we peeled off during the day.

The travel agency catalog rated this trek as one of the toughest in the Himalayas, but we thought that statement was for city softies and not for people who had trained with jogging and hikes.

The first day sobered everyone. After a two-hour bus ride into a valley of the Himalayas, surrounded by green paddy terraces and no snow-covered mountains in sight, we started walking up a rocky trail at 20 degree pitch. The steepness never let up as we panted up to 7,000 feet elevation at six in the afternoon. Our campsite that night was an alpine meadow with grazing cattle and goats. Our bright yellow and blue tents drew from a neighboring village a crowd of children who stared as the Sherpa kitchen crew produced a dinner of scrambled eggs, boiled potatoes in the skins, cauliflower, Indian-style *chapatis*, and dessert of one fresh apple. By darkness at eight we were all in our sleeping bags.

That first day our procession had stretched out several miles. We could count 52 porters, each assigned 80 pounds of gear: duffle bags, tents, ground cloths, kitchenware, and food for 25 days. We also had six Sherpas, the elite tribesmen in the mountains around Everest; they hired the porters, chose the campsites, erected the tents, and kept company with the laggards on the trail, frequently me. In a very gentle way the Sherpas offered advice to us novices: "When you are climbing, lift each boot only two inches. Advance each foot only 12 inches. The short, easy steps will get you to the top in fresher condition." They followed their own advice.

Day number two we learned about tightness of schedule. At 5:30 A.M. a cheerful Sherpa called out "Bed tea!" It was still dark, but we were already packing sleeping bags into stuffbags and trying to reorganize our overfilled duffle bags. By six a porter was standing outside the tent, impatient to take the duffle bag and set off on his day's trek. He was supposed to reach that night's campsite before we did.

At 6 A.M. we ate a breakfast of oatmeal and evaporated milk, Swedish crackers and a choice of hot drink—tea, coffee, or a drink called *Chocomalt*, which was said to give the best energy for the day. This was a meager meal, but it had to be prepared by cooks starting at 4:30 A.M. at an elevation where water boils very slowly.

We were on the trail at 6:45 A.M., stopping beside a stream at 10:30 to eat a lunch already prepared by the Sherpas. Back on the trail by 11:30, we arrived at the campsite by 3 P.M. Then came tea and cookies. Dinner followed at 6:30 P.M., and we were back in our sleeping bags by 8. The more energetic ones found time to keep a diary and to wash clothing every day. Others, like me, were stretched out in a tent between tea and dinner. Eric was my tentmate.

For 14 days we went up one side of a ridge one day, down the other side the next day: 3000 to 4000 feet up, and the same distance down. Generally at the bottom of the ridge we came to a stream, and our trail wound along the steep hillside above the roaring torrent of green water that threw white spray several hundred feet up the mountainside. Many times we crossed these streams, sometimes on suspension bridges with husky steel cables and good protective netting on the sides; sometimes on temporary bridges constructed of two or three logs, or even one log, stretching 15 feet above the roar of the water—without a railing. On slippery one-log bridges, I swallowed my pride and accepted the help of two Sherpas, one ahead of me holding a hand, the other behind me clutching my belt. The log crossings were an experience that still gives me bad dreams.

The changes in scenery were magnificent. At 10,000 feet we reached pine forests with a rich grass undercover like a national park, then passed the treeline into alpine meadows. Twice we walked through magnolia forests at the treeline where extreme cold had caused trees to become gnarled. In the lowlands, along streams, we walked under tropical trees 300 feet high, with 50-foot Spanish moss hanging like veils. We heard south Asian birds in the forest but seldom saw them.

Several viking-type men, including Eric, bathed in the icy streams. They avoided the rushing current in the middle but found quiet pools along the river bank. Early in the trek our trail twice crossed mountain roads where trucks had brought in the luxuries of the outside world—beer in liter bottles and Cadbury chocolate bars.

Our camp toilets consisted of two blue tents, both unisex, with a shallow slit trench in the earth, like an Asian toilet. Stories circulated about people who fell into the trench when making a service stop at night. In daytime, we just headed into the bushes along the trail.

Our trek leader said other expedition groups frequently grew quarrelsome and irritable. Ours was an exceptionally pleasant group, with much chatter and story-telling. Laundry efforts became fewer because clothes did not dry. Personal hygiene became less and less important.

After the fourteenth day our route turned from west-east to south-north, straight up a series of valleys leading to Everest. Each night we camped about 1,000 feet higher. Long underwear came out of the duffle bags. We passed through Namche Bazar, town of the Sherpas (80 houses, 400 people clinging to the cliffside); most of our Sherpas disappeared that night to visit their families. There was a post-office at Namche Bazar where good tourists could mail their postcards to friends back home.

For two days before Namche we were accompanied on the trail by tradesmen toting fruits and vegetables to the Sherpas' fortnightly market. One night we camped outside a huge rock cavern where the trading people, enroute to Namche, danced and sang by firelight. The rhythms probably were descended from prehistoric times.

At Namche our barefoot, shivering Nepali porters were paid off. The carrying job was taken over by yaks, which resemble short-legged cattle with enormous carrying and climbing strength. Yaks generally do not live below 11,000 feet, and the porters do not work above that elevation, so Namche was the transfer point. Each yak carried the loads of two porters. It was a great sight to see the Sherpas loading 25 yaks in a crowded area around our tents.

The medical doctors in our group constantly checked us for mountain sickness: Do you have a headache? Are your ankles swollen? Have you diarrhea? I had none of those, but I got another symptom—above 10,000 feet I lost my appetite for the starchy, greasy food. The less I ate, the harder it was to maintain the trekking pace.

One constant plea of the doctors was that we maintain our fluids. We all carried one-liter water bottles; we stopped to drink frequently and refilled at lunch and dinner. The saying went: If your urine looks like dark tea, drink enough water to make it look like gin. I drank as directed, but mine never looked like gin.

One night under a Coleman gas lantern in the mess tent, our group pressed the trek leader, Charlie Houston, for a talk on mountain sickness. He had spent much of his adult life studying this curse of mountaineers. My notes can't do justice to Charlie's elegant language, but his talk stopped all yawns because we realized we were all at risk.

People who go rapidly up to 10,000 feet, Charlie began, will notice headache, pounding pulse, and may feel mentally confused and often nauseated. Of those who continue rapidly up to 18,000 feet, 5 out of 100 will faint and a few may have convulsions.

This response to altitude, we were told, is determined by the speed of ascent, the altitude reached, and the length of stay—plus individual characteristics that are not presently understood. (Our own trekking schedule, he assured us, had been planned for its gradual three-week approach to Everest and allowed two days for acclimatization at 11,000 and 13,000 feet.)

Altitude sickness can be identified as a series of illnesses of increasing severity. Dr. Houston described three.

The first, *acute mountain sickness*, called *soroche* in South America, occurs above 7,000–8,000 feet after rapid ascent. It is characterized by headache, nausea, shortness of breath, disturbed sleep, and difficulty with thinking. The symptoms resemble seasickness, or some would say, a bad hangover. This can be a miserable affliction. Few people die from it but some wish they would.

The second form, *high-altitude pulmonary edema*, occurs mainly above 9,000–10,000 feet. It is characterized by shortness of breath, cough, and often a slight fever. The symptoms may take 36–72 hours to become obvious, but they can rapidly worsen to unconsciousness and death. Getting the patient down a few thousand feet on the mountain is usually very helpful.

The third form, *high-altitude cerebral edema*, is less common but frequently more deadly. Since the brain has the greatest need for oxygen, it is not surprising that lack of oxygen affects brain functions early—that is, judgment, decision making, and appreciation of one's condition. A curious staggering walk appears early.

Acclimatization, of course, is a partial safeguard against all forms of mountain sickness. Almost 200 persons have reached the top of Mount Everest, at least a dozen of them using no auxiliary oxygen. To reach such a summit mountaineers must allow time for the body to adjust to less oxygen, but even with superb acclimatization, a climber on the top of Everest is at his utmost limits. The Himalayas, Houston cautioned, are not for everyone, and even at much lower altitudes, illness and death can strike the incautious.*

Sixteen miles from Everest base camp we came to a magnificent Buddhist

---

*Charles S. Houston is the author of a book filled with joyful anecdotes on mountain climbing—and grim medical accounts of those who failed to follow reasonable precautions. See *Going Higher: The Story of Men and Altitude*, 1986.

monastery, Thyangboche, perched on a ridge at 13,000 feet, completely surrounded by ice-covered peaks. To the north were Everest and Lhotse; to the east, Ama Dablam; to the south and west, mountains without names because they were less than 25,000 feet. Here the trek leader urged everyone who was in doubt about his performance at 19,000 feet to stay with the 32 monks. Three of us halted here, while Eric and the others went on to the glacier. I spent the three days photographing and visiting other monasteries up to 16,000 feet. One claimed to have the hand and skull of a *yeti*—the giant abominable snowman—which I examined. The hand was human size; the skull was about 15 inches high, but looked to me like an animal skull.

Anyone who has read James Hilton's *Lost Horizon* will recall the atmosphere of the Himalayan monastery—gongs for worship call, murmuring of prayers, yellow-robed monks washing their clothes at a spring in the middle of a meadow or tending vegetable gardens.

When we resumed our trip, our trek consisted of three days, mostly downhill, to a tiny airfield at the village called Lukla. Here a 20-passenger, Canadian-built plane, the Otter, landed on a steep uphill runway; it then took off down the slope for the 30-minute flight to Kathmandu. It was disheartening to learn that the distance of our three-week overland hike could be covered in 30 minutes by a modern machine.

We observed that many trekkers—especially Germans—fly in to the Lukla airfield and start their trek above 10,000 feet, walking from there to Everest. And some of them are carried back to the airfield in litters with severe mountain sickness. Few people who walk from Kathmandu get sick from altitude.

Did you enjoy it? everyone asked. Yes, enormously. It was a superb experience, but better recommended for persons the age of Eric than for me. Eric calculated from the map that we climbed 52,000 feet in the first 16 days—about twice the height of Mount Everest—in crossing mountains of 10,000 feet or less.

Did I lose weight? Yes. I didn't step on a scale until 30 days after leaving Nepal, and then I was down 13 pounds. I may have lost as many as 20 pounds in Nepal.

Was I satisfied with my training schedule? No; my training before the trek was inadequate. I had climbed up and down 300 meters (1,000 feet) in an hour of exercise every afternoon for six months in Mexico. The Nepal trek required that kind of climbing daily for seven hours. My Mexico regimen did not give me adequate endurance.

All the same, my trek to Chomo in 1981 revived a hope I had nurtured for many years—to retrace the Red Army's Long March of 1934-1935, and the opportunity was nearer than I realized.

*"March on, march on, march on, on."*
Chinese national anthem

PART SEVEN

# WE RETRACE THE LONG MARCH AFTER 50 YEARS

For years I had fantasized I would take a journey over the route of the Long March. The terrain was not open to me during the Japanese war (1937-1945), or during China's war of liberation (1946-1949), or during two decades when the PRC shut out most Americans (1950-1972). But the attraction of this trip never diminished. I recognized three appealing motives.

1. The Long March could help explain a major revolution in modern history. When a quarter of mankind swings in a new direction, the balance of history is altered.

2. The Long March crossed dramatic countryside—the green rice fields in the south, the frozen Tibetan heights in the west, and the dry brown loess lands of the northwest—all good subjects for photography.

3. The Long March passed through impoverished areas. A visit half a century later should help answer the question, How successful was Mao Zedong in improving the peasants' livelihood? The third motive was my primary interest.

In November 1981 Berni and I visited the Chinese Military Museum in Peking. This museum was the appropriate place, I had decided, to deposit the 152 photographs that I had taken of the Chinese guerilla armies in 1938 and the dispatches I

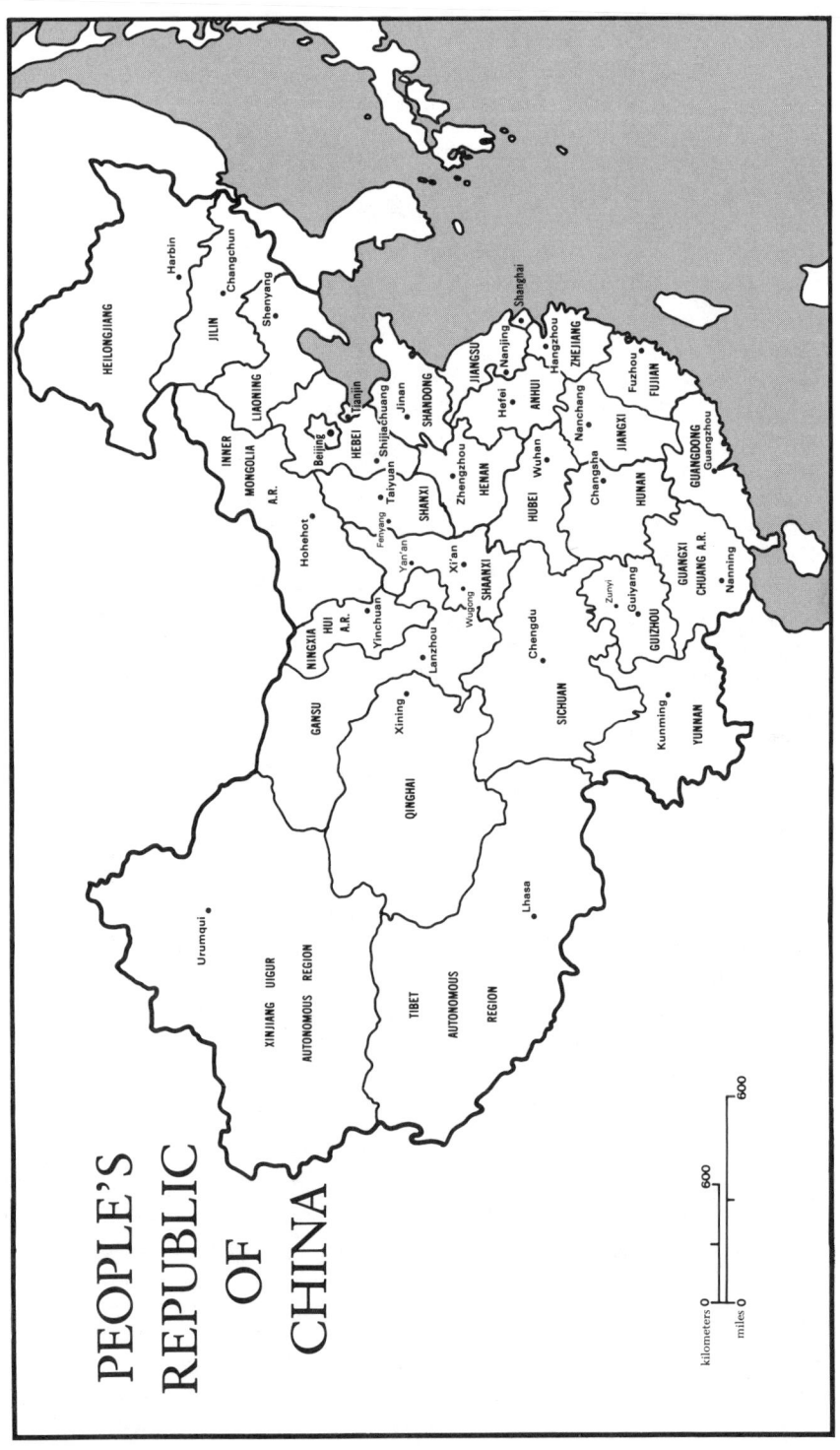

had written for the Associated Press in north China. My photos included early shots of Mao Zedong, Zhu De, Peng Dehuai and other Red Army leaders. I had these photos and stories bound and I presented them to the museum under the title "American News Reporter with the Chinese Guerilla Armies in north China." The deputy curator with whom I dealt was a scholar named Qing Xinhan, a combat soldier turned historian. I confided to him my hopes of making a trek over the route of the Long March and asked what plans the museum had for celebrating the fiftieth anniversary of the march in 1985.

One year later—in November 1982—a telephone message at my office in Mexico said the Chinese defense attache, an official of the Chinese Embassy in Mexico, wished to pay a call on me at 5 P.M. the following day. I did not know the man who gave his name as Chen Jinyang. When Chen arrived, he was a slender, athletic Hunanese of 52, a college graduate who had served five years in Moscow as assistant defense attache, a similar assignment in Bulgaria, and now had a twin posting to Mexico and Cuba. Such a career, I calculated, must place Chen fairly high in the Chinese defense intelligence service. He asked to speak in Chinese, and I was soon beyond my depth. As I got his message, the army museum at Peking was inviting Berni and me to travel with a group of army officers along most of the route of the Long March in June and July 1983. Nothing specific was said about itinerary, the means of transport, the escorts, and the cost. When I asked Chen about these matters, he suggested I write a letter to the museum, proposing my own answers, and send the letter in the Chinese diplomatic pouch from his office. I liked his directness.

The itinerary I proposed would pass through most of the famous battle sites and the location of other exploits of the Long March, omitting the climb over the Great Snowy Mountains and the trek across the swampy grasslands of northern Sichuan.

I suggested interviews with Red Army survivors, commune secretaries, school teachers, and talks with the planning department of each province. As for escorts, we needed at minimum one army interpreter and one army photographer. Berni and I would pay our own travel to and from China, and I suggested we discuss the travel costs within China.

Five months later we received a written reply that approved these proposals. The Chinese army offered to pay all the travel expenses in China. Only much later did we learn the cause of delay in the reply: the People's Liberation Army had sent jeeploads of officers to inspect roads, guest houses, and food stops along the route and to ask for help from civilian government agencies for briefings on the people's livelihood. These precautions later paid off. The entire trek went off without a hitch.

In earlier years Berni and I had made two unusual trips in Asia, each following the footsteps of a famous traveller. In 1961 we spent weeks on muleback in the Bakhtiari mountains of southwest Iran. We were following the route of a British archeologist and diplomat, Sir Henry Layard, who described the trek in his diary, *Early Adventures in Persia, Susiana and Babylonia: 1840–1844*.

In 1963 we walked the roads of ancient Bokhara and Samarkand in soviet Asia, using as our travel guide the diary of a British diplomat, Fitsroy MacLean, entitled *Eastern Approaches* (1936). MacLean was a romantic who liked to see great Asian mosques by moonlight. In spite of the suspicions of our Russian guide, we managed to get those same nighttime glimpses.

In preparing to follow the Long March we turned for help from writers who had described the events of the Long March or the related Chinese geography. We put into our shoulder bag five books:

George Cressey, *China's Geographic Foundations* (1934)
Agnes Smedley, *The Great Road* (1956)
Edgar Snow, *Red Star Over China* (1937) and *Red China Today* (1961)
Dick Wilson, *The Long March 1935* (1971)

Scores of other books were worth carrying, but we had learned that the fewer books you carry, the more likely you are to use them.

When we arrived at Beijing airport in May 1983, we were full of questions. Five PLA officers in green dress uniforms awaited us. Only one was familiar—he was Old Qing, the deputy museum curator to whom we had presented the photo album two years earlier. He would accompany the trek. The other four greeters were the deputy chief of foreign affairs for the Army General Staff, Sui Guokuen, about 50 (it was he who had labored over the trip logistics); the interpreter, youthful-looking Tong Jinrong who became our eyes and ears for the next two months; a lanky army photographer named Qi Baolong, age 43, who produced extraordinary pictures by shinnying up walls or standing on vehicles; and finally a young man from the army logistics staff who extracted our luggage from customs, produced a Red Flag limousine for the drive into Beijing, and wheedled us a room at the Beijing Hotel after the manager said the hotel was full.

We were now eager for our first Beijing interview.

> Turning the Chinese army from Mao Zedong's chaotic "millet and rifle" brigade into a modern fighting force will be hard.

The Economist, January 1986

CHAPTER 40

# A Briefing on the Peoples Liberation Army

On our first day in Beijing, Berni and I needed current information about the Peoples Liberation Army (PLA), which had invited us to China. We were about to travel during June and July with PLA companions, stay often in PLA guest houses, and take frequent meals with PLA commanders. So we asked Old Qing, our sponsor, to arrange a briefing at the PLA military academy, the topmost army school, located north of the Summer Palace about 15 miles outside Beijing. We hoped to learn answers to three questions like these:

- How much has the PLA changed since the days of the Japanese war? Does the Chinese Army with 4.2 million armed men—the largest in the world—still teach the guerilla song which begins "When the enemy advances, we retreat"?
- What progress is the PLA making in modernizing its equipment?
- What wars are studied in the academy? (The answer might suggest the kind of conflict the academy is preparing for.)

When our sedan approached the academy at 8 A.M. one spring morning we passed a guard post displaying a sign in English: NO FOREIGNERS BEYOND THIS POINT WITHOUT SPECIAL PERMIT. Our driver handed over a permit.

Inside the academy gate, we soon found ourselves in a classroom of a modern university building, seated with a group of ten PLA briefing officers. Our principal briefer was identified as Deputy Commandant Yang Zhen, age about 55, lean, with a crewcut, gold-rimmed glasses, a trim green summer uniform, and a pleasant smile. Yang went straight into his introduction:

"First, China is a socialist country that needs a long period of peace to accomplish its development. Any future war we can now foresee will be a war of resistance against invaders. China will be weaker in armaments. This academy emphasizes military strategy whereby inferior equipment can overcome a stronger enemy.

"Second, our past experience with the war of resistance against Japan remains relevant.

"Third, this academy teaches Mao Zedong's 'Thoughts on War,' but has updated them.

"Fourth, the PLA is gradually equipping itself with modern armaments made in Chinese defense industries. That includes artillery, tanks, and jet airplanes. We will not depend on imports although we seek to buy prototypes of new weapons for adaptation in China."

Commandant Yang asked that we postpone our questions to the end of the three-hour program: first, a slide presentation on the work of the academy; second, a walking tour of the exhibition rooms presenting—on maps and lighted table models—the wars that the students study; third, displays of miniature modern equipment used by the Chinese navy, air force, and armored corps; fourth, a movie on the 1981 combined field exercises of the PLA; and finally, a question-answer period.

During the slide presentation I took some skeletonized notes: This academy was established in 1957, four years after the Korean War. The faculty numbers 60, the student body about 1,000. The abbreviated course for divisional commanders (major generals) takes 100 officers for one year. Students average 45 to 50 years of age, and their military experience has been 25 to 30 years. Their studies are 70 percent military, 25 percent political (Marxism, Leninism, "Thoughts of Mao") and 5 percent army administration. A more junior course lasts two years, enrolls about 600 officers. Their average age is 35, and their average army experience is 15 years.

Our walk through the exhibition rooms was interesting for the range of wars that they included: the Jiangxi revolutionary war and Long March (1927-1936); the Japanese war (1937-1945); the Russian seizure of Manchuria (1945); the war of liberation (1946-1949); the Korean war (1950-1953); the Russian-Chinese border warfare (1969); the Arab-Israeli war (1977); China's 16-day war in Vietnam (1979); and the British-Argentine war in the Malvina or Falkland Islands (1982).

Next we were taken across an overhead walkway joining the second floors of two buildings—like the drawbridge over a moat—to a locked part of the academy devoted to the study of foreign military forces. The principal room was devoted to the USSR and a second room to the United States. We passed the U.S. display briskly without time to pause. Briefer Yang made no unfriendly comments, but a visitor could draw the conclusion that the USSR was the potential enemy on which the academy was now focused, and the United States had been considered the most likely threat before the 1970s.

Next we entered a small theater. The lively color film showed a 1981 field operation in which Chinese infantry, airborne troops, armored corps, air force, and navy were all firing live ammunition. The closing scene showed Deng Xiaoping standing in a command car taking salutes from the combined forces. Deng's role was presumably based on his position as chairman of the military affairs committee of the Chinese communist party.

Now came the question-answer period, and Briefer Yang was unflappable in answering all questions from his American visitors. The hour's discussion can be reduced to Questions (Q) and Answers (A) that proceeded from elementary to delicate. (We expected that at any moment the briefer might close the interview.) Here is how the talk proceeded:

Q. *How does your selection of PLA officers in the 1980s compare to your selection in the old Red Army?*
A. Requirements for officers have changed. During the revolution most officers were uneducated peasants who were chosen for bravery on the battlefield and loyalty to the communist party. Today we aim to combine correct political attitudes with better education and greater military expertise. All appointments of new officers above platoon level now require a university education. For enlisted men we are teaching mathematics, chemistry, and physics to many former peasants and laborers who never finished high school.

Q. *Do women attend the academy?*
A. No, we have no women students, but we have women faculty. The PLA enrolls women in the medical corps, communications service, and administrative staff. We do not assign women to combat.

Q. *Has the PLA maintained its close relationship to the people that Mao Zedong once said was "as close as fish to water"?*
A. After 1949, many PLA barracks were located in cities and the contact of soldiers with the people was less frequent. But recently the PLA leaders have tried to remedy this isolation by involving the PLA in civilian activities. In 1982 alone the army joined in more than 10,000 construction projects (factories, mines, railroads, bridges, oil fields, and hydro-electric stations). We think the fish-and-water relationship is reviving.

Q. *How is the PLA progressing on modern armament?*
A. Our national budget has been adjusted (cut back). We have streamlined our PLA organization, reducing staff and using the savings for armaments. We procure weapons only within our own defense industries, as mentioned earlier. The modernization of our weapons will be a long process.

Q. *Does the academy continue to teach Mao Zedong's essay "Thoughts on Warfare"?*
A. Yes, but you will recall that Mao himself revised his writings on war after liberation, and our academy continues to update Mao's thinking to reflect recent military experience. We teach people's war because our foreseeable defense will be a war within China against outside forces. We still believe it is men, not weapons, that will decide the outcome of national defense.

Q. *Are some of Mao's thoughts on war obsolete?*
A. Yes. During the Japanese war the Eighth Route Army grew much of its own food. That would not be possible in a modern war. Also during the Japanese war, our guerilla forces obtained most of their weapons from the enemy.

Q. *Are you aware that some western military writers are critical of the writings of Mao on war, using such comments as "You can't fight guided missiles with broadswords"?*
A. Yes, we know our army is regarded as backward, but we know we are stronger than the Afghani guerillas, and the Afghans have stood off the Russians for four years.

That last answer of briefer Yang brought to mind an appraisal of the PLA in the official United States history of the Korean War. The appraisal reads in part:

> The Chinese coolie in the padded cotton uniform could do one thing better than any other soldier on earth; he could infiltrate around an enemy position in the darkness with incredible stealth .... It was not mass but deception and surprise which made the Chinese Reds formidable.
> The coolie in the PLA ranks had no superior in the world at making long approach marches by night and hiding by day, with as many as 50 men sharing a hut or cave and subsisting on a few handfuls of rice apiece .... Once engaged and under fire, the attackers hit the ground. Rising at any lull, they came on until engaged again; but when fully committed, they did not relinquish the attack even when riddled with casualties. Other Chinese came forward to take their places, and the buildup continued until a penetration was made ....

As we left the military academy, I asked briefer Yang if he could give me papers on the Long March that are studied by officers at the academy. Three days later we got the answer: No. The papers are still classified, almost 50 years after the march.

## Postscript

In 1985 the PRC announced plans for a reduction of 1 million soldiers in the standing army, still leaving 3.2 million men in uniform. Several dozen generals and 47,000 lesser officers had already been persuaded to retire from the army during 1985–86. This made room for better-educated officers at the top and permitted a shift in military expenditures, which were reported to consume 14 percent of the national budget. The smaller standing army would be offset by part-time training for 50 million high school and university students in a program resembling the U.S. Reserve Officers Training Corps (ROTC).

*I had long desired to stand face to face with Chinese farmers; to walk through their fields and to learn by seeing some of their methods which centuries of stress and experience had led them to adopt.*

F. H. King, 1911

CHAPTER 41

# Great Changes in the Countryside

Next Berni and I needed a briefing on the changes in the Chinese countryside; for this we approached friends in the Chinese Academy of Agricultural Sciences.

"You should expect great changes in the villages," they said. They reminded us that after Mao Zedong died in 1976, the government passed through two indecisive years in which Maoist policies remained essentially unchanged. Then the new regime led by Deng Xiaoping began a second rural revolution that swept aside some of Chairman Mao's favorite revolutionary ideas. The resulting boost to farm production was incredible. Consider these four results:

- China's grain harvest rose to new historical records for five years out of the next six, starting at 305 million tons in 1978, reaching 387 million tons in 1983, and continuing upward to 407 million tons in 1984.

- The ginned cotton harvest rose 66 percent in four years, so successful that the PRC was able to abolish cotton rationing after 30 years of short supply.

- Production of cooking oil rose 165 percent in four years, causing a glut that persuaded the authorities to lower the future purchase price. (Any housewife who has stir-fried in a Chinese wok appreciates the importance of cooking oil.)

- Peasant incomes doubled in the four years 1978–1982—albeit from a very low starting base. Rural income in 1978 averaged yuan 133.37 according to the State Statistical Bureau. By 1983 this income reached yuan 309.08. Since one Yuan was then worth US$0.50, the rise in average annual income per person was from US$67.00 to US$155.00 per year.

What were the new policies, we asked, that so stimulated the peasants? Our friends summarized the new strategy in five points.

1. The government released the 800 million peasants from Chairman Mao's compulsory collective farming. Villagers were no longer required to share labor among 30 or 40 families and to split their earnings. Instead, each family could contract for its own piece of land to be cultivated by the family, and it could sell on the open market whatever it produced above a modest quota that must be sold to the state. The system was similar to fixed rent.

2. Chairman Mao's system of central planning for agriculture was relaxed, permitting substantial freedom for the peasant to decide what to grow. Many peasants shifted from grain to more profitable cash crops such as cotton, oilseeds, and sugar.

3. The purchase price paid by the government for major agricultural products was raised: the price for "quota" production rose 20 percent, and "above-quota" prices jumped 50 percent. As expected, production shot up. Peasants may be illiterate but they can figure.

4. Peasants were urged to undertake specialized production such as raising hogs, tending silkworms or managing fish ponds. These functions had previously been managed by the whole village but were not profitable because the collective system gave no incentive for a peasant to acquire specialized skills. Under the new contract, the peasant was committed to deliver a stated quota to the government, and all production above the quota became family profit.

5. The government restored and enlarged the "private plots"—equivalent to kitchen gardens—and encouraged "free markets" where peasants could sell produce outside of government control. One government report said private plots covered 5 percent of total PRC cropland but produced 37 percent of all produce, a remarkable tribute to private enterprise.

These policy changes represented as great a revolution in the Chinese countryside as the earlier adoption of Mao's commune system in 1958 and the introduction of central controls. No other Marxist government had gone so far in using a profit motive to stimulate family agricultural production.

Great changes usually have negative side effects. What were the disadvantages of this new revolution in the countryside? we asked our friends. At first our friends said there *were* no negative consequences, but we persisted in the question and gradually assembled a list of disadvantages that had not yet been publicized. For example:

*Subsidies*: When the prices payable to the peasant were increased, the government decided not to pass on the higher cost to the urban consumer. In 1978 subsidies to all sections of the Chinese economy, as a share of government expenditures, were only 7 percent, but by 1981 these subsidies had risen to 30 percent—a level that approached some Eastern European countries. The financial problems of Poland, for example, are partly attributable to the subsidies granted to urban consumers. PRC cannot continue to buy up all the surplus crops without increasing this subsidy problem.

*Machinery*: The machinery pools from 1978 and earlier were no longer suitable. The size of tractor, for example, had been chosen to fit the amount of land cultivated by a production team—then about 20 hectares (50 acres). When the household became the new unit of farming (average less than one hectare), the old machinery was too large. A few families began to purchase garden-size tractors, as the Japanese did after World War II; the next step might be for families to rent medium-size tractors for custom work, as is done in Mexico. An intermediate step is likely to be the continued use of the ox and the donkey.

*Population*: The population policy of "one-couple, one-child" was weakened by the new farm policies. Since the peasant was now paid on the basis of his productivity, there was an advantage in having more children as field hands. County magistrates confirmed that there was some rural backsliding in the one-child program.

Other side effects were foreseeable. A social welfare fund in the old communes had provided support to the aged who lacked close relatives. Maintaining a welfare program would be more difficult under the household responsibility system.

Finally, production teams that were handicapped by poor soil or difficult topography had benefited previously by pooling their production with other teams within the same commune. This problem would be more difficult to solve under the household system. All these side effects are solvable, our Chinese friends assured us, but solutions take time.

On December 7, 1984, the newspaper of the Chinese communist party, the *Peoples Daily*, startled the political world with a front-page commentary declaring that Karl Marx's doctrines were obsolete as a guide for China. The Chinese were the only ruling communists who had openly questioned the tenets of Marxism and Leninism. "Marx died 101 years ago," the editorial stated. "His works were written more than 100 years ago. There have been tremendous changes since his ideas were formed. Some of his ideas are no longer suited to today's situation."

Some western news commentators concluded that China was returning to capitalism, but that seemed unlikely. A central feature of Marxism is that the key means of production are under state ownership; that arrangement in China has not changed. Another maxim of Marxism is the so-called "dictatorship of the working classes under the leadership of the communist party"; in China the communist party remains firmly in commmand.

So what was new? China proposed to link wages and bonuses to job performance, which is a market-style strategy. And China would gradually deregulate some industries and services and let the market—or profit system—replace soviet-style central planning. The state would no longer manage these freed enterprises directly.

Chinese leaders acknowledged that the new system involved risks. Inflation was one danger, unemployment another. And if these changes got out of control, the experiment would jeopardize the rule of the entrenched bureaucracy. But without this gamble, the Chinese leaders argued, China would remain in the third world—a backward country.

For almost 70 years Moscow had been the Rome of orthodox communism, claiming infallibility. Some countries in Eastern Europe—Yugoslavia, Hungary, East Germany and Poland—had tinkered with free-market reform, but none had gone far in challenging the Russian system. Now China was playing the role of Martin Luther in a Protestant departure from Marxism. Protestants did not cease to be Christians, of course, and the Chinese did not cease to be socialists. But China renamed its system "socialism with Chinese characteristics," a course uniquely suited to Chinese conditions.

Still digesting all this information and planning to look for confirmation, we began our journey.

*I have become painfully aware of the difficulties and dangers of writing contemporary history.*

Maurice Meisner, 1977

CHAPTER 42

# The China Daily Reports Our Trek

On a breezy day in late May 1983, Berni and I flew from Beijing to Nanchang, capital of Jiangxi province. We were starting our journey over the route of the Long March, accompanying a party of PLA officers. I planned from the start to write a series of articles describing the changes we observed along the route of the march. These articles would contrast the 1930s and 1980s. But almost immediately I found this difficult because it provided no continuity for the story. So at the end of the journey I gave an interview with the *China Daily*, the English language newspaper at Beijing; this summarized our itinerary and tied our experiences together. The interview appeared August 1 and 2, 1983. I realize this puts the interview before the journey—but the *China Daily* will make this report more coherent.

> An American husband-wife team has completed a 9,000 kilometer journey following the approximate route of the Red Army's Long March of 1934–35 and has recounted some of their experiences to *China Daily*.
> 
> "The Long March is still a good news story, one of the greatest of the twentieth century," said Haldore Hanson, 71, an agricultural research administrator from Mexico. He and his wife, Bernice, 68, lived in China at the time of the Long March in the 1930s. Hanson was later the Associated Press correspondent assigned to the Eighth Route Army, and his wife (before their marriage) was an English teacher in a middle school at Fenyang, Shanxi province.
> 
> Hanson said theirs was no heroic journey. "We stayed in army guest houses. We visited with magistrates in 30 counties. We crossed the 3437-meter Erland mountain in western Sichuan province in an air-conditioned minibus. Mao Zedong and his army of 20-year-olds struggled over the same ridge through a roadless forest."
> 
> The Hansons visited not only the sites of military exploits but talked to

peasants and officials to learn what changes had taken place since 1935. They looked at agriculture, education, health, and the critical population problem. "Those developments might be called another long march for the younger generation," Hanson observed, "and it still goes on."

"Our top experiences were the Luding chain bridge and a revisit to Mao Zedong's cave at Yan'an where I interviewed him in 1938," Hanson said.

From Beijing, the Hansons flew in May 1983 to Nanchang, capital of Jiangxi province in southeast China, where the Red Army was born on August 1, 1927, the result of the Nanchang Uprising. That uprising was a revolt by 20,000 Kuomintang troops led by five officers who later became famous as Red Army leaders: Zhou Enlai, Zhu De, He Long, Liu Bocheng and Ye Ting. The date, August 1—or *bayi* in Chinese—is commemorated as People's Liberation Army Day.

The Hansons travelled 1,100 kilometers by motor car in Jiangxi to visit revolutionary sites. They stopped at Ruijin, the small town that served as capital of a 14-county Red Army base (1930-1934) that Chiang Kai-shek's five annihilation campaigns set out to destroy. The Jiangxi soviet base tested Mao's ideas on land reform, on developing an economy under military siege, and on how to win peasant support, which proved critical in the Chinese revolution.

At the town of Yudu in south Jiangxi, regarded by historians as the starting point of the Long March, the Hansons made a night march with a group of young soldiers to get the "feel" of the march. They retraced Mao Zedong's footsteps at the start of the Long March when he left the north gate of Yudu town (5:30 P.M., October 16, 1934), walked downstream along the bank of the Gan River, and crossed a 400-meter pontoon bridge built by Red Army engineers. From there the Red Army pressed westward by night marches for two weeks before the enemy realized that the Jiangxi soviet had been evacuated.

In south Jiangxi, little Xingguo county boasts that it sent more volunteers to the Red Army than any other county in China, and more than 100 Xingguo boys rose to the rank of major-general. Here, as elsewhere, the Hansons interviewed men over 70 who were Red Army veterans.

Next, the Hansons drove to Jinggangshan, the formerly wild and impoverished area where Mao Zedong created the first Red Army base (1927-1929). Here Mao put into practice in eight counties some of his ideas on how to create a soviet area.

Near Changsha, capital of Hunan province, the Hansons visited the boyhood home of Mao Zedong which is now a national shrine. The 1.5 hectare farm of the Mao family serves as an ethnographic museum to illustrate how a fairly prosperous peasant family lived in south China at the beginning of the twentieth century.

The Hansons crossed Hunan province by train, passing quickly over the Xiang River by railroad bridge, whereas part of the Red Army fought a seven-day bloody battle there.

In Guizhou province the two Americans travelled 1,000 kilometers by car, following the Red Army path to the Wujiang River battle, to Zunyi, to the

Loushan Pass, and to the many crossings of the Chishui River. These were sites of the great events of the Long March in Guizhou.

At Zunyi in Guizhou the Hansons sat in the meeting room where an enlarged meeting of the Political Bureau of the Central Committee of the Communist Party elected Mao Zedong head of the Military Command Group, thus assigning him military leadership for the balance of the Long March.

At Loushan Pass—a hilltop on the Guiyang-Chongqing highway—the Hansons retraced the biggest military victory of the Long March, a battle in which 20,000 Kuomintang troops surrendered. The surrender site on the Wujiang River is now marked by a new hydro-electric dam.

The Hansons next arrived by train at Chengdu, capital of Sichuan province, and from there set out on a road journey of 1,700 kilometers to see the Long March events on the Dadu River and the crossing of the Great Snowy Mountains of western Sichuan. (In 1935 this area was known as Xikang province.)

At Anshunchang two old boatmen now in their 70s—men who guided ferry boats for the Red Army in 1935—escorted the Hansons to the river bluff and showed where three ferry boats worked for a week to move one division of the Red Army across the swirling Dadu River. One boat overturned, spilling 50 soldiers into the river where all apparently died. The balance of the Red Army—perhaps 20,000 men—marched farther upstream to Luding, a heavily fortified chain bridge—from which the defending Nationalist troops had removed most of the wooden flooring.

Here the Dadu River passes through a deep rocky gorge 104 meters wide. The suspension bridge, built shortly after 1700 on 13 iron chains, pitches and sways when several people cross at the same time. A Red Army death squad of only 22 soldiers captured the bridge in the face of machine-gun fire by Sichuan warlord troops. Red Army reinforcements cleared the small town of Luding of enemy troops, thus enabling the balance of the Central Red Army to cross in safety during the next six days. The Luding crossing is rated as the most critical single event of the Long March.

The Hansons walked across the bridge which they found in excellent condition in 1983. "We tried not to look down at the water 10 meters below us," Mrs. Hanson admits.

Crossing the Great Snowy Mountains at an elevation of 4,200 meters was the next exploit of the Red Army. Led by Tibetan guides, the marchers in thin cotton uniforms climbed through snow in passes 18 kilometers long. The Hansons went to Baoxing, a county seat in western Sichuan for a briefing by a Red Army veteran, survivor of the Snowy Mountain crossing.

The Hansons travelled by plane over the marshlands of northern Sichuan where thousands of Red Army soldiers perished in the swamps. From Xi'an, capital of Shaanxi province, they drove 1,700 kilometers to see Wuqi village, regarded as the end of the Long March, then to Bao'an where the soviet government made its headquarters in 1935-1936, and to Yan'an where the border government flourished for a decade (1936-47). This is where thousands of young people were trained for guerilla action against the Japanese invaders.

Wuqi had good reason to be called the end of the Long March. This was a desolate village of less than 100 households in 1935, situated near the common boundary of Shaanxi, Ningxia and Gansu provinces. Here, the weary Red Army arrived on October 19, 1935, still with the Muslim army of General Ma Hongkui at its heels.

The Hansons walked the last few kilometers into Wuqi, following the path of Mao Zedong on his last day of the Long March. Next day, after one night's rest, Mao directed the last battle of the march, in which the Red Army trapped and destroyed four regiments of cavalry, frightened one infantry division away, and captured 500 horses. Thus Wuqi village got its place in history and the Long March ended.

Hanson says he choked up with memories when he visited Mao's cave at Phoenix Hill and sat in the same chair in Mao's bedroom where the two men had talked all one night in September 1938—Hanson taking notes for the Associated Press, and Mao outlining his ideas on a protracted war with Japan.

Hanson says that in his trip, as he was briefed by provincial historians, he picked up small changes in the classical accounts. For example, the museum curator at the Luding chain bridge said that the Red Army's squad did not swing from the chains, as reported in early accounts, but each man sat upon two of the chains, holding his rifle with one hand and pulling himself along with the other hand. This version is less dramatic, but more plausible.

Also at Luding, the curator said that the defending warlord troops set fire to the gatehouse at one end of the bridge but not to the floor planks on the bridge, as previously reported. The gatehouse in 1983 still shows fire damage.

"We thought it was not enough to revisit military sites of 50 years ago," said Hanson. "We tried to learn what changes the Peoples Republic had brought about in the countryside. Some of the areas we travelled were among the poorest districts in old China before 1949, especially the mountainous areas of southern Jiangxi, northern Guizhou, western Sichuan and northwest Shaanxi."

The eight counties in the Jinggangshan mountains, which served as the first Jiangxi guerilla base in 1927-1929, now have a population of more than one million. Each county has not only reached self-sufficiency in food, but delivers surplus grain to the government. Back in the 1920s, mountainous Jinggangshan was a wild and impoverished area with no roads and no government services. Today Ciping, the Red Army headquarters of the 1920s, is a town of 6,000 with paved streets, electricity, running water and an impressive business district that includes a revolutionary museum with six researchers.

The Jinggangshan area now supports primary schools that enroll 96 percent of the school age children, and the Jinggangshan literacy rate—those who read 1,500 Chinese characters—has been pushed up from about 20 persons per 100 in 1949 to more than 60 persons in the 1980s.

Many farmers told the Hansons that they are earning more money than ever before especially because of the responsibility system introduced in 1978. This system permits households that produce more to keep more.

Greater prosperity can be seen in the new homes being built with burnt brick walls and burnt tile roofs—replacing older homes made of mud bricks with thatched roofs. Many new village homes in Jiangxi and Hunan have eight to ten rooms and up to 200 square meters of floor space, which is several times larger than the average apartment in Beijing or Shanghai.

"We passed villages of 10 to 20 homes, all new." Hanson said.

"Many peasants now earn more than I do," was the frequent comment of county magistrates.

What about population growth?

They inquired about family planning programs wherever they visited. All provinces said the one-child family policy was "on schedule" in the cities and towns, but lagging in the countryside. Rates of natural increase ranged from under ten per 1,000 to more than 17 per 1,000. That means an annual population increase of 1.0 percent to 1.7 percent.

Baoxing county in western Sichuan province—at the foot of the Great Snowy Mountains—reported extraordinary success. It has a birthrate of 11 per 1,000 and a death rate of six, which means a natural rate of increase of five per 1,000, about the same as Shanghai. Progress like this is always associated with a local woman leader who is committed and persuasive, and there is such a leader in Baoxing.

Hanson said the strongest evidence of change along the Red Army route came from Red Army veterans, men in their 70s with children and grandchildren. When asked whether their children were better off than they had been, all the veterans grinned and nodded. Asked in what way the children were better off, the usual answer was: better education, better health, better jobs, better homes.

That ends the news story, and we go back to our experiences on the road.

*When you travel in remote places, never pass up an orange or a toilet.*

U Hpu, Burma's director of agriculture, 1957

CHAPTER 43

# On the Road in Jiangxi

June 1983: Our daily routine on the road with the PLA usually began with breakfast at 7 A.M. and departure at 7:30. If the day's schedule was unusually full, we began at 6.

Breakfast consisted of western continental menu: toast, marmalade, and coffee, or a standard Chinese breakfast: rice porridge, steamed bread, cold vegetables, and tea.

Each traveller in the group carried his (or her) own luggage from hotel room to bus. There were no porters.

Over south China roads we travelled in a 16-passenger Toyota bus, a vehicle rented by the PLA from the government's International Travel Service. All tour buses we saw in China were imported from Japan—some were as small as 9-passenger combis, others as large as 50-passenger Greyhound types. China has its own automobile industry and the local buses we saw on the city streets were Chinese-made, but a decision had evidently been made to use Japanese vehicles for visitors. We experienced no vehicle troubles on our entire visit, except for an occasional flat tire. Most driving was conservative.

Besides ourselves our bus party in Jiangxi consisted of the three army escorts from Peking and four additional army men picked up at the Jiangxi provincial headquarters. The provincial men managed the transport, food, and overnight lodging, since this was their turf. There was also an army doctor.

Chatter in the bus was continuous, and the interpreter kept us involved. Occasionally there was singing of old army songs or local folk songs. Old Qing, the museum curator, had a particularly good baritone voice.

At mid-morning we stopped at a government building for a wash up and a soft drink. The Chinese phrase "You wash" could be interpreted either as an invitation or a command; we accepted it as a courteous offer. If our mid-morning stop were made on the open road, Berni walked discreetly down the road while the men passengers disappeared into the bushes.

Noon meals were provided by a local magistrate, a commune secretary, or the local army commander. For our luncheon of about ten participants, the host generally offered ten Chinese dishes featuring the local favorites, some dishes hot with chiles and others bland for visitors. We favored the bland ones, although an officer once reminded us of Mao Zedong's saying in Hunan province: "You can't be a good revolutionary if you don't eat chiles."

After lunch our escorts favored a siesta lasting one hour, usually in a county hotel where beds permitted a short sleep. This surprised us. We could not imagine the original Long Marchers stopping for a siesta, and at first we were impatient at losing that much time in our daily schedule; neither Berni nor I was able to sleep at midday. But after using the time to review notes from the morning and prepare questions for the afternoon, we came to value the siesta. By the time we had travelled for two months without pause for weekends, I could see the reason for the Chinese midday rest.

At 2 P.M. we were on the road again. We halted for the day at 5 or 6, having covered 200-250 kilometers if most of the day had been given to road travel.

Our overnight accommodations were in army quarters or county hostels. These provided single beds, an attached bath with western-style toilet, and a color TV set that showed two channels after 6 P.M. These rest houses of the 1980s were better than any rural accommodations we recalled in China of the 1930s. But our facilities would not be considered adequate by the China International Travel Service for today's western tourists paying US$80 a day for their three-week tours. The areas we travelled were mostly closed to tourists.

Some comments on meals. Berni and I were often segregated at meal times in a corner of the dining room, screened off from the rest of the diners. We considered this a courtesy to give some privacy to both visitors and their escorts. It also gave the interpreter an hour to relax.

A second observation: A banquet was given by the local army commander or magistrate the first evening our party spent at his post. Sometimes a banquet was offered both noon and night when we passed through two jurisdictions. Ironically, this superabundance of food and drink was one of our trials. The food was delicious, and we enjoy Chinese cooking. By Chinese tradition the host heaps food on the guests' plates. But the alcoholic side of the meal was beyond our capacity. Each place setting was usually provided with three glasses containing beer (8 ounces), sweet grape wine (4 ounces) and a distilled liquor (1 ounce). The distilled beverage was often a fiery liquor called *Maotai*, produced from sorghum and other grains at the town of Maotai in Guizhou province. The host usually opened the meal by standing to deliver a short speech extolling the honored guests, calling them old friends of China, then proposed a toast of distilled drink with the call for *ganbei* (dry glass). A waitress immediately refilled the glasses. Frequent toasts continued through the meal, and if there were two or more tables, the toasters moved between tables, calling again and again for *ganbei*.

When the celebration occurred twice in one day, it was more than we could absorb. We tried turning a liquor glass upside down to signal no more, but that seemed to be poor manners. The only successful way to slow down alcohol consumption was to respond to each toast by wetting the lips with liquor and calling out *suibian* ("as you wish," instead of "bottoms up").

In all our travels with the PLA, we never experienced a stomach upset. That is a remarkable contrast to experiences in these same provinces in the 1930s when contamination lurked in every teahouse kitchen.

The Chinese army's concern for our health and safety was at first irritating and later amusing. People whose ages are near 70 are considered by the Chinese to be approaching the grave. Old Qing, the curator, often called out "Be careful" (*xiao xin*!) or "Go slowly" (*manzou*!). When we went downstairs, an officer might offer to hold an elbow. A military doctor travelled with us in Jiangxi and Sichuan provinces, explaining that local medical help might not be available if there were an accident. These doctors wanted to take our blood pressure periodically, but we laughingly declined. Neither Berni nor I suffered anything worse than a cough and sore throat, and for that we accepted the army doctor's herbal medicines. In two or three days, the affliction disappeared, as it probably would have without medication. Once an army officer asked Berni if Mr. Hanson had his "real teeth." Berni said yes with a chuckle.

Sometimes I had a feeling of being closely watched. If I tried to go for an hour's walk alone in the streets of the town where we made an overnight stop, say from 5 to 6 P.M., I was soon joined by the army doctor (with his ten-pound medical kit), by the army interpreter, or by a local official who offered to read the signs on buildings ("Here is a technical school."). I had brief conversations with street peddlers who sold drinks, T-shirts, or plastic sandals. But this overprotectiveness was irritating and gradually diminished; by the end of our trek I was trusted to take a walk alone. But Old Qing still offered his parting advice, "Be careful of the bicycles!"

When China's premier, Zhao Ziyang, visited the United States and Canada in 1984, he likewise acquired a sore throat. Evidently both east and west have viruses for which the visitor lacks resistance. Nor was Premier Zhao allowed to wander through the streets of Washington alone!

Our minibus rolled along the Jiangxi roads that the Red Army had tramped a half century earlier. The countryside was serene with deep green paddy fields extending to forested hills, under a bright blue sky. We watched the farm families at work. An older peasant, barefoot and wearing a conical bamboo hat, was guiding a water buffalo through the paddy muck, dragging a log to smooth the bed for transplanting. A younger man in blue peasant clothes was spraying an insecticide on an earlier rice crop (that's new). Several young women in flowered blouses worked singly, pulling weeds from the beds of rice seedlings. The nurseries reminded us that every rice plant in China—covering thousands of square miles—is still transplanted by the hand of a stooping peasant, an incredible commitment to productivity.

Rice fields, we noticed, came right up to the roadside embankment and the embankment itself was covered with plants of soybeans or sweet potatoes. Even the paddy bunds (foot paths) were covered with soybeans, thus wasting not a single square foot.

Around each village were the private plots assigned to individual families. These could be recognized by the meticulous trellises that held up vegetable crops. In many private plots we saw at least one young person with shoulder pole bearing two wooden buckets of sloppy compost that would be applied by a long-handled dipper, one cupful of black ooze for each plant.

Jiangxi province, we were told, was now triple-cropping approximately half its agricultural land, frequently with a rotation of rice-rice-vegetables within one year. This was more intensive agriculture than I remembered in the 1930s.

Another conspicuous change was the method of lifting irrigation water. In the old days every stream passing through a rice field was lined by water wheels—some 10 or 15 feet high—that lifted water from the streambed to the fields. Water wheels were then powered by one or several peasants treading on the spokes of the wheel, the water rose in small cups that emptied at the top of the wheel into a trough and spilled into the field. Powering the water wheel was a drudgery that had lasted several thousand years. Now we saw electric power lines crossing the rice fields with drop lines at small pump houses where water was lifted by electric pumps. The era of manpower propelling the wheels was finished, at least in this area.

One more change: Berni was the first to point out that grave mounds no longer dotted the agricultural fields. Burying the dead in productive farmland was an ancient custom, still practiced down to 1949. A typical grave mound was ten feet in diameter and four feet high. Frequently there was a cluster of mounds a few hundred feet from the family dwelling, making it convenient for respectful descendants to pull the weeds from the graves of their ancestors.

In the 1930s the American economist, Lossing Buck, had made a survey of grave mounds in his monumental study *Land Utilization in China*. Buck estimated that mounds then covered a million hectares or about 1 percent of all cropland in China.

In a no-nonsense approach, the communist government ordered graves removed from cropland and advocated cremation for future deaths. Cremation never took hold in rural areas, but it does prevail in the cities. We spotted new peasant graves dug into the steep hillsides with coffins inserted horizontally into tombs, and a stone or concrete seal to cover the opening.

If Lossing Buck had been correct in his estimate that grave mounds covered 1 percent of China's cropland, it is possible that Peoples China gained 3 to 4 million tons of grain each year by eliminating the mounds from agricultural land.

*Rice has been cultivated in China for more than 6700 years.*

Shen Jin-hua, 1980

CHAPTER 44

# The Rice Revolution in Hunan

Rice we saw growing along the roads of Hunan province in June 1983 looked exceptionally good. The rice plants were shorter than I remembered when I visited these areas in the 1930s. They were also more uniform and showed no rogues (outsized plants), no lodging, no visible disease, and fewer weeds. These improvements suggested that peasants were applying better production practices than 50 years earlier.

Farmers we talked to said their rice yields were at least double those before liberation. They quoted their yields in *jin* per *mu*; when we converted their harvest figures to our western measure, they were reporting that yields had risen from about two tons per hectare in the 1940s to more than four tons per hectare in the 1980s. These estimates were confirmed by county magistrates and commune officials. Doubling the yield of a major crop would be an extraordinary achievement anywhere in the world. It would match the experience of American farmers with hybrid corn.

When we visited the Hunan Academy of Agricultural Sciences, a few miles from the capital city of Changsha, we naturally asked about these remarkable rice yields and how they were achieved. The academy researchers spent half a day piecing together for us a three-decade story.

Chinese rice scientists had contributed three breakthroughs. First, by shortening the growing period, they enabled more farmers to grow two rice crops on the same land in the same year. Second, by dwarfing the stems of some rice varieties, they enabled the plants to put less energy into foliage and more into grain. Third, by using hybrid vigor, they achieved still higher yields. The three steps occurred in successive decades—the 1950s, 1960s, and 1970s—and together they doubled the rice yields.

Hoping to identify some of the Chinese scientists involved and to compare their accomplishments to similar work at the International Rice Research Institute (IRRI) in the Philippines, we asked more details.

The first breakthrough, further shortening the period that each rice crop spends on the land, occurred in the lower Yangtze valley. Before 1960 a typical rice variety in that region was in the main paddy field 150 days. It was then uncommon to grow two rice crops within one year on the same land. Later, during the 1960s, double-cropping spread rapidly. In southern China scientists found that a first crop of 135 days (March–July) and a second crop of 105 days (July–October) was generally feasible. In northern China the double-crop pattern of rice-rice was impossible because the frost-free period was too short, but it was possible to use a double-crop pattern of rice and winter wheat wherever irrigation was available. All told, double-cropping had added 50 percent to China's national rice harvest.

A second breakthrough, dwarfing the rice plant, was credited to a group of rice breeders at the Guangdong Academy in Guangzhou (Canton). After the People's Republic was established in 1949, the government conducted a campaign to collect rice seeds—both domesticated and wild—from within China and abroad. From this search the rice breeders acquired 40,000 rice samples for their seed bank, including duplicates. These seeds were tested in the research station. Only one type among the 40,000 was found to have a very short stem—about 80 centimeters (32 inches), compared to 125–150 centimeters for traditional varieties. This short plant, designated a *semidwarf*, had the capability when crossed to other rice plants to transfer its shortness to the progeny.

In 1956 the breeding team at Guangzhou crossed this semidwarf, named *Ai-Zai-Zhan*, with a taller plant of outstanding quality named *Guang-Zhang 13*. The succeeding generations looked outstanding, and the best among many progeny was selected in 1959 and given the name *Guang-Zhang-Ai*. That became China's first semidwarf rice variety to enter field production. *Guang-Zhang-Ai* has since become a parent of at least 45 other semidwarf rice varieties, all of them less than 100 centimeters tall and all high yielding.

On average, semidwarf rice varieties in China have given a yield increase of 50 percent above the older, taller plants. The short, stiff stems of the semidwarfs have also reduced the problem of lodging.

The third breakthrough, using hybrid vigor, was an achievement of Hunan Academy at Changsha, the first place in the world to produce hybrids of rice. The Hunan breeding work was supervised by a scientist named Yuan Longping, a little known instructor in Hunan's Anjiang Agricultural School. Yuan began experimenting with hybrid rice in 1964 at age 34. His work speeded up in 1970 when a fellow teacher from Anjiang found a sterile wild rice plant (it was called *wild female abortive*) on Hainan Island. This wild plant was naturally sterile, yet when crossed to a *restorer* parent, it commonly produced plants with hybrid vigor that yielded 20–30 percent higher. The principle is the same as that of hybrid corn in the United States. For this achievement the State Council of China in 1980 awarded Comrade Yuan a gold medal.

Hybrid rice is not yet adapted to all areas of China. So far it will grow only in the southern part of China, only in the second crop, and only with Indica-type rice, not Japonica. Nevertheless, hybrid rice has added many million tons of rice to China's annual harvest.

We asked the Hunan scientists, How does the work of Chinese rice scientists compare to similar research work outside China? An oversimplified answer would be this: China released its first semidwarf rice variety in 1960, about five years before the best known IRRI semi-dwarf, *IR 8*, became available in 1965.* China was the only country to grow hybrid rice on a commercial scale in the 1970s. IRRI was also working to develop hybrid rice, but China was clearly the front runner.

This story of a rice revolution, as told by Hunan Academy, is not a full explanation. More irrigation water and more fertilizer also played a part in raising rice yields. I have described elsewhere how China has expanded its irrigated land by 33 million hectares since 1950—an achievement no other country has remotely approached. China also increased its use of chemical fertilizer from almost none in 1950 to more than 15 million tons of nutrients in the 1980s, making China the third largest user of chemical fertilizer in the world (after the USA and the USSR). Important as added water and fertilizer were, they could not have produced such an increase in the harvest without the responsive rice varieties developed by Chinese scientists.

PRC has now set these rice scientists an ambitious goal—to raise the national rice harvest from 140 million metric tons in 1980 to 200 million tons in the year 2000. To reach this goal China would need to achieve average rice yields of six tons per hectare, thus equalling Japan's world leadership. Whether China can do this remains to be seen. But young men like the breeders at Changsha are confident.

---

* An even earlier semidwarf rice named *Taichung Native I* was reportedly bred on Taiwan in 1949 and named in 1956.

*The Liang family deserves their success.*
Commune secretary, 1983

CHAPTER 45

# Communes Where Some Get Rich First

Our three sedans left Changsha early one morning in June 1983 and travelled eastward for an hour over a good asphalt road to Zhong Hua Shan commune (literally Central Flowery Mountain collective). Shortly before we reached the commune headquarters, the road passed under a high-arched aqueduct 1½ miles long and 60 feet above the road, delivering water from one low hill to another.

A commune secretary named Liu invited us to sit down in his office, where he gave us the basic commune statistics.

*Population*: 11,000 people or 2,200 households.
*Cultivated land*: 2,300 acres, mostly rice
*Irrigation*: 100 percent of cropland, thanks to the new aqueduct.

In translating these numbers into U.S. terms, I recalled the phrase "family-sized farm," which in America usually means a farm of 160 acres operated by one family. If it were required to accommodate the same density of population as Central Flowery Mountain commune, the American farm would need to support 140 Chinese families. That suggests the degree of crowding in rural China.

We stood with Secretary Liu under the aqueduct as he explained the irrigation system. This commune, he said, and its two neighboring collectives had half their cropland on the valley floor and half on the hillside. The bottomland supported flooded rice; the hillsides produced dryland crops. The harvests on the hillside were meager, while those on the bottomland were five times larger.

Before 1949 no landowner had wanted to invest in irrigation for the hillside; each had been satisfied to take his cut on a meager hill crop. When the landlord's property was distributed among the peasants, each household received about one acre. It was still not possible to organize a big irrigation project.

Then came the communes in 1958, and for the first time a big irrigation project was discussed. It still took another six years of negotiation with the two neighboring communes before they agreed on the first step—to build a dam on a nearby river and to distribute water through two canals in the bottomlands. When it was built, the dam generated electricity, and electric lights were installed for the first time in 400 villages.

But the principal problem remained unsolved: there was no irrigation for the hillsides. Younger men were bold enough to propose (1) that water from a dam be led to the top of one hill, (2) that an aqueduct 1½ miles long carry water from one hill to another, and (3) that water be distributed by gravity on all the hillsides. For five years that proposal was debated while alternative designs were drawn and finances sought. The 400 villages (three communes) agreed to provide the labor. They built brick kilns at the site and stockpiled millions of bricks. The county government agreed to contribute 4 million Chinese yuan (then US$2.0 million) toward the cost of cement and other purchased materials. Construction took place during 1976–1978. Water began flowing over the aqueduct in 1978, and crop production of the 400 villages soon doubled.

"The year 1978 will go down in local history as our greatest moment," said Old Liu. "Now we know that 400 villages working together were able to accomplish something that rich landlords failed to do."

"Okay," I said, "there have been many changes in the commune system since 1978. What was the biggest change here?"

"Sidelines," he answered. "We have transferred to individual families our commune enterprises for pig raising, fish ponds, and other profit-making activities. We also permit private households to set up retail shops and restaurants in competition with our commune. Some families have been very successful in these activities."

As we walked through one village, I spotted a large new brick house, its exterior so handsome that it might have been in a city suburb of Minneapolis. "Who lives there?" I asked. "A leading cadre?"

"Oh no," said Secretary Liu. "That house belongs to a peasant in the commune, a Mr. Liang, who started several small businesses." We asked to call on the Liang family and were invited inside. In the living room was a display case containing hardware and electrical goods for sale. That was one of six specializations of the Liang family. Behind the house the family was fattening 60 hogs in a brick pen. At the side of the house they had a flock of laying hens. Along the drainage ditch of the commune road they had planted 35 citrus trees and were selling both oranges and lemons.

We asked Secretary Liu how the Liang family was able to compete with the commune. Liu scratched his head. On pigs and chickens and citrus trees, he said, this family gives more careful management than the commune can. And on the retail shop for hardware and electrical goods, the family chooses its small stock of merchandise with a careful eye to the needs of the commune members. "The Liang family deserves their success," Liu conceded.

"Are there other families like the Liangs?" I asked.

"Oh yes; in 1982 there were seven families in this commune who had incomes over Yuan 10,000 (US$5,000). The Liangs earned Yuan 16,000 last year (US$8,000), and they have paid for this house since 1978. So have several other families."

"Do some of your commune members earn more than their leaders?" I asked.

"Of course," Liu said with a nervous laugh. "Some make far more than the commune heads. But we are proud of them. The new slogan of the communist party is that some shall get rich first, and these are our first success stories."

We found examples in other provinces under this slogan, "Some shall get rich first."

In Guizhou province, not far from the city of Zunyi, we visited Mrs. Zhang of Long Kang commune, who was runninng a dumpling restaurant in the town center. She had earned enough in four years to pay for construction of a new brick house of five rooms in which we observed a color TV, a sewing machine, and a washing machine. Mrs. Zhang was dressed in colorful clothes that she had made on her sewing machine. "A private restaurant had no difficulty," she said, "in winning customers away from a commune-owned restaurant."

In the same commune we saw a dump truck parked in front of a house and asked to pay a call. This was a hot day when we found Mr. Fu in his red undershirt in front of an electric fan. He confirmed the truck was his. He had bought it second-hand from his commune and used it for hauling coal from a mine to his neighbors' houses. In two years he had paid for the truck and now was negotiating for a larger vehicle. Did he also farm? He laughed. "I can't afford to spend time farming. I leave the five *mu* (0.84 acres) of land to my wife." Children? Yes, he had three children: two girls, eight and five, and a son aged one. We asked how he managed to have a third child during the period of government policy for one-child families. He hung his head and said he was fined Yuan 100 by his commune for having a third child. "But it was worth it," he asserted. Would he have more? No, he said. He had learned his lesson.

In Sichuan province we stopped at a commune in Chonglai county, west of Chengdu, where we observed a fine brick house, obviously new, and rightly guessed this was a "specialized household." What is the family's skill? we asked. In the living room we found a small factory producing yeast for a brewery. Every five days this household set out hundreds of pans with raw materials for yeast, and on the fifth day they delivered their product to the brewery. Why didn't the brewery do this for itself? It had tried and found yeast required attention 24 hours a day. Only a well-motivated family could succeed. This parlor industry had paid for the house.

As we prepared to leave the Hunan commune that prompted this narrative, Secretary Liu confirmed that specialized households were still few but that competition was growing and new specializations appeared each year. Where would this lead by 2000 A.D.? He preferred not to speculate.


Like Secretary Liu of Central Flowery Mountain collective, most Chinese we met in our travels were unwilling to speculate about the future. We thought of several explanations.

First, any social change in China is likely to alter existing communist policies; therefore, anyone who predicts future change could be accused of opposing today's party policies. It is safer for a Chinese to avoid speculation.

Second, Chinese adults now 60 years or older have witnessed many reversals of government policy: the Guomindang repressions of the 1930s and 1940s, the celebrations that followed liberation, the jailings that ended the "Hundred Flowers" period of the 1950s, the harassments during the Cultural Revolution, the uncertainties at Chairman Mao's death and the arrest of the Gang of Four, and the startling reversal of policies under Deng Xiaoping and the post-Mao leadership. Who could say what new changes might be ahead?

Third, the younger generation has grown to adulthood with little knowledge on which to base speculation. Under Mao's leadership the government tightly controlled the release of information.

In these circumstances only a brave or foolish Chinese would speculate about the future form of socialism in China.

> Guizhou province has "three nevers": The climate never provides three consecutive days without rain; the topography never provides three adjacent mu *of level land;* and the population never contains three neighbors with coins in their pockets.

Popular saying

CHAPTER 46

# Through a Poor Mountainous Province

When we passed by auto through the capital city of Guiyang in July 1983, I saw a remarkable contrast to the same city 40-odd years before. Wartime Guiyang, as I remembered it, was a walled city of muddy streets, mildewed one-story houses, and thousands of wartime refugees living in shacks under the shadow of the city walls. The economic mainstay of Guizhou province in wartime was opium; it was the only agricultural product with high enough value and low enough weight to be carried over the mountain paths on a peasant's shoulder pole.

By 1983 the city had grown from 200,000 to 1.3 million. PLA sedans whisked us through the city to the Hotel Hua Qi in the suburbs, travelling wide paved boulevards with traffic circles and row on row of six-story apartment buildings. All the rooftops displayed television aerials.

We were told that eight tourist hotels in Guiyang were filled during summer months by planeloads of Hong Kong Chinese who regarded Guiyang's cool climate at 4000 feet elevation a welcome escape from Hong Kong's heat and humidity. We passed factories that made Guiyang one of China's secondary industrial centers—a producer of steel, diesel engines, chemicals, textiles, leather goods, television receivers, watches, and cement.

A provincial planning officer came to our hotel and briefed us. He reminded us of two popular sayings about Guizhou province. The first was the 80–10–10 rule: The surface of Guizhou province contains 80 percent mountains, 10 percent water, and 10 percent cropland. The second saying might be called Guizhou's "three nevers" (see chapter heading).

My travelling bookbag provided two other facts to suggest that despite the tidiness of its capital city, Guizhou was still one of the poorest provinces. The *China Agricultural Yearbooks* for 1980 and 1981 (official publications from Beijing) provided data to calculate average food supply—in calories per day—for each Chinese province. These calculations were crude but adequate to distinguish the hungry areas from the food surplus areas. By these data, Guizhou had the lowest food supply of all the provinces (about 1600 calories per person per day in 1979 and 1980). Heilongjong province had the highest food supply (about 3000 calories). China's national average for the same two years was 2333 calories. This indicated that Guizhou had a food supply that was slightly above half the food supply of the leading province and only two-thirds of China's average. These comparisons did not include food shipments across provincial boundaries but such shipments were negligible—about 7/10 of 1 percent of China's total food production—and most of that moved to the large coastal cities. This explained the lean appearance we noted in the Guizhou people.

A second fact about Guiyang concerned childbirth. In 1981—by official count—Guizhou had the poorest record among all provinces in reducing its fertility rate. China's "average fertility" rate in 1981—the number of children in a completed family—was 2.6. Guizhou had 4.4 children.

A related statistic: In the year 1981 approximately three-quarters of all babies born in China were the first child in each family; one-quarter were the second child or higher sequence. Guizhou had the reverse ratio: three-quarters of all Guizhou babies were second or higher sequence, and only one-quarter were first child. (These figures came from the official journal, *Beijing Review*.)

If population growth in Guizhou continues to be the highest among provinces and food production per person continues to be the lowest, this province will remain one of China's poorest.

On the mountainous three-hour drive from Guiyang to Zunyi, the most dramatic sight was the hydroelectric dam on the Wu River and its adjoining aluminum factory. The dam was of the concrete eggshell style, 500 feet high, with a generating capacity of 630,000 kilowatts. The factory converted local bauxite into aluminum with power from the dam. We did not stop for a briefing, but we were told an interesting sidelight. Both the dam and the factory had been completed in the late 1960s but had stood idle until the late 1970s because of the chaos of the Cultural Revolution. Was the delay typical? we asked. Yes, came the answer; many major development projects had come to a halt during interference by the Red Guards. In the post-Mao period, the hydroelectric generators and factory were operating at capacity.

Villages along the Zunyi road looked impoverished in 1983—mostly one or two-room huts constructed of mud-blocks with thatched roofs. In villages visible from the road, less than one hut out of ten had been rebuilt with burned brick and tile roof. The rural housing of Guizhou had not greatly changed since the nationalist China era, or possibly since the Qing dynasty of the nineteenth century. Nevertheless, crops around the villages looked good. Only one crop of rice per year could be grown at this elevation because of the short frost-free season, and corn prevailed on the hillsides. Compared to Hunan the responsibility system for peasants had not yet produced much benefit here.

Our route through mountainous Guizhou suggested that Chairman Mao's development strategy was far from egalitarian—in fact, was quite discriminatory. Mao believed that each province should be self-supporting, regardless of its resources; it should not rely on handouts from the central government. This meant poor provinces like Guizhou should finance their own rural progress—that poverty should overcome poverty. After a full generation of socialism, the poorest provinces were still the poorest. If a line were drawn from north to south across PRC, dividing the nation into two halves, the provinces in the coastal half are still the most productive, including Jiangsu, Zhejiang and Hunan; the provinces in the inland half of the country are still the poorest—embracing Guizhou, Shaanxi, Gansu and a half dozen others. Many economists endorsed Chairman Mao's strategy that rural investment should be concentrated in the areas of best soil and rainfall—that is, the coastal half.

There were other biases. The PRC investments under Mao were skewed in favor of the cities. The income of city workers rose to a level double that of peasants. In Guizhou province—as we observed—investment clearly favored industrial growth in the capital city.

The countryside was not wholly neglected. We saw village schools and village clinics where none had existed before 1949. The peasants we met acknowledged that they no longer paid half their crops to a landlord. These changes could be credited to the PRC government, and the benefits to peasants were not small.

But other countries that confronted entrenched rural poverty had found it necessary to establish rural assistance programs that went beyond the scope of agricultural extension and crop price supports. The U.S. Farm Security Administration was one example. Mexico's Plan Puebla to help subsistence farmers was another.

Under Deng Xiaoping after 1978, PRC has found it desirable to give greater attention to the problems of regional equity. After all, who is going to buy the consumer goods produced in the city of Guiyang if the peasants of the surrounding countryside cannot afford them?

*The Yangs live in a city apartment of 28 square meters; that is the quota of floorspace permitted for persons of the Yangs' employment.*

Interview with a government employee, 1983

CHAPTER 47

# A Family Lives Well on US$18.27 a Week

For three days in Guizhou province in July 1983 Berni and I accompanied a slender, bespectacled government employee whom I will call Yang. We avoid his real name because this chapter will report on his family income and expenses—a private affair.

Our conversations with Yang clarified two questions: First, was it possible that the average Chinese income was only about US$300 per person per year, whereas in the United States the average was over US$14,000? Both figures come from the *World Bank Atlas, 1984*. Second: if these average incomes were correctly stated—and I assumed they were—how could a Chinese family support itself on an income so far below the poverty line, yet appear to lead a normal middle-class life? The United States government had determined in 1982 that US$9,862 a year was the theoretical poverty line for a family of four in the United States. The average Chinese family of five persons, with average income of US$300 per person per year, would have family income of only US$1,500 a year—far below the U.S. poverty line.

The man riding in the front seat of our automobile was well dressed in a blue nylon shirt and sport jacket, both made in China. He wore a stainless steel wrist watch made in China. He carried a good-quality overnight bag, made in China. He took notes with an expensive-looking ballpoint pen, made in China. He spent his spare moments reading a Spanish-language novel printed in Beijing. How impoverished was this man? I asked myself. If he were willing to discuss his family income and expenses, he might clarify for us the average cost of living in China.

Yang showed no sensitivity when I suggested we talk about family finances. First, we established his background. Yang was Shanghai born, age 36, son of a factory supervisor—a blue collar worker. Yang graduated from

Shanghai Foreign Languages Institute. His wife, a little older, was a dentist in a government hospital. They had one son, age 2½, and would have no more children under present Chinese policy—although Mrs. Yang wished she could add a daughter.

The Yangs were a two-income family: an interpreter's monthly salary of yuan 83 (Chinese dollars) and a dentist's salary of yuan 70. In addition the Yangs received a reward of yuan 5 a month for having only one child. Their total income thus came to yuan 158 a month or yuan 1900 a year.

The official exchange rate in 1983 (two Chinese yuan equalled one American dollar) appeared to give the Yang family an income of US$950 a year, or US$79 a month, or US$18.27 a week. I say "appeared" because confusion arises when we try to compare a Chinese family budget to the cost of living in the United States.*

As we talked, I recalled my financial situation at age 36 in postwar Washington, D.C.. I too was a government civil servant working on foreign affairs; I too had a wife and one child. My salary was US$5600 a year, and Berni was selling real estate part time. Our total income probably reached US$8,000 in 1948 dollars. We lived in a three-bedroom house for which the mortgage payments consumed a quarter of our income. Food bills probably took another 25 percent. We drove a second-hand Ford. We ate rather simply, bought some clothes from mail order catalogues, and did some entertaining. In short, we considered ourselves comfortable but in a low tax bracket.

I asked Yang to tell us what he bought with his income.

About housing: The Yangs lived in a city apartment that was measured by the government at 28 square meters; that was the quota of floorspace permitted for persons of the Yangs' employment. The government housing charge was yuan 3 a month or US$18 a year. That sounded impossible, so I asked Yang to repeat it. Later I encountered city housing charges in Beijing and Harbin ranging from two to ten yuan a month, suggesting that Yang's housing charge was within the government pattern. Yang's apartment

---

*One source of distortion here: The exchange rate quoted by banks between two currencies like the U.S. dollar and the Chinese yuan does not provide a realistic comparison of purchasing power. The conventional exchange rate overstates the income gap. The Chinese yuan in 1983 would purchase more goods in China than 50 cents would purchase in the United States. A more useful comparison—if we had it—would be the purchasing power parity, which measures how much of two currencies is needed to purchase equal goods. Such a parity calculation is not readily available for China. Available evidence on purchasing power parity indicates that for low-income countries like China, per-capita income should be just over three times greater when stated in U.S. dollars. By that standard the Yang family income would be US$2850 a year, rather than US$950 in conventional exchange rate terms.

included a modest living room, a single bedroom, a toilet and kitchen located on a different floor but assigned for one-family use, and a vegetable or flower garden of 20 square meters (call it 10 by 20 feet). Obviously space was one of the limiting aspects of family life, and one of the reasons why living costs were low. We never saw the Yangs' apartment, but I visualized it about the size of a one-room efficiency apartment that Berni and I had rented in Chicago after our marriage. We were in our twenties. The Chicago apartment had a roll-away bed and cooking facilities the size of a closet. Such tight space required orderly living.

The Chinese housing charge was not actually rent but a maintenance fee. The government treated the construction cost of housing in the cities as part of its capital budget and made no effort to recover the cost.

About food: Mrs. Yang did the food shopping, a little every day because the Yangs had no refrigerator. (In our China travels in 1983 we rarely encountered a *ganbu*, or government employee, who owned a refrigerator although they were on the market in increasing numbers.) Yang guessed the family food bill was a little more than half the family income, about yuan 1,000 a year (US$500 or US$9.60 a week).

By American standards, this sounded unbelievably low, so I asked Yang what they ate. The Yangs cooked three meals a day at home because their places of work were close to their apartment. Breakfast was the familiar rice gruel served with deep-fried pastries (*tiaozi*). Lunch was often a large bowl of wheat noodles in soup, with pieces of chicken and vegetables spread on top. Evening dinner was the principal meal, consisting of steamed rice and four center dishes, often two of stir-fried vegetables, one of bean curd, and perhaps a fish. Mrs. Yang shopped at the government market for rice and cooking oil, which were rationed and subsidized in 1983; and she went to the farmers' open market—nongovernmental—where meats and vegetables were higher priced but better quality. As I wrote down the family menus, I noted that Yang—sitting in front of me—appeared healthy on this diet.

About clothing: Mrs. Yang made most clothes for the baby and herself on her sewing machine, and Yang bought two *ganbu* uniforms a year. The annual cost of family clothing was placed at 10 percent of the family budget (about yuan 190 or US$95). Yang thought that Chinese cotton and wool cloth was lower priced than in other countries, but cloth purchased outside of China had a greater variety of patterns. Yang himself had travelled abroad as an interpreter with government missions and had brought home some material.

About utilities: Electricity for household lighting cost yuan 2 a month and household water service yuan 1 a month. I told Yang that utilities were considerably higher in the United States, and in Mexico, too.

About recreation: Here the family tastes diverged. Mrs. Yang enjoyed a first-run movie (yuan 0.20) or a stage show (from yuan 0.30 to yuan 1.00). Yang prefered a soccer game (yuan 0.10) or best of all, an armful of new books from the government bookstore. Recreation may cost the family yuan 100 a year (US$50). Fortunately for Yang, books from the government printer are low in cost.

About the baby's nursery school: This was an acknowledged luxury. The baby, age 2½, was in preschool from 7:30 A.M. until 6 P.M. at a fee of yuan 20 a month (US$120 a year). Children in this preschool received two meals a day including milk. Until the Yang's son had reached two, his grandmother had come from Shanghai to live with the Yangs in Guizhou, caring for the baby at home and permitting both parents to work.

I asked Yang if we had forgotten any budget item. No, he said; the family paid nothing for transportation from home to work: his wife walked the short distance, and he rode his bicycle 15 minutes; nothing for medical care, which except for a token registration fee was free to government employees; and nothing for income tax. The first 600 yuan of income per month were exempt from income tax in 1983. Since yuan 600 (or US$300) was then the maximum monthly salary for government employees, this meant that Chinese were free from income tax, except those engaged in private enterprise earning over yuan 600. The Yangs had no vacation time except seven government holidays a year.

I summed up this one-year family budget and asked Yang to review the table. Here is what it showed:

### Family Budget of One Ganbu

| Item | 1983 Chinese yuan | Equivalent American dollars |
| --- | --- | --- |
| Housing maintenance | 36 | $ 18 |
| Food | 1,000 | 500 |
| Clothing | 190 | 95 |
| Utilities | 36 | 18 |
| Recreation | 100 | 50 |
| Baby's nursery school | 240 | 120 |
| Medical costs | 0 | 0 |
| Income tax | 0 | 0 |
| Subtotal | 1,602 | 801 |
| Savings | 298 | 149 |
| Total | 1,900 | $ 950 |

Yang said the table was satisfactory and added, "We think we are living fairly well."

I asked Yang what he did with his savings. He said during the first ten years of his marriage no money remained long in the bank because the family was acquiring the basic household goods that most young couples seek. I asked if he could recall the possessions he had bought and what they cost. His mind was like an account book as he recited the purchases, all manufactured in China.

Furniture: 600 yuan for the original wicker furnishings, some of which had already been replaced with better quality. To this he added:

|  | yuan |
|---|---|
| 2 bicycles, each | 110 |
| 2 wristwatches, each | 50 |
| 1 shortwave radio | 100 |
| 1 sewing machine | 100 |
| 1 14-inch color TV | 800 |
| 1 electric fan, table model | 50 |
| 1 washing machine | 200 |

These items totalled about yuan 2,250 or US$1,125.

Yang at 36 had no complaints about his economic situation. His family was living surprisingly well on yuan 1,900 a year.

There was one thing unique about Yang. Several times he mentioned his wife's role in keeping the family expense records, so I asked who managed the bank account. He and his wife had separate bank accounts, he said, but Yang handed his salary checks to his wife; she kept the records. When I asked other Chinese men who kept their family finances, they always said, "I do, of course."

## Reflections

The *World Bank Atlas, 1985* listed 37 countries with an average per person income of $400 per year or less; the countries were all in Africa or Asia. These included almost half the people in the world and covered such countries as Bangladesh at $130 average income (the lowest), Ethiopia $140, Zaire $160, Burma $180, India $260, China $300, Ghana $320, Pakistan $390 and Sudan $400.

Of course the purchasing power of these average incomes varied greatly, and the life style in the low-income countries also covered a wide range. If I were required to be reborn in the 1980s in any of these poorest countries, I believe I would most likely achieve a satisfactory life style in China.

> The PRC has completed railroads since 1949 that link all the provincial capitals except Llasa in Tibet (elevation 14,000 feet).
>
> Government briefing, 1983

CHAPTER 48

# Sichuan Transport, Old and New

Now back to the journey with our PLA companions.

From Chongqing to Chengdu in Sichuan province, we travelled by first-class railroad sleeper car on a train that was labelled, surprisingly, the Chongqing-Beijing Express. When we alighted at Chengdu we checked the station signboard and confirmed that this was a through train travelling 1600 miles by way of Xi'an and Zhengzhou, scheduled to arrive in the national capital in two days. Other trains on the signboard were Chengdu-Shanghai via Xuzhou; Chengdu-Guangzhou (Canton) via Wuhan; Chengdu-Kunming through the gorges of the Tibetan plateau; and most remarkable of all, Chengdu-Urumqi, capital of Chinese Turkestan, via Lanzhou. This brought back memories: When I arrived in China in the 1930s not a single rail line entered Sichuan province; travel to Chinese Turkestan (now Xinjiang Uigur Autonomous Region) was generally by camel caravan. The Peoples Republic had built many of these railroads since 1949, linking together all the provincial capitals of China except one—Llasa in Tibet, where the elevation is 14,000 feet, and even there a rail line is now under construction.

Trying to comprehend these changes, I recalled that the last time I had travelled between Chengdu and Chongqing had been in October 1938. At that time deluxe travel was by an ancient bus. It accommodated 25 passengers, making the "run" between the two cities in three days, stopping twice overnight at wayside inns.

The quality of travel in those days was well described by my old friend, Graham Peck, an American artist who visited Sichuan in 1936. He reported:

> On a misty January dawn I walked to the bus station in Chongqing's western limits and in company with two dozen Chinese climbed into a ramshackle

carryall about the size of a station wagon. When we had assumed our positions on the narrow seats, attendants and friends of the passengers began thrusting through the windows quantities of luggage: suitcases, baskets, bedding, babies, fiddles, fireworks, thermos bottles, melons, rugs, parasols, cooking utensils, clocks, chickens and other portables. The engine started, the car began to tremble, and gradually the paraphernalia shook down into a compact mass little more than waist high. Thus wedged in, a three day-journey began.

In 1983, comfortably asleep on a train, we covered the same route in eight hours.

*During the 1970s China's fertility fell at an extraordinarily rapid pace not previously experienced by any other population over a comparable span of time.*

John Bongaarts and Susan Greenhaigh, 1985

CHAPTER 49

# A Population Program Called 1 × 1 = 1

Population statistics can be boring, but when Berni and I spent an afternoon at the Health Secretariat in Chengdu, we expected Sichuan's population story to be fascinating. It was.

Sichuan is China's most populous province. In the 1982 national census the province counted 102 million people, which means that one of ten Chinese was living in Sichuan. Moreover, among the 29 Chinese provinces, Sichuan achieved the greatest drop in population growth rate during the 1970s. We asked how they had done it.

Four briefing officers awaited us in the conference room of the Health Secretariat; the chief was Dr. Liang M.D., director of the population program. A man about 50, Dr. Liang had several qualities that communicated confidence: He was vigorous in appearance, handled his facts clearly, and never evaded a question. Since I previously had administered Ford Foundation grants to support population activities in southern Asia and western Africa, I thought I would recognize any false claims. I detected none.

I suggested to Dr. Liang that he tell his story in his own manner and my questions would follow. He chose an unusual opening: If Sichuan province should become an independent country today, it would be the eighth most populous country in the world. He was right. The *World Population Data Sheet* for mid-1983 listed the most populous places in this order:

| | |
|---|---|
| 1. China | 1,023 million |
| 2. India | 723 million |
| 3. USSR | 272 million |
| 4. USA | 234 million |
| 5. Indonesia | 156 million |
| 6. Brazil | 131 million |

| 7. Japan | 119 million |
| 8. Sichuan province | 102 million |

Dr. Liang next traced how the people of Sichuan had multiplied in Chinese history. For this he used four benchmarks from the provincial archives:

| 1 A.D. | 3.5 million |
| 1840 A.D. | 38.0 million |
| 1949 A.D. | 57.0 million |
| 1982 A.D. | 102.0 million |

The old records may not meet today's standards of census accuracy, but they were good enough to serve the comparisons that Dr. Liang was about to make. Between 1840 and 1949, he pointed out, Sichuan's population had expanded only 19 million in 109 years, or about 170,000 a year (simple average). In those years, Dr. Liang thought, population growth had been held in check by civil wars, epidemics (cholera, typhoid, typhus, plague), and lack of medical services.

Next Dr. Liang looked at the period of the People's Republic. In the 33 years from 1949 to 1982, Sichuan's population had jumped 45 million or about 1.4 million a year (simple average). This was eight times the growth rate of the Qing and Republican eras that preceded the communist government. To explain what had happened, Dr. Liang gave as his opinion: civil wars had ended, major epidemics had been brought under control, and a new national health service—still with limited resources—had worked well enough to put an end to most infant deaths from contagious diseases. The result was a spurt in population growth.

This brought Dr. Liang to the on-going national campaign for reducing the birth rate. Launched in 1971, the "later-longer-fewer" campaign had introduced three reproductive goals—later marriage, longer spacing between first and subsequent children, and fewer children. By later marriage the policy makers generally meant ages 29 and 25 for men and women in the countryside. Longer spacing was generally interpreted as four years between first and subsequent children in the cities and three years in the countryside. Fewer children generally meant three for rural dwellers and two for couples in the cities, but in 1977 the limit of two children was established for all couples.

To summarize Sichuan's accomplishments under the national campaign— that is, during the 11 years 1971-1982—Dr. Liang dictated slowly the following three statements and asked me to read back the numbers for double-checking:

- By 1982 Sichuan's birth rate was 15.83 per 1,000, down from 40 in 1971.

- By 1982 Sichuan's death rate was 6.87 per 1,000, down from 8.79 in 1971.
- By 1982 Sichuan's rate of natural increase (that is, birth rate minus death rate) was 8.96 per 1,000, down from 31.21 in 1971.

I told Dr. Liang that no nation with a population of 100 million had achieved a drop in birth rate equal to Sichuan province. None had ever come close.

He waved his hand from side to side, protesting my comment; his report had not yet reached the current difficulties. All through the 1970s, he continued, the population program had been aware of an approaching problem. A bulge of new marriages would occur starting about 1981, caused by a corresponding spurt of births in the 1960s. The bulge occurred on schedule. Marriages in Sichuan in 1981 totalled 1,180,000—half above the trend—and the birth rate began to increase proportionately.

In anticipation of the marriage boom, China adopted in 1979 the campaign for "one-couple, one-child" sometimes called $1 \times 1 = 1$. The change came none too soon. Dr. Liang said Sichuan now has family pledges for one child from 2.85 million Sichuan couples in their twenties, and he expected the pledges to keep increasing during the 1980s.

"You can't prohibit new families from having babies," continued Dr. Liang, "so we set up a system of rewards. In the cities we pay a monthly reward of yuan 5 (US$2.50) to each couple that limits its offspring to one. The payment continues until the single child reaches age 14. This reward may sound small to a westerner but here it is a significant addition to a Chinese family income. In the countryside some communes pay the reward in cash; others may reduce the family quota for grain delivered to the state."

Dr. Liang then put aside his papers, leaned back in his chair, and said he would answer questions.

"Tell us about your experience with contraception," I suggested.

There were 15 million women of child-bearing age (15-49 years) in Sichuan, living with a husband, he said, and 13 million families were practicing contraception.

"What contraceptive methods were used by 13 million families?" I asked. He produced a chart that summarized:

| | |
|---|---|
| Sterilization | 47% |
| Female tubal ligation | 37% |
| Male vasectomy | 10% |
| IUD (intrauterine device) | 45% |
| Pill and injectibles | 6% |
| Condom | 2% |

The percentage for sterilization seemed high, I said. He explained that the Sichuan program had encouraged married women with two or more children to be sterilized. For those who were sterilized, there was no need to maintain a contraceptive supply service. All contraceptives were free, he added. Abortions were freely available but were recommended only as last resort after contraceptive failure.

"Tell us about your staff," I said. "How many do you have and how are they trained?" I recalled that staff training was the most important factor in the success of family planning programs in countries of southern Asia like India.

Dr. Liang said his full-time staff numbered over 10,000, stationed in villages and towns. They were divided into three categories: administrators, medical personnel, and motivators (those who spread propaganda among married couples). There were training courses for each type of staff, and every staff member in the province took a refresher course each year. Dr. Liang offered the opinion that Sichuan had achieved leadership among Chinese provinces because it had the largest and best trained staff for population work.

My next question: "How do you change the mind of a woman who has decided to have a second or higher child?"

There was no single method, Dr. Liang said, but "first we use peer group pressure—that is, meetings among women in the rural commune, or the urban neighborhood, or the urban employment unit." These meetings reviewed the advantages to the family and the community to have fewer babies. Peasant women recalled how limited their land was, and each child caused greater land pressure. City women discussed their limited housing, education, jobs and food. Most women, Dr. Liang added, were persuaded at this stage. He did not describe the further steps.

Family planning workers in other Chinese provinces had already described to Berni and me the penalties sometimes invoked in the one-couple, one-child campaign. The parents of an unauthorized child might be required to pay back any reward received for a one-child pledge. Added housing space, kitchen garden space, educational support, and other privileges might be withheld. The pressures were open ended.

My last question was political, and Dr. Liang answered it diplomatically. "How do you explain your greater success in dropping the birth rate than has been attained in similar programs of south Asia, say in a country like India, for example?"

"I would rather that countries of south Asia draw their own conclusions," Dr. Liang replied. "In China we find our organization of the people has given us effective channels for public persuasion. China has a long tradition of community activity. We use this tradition in family planning, and we get public support. I can speak only about China and can say the system is effective here."

Ending the three-hour interview I congratulated Dr. Liang on the leading position that Sichuan had established among the provinces. It was my impression that the progress of China down to 2000 A.D. in its four modernizations—that is, in agriculture, industry, science, and defense—would depend to a significant degree on China's success in limiting population growth. He agreed.

## Reflections

China's birth and death rates have declined nationally at more rapid rates than in other developing countries—to levels only slightly above those in industrialized countries including the United States. China's actual growth rate may be a little higher than the published figures because of underregistration; but even allowing for some undercount, China's success in slowing its national growth has surpassed that of almost all third world countries. Among the few countries that have excelled China's performance are Singapore and Hong Kong, both urban ministates composed largely of ethnic Chinese.

In retrospect, China's national rate of natural increase (birth rate minus death rate) was 33.3 per thousand in 1963, fell to 23.4 per thousand in 1971 when the current major family planning campaign began, to 12.05 per thousand in 1978 when the post-Mao leadership took command, and to 11 per thousand in 1985.

The drop in growth from 12 per thousand in 1978 to 11 in 1985 was more remarkable than it appears—in fact, it was probably as big an achievement as all the successes of the 1970s. Why? Because the number of Chinese women reaching marriage age rose by more than half during the years 1980–1985, yet the population growth rate continued to fall.

By 1980 seven out of ten married couples were reported to be using some form of contraception. The two most common birth control methods were the IUD and sterilization.

News reports on China's population program generated widely differing reactions in the outside world, ranging from admiration for Chinese discipline, to skepticism about the statistics, to a belief that the government had employed compulsory abortion, that families had practiced female infanticide and even speculation that China's one-couple, one-child policy would produce a generation of maladjusted young people. These thoughts deserve comment.

About abortion: Induced abortion occurs in all societies whether legislation permits it or not. An estimated 55 million abortions are performed throughout the world annually in recent years—about 70 abortions for every 1000 women of reproductive age. More than half of all abortions occur in developing countries.*

In the United States the 1978 abortion rate was 23 per thousand women of reproductive age; in China for the same year it was 25—approximately the same. Eastern bloc countries had higher rates. In the USSR there were 180 abortions per 1000 women of reproductive age in 1970, the latest available data.

Induced abortion was legalized in China in 1956. Since then the procedure has been readily available, free of charge, and granted to women on request. During the 1970s the number of abortions performed in the whole of China rose from 3.9 million in 1971 to 5.5 million in 1978. The Chinese statistics are consistent with the official Chinese policy that abortion is not to be used as a method of contraception but only as a last recourse in the event of contraceptive failure. China has about 150 million married couples of reproductive age. Clearly five million abortions could not represent their principal method of contraception.

Chinese national health authorities have consistently denied that they encourage or sanction involuntary abortion, involuntary sterilization, or any other form of compulsory family planning pressures. My interviews and reading had given me no reason to question that official viewpoint. But compulsory abortions have been reported in the Chinese press, suggesting there have been deviations from the national policy in some provinces and some time periods. These reports have been particularly frequent in the Hong Kong press, citing Guangdong province in the early years of the one-couple, one-child policy.

What about female infanticide, the ancient practice of letting newborn girl babies die? Peoples China hoped it had put a stop to this criminal practice. But in the early 1980s, at the beginning of the one-couple, one-child campaign, there were reports of female infanticide by families whose first child was a girl and who still hoped for a boy on the next try. These reports were indirectly confirmed in a 1982 speech by Premier Zhao Ziyang in which he declared, "The whole society should resolutely condemn the criminal activities of female infanticide."

---

*My information about abortion is taken from Chinese official sources, as reprinted by the United States Congress, Office of Technological Assessment, in its 1982 publication, *World Population and Fertility Planning Technology.*

In my judgment it is unlikely that female infanticide has been more than an occasional happening in the PRC. The lack of reports since 1982 seems to indicate that the government has generally succeeded in ending this homocidal behavior.

Finally, what about the consequence of creating a nation of one-child families? In America the child without siblings has been thought to have a difficult personality—self-centered, demanding, quarrelsome and overprotected.

In my reading on the single child, I have encountered surveys of American scholarly literature that reach favorable judgments. In "The Only Child" in the *Journal of Individual Psychology*, T. Falbo concluded in 1977 that no professional evidence supports the stereotype that singletons are maladjusted, asocial, lonely, self-centered, or "spoiled." In fact, one study after another found the single child to be intellectually advantaged.

Another review of literature by three psychologists—Claudy, Farrell, and Dayton's "Consequences of Being an Only Child," published by the American Institutes for Research, Palo Alto, California— found in 1979 that American singletons are more mature, socially sensitive, and cultured but are somewhat less sociable. The occupational interest of the single child, they found, favors science, mathematics, music, and literature, whereas children from multichild families veer more toward sports and mechanical pursuits. The single child prefers more solitary activities like reading rather than group-oriented activities. The single child has higher academic skills. When American singletons were interviewed at age 29, they had greater academic achievement, had chosen better-educated spouses, had fewer children, and were less likely to divorce.

Chinese parents of the present generation can take comfort that a single child is likely to become a superior adult.

The Population Council, a scholarly demographic body in New York, has published its belief that Peoples China could succeed in holding its population below 1.2 billion in year 2000 even if it switched to a two-child family goal, provided it was able to meet three conditions: (1) a delay of first birth to age 25 of the mother, (2) a spacing of four years between first and second births, and (3) a strictly enforced stop-at-two policy. That would entail fewer difficulties than the one-child policy and would probably be more acceptable to the Chinese poeple. The struggle to limit Chinese population is one of the truly important happenings in the third world in the 1980s and 1990s.

> *We in North America are wont to think that we may instruct all the world in agriculture, because our agricultural wealth is so great and our exports to less favored peoples have been heavy.*

Dr. L. H. Bailey, 1911

CHAPTER 50

# A Shaanxi Harvest Seen Through American Eyes

On a warm July morning in 1983 Berni and I left our hotel at Xi'an with our PLA companions for a drive of 60 miles westward through the narrow Wei River valley. Anthropologists have determined that 8,000 years ago this valley was the center of prehistoric China. Here the domestication of China's first grain crop—millet, not rice—enabled the ancient migratory Chinese to give up their hunting and gathering and settle in permanent villages. Millet is a member of the sorghum family, and a plant native to China. After many centuries of millet cultivation, the Chinese learned to grow flooded rice. The center of Chinese population then shifted southward to the Yangtze Valley.

West of Xi'an we drove through fields that had been cultivated as long as any fields on earth—about 300 generations. Once when our car stopped, I picked up a handful of brown soil to see how it looked after 80 centuries of cultivation.

Not far from Xi'an we began to see pump houses in the fields. These were one-room sheds recognizable by their overhead connection to a power line. Electric pumps were lifting ground water from tube-wells and gushing the life-giving liquid into ditches. Less frequently we passed overhead aqueducts 15 to 20 feet above the road, bringing pumped water from the river to the low hills where water was distributed by gravity.

Our journey through this valley occurred during harvest of winter wheat and turn-around time for planting summer maize. Everywhere along the road, wheat harvest was in progress. Thousands of people were busy using the traditional methods for bringing in the crop. The road was filled with a procession of carts pulled by peasants or by oxen or peasants carrying one sack of grain on each end of a shoulder pole. Rarely did we pass a hand tractor in 1983 and there were no trucks.

Suppose our farming neighbors from Aldie, Virginia were here today, Berni suggested. How would they view this harvest? What would Ferne Marshall see along this road? (Ferne Marshall was an 80-year-old Virginia farmer—a neighbor who has managed a grain and cattle farm of 110 acres and put five children through college on the proceeds.) What would the Marshalls see in the Wei River Valley? We made a list.

The peasants were cutting wheat with hand sickles, tying the bundles with a few straws, and carrying the sheaves to the threshing floor—a hard sun-baked area—where the sheaves are dried. The crop was threshed—grain separated from the straw—by trampling of animals, and the grain was spread out to dry along the side of the highway. When dried, the golden grain was winnowed by tossing it in the air with a wooden shovel; this permitted a breeze to separate the lighter chaff from the heavier kernels. Finally the peasants bagged the grain by hand and carried it home. Ferne Marshall, seeing this, would doubtless conclude that Chinese farming procedures along the Wei River were several generations behind the west. In some respects they were comparable to American practices at the time of the Civil War (1861–1865) or even the eighteenth century before development of the reaper and binder. Some American farmers might despair of China's backwardness.

Then Berni raised the question, Would Chinese see more in this harvest scene? People all over the world tend to measure progress by the changes in their own vicinity and during their own lifetimes. So we looked again at the Wei Valley, trying to see it through Chinese eyes.

First the road. At China's liberation in 1949 this motor road was a sunken cart track, deep in mud during the rainy season. Today the roadbed has been raised six feet above the surrounding fields, lined with poplar trees and weatherproofed. The road connects all the villages along the Wei valley and leads to markets in Xi'an. True, the road is narrow and bumpy, but it is an improvement for the peasants of the area.

What about irrigation? Thirty years ago this valley was rainfed—that is, the crops depended on the weather. The valley suffered a mild drought at least five years out of ten, and once a decade on average the valley experienced a drought so severe that entire families departed as refugees to beg on the streets of Xi'an. It was not unusual for some families to sell their children to save them from starvation. That harsh era ended when the PRC introduced irrigation. Power lines were installed and water for irrigation was lifted out of the ground.

What else was new? We looked at the children participating in the harvest.

They no longer had angry sores on their scalps and sticky discharge from their eyes. Rudimentary clinics in the villages with their "barefoot doctors" had reduced contagious diseases and brought under control the killer epidemics like smallpox and cholera.

About schools? Officials in Xi'an had told us that 96 percent of the school age children of the Wei River valley were in school. Perhaps the estimate was too high, but education—as the villager sees it—was greatly expanded.

And housing? In villages that we could see along this road, about a quarter of the houses so far had been reconstructed with red bricks and black tile roofs. That suggested savings from crops and animals since liberation.

The Chinese peasant would probably say that the Wei River valley was now a place of hope.

*Very few wheat breeders achieve in their lifetime the goals they set out to accomplish. These two Wugong men had reached their goals.*

Briefing, Shaanxi Academy
of Agricultural Sciences, 1983

CHAPTER 51

# Two Wheat Breeders at Wugong

Having witnessed the Wei valley wheat harvest, Berni and I drove on to Wugong, a small town 60 miles west of Xi'an that is best known for its Northwest College of Agriculture and Shaanxi Academy of Agricultural Sciences. The academy is the leading research center for crops in northwest China, especially for wheat and maize, the two basic foods. By a visit to Wugong we wanted to judge the prospects for future food production in the dry northwest. During the first three decades of Peoples China, agricultural improvement had focused on the irrigated coastal provinces. For the remainder of the twentieth century—if China were to achieve its food goals—it would be necessary to show rapid improvement in rainfed areas, including the northwest.

President Liu met us at the front door of the academy with his senior staff, and we went through a familiar routine of courtesies: a tour of the laboratories to show off the academy's new equipment; a briefing in the conference room, giving the history of the academy and list of national awards received by this center; then lunch in the staff cafeteria and an afternoon tour of the field plots.

I was most interested in two famous wheat breeders whom I had heard about. One was Professor Zhao Hongzan, the other, scientist Wang Yucheng. Both were 63 years old, and both had spent their scientific careers at Wugong. Zhao was head of the Plant Breeding Department of the college, and Wang headed the Crops Research Institute at the academy. They had been fellow graduates in the wartime college class of 1942 and had done all their wheat breeding as partners.

Old Zhao was a gaunt man with crewcut hair still black, a deeply tanned face, prominent cheekbones, and a confident manner. Wang was the shorter, a balding man with two thatches of white hair over his ears and a most contagious smile.

Local wheat in the 1940s, Zhao explained, had three major shortcomings. First, the available varieties were susceptible to the rust diseases and especially to stripe rust. Second, the available winter wheat varieties required a growing season of 300 days—too long for double-cropping with a summer crop. Third, the wheat grew too tall when fertilized and irrigated, and lodged (fell over). In 1942 these two young breeders were bold enough to think they could solve all three problems in their lifetime, and they have.

Zhao and Wang made about 300 crosses a year, rejecting most of the progeny after one year of observation, as is usual in plant breeding. They used students as their field assistants, training a large number of future breeders. In 1950—after eight years of work—they released their first two varieties, called *Bi Ma 1* and *Bi Ma 4*, two sisters that gave encouraging resistance to stripe rust.

Zhao and Wang worked another 15 years before they achieved in 1965 their second outstanding wheat called *Feng Zan 3*, which translates "Abundant Harvest 3." Feng Zan 3 had three outstanding qualities: it yielded 4.5 tons per hectare compared to 3.0 tons for the Bi Ma sisters; the plant height was 90 centimeters (36 inches) compared to 120 centimeters (48 inches) for the Bi Ma line; and the new variety shortened the maturity period (growing season) from 300 days to about 250 days. After its release, Feng Zan 3 was grown widely by farmers and used for breeding in other provinces.

A third success was *Ai Feng 3*, meaning "Short Plant Abundant Harvest." This was released to Chinese farmers in 1970. Its yield potential jumped to seven tons per hectare; the plant height was further shortened to 80 centimeters (32 inches); and the growing season was shortened to 220 days. The two breeders were delighted, but they did not immediately realize the cause of their third success. By using as one parent a Korean variety called *Suwon 86*, they had incorporated the dwarfing genes of a famous Japanese wheat line called *Norin 10*. Thus Ai Feng 3 became a distant cousin of all the Mexican semidwarf wheats that had spread throughout the developing world; it was also a close relative of Gaines, the American winter wheat that held the American yield record of 14.1 metric tons per hectare. Not surprisingly, during the 1970s Ai Feng 3 became the favorite parent material for Chinese breeders who sought short, stiff straw to prevent lodging.

I asked President Liu whether double-cropping of winter wheat with summer maize was now common. He said double-cropping had spread rapidly in the 1970s, using wheat bred by the Wugong team (220 days) and a hybrid maize variety from the United States called *Missouri 17* (110 days). The combination had approximately doubled the harvest of grain per hectare in irrigated areas of China's northwest. The best commercial yields of the double crop had been 15 tons per hectare, a great achievement by world standards.

So far the two wheat breeders had spoken to us only about wheat under irrigation, and we knew there was little possibility for increasing irrigated land in China's northwest. The principal sources of water—rivers and underground water table—were already being exploited wherever the cost was acceptable. What was the prospect, I asked Zhao and Wang, for increased wheat in rainfed areas? The two men glanced at each other and smiled ruefully; then Old Zhao offered an answer.

National authorities, he said, had high expectations for increased rainfed production before the year 2000. More wheat from rainfed areas is easy in theory but difficult in practice. It takes three inputs. First, you conserve the moisture when rain falls on the loess soil.* That means you stir the soil to reduce evaporation, and stirring the soil requires animals or machinery to pull a cultivator. Second, you add fertilizer in dryland farming where little or no fertilizer has been used before. That means more cost and more risk for the farmer. Third, you plant wheats that will grow well under low-moisture conditions. This means breeders like Wang and Zhao and their assistants must develop them. Each of the three inputs requires new research for which China has little experience. "We think Wugong will succeed," Zhao said, "but this is a 15 or 20-year assignment."

The government in Beijing has announced its goal to raise the national wheat harvest from 60 million tons in 1980 to 85 million tons in 1990 to 104 million tons in 2000. These are ambitious aims, and they are to be achieved with no increase in crop area. I believe the 1990 goal will be met ahead of schedule, but the goal for year 2000 depends on the success of dryland research. These two Wugong breeders carry much of the responsibility. Since they are both 63, the ultimate burden in 2000 A.D. will fall upon younger men. Berni and I wished them success and secretly hoped we could return in 2000 A.D. to see the outcome.

Before leaving Wugong, I asked President Liu what damage this academy had suffered during the Cultural Revolution. His answer: nothing. There were no Red Guard visitors. The academy lost no equipment, no library books, no germ plasm, no staff. President Liu attributed this good fortune to the fact that the academy is 60 miles from Xi'an and not on a major road. The neighboring Northwest College of Agriculture also lost nothing in the

---

*For a description of loess, see footnote in chapter 11, page 71.

national chaos. Most colleges and research institutes in the coastal area suffered not only building and equipment damage, but also loss of germ plasm that may never be replaced.

As darkness approached on the road returning to Xi'an, the wheat harvest crews were still engaged in their laborious work. In addition, we saw young women in gaily flowered blouses hoeing weeds in the emerging corn. They looked tired.

*There is perhaps no better test of the progress of a nation than that which shows what proportion are in poverty.*

Professor A. L. Bowley, London School
of Economics, 1923

CHAPTER 52

# How Well Is the PRC Meeting the Basic Needs of Its People?

Having completed our journey over the route of the Long March, we returned to Mexico in August 1983, still pondering the question: How well is the PRC meeting the basic needs of its people? We wanted to compare China with other countries of the third world.

We had seen changes along the route of the march, including better food production, better housing, more schooling, and widespread health clinics. But these observations covered only a few provinces. To get a more comprehensive picture, we needed to draw on the World Bank's annual *Development Report* (containing the best comparative statistics on the third world), the *World Population Data Sheet* of the Population Reference Bureau, the *China Outlook and Situation Report* issued by the U.S. Department of Agriculture (an excellent annual pamphlet), the yearbooks of the UN Food and Agriculture Organization, and the annual communique of the PRC State Statistical Bureau. From this wealth of information we tried to formulate what is happening to China on five fronts: population, hunger, health, literacy, and status of women.

*Population.* The Chinese population story starts with a sobering fact: Approximately 470 million people were added to PRC between liberation in 1949 and the census of 1982. During that span of 33 years the excess of Chinese births over deaths equalled the total population of Europe. Each year in that period, on average, China added 14 million to its population, the equivalent of another Australia. This expansion reflected Mao Zedong's statement in 1949, "It is a very good thing that China has a big population. Even if China's population multiplies many times, she is fully capable of finding a solution." That was China's population policy—or lack of one.

Mao's leniency on population matters during the first two decades of the PRC permitted a "people boom" that now makes it exceedingly difficult for the Deng Xiaoping regime to achieve a rapid improvement of living standards on a per-person basis.

It is doubtful that the Dengist policy of one-couple, one-child will survive in its present form to the year 2000 because of rural resistance. But a modified two-child strategy, combined with a delayed first child, several-year spacing and a rigid cutoff of third births and higher, will come close to meeting China's target of 1.2 billion population in the year 2000. This would preserve China's status as the most successful population regulator in the third world.

*Hunger.* A revolutionary government in China was expected above all else to provide adequate food for a country that had suffered recurring famines for 40 centuries.

According to figures published after Mao's death, the Peoples Republic doubled the foodgrain harvest during its first three decades—from 147 million tons of foodgrain in 1951 to 320 million tons in 1980. That increase was impressive. But population was also zooming in that period—from 589 to 983 million people by official estimate, or about 75 percent. Most of the food increase was consumed by extra mouths.

How much hunger is there in China? An FAO survey in 1975 put average Chinese consumption at 2300 calories per day. A World Bank study in 1983 placed average consumption at 2550 calories. It should be possible to feed a nation satisfactorily on that daily food allowance, provided the supply is distributed equitably. But food distribution in China, despite rationing, has had two flaws: (1) food supply in the cities was said to be 20 percent higher than in the countryside; and (2) the food supply varied greatly between the richest and poorest rural areas. These differences have never been fully balanced by the movement of food.

The rapid growth of food output per person in post-Mao years suggests that Chinese agriculture could take great strides in the remaining years of the twentieth century, outstripping other large countries of the third world such as India, Pakistan, Bangladesh, Nigeria, and Brazil.

*Health.* Better health ranks high among the people's expectations from a revolutionary government. No statistic expresses more clearly the difference between a healthy society and a society undergoing great stress than the number of babies out of each thousand live births who die before they reach age one. Rates of fewer than 10 baby deaths per 1000 have been achieved by prosperous nations like Japan. The *U.N. Demographic Yearbook* lists China with an infant mortality rate of 35 deaths per 1000 live births. That compares with an average of 107 babies dead by age one for all developing countries in the 1980s. Judged by infant mortality in the developing world, China's health status ranks close to the top.

Life expectancy at birth is the most comprehensive indicator of a nation's health. The *World Population Data Sheet, 1984*, places Japan and several other industrialized countries at the top of the list for long-lived populations; Japan's average life expectancy at birth was 76 years. Suffering the poorest health were 42 developing countries in tropical Africa with an average life expectancy of 47 years. China, in the same publication, had life expectancy of 65. This placed the Chinese substantially above India, Pakistan, Indonesia, and Bangladesh, all in the 47–51 range, but a little lower than South Korea (66), Argentina (70) and Cuba (74).

Medical facilities in Peoples China have impressed many visiting public health officials. Peoples China has provided more widespread medical care than did the previous nationalist government and more health services than do most developing countries. A baby sick with diarrhea in a Chinese village has more chance for prompt treatment than a baby in northeast Brazil, in tropical Africa, or even in India with its thousands of doctors.

All this suggests that the government of PRC is fulfilling well its obligation to the people for health protection.

*Literacy.* Before 1949, J. Lossing Buck at Nanking University found that something like five out of six adult Chinese were illiterate. This indicated that the Peoples Republic inherited from the nationalist regime 300 to 400 million illiterates out of a population of 537 million. How much of that inherited illiteracy, we asked, has Peoples China eliminated?

Because different definitions are used, statistics on illiteracy are controversial. An urban worker's "functional literacy" may mean the ability to read the destination on a trolley car. A villager's literacy may mean the ability to understand notices on a public bulletin board. The PRC government defines literacy as the ability to read 1500 Chinese characters. This requirement is certainly minimal; a six-year primary school graduate is expected to read 3000.

If we combine the primary school graduates since 1949 with those who took a cram course for literacy, and then add those who were literate before 1949, we arrive at a literacy rate in China of 60 to 70 percent at Mao's death in 1976. A reasonable figure would be 67 percent.

At that level, China would be far ahead of India and Pakistan (36 and 24 percent), but still behind Thailand (84 percent), the Philippines (89 percent), South Korea (93 percent), and Japan (99 percent). At 67 percent literacy, China still has over 300 million illiterates, only a slight reduction in absolute numbers since 1949, but a great achievement nevertheless.

*Status of women.* Before 1949 women constituted the most underprivileged Chinese social group. Four forms of discrimination against women were evident: (1) fewer than 2 percent of females over age 12 had any education; (2) women generally lacked access to employment except in subsistence agriculture and domestic service; (3) a large number of females became victims of ancient forms of crueltry such as footbinding, infanticide, and girl slavery; and (4) archaic marriage practices still prevailed, including child betrothal and extortionate dowries.

Mao Zedong saw in the lowly status of women a great opportunity for the Chinese revolution. By supporting a Chinese form of "women's liberation," the communists could gain political adherents. By urging women to enter the work force, China could increase its production. And by educating women, China could double the nation's brain power. Mao often said that women held up half the sky.

How much has Peoples China changed the status of women? In a 1978 survey, the Chinese Ministry of Education found that girls made up 50 percent of primary enrollment, 40 percent of high school pupils, and 30 percent in colleges and universities. Women's education had come a long way since 1949. Still, the All-China Women's Federation found reason to complain in 1978 that 80 percent of the remaining illiterates in China were women.

Employment? Nonagricultural jobs are the most attractive because they tend to pay better and are less dreary. In 1980 there were estimated to be more than 100 million nonagricultural jobs, and—according to Beijing—women filled about one third. That is a high proportion by standards of the third world.

What about the old cruelties? Footbinding was a bizarre custom prevalent in China from the tenth century until 1949. Chiang Kai-shek's government outlawed footbinding but was unable to stop it completely. The practice was ended promptly by the communist government in 1949 through intense peer group pressure.

New marriage laws were another approach, but PRC soon learned it is easier to change laws than social practices. A new Chinese constitution of 1980 declared that "Women enjoy equal rights with men in all spheres of political, economic, cultural, social, and family life." Chinese women thus attained—on paper at least—constitutional guarantees that women in the United States are still seeking through an equal rights amendment.

Despite such laws, China remains a man's world. Until 1985 there was no woman on the ruling communist politburo, and only 2 women vice premiers among 20. Cooperatives were still dominated by men.

Overall, few countries of the world have enabled women to come so far in so short a time, but China's effort toward equality of the sexes still goes on.

## Reflections

China has done reasonably well in meeting the basic needs of its people. This does not mean it has ended destitution. In its *World Development Report, 1982*, the World Bank concluded, "China's nationwide food security ... may blunt the impact of poverty; nevertheless it is probable that at least 150 million people there have living standards little better than those of the absolutely poor in other countries."

Yet the number of people at the margins of survival in China fell dramatically under PRC. No other large country in the third world—not India, not Indonesia or Bangladesh, not oil-exporting Nigeria or industrializing Brazil—could say the same.

Does this suggest that the "China model" could serve other poor countries? Probably not. China has historic advantages that make very unlikely a successful effort by any third world nation to follow a "Peking model." Among these differences:

- China is the oldest continuously self-governing nation in the world. It has ethnic homogeneity and discipline.
- China has a long tradition of peasant insurrections and revolutionary leaders that played a role in the revolution.
- The communists came to power unassisted by any foreign country, beholden to no one.
- The heart of the "Maoist model"—and the "Dengist model," too—is the relation of the communist party to the Chinese people, a relationship dissimilar from any poor capitalist country, and substantially different from any other socialist country.
- The Chinese communist party had Mao Zedong as leader—followed by Deng Xiaoping—both men of political genius.

I doubt that these advantages of the Chinese experience can be achieved in another developing country.

EPILOGUE

# The Third World in the Year 2000

A calculation about the third world in the year 2000 is certainly hazardous. If anyone had made a 15-year projection at the start of World War II, he could not have foreseen the great scientific developments of radar, antibiotics, jet propulsion, and atomic energy. Likewise, a 15-year projection in 1970 could scarcely have forecast the revolution in computers and the emergence of industrial robots.

Most speculations about the future are wishful thinking. But some forward calculations, it seems to me, can draw on current knowledge and apply to the future the most plausible expectations—like tracking heavenly bodies from their present position in the sky, using their past speed of motion and their curving direction of flight. Such speculations warrant a modest degree of confidence.

If I start with speculations about China in 2000, there are some obvious facts. Fifty years will have passed since liberation. Seven Chinese out of ten will have been born after the revolution. They will have lost touch with the forces that drove the generations of their grandparents and parents to embrace communism. These late-comers will never have known a landlord. The young people of 2000 will be better educated, more materialistic, more outspoken, and better informed about the outside world. They will be less impressed than their elders with the achievements of the PRC because they never knew the old China.

I anticipate that China will reach at least three of its major development targets for 2000.

1. China's population will remain below 1.2 billion (the principal goal under the one-couple, one-child campaign).

2. China's annual grain harvest will reach 480 million tons by 2000, a gain of 50 percent above 1980. (The grain campaign was already ahead of schedule in 1985.)

3. China's average per-person income will reach $800 in 2000, up from $300 in 1985. (But that will be less than 10 percent of the average income in industrialized countries.)

Three political areas remain unclear:

- Will PRC call itself communist?
- Will PRC again become a partner with the USSR?
- What is the future of Taiwan?

1. *Ideology.* Already in the mid-1980s Deng Xiaoping, the Chinese paramount leader, dropped the label *communism* and adopted the phrase *socialism with Chinese characteristics.* This switch of labels reflected—among other things—the pride of Chinese leaders who no longer attributed their form of government to the borrowed thoughts of a nineteenth-century German political philosopher (Marx) and a leader of the Russian revolution (Lenin). China was moving toward middle ground between communism and capitalism, trying to retain the best features of each and to escape the extremes of both—a strategy suited to the needs of China.

2. *Russian relations.* The two revolutionary giants split apart in 1960 over soviet detente with the United States, soviet reluctance to share atomic technology with China, and other issues. During the 1960s the two sides denounced each other, and in 1969 armed clashes occurred along China's northern border. Mao Zedong's fervent nationalism and his desire—after Stalin's death—that the PRC should become the leader of the communist world, added to the ill will.

Under Deng Xiaoping after 1978, many factors worked against a return to the Chinese-Russian partnership: China protested Russian armed forces on its northern border and the Russian armed incursion into Afghanistan; China increasingly turned to democratic countries for advanced technology; and the soviet economy was under visible strain.

China's growing economic success, as now seems evident, strengthened the PRC decision to maintain an open door toward the democracies—a posture she will probably maintain to 2000 and beyond.

3. *Taiwan.* Economic circumstances clearly visible in the mid-1980s are pushing Taiwan toward an agreement with the PRC that would make

Taiwan a "special province" under the formula "one country, two systems." This settlement seems likely in the 1990s before the return of Hong Kong to the PRC in 1997. The Taiwan agreement might follow the Hong Kong pattern, guaranteeing that a free market economy will continue for half a century. There are several pressures for this settlement.

- More than half of Taiwan's trade passes through Hong Kong. This trade will come under PRC control in 1997.
- PRC is developing numerous duty-free ports along the China coast that will gradually rival Taiwan as free trade zones.
- The emotional attachment of the United States to Taiwan and to the two-China formula is fading as the volume of American investment and trade with PRC increases.
- President Chiang Ching-guo of Taiwan, the second generation of the Chiang Kai-shek dynasty, will be 90 years old if he lives to 1997. Chiang Kai-shek's grandson has been suggested as the third generation leader in Taiwan, but this appears unlikely. He lacks the charisma.

Before 1997 Taiwan has much to offer PRC. Its strongest bargaining point is its supply of business executives, experienced in world trade.

Taken as a whole, what do we foresee in 2000 for the third world?

Suppose I start with a population projection. Demographers at the Population Reference Bureau have estimated that more than 1 billion people will be added to the developing countries between 1985 and 2000. This means the equivalent of two more Europes will be populated in 15 years. It takes no wisdom to visualize the difficulties in providing them with food, clothing, housing, schooling, and jobs.

These additional people will live longer than today's population. Life expectancy at birth in the third world now averages 58 years. By 2000 a reasonable estimate would be 70 years. Longer life will be made possible by better control of epidemics like cholera and the reduction of children's diseases like measles.

Literacy will continue to rise. In the third world between 50 and 60 people out of every 100 over the age of 12 can now read and write. By 2000 the rate could reach 80 to 90 out of 100. This gain could be accomplished just by continuing the present proportion of children in primary schools. Some poor-quality education is counted in this estimate.

Food supply in the third world in 2000 will be better than it was in 1970 and 1980, but distribution will still be uneven. A few African countries may achieve a green revolution—for example, Cameroon, Ivory Coast, and Zimbabwe; but most African countries will still be food importers. In Asia, some countries will still have rising food production from their outstanding agricultural research in the 1980s; these will include India, the Philippines, and Indonesia. But the greatest cause of hunger will continue to be poverty.

What can we assume about individual incomes in the third world? If each of the 37 poorest countries in 1985 were able to double its per-person income by 2000—a very optimistic assumption—the average income of Bangladesh would reach $260 per year, Ethiopia $280, Zaire $320, Pakistan $780, and Sudan $800—all measured in 1985 dollars. The increases would help some families to purchase the food that they could not afford in the 1980s, but these people would remain very, very poor.

Government-owned industries in the third world will probably be greatly reduced by 2000 if we interpret correctly the present trend; many governments are selling publicly-owned industries to private investors. In the 1960s newly independent countries often adopted socialism as a reaction against the economic system of former colonial masters. Also many leaders of the newly independent countries had been educated at London, Paris, Brussels, and Amsterdam, where socialism was in vogue in the universities. After a quarter century of government-managed industry, many countries found they were losing ground because they failed to provide incentives for economic growth. The result: a swing toward private enterprise. Many third world countries once looked to the Soviet Union as a model for economic development. Most of those same countries are now looking westward toward the United States, or eastward to Japan, South Korea, Hong Kong, and even to Deng Xiaoping's China.

In 2000 the entire world will be better off, if my expectations prove correct. There will also be new problems that we did not foresee. If I am still around—at age 88—I shall see how the third world measures up—and acknowledge my errors.

# Selected Bibliography

The titles in this bibliography are those (1) cited in the text, (2) quoted in the chapter headings, and (3) consulted in preparation of the manuscript.

Ayub Khan, Mohammed. *Friends Not Masters.* Lahose: Oxford University Press, 1967.

Bailey, L.J. Preface to F.H. King. *Farmers of Forty Centuries.* Emmaus, Pennsylvania: Rodale Press, 1911.

Bauer, P.T. and John O'Sullivan. "Foreign Aid for What?" *Commentary*, Dec. 1978, July 1979.

Bauer, P.T. and B.S. Yamey. "Against the New Economic Order," *Commentary*, July 1977.

*Beijing Review.*

Belden, Jack. *China Shakes the World.* New York: Harper, 1949.

Bickel, Lennard. *Facing Starvation: Norman Borlaug and the Fight Against Hunger.* New York: Reader's Digest Press, E.P. Dutton and Co., Inc., 1974.

Buck, J. Lossing. *Land Utilization in China.* Shanghai: Commercial Press, 1937.

Carlson, Evans F. *Twin Stars in China* (reprint). Westport, Conn.: Hyperion Press, 1975

Chesneaux, Jean. *Peasant Revolts in China, 1840–1949.* Stanford: Stanford University Press, 1973.

Chiang Kai-shek. Speech in 1948 quoted in Lloyd Eastman, "Who Lost China?" *China Quarterly*, June 1973.

Clubb, O. Edmund. *Twentieth-Century China.* New York: Columbia University Press, 1964.

Cressey, George. *China's Geographical Foundations.* London: McGraw-Hill, 1934.

Eastman, Lloyd. *The Abortive Revolution.* Cambridge: Harvard University Press, 1974.

Eberstadt, Nicholas. "Has China Failed?" *New York Review of Books,* April 5, 1979.

Fairbank, John King. *Chinabound: A Fifty-Year Memoir.* New York: Harper & Row, 1982.

Fairbank, John King. *China and the United States.* Cambridge: Harvard University Press, 4th ed., 1980.

Fei, Hsiao-tung. *Peasant Life in China.* New York: Dutton, 1939.

Gramling, Oliver. *AP: The Story of News.* New York: Farrar and Rinehart, 1940.

Hanson, Haldore. *Humane Endeavor: The Story of the China War.* New York: Farrar and Rinehart, 1939.

Hanson, Haldore et al. *Wheat in the Third World.* Denver: Westview Press, 1983.

Joint Economic Committee of U.S. Congress. *China: A Reassessment of the Economy.* Washington: Government Printing Office, 1975.

Jones, Joseph M. *The Fifteen Weeks.* New York: Viking Press, 1955.

Kahn, E.J., Jr. *The China Hands.* New York: Viking, 1972.

King, F.H. *Farmers of Forty Centuries.* Emmaus, Pennsylvania: Rodale Press, 1911.

Layard, Sir Henry. *Early Adventures in Persia, Susiana, and Babylonia, 1840–1844.* London: John Murray, 1894.

Mao Tse-tung. *Selected Works of Mao Tse-tung.* Peking: Foreign Languages Press, 1961 and 1983.

Mathews, Jay and Linda. *One Billion: A China Chronicle.* New York: Ballantine Books, 1983.

MacLean, Fitsroy. *Eastern Approaches.* London: Mayflower Books, 1961.

Meisner, Maurice. *Mao's China.* New York: Free Press, Macmillan, 1979.

Miller, Arthur and Inge Morath. *Chinese Encounters.* New York: Penguin, 1981.

Montrose et al. *U. S. Marine Operations in Korea, 1950–1953.* Washington: Defense Department, 1969.

Myrdal, Jan. *Report from a Chinese Village.* New York: Pantheon, 1970.

Pahlavi, Mohammed Reza Shah. *Mission for My Country.* London: Hutchinson and Co., 1961.

Peck, Graham. *Through China's Wall*. Boston: Houghton Mifflin, 1940.

Reeves, Thomas. *The Life and Times of Joe McCarthy*. New York: Stein and Day, 1982.

Reischauer, Edwin O. *The Japanese*. Cambridge: Harvard University Press, 1978.

Rice, Edward E. *Mao's Way*. Berkeley, Cal.: University of California Press, 1972.

Selden, Mark. *The Yenan Way in Revolutionary China*. Cambridge: Harvard University Press, 1971.

Seybolt, Peter. *Through Chinese Eyes*. 2 vols. New York: Praeger, 1974 and 1975.

Shewmaker, Kenneth E. *Americans and Chinese Communists, 1927-1945*. Ithaca: Cornell University Press, 1972.

Smedley, Agnes. *The Great Road: The Life and Times of Chu Teh*. New York: Modern Reader, 1956.

Snow, Edgar. *Red China Today*. New York: Random House, 1971.

Snow, Edgar. *Red Star Over China*. New York: Random House, 1938.

Stakman, Bradfield, and Mangelsdorf. *Campaigns Against Hunger*. Cambridge: Harvard University Press, 1967.

Tuchman, Barbara W. *Stilwell and the American Experience in China, 1911-1945*. New York: Bantam Books, 1972.

Van Slycke, Lyman, ed. *The Chinese Communist Movement: A Report to the U.S. War Department*. Stanford, Cal.: Stanford University Press, 1968.

White Theodore. *In Search of History*. New York: Harper & Row, 1978.

White Theodore H. and Annalee Jacoby. *Thunder Out of China*. New York: Sloan Associates, 1946.

Wilson, Dick. *The Long March*. New York: Viking Press, 1972.

Wilson, Dick. *Mao in the Scales of History*. New York: Cambridge University Press, 1977.

World Bank. *World Development Report 1985*. New York: Oxford University Press, 1985.

Zhang Rongzu. *Mount Qomolangma: The Highest in the World*. Beijing: Foreign Language Press, 1981.

Zwicker, Brig. Gen. Ralph W. Quoted in Thomas Reeves, *The Life and Times of Joe McCarthy*. New York: Stein and Day, 1982.

# Index

Abortions, 310
Act for International Development, 107, 133
Africa
  agricultural problems, 174
  political upheavals in 1950s and 1960s, 169
  wood carvings, 179
Albrecht, Herbert, research administrator, 172
Allen, Ambassador George, 108
Anderson, Glenn, wheat researcher, 189, 246
Aresvik, Oddvar, Norwegian economist in Pakistan, 157
Associates Press, 28, 76, 87, 58, 203, 216
Ayub Khan, President Mohammed, 144, 150, 152, 160

Bangladesh, 158
Bauer, P.T., economist, 133
Beal, Edwin, Chinese language scholar, 11
Beijing. *See* Peking
Belden, Jack, war correspondent, 46
Bennett, Henry, U.S aid administrator, 110
Benton, William, assistant secretary of state, 103, 122
Bethune, Dr. Norman, Canadian medical doctor in China, 29
Bhutto, Zulfikar Ali, Pakistan political leader, 158
Biafran war, 176
Biggerstaff, Knight, Chinese language scholar, 13, 18
Bloom, Rep. Sol, 105

Bodde, Derk, Chinese language scholar, 18
Boerma, Adekko, FAO director general, 207
Borlaug, Norman, wheat scientist, 189, 195
  biographic sketch, 195
  China wheat visit, 246
  in Pakistan, 154
Borodin, Michael, Russian revolutionary in China, 16
Brown, Bernice (wife of author)
  letter from Pakistan, 160
  school teacher in China, 24
Brown, Lester, agricultural economist and author, 174
Brown, Dr. Richard, Canadian medical doctor in China, 62, 64
Brunauer, Esther Caulkin, State Department officer, 114
Buck, John Lossing, American economist in China, 35, 286, 321
Budenz, Louis, ex-communist, 118
Bundy, McGeorge, president of Ford Foundation, 206, 210
Burma, 135

CAAS. *See* Chinese Academy of Agricultural Sciences
Carleton College, 5, 24
Carlson, Capt. Evans, U.S. attache in China, 60
Carnegie Endowment for International Peace, 5
Carter, Pres. Jimmy, 57
Central China University, Wuchang, 77
CGIAR. *See* Consultative Group on International Agricultural Research

Chang Yu-ch'uan, Chinese counsellor, 12, 15
Changsha, Hunan, China, 279, 288, 291
Chen Yi, Gen., 20
Chengdu, Sichuan, China, 76, 280
Chiang Kai-shek, 136
    and the united front, 1937–1941, 42
    detention at Sian, 38
    profile of early life, 17
    speech in 1948 in Taiwan, 83
Chicago, 5, 87
*China Daily*, Beijing, 278
Chinese Academy of Agricultural Sciences (CAAS), 231, 247
Chinese agriculture
    comparison to India, 255
    policy changes after 1978, 161
    why important, 253
Chomolungma. *See* Everest, Mount
Chongqing, Sichuan, China, 77
CIAT. *See* International Center for Tropical Agriculture, Colombia
CIMMYT. *See* International Center for Maize and Wheat Improvement, Mexico
CIP. *See* International Potato Center, Peru
Clifford, Clark, presidential aide, 107
Clubb, O. Edmund, foreign service officer, 36, 123
College of Chinese Studies, Peking, 13, 24, 51
Consultative Group on International Agricultureal Research (CGIAR), 120, 192, 207
Contraception. *See* Family planning
Cost of living in China, 298
Culture shock, 182

Dadu River, Sichuan, China, 280
Davies, John Paton, foreign service officer, 123
DeFrancis, John, Chinese language scholar, 18, 27
*Democracy* magazine, Peking, 39
Deng Xiaoping, general and political leader, 68, 70, 269, 274, 294, 297, 323
Dez Dam, Khuzestan, Iran, 144, 147
Dickey, John, State Department officer, 104
Dollar, Mexican silver in China, 6
Duluth, Minnesota, 5, 80

Eberstadt, Nicholas, 133
Eighth Route Army, 58
    discipline, 65
    mass meetings, 68
    radio transmitters, 67
    why successful, 63
Everest, trek to Mount, 258

Fairbank, John, professor of Chinese history, 18, 92
Fairbank, Wilma, State Department officer, 18, 93, 95
Family planning
    in Pakistan, 167
    in Peoples Republic of China, 196
    in Sichuan province, China, 186
    in west Africa, 100
FAO. *See* United Nations Food and Agriculture Organization
Fenyang, Shanxi, China, 25
Fisher, Adrian, State Department officer, 116
Fisher, F.M., war correspondent, 18
Ford Foundation, 206
    in Nigeria, 169, 177
    in Pakistan, 150, 160, 167
    in USA, 150
Friggins, Paul, magazine writer, 219
Fulbright, Sen. William, 106

Gowon, Gen. Yakubu, 170, 177
Grave mounds, 286
Great Snowy Mountains, Sichuan, China, 280
Green revolution controversy, 210
Griffiths, Gen. Samuel, U.S. attache in China, 19, 58
Guerillas
    in Hebei, 51, 58
    in Shanxi, 61
    singing, 56
    train wrecking, 58
Guilin, Guangxi, China, 76, 78
Guiyang, Guizhou, China 295
Guizhou province, 178

Hamilton, Josephine, teacher in China, 24
Hanson, Eric, son of the author, 140, 162, 258
Hanson, Signe, daughter of author, 140, 162
Harlan, Jack, plant historian, 195

Harrar, George, president of Rockefeller Foundation, 106, 209
Harris, Morris, AP correspondent in China, 81
Havener, Robert, agricultural administrator in Mexico, 193
He Long, Gen., 20, 26, 279
Hersey, John, war correspondent, 41
Hickenlooper, Sen. Bourke, 117
Hill, F.F., Ford Foundation vice-president, 176, 206
Hiss, Alger, State Department officer, 112
Houston, Dr. Charles, researcher on mountain sickness, 258, 262
*Humane Endeavor: Story of the China War*, 82, 112, 116
Humelsine, Carlisle, State Department officer, 116
Huq, Mabub ul, Pakistan planning officer, 159
Hurley, Patrick, Ambassador to China, 51, 202

ICARDA. *See* International Center for Agricultural Research in Dry Areas, Syria
ICRISAT. *See* International Center for Research in the Semi-arid Tropics, India
IITA. *See* International Institute for Tropical Agriculture, Nigeria
Interdepartmental Committee on Scientific and Cultural Cooperation with Latin America, State Department office, 60
International Center for Agricultural Research in Dry Areas, Syria (ICARDA), 257
International Center for Maize and Wheat Improvement, Mexico (CIMMYT), 210, 257
  directing staff, 189
  origins, 188
  trustees, 189
International Center for Research in Semi-arid Tropics, India (ICRISAT), 257
International Center for Tropical Agriculture, Colombia (CIAT), 257
International Potato Center, Peru (CIP), 257
International Institute for Tropical Agriculture, Nigeria (IITA), 257, 172
International Rice Research Institute, the Philippines (IRRI), 257

Iran, 106, 142
  coin collecting, 181
IRRI. *See* International Rice Research Institute, the Philippines

Japan, empire building, 9
Jinggangshan, Jiangxi, China, 279, 281
Johnson, Elmer, maize breeder, 218
Judd, Dr. Walter, missionary in China, 5, 24, 105

Karun River, Iran, 144
Khuzestan Development Service, 146
Khuzestan province, Iran, 144, 180
Khuzestan Water and Power Authority (KWPA), 144, 147
Klatt, Arthur, wheat researcher in Mexico, 193
Kung, H.H., Chinese finance minister, 77
KWPA. *See* Khuzestan Water and Power Authority, Iran

Lattimore, Owen, scholar on China, 114
Li Xiannian, Gen., 20
Liberation in China, 200
Lilienthal, David, Tennessee Valley Authority administrator, 143, 148
Lin Biao, Gen., 20
Liu Bocheng, Gen., 20, 279
Liu Dajong, Chinese university president, 257
Long March
  comparison to other epics, 20
  definition, 19
  end, 25
  our trek over route, 265
  start, 19
  veterans in Shanxi, 62
Louisell, David, lawyer, 117
Loushan Pass, Guizhou, China, 280
Lu Hsun, Chinese writer, 36
Lu Liangshu, Chinese research administrator, 144
Lu Zhenco, Gen., 37, 55, 56
Lugouqiao. *See* Marco Polo Bridge

Ma Haide, Dr., medical doctor in China, 37
MacLeish, Archibald, assistant secretary of state, 102
Macmahon, Arthur W., political scientist, 102, 104

Maize
  China production goal for 2000, 195
  CIMMYT research, 213
  definition, 213
  hybrid development, 215
  recurrent selection, 215
  third world production, 214
  unique features, 214
  world production, 214
Manchester, William, author, 85, 107, 201
Mao Zedong
  Capt. Evans Carlson's appraisal, 60
  essay "Thoughts on War," 159
  essays on "Protracted War" and "New Democracy," 73
  in Canton 1924, 17
  interview 1938, 71
  profile to 1928, 21
  views on women, 322
Marco Polo Bridge, 45
Marshall, Ferne, Virginia farmer, 124, 313
Marshall, Gen. George C., 105
McCarthy, Sen. Joseph, 112
  characterization, 123
  death, 123
McNamara, Robert, World Bank president, 180, 207
Mendel, Gregor, nineteenth-century crop scientist, 196
Mijares, Rafael, Mexican architect, 223
Missionaries in China, 32, 111
Mount Fuji, Japan, 8
Moyer, Raymond, agricultural missionary, 32
Mundt, Rep. Karl, 105

Nanchang, Jiangxi, China, 20
Nanchang uprising, 20, 279
Narvaez, Ignacio, Mexican wheat scientist, 154
Nathan, Robert, economist, 127, 135
Ne Win, Gen., president of Burma, 140
New Fourth Army, 42
Nezahualcoyotl, Aztec king, 227
Nie Rongzhen, Gen. 20, 61
Nigeria, 169, 176
Nobel Peace Prize, 203
Nu, U, 135

Ojukwu, Lt. Col. E.O., Nigerian leader, 176

Opium
  Amoy, 31
  Peking, 30
  smoking procedures, 31
Osler, Robert, research administrator in Mexico, 203, 189

Pahlavi, Mohammed Reza Shah, Iranian king, 142
Pahlavi, Reza Shah, Iranian king, 142, 148
Pahlavi Foundation, 143
Pakistan, 150, 160, 181
  coin collecting, 181
  technical assistance program, 164
  war with India 1965, 161
Papanek, Gustav, economist, 110
Pearl Harbor, 85, 86
Peking (Beijing)
  airport, 237
  changes since 1949, 238
  city walls, 11
  foreign population in 1930s, 17
  residential housing in 1980s, 241
Peiping. *See* Peking
Peng Dehuai, Gen., 67
Peoples Liberation Army (PLA)
  briefing, 269
  invitation for trek, 265
  military budget, 273
Peoples Republic of China
  cost of living, 181
  Cultural Revolution, 234
  departure of Russians in 1960, 234
  economic indicators, 236
  end of unequal treaties, 17
  land reform, 232
  liberation, 232
  major events, 1949–1975, 232
Peurifoy, Jack, State Department officer, 115
Phillips, Ralph, animal scientist, 96
Pinyin spelling, 12
Plan Organization, Iran, 143
Point Four. *See* Technical assistance program
Powell, J.B., American editor in China, 27, 36
Pradilla, Dr. Alberto, Colombian researcher, 220
Price, Byron, Associated Press administrator, 88

Qing Xinhan, military historian, 267, 285

Railroads in China, 11, 185
Reck, Dickson, advisor in China, 97
*Red Star Over China*, 20
Rice
  Chinese production goals for 2000, 195
  Chinese research, 288
  crop in Hunan, 288
  third world production, 214
  triple cropping, 170
  world production, 214
Rockefeller Foundation, 34, 195, 205, 213
Roosevelt, Eleanor, 90
Roosevelt, Pres. Franklin D., 49, 102, 122
Russo-Japanese War, 1904-1905, 9

Saari, Eugene, wheat pathologist, 246
San Nicolas Tlaminca, Mexico, 222
Service, John S., foreign service officer, 114, 123
Shaanxi province, China, 10, 166
Shen Jingpu, agricultural administrator, 257
Sian incident, 38
Sichuan province, 303
  population program, 305
Sino-Japanese War, 1894-1895, 9
Smedley, Agnes, correspondent in China, 20, 36
Smith, Sen. Alexander H., 105
Snow, Conrad, State Department officer, 65
Snow, Edgar, author, 18, 19, 20, 27, 237
Snow, Helen Foster, correspondent in China, 20
Sprague, Ernest, maize scientist, 189, 193, 219
Stakman, Charles, wheat scientist, 195
Stevenson, Adlai E., political leader, 102
Stilwell, Gen. Joseph, 76
Subramanium, C., Indian Minister of Agriculture, 202
Sun Yat-sen, 16, 17

Taigu, Shanxi, China, 25, 28
Taiwan, Shanxi, China, 9, 326
Tanggu, Hebei, China, 11
Taylor, Gen. Maxwell, 81
Technical Advisory Committee (CGIAR), 208

Technical assistance program of the United States (Point Four), 103, 107
Technical Cooperation Administration (TCA), 109
Third world
  common characteristics, 129
  definition, xi
  international assistance to, 133
Thorp, Willard, assistant secretary of state, 112
Tokyo, 8, 81
Trager, Frank, author, 135
Truman, Pres. Harry, 102
Tuchman, Barbara, author, 76, 78
Tucker, William, author, 212
Tydings, Sen. Millard, 117
Tydings Subcommittee, 113

United front, 42
United Nations Economic and Social Council (ECOSOC), 108
United Nations Expanded Program of Technical Assistance, 103, 109
United Nations Food and Agriculture Organization (FAO), 125
United States Department of Agriculture, 198, 199
United States Department of State
  cables and correspondence routing, 97
  Division of Cultural Relations, 94
United States Information Agency, 103

Vasal, S.K., maize researcher in Mexico, 218, 220
VE Day, 85
Villegas, Evangelina, laboratory scientist in Mexico, 220
Vincent, John Carter, foreign service officer, 123
Violic, Alejandro, maize scientist in Mexico, 193
Vogel, Orville, wheat breeder, 114
Voice of America, 103

Walinsky, Louis, economist in Burma, 136
Wallace, Henry A., vice-president of the United States, 127, 209
War correspondents in China, 41
Ward, Barbara, author, 205
Washington war agencies, 94
Washington wartime living, 100
Wei Lihuang, Gen., 69

Wellhausen, E.J., maize scientist, 204, 216
Whampoa Military Academy, 61
Wheat
  breeders at Wugong, 315
  China's production goals for 2000, 317
  description of semidwarfs, 154, 200
  development of semidwarfs in Mexico, 197
  how crosses are made, 198
  in Pakistan, 154, 164
  In Wei River valley, 312
  production in Pakistan, 157
  promotion of semidwarfs, 200
  world seed collection, 198
White, J.D., news correspondent in China, 18, 46
White, T.H., author, 1, 41; and Annalee Jacoby, 1
Winklemann, Donald, economist in Mexico, 189
Wolf, Charles, economist, 110
Women's status in China, 198
Wong Wenhao, Chinese minister, 77
World Bank, 252, 302, 320, 323
Wortman, Sterling, Rockefeller Foundation officer, 212

Wugong, Shaanxi, China, 315
Wujiang River, China, 280
Wuqi village, Shaanxi, China, 280

Xi'an incident. *See* Sian
Xu Yuntian, Chinese research administrator, 231, 257

Yale-in-China Medical School, 77
Yan Xi-shan, Chinese governor, 28
Yan'an, Shaanxi, China, 75, 166, 344
Yang Hou-cheng, Gen., 39
Ye Jianying, Gen., 20
Ye Ting, Gen., 279
Yuan Shih-kai, Gen., 164

Zhang Xue-liang, Gen., 25
Zhang Zuolin, Gen., 24
Zhu De, Gen., 20, 279
  biography, 37
  Capt. Evans Carlson's appraisal, 60
  description, 68
  profile to 1928, 21
Zia ul Haq, president of Pakistan, 158
Zunyi, Guizhou, China, 280